LIFE WITHOUT DARWIN

Reclaiming Evolution
from Capitalism

Peter C. Reynolds

A Great Divide Book

Life Without Darwin

A Great Divide Book

Borderland North Publishing

https://www.borderlandnorth.com

ISBN 978-0-9629261-4-3
Edition POD. v.1.6.

Prologue

Chapter 1   The Father of Social Darwinism
Bipolar science and congruent belief.

Chapter 2   Evo-Revo: Evolution as Revolution
Darwin makes his mark as a theologian of modernity.

Chapter 3   The Corporate Moral Order
Science and Progress replace religion.

Chapter 4   The Takeover
The coevolution of Darwinism and capitalism.

Chapter 5   The Tree of Life Needs Pruning
Eugenics, the sequel.

Chapter 6   Social Darwinism, The Sequel
The fallacy of reducing society to genes.

Chapter 7   Darwin's Contributions
A summary.

Chapter 8:   Postcapitalism
From Darwinism to social justice.

Glossary of terms in Religion, Society, and Evolution

Index of Persons and Index of Topics

About the Author

Acknowledgments

Without the encouragement and support of my dissertation advisors, Harold C. Conklin of Yale University and Karl H. Pribram, M.D., of Stanford University, I would not have had access to many of the people and events that I describe in this book. I wish both were alive to read it—though both would be dismayed by what the university has become.

I owe a special debt to the late J. Bronowski and to the late Jonas Salk for the opportunity to observe the practice of molecular biology at the Salk Institute for Biological Studies in La Jolla, California. Due to the kindness of the late Professor James Dewson, I obtained a postdoctoral fellowship at Stanford University Medical Center, which gave me a front-row seat on Big Science and technocratic medicine. Also, the late Professor Roger Keesing of the Australian National University gave me the opportunity to participate in British social anthropology. My friend Hilary Yerbury first introduced me to the work of the Frankfurt School, thus awakening me from my dogmatic slumbers.

My fieldwork in Silicon Valley was made possible by Joanne Rampelburg, who found me my first high-tech job at the pseudonymous Falcon Computer Company. My first boss, marketing manager Sunny Baker, provided a seasoned perspective on corporations that helped to clarify the social dynamics of Silicon Valley.

I want to thank those academic colleagues who made it possible for me to do research at their field sites: Nancy Lutkehaus for my visit to Manam Island, Papua New Guinea; Kirk and Karen Endicott for two visits to the Batek De' of Kelantan State, Malaysia; and Steve Gartlan for welcoming me on his survey of nonhuman primate populations in Cameroon, West Africa. Janet Kreft was essential for logistics and field support in Malaysia.

The following people read drafts of chapters, raised strategic issues, checked facts, corrected errors, and, above all, gave me the encouragement that I needed to complete the project: Eugene Anderson, Myrdene Anderson, Gregory J. Claeys, James Davis, William Ditewig, Ruth Dixon-Mueller, Mark Dowie, Marc Flandreau, Jean Heriot, Barbara Honegger, Diane Jonte-Pace, Paul Keal, Alice B. Kehoe, Robert Klotz, Jane Lancaster, Carol Marujo, Bill Meacham, Eileen Menteer, Ken Morris, Raymond Pierotti, Stanley N. Salthe, Sarah Saul, Alfredo Saynes, Barbara Smuts, and William Warburton.

Scott Alkire and Elizabeth Collison provided strategic editorial advice.

Others contributed important references: Marcos Guevara, Steve Harrington, Liam O'Connell, Felix Concubhair Ó Murchadha, David Pleins, and Dana Sawchuk.

Irwin Bernstein and David K. Smith validated some key findings. Reference librarians Helène LaFrance and Helen Ryan gave me access to sources that I needed, while suggesting others that I needed to know about.

Two of the founders of Park Slope Food Cooperative, Joe Holtz and Morris "Moe" Kornbluth, kindly allowed me to interview them. Michael T. Bianco and Susan Draper-Bianco, members of the Co-op for thirty years, shared their recollections.

I am grateful to the following people and organizations (in chronological order) for the opportunity to present some of the topics in this book before a live audience: Mary Coady and James Davis of the Thomas Merton Center in Palo Alto, California; Diane Jonte-Pace, professor of religious studies at Santa Clara University in California; Maria Rosa Obiols and her colleagues in Barcelona, Spain; the staff of The Peace Center in San Jose, Costa Rica (Centro de los Amigos Cúaqueros de la Paz); Orlando V. Bedoya Pineda and Ursula Podestá at the Universidad Nacional de San Augustín in Arequipa, Peru; Andy Kafel, School of Americas Watch in New York City; Sonny Saul at Pleasant

Street Books in Woodstock, Vermont; and the late Rev. Robert Andrews, host of the Ticodel lecture series, Ciudad Colon, Costa Rica.

I especially want to thank all of those (in first-name alphabetical order) who offered their libraries, guest rooms, houses, apartments, and house boats while this book was being written: Ann Marie, Barbara H., Bill and Sandy, Carl and Helen, Carol M., Carol R., Chris and Lady, Christopher B., Eric and Lynne, Fred and Pat, Isabel M., Jaime and Martha, John and Marlene, Maria Elena L., Maria Rosa O., Ruth D., Sarah S., and especially Stacey C. This work would not have been possible without their hospitality and generosity.

Professor Eugene Anderson of the University of California at Riverside brought his erudition to bear on the penultimate draft of the manuscript, making many constructive comments on my treatment of evolutionary biology, anthropology, and the philosophy of science. I owe him a special debt of gratitude.

Helen Drachkovitch has never ceased to provide encouragement and support.

Finally, I want to thank my wife Dr. Nicole L. Sault, whose unstinting encouragement, inspiration, and good humor, combined with her intellectual abilities and broad ethnographic knowledge, made this a better book.

Preface

This book deals with the intersection of three areas of intellectual life that are usually kept apart: religion, social science, and evolutionary biology. I have tried to make the content of these fields accessible to a general reader, but when necessary I make use of technical terminology, such as *genotype* and *phenotype*, so as to avoid cumbersome circumlocutions. But as few people have command of the jargon of all three fields, I have added a glossary at the end of this volume. When a technical term is used for the first time in the body of this book, I have marked it with a superscript (G) to indicate whether it is found in the glossary. For example: matriline,G methylation,G modernism.G If a term consists of multiple words, I place the superscript after the first word, as for example natural G selection, so as to clarify where the term is located in the glossary. However, if the multiple words in a term are capitalized, I place the superscript after the last capitalized term, as for example New Deal G and Chicago School.G

Not all technical terms mentioned in the text are included in the glossary. If a term is important to the argument, as for example *epigenetic,* I usually define it twice, once when first introduced and then again in the glossary. However, many other technical terms, such as *Drosophila* (a genus of fruit fly) and *Macaca* (a genus of monkey), are defined when first mentioned in the text; but as their names are incidental to the argument they are not included in the glossary. In a few cases, I have added terms to the glossary as a convenience to the reader, such as geological epochs (e.g. Cambrian). Familiar terms are included if they are open to various interpretations and definitions, such as *Puritanism* and *capitalism.* Finally, I include in the glossary any new terminology that I introduce in the text: specifically, the terms *bio-immortality,* the *bipolar theory of science, complementation, congruent systems of belief,* and *keystone ideology.*

Book I
Prologue

Until Darwin, evolution was bundled with demands for liberty, equality, and fraternity; but after Darwin, it was bundled with competition, eugenics, and the selfish gene.

Darwin's theory of evolution was born of a particular moment in history when the capitalist class was wresting control of mainstream intellectual culture from the clergy and the aristocracy, and his theory bears the imprint of that formative struggle. In Darwinist thought, religion is an obstacle to science (as Victorian progressives contended); competition makes the world go 'round (as the capitalists proclaimed); and superior social qualities are determined by superior bloodlines (as the aristocracy believed). Darwin merged these beliefs with the concept of natural selection—and brought organic evolution into the intellectual mainstream.

Darwin is best known for organic evolution, but his theorizing extended well beyond plants and animals to include the social and political issues of the day. Indeed, Darwin's place in history owes less to natural science than to the social forces that he set in motion. Darwin and his colleagues were instrumental in the professionalization of science and the establishment of modern biomedical education. Their educational policies made the university into a force for modernization while leaving intact the academic culture of intellectual orthodoxy. Thus, the Darwinian revolution was not confined to biology but involves social science, higher education, political advocacy, and moral philosophy as well.

Nowadays, empirical research using Darwin's key concepts of adaptation and selection is known as evolutionary biology, but the empirical science has from the beginning shared the stage with a system of belief known as Darwinism. The latter uses findings derived from evolutionist science but combines them with social and metaphysical ideas that have no necessary connection to evolution at all. As if to complicate the situation even further, many eminent evolutionary biologists have been enthusiastic Darwinists, while captains of industry have long funded evolutionist science.

Darwinism is not reducible to the writings and personal beliefs of Charles Darwin. What an individual believes is essentially unknowable to scholarship, so anthropology focuses on public acts such as books, speeches, and scientific research. Moreover, a belief system is a collective product that requires followers as well as leaders. One can, of course, return to the seminal works of an inspirational figure and provide evidence of belief in this thesis rather than that, but this in no way alters the fact that history is irreversible and runs in a channel wider than a single person.

Whether assessing Darwin or Marx, Jesus or Calvin, it is important to bear in mind that collective understanding of a belief system always reflects the interpretations of a particular social class and period of history. For this reason, the tenets that are emphasized may differ from one age to another, and the emphasis may also differ from that of the founder. Yet an influential shaper of thought typically inspires a community of disciples with a specific configuration of beliefs that may endure unchanged for centuries. Darwinism first emerged in the England of the 1860s and has continued to the present day, expressed through the actions of a community of believers that I refer to as *Darwin's cohort*.

In my definition, *Darwinism* consists of four core beliefs. These are (P) Progress through genetic change, (H) hostility to religion, (A) atomistic individualism, and (G) the genetic inheritance of social behavior. The initial letters of these four tenets spell the acronym PHAGe, which rhymes with *page* as in a a book.

In the following pages, I explore the interaction of Darwinist ideology with evolutionary biology, higher education, corporate capitalism, and the moral order. To this end, I discuss the shift from Christianity to modernism in universities in the United States and England in the late nineteenth century. I also review the corporate takeover of American higher education in the course of the twentieth, especially its effects on medicine and bioscience. In the process, I explicate the inherent limitations of Darwinist thought both as social policy and as a science of human evolution. Finally, I present my personal vision of life without Darwin based on Christian ethics and libertarian socialism.

Chapter One

The Father of Social Darwinism

For most of his life Charles Darwin lived as a country gentleman in a spacious home full of books, specimens, children, and domestic animals: a scientist absorbed with the minutiae of experimentation, dissection, and selective breeding, a man seemingly far removed from the class^G conflict of industrial^G England and the violence of its colonial wars. Yet it is not his encyclopedic grasp of the facts of biology that made him a household name among people who could not tell a barnacle from a limpet.

Charles Darwin, Political Economist

The use of evolutionary^G biology to justify the social order is known today as Social Darwinism,^G and the conventional wisdom is that it is an aberration of Darwin's theory that emerged in the last decades of the nineteenth century, trumpeted by the nouveau riche of the Gilded Age.^G House historians split the historical Charles Darwin into two different people: Charles Darwin the scientist, the brilliant theoretician of evolutionary biology, and his evil twin Herbert Spencer, a discredited social philosopher who taught that evolution is supportive of capitalism.

A prominent historian, Richard Hofstadter, helped to sever Darwin from Social Darwinism by treating the latter without reference to the former, focusing instead on the "general acceptance of unrestrained competition"—as if Darwin did not help

to create this climate of opinion.[1] Interpretations such as Hofstadter's require that we divorce Darwin's system of thought from
its social implications while ignoring the fact that Darwin saw
himself as contributing a biological perspective to the social issues of the day.

Michael Ruse, a prominent Darwin scholar, traces Social
Darwinism to *both* Charles Darwin and Herbert Spencer. Both
thinkers were responding to Malthus's Law of Population,^G but
their responses took divergent paths. Darwin emphasized nat-
ural^G selection, whereas Spencer emphasized the inheritance of
acquired characteristics.[2]

Another scholar of the Victorian period, Gregory Claeys,
points out that "in the mid-1860s Darwin himself became in
effect a Social Darwinist, and came increasingly to hope that the
optimal outcome of human natural selection would be the triumph of 'the intellectual and moral' races over the 'lower and
more degraded ones.'"[3]

Charles Darwin's work is always viewed as "biology," but at the
time when he was formulating his theory the line had not yet
been drawn between social and biological science. People who
studied plants and animals were known as natural historians,
while inquiry into the workings of government^G and the economy was known as political^G economy. In the twentieth century,
the term political economy fell into disuse because it implies that
politics and economics are functionally inseparable, whereas capitalism demands that the economy be presented as a mechanistic
process that is independent of government. At the same time,
modernism^G urged students of political policy to define themselves as political "scientists," thus encouraging the conflation of
value with fact.[4]

In the British Isles of Darwin's day, the study of politics and
economics was epitomized by Thomas Robert Malthus, a professor of political economy in a school founded by the East In-

dia Company to train its future administrators and managers. Charles Darwin is straightforward about his debt to Malthusian[G] theory. In the introduction to *On the Origin of Species* he explicitly informs the reader that evolution by natural selection is "the doctrine of Malthus, applied to the whole animal and vegetable kingdoms."[4] Decades later in his autobiography Darwin reaffirms Malthus's inspirational role:

> In October 1838, that is, fifteen months after I had begun my systematic inquiry [into the origin of species] I happened to read for amusement Malthus on Population, and being well prepared to appreciate the struggle for existence which everywhere goes on from long-continued observation of the habits of animals and plants, it at once struck me that under these circumstances favourable variations would tend to be preserved, and unfavourable ones to be destroyed. The results of this would be the formation of a new species. Here, then I had at last got a theory by which to work.[5]

In popular histories of science, Malthus is usually positioned as the founder of demography, suggesting a scientific companion on Darwin's evolutionary journey, but to his contemporaries he was one of the best-known and controversial figures in British politics, a prominent economist and advocate of the Whigs,[G] who was, in the words of biographer William Petersen, "at the storm center of every important controversy during his lifetime."[6] Malthus first earned his reputation as a critic of the French Revolution, giving him the support of the aristocracy,[G] while his Law of Population, which implies that the poor reproduce faster than their food supply (and so have only themselves to blame) was enthusiastically embraced by the capitalists.[G][7] To Malthus, demography was inseparable from political advocacy, and he railed against public charity, arguing that it encourages the poor to have more children.

In the England of the 1830s, as with the Republican Party in the United States today, it was widely believed that poverty is due to an insufficiency of moral character. From this it follows that the solution to poverty is to eliminate free lunches for the poor and force the lazy back to work. In 1834, only a few years before Darwin's inspirational moment, the Whigs had put Malthus's theories into practice by abolishing church-supported charity and replacing it with a national system of workhouses.[8] The Whig legislation, commonly known as the New Poor Law, provided state aid to the homeless and the unemployed only if they had been accepted into state-run residences where husbands and wives were separated from each other and required to work for their food. The concept was based, in Petersen's words, "on the Benthamite[G] principle that relief should be available to the able-bodied poor only under conditions deliberately set out to be worse than those of the lowest-paid independent worker."[9]

The workhouse system was widely hated by people who were in danger of falling into it, and it provides the setting for Charles Dickens's novel *Oliver Twist*, which was first published in serial form between February 1837 and April 1839, making it contemporaneous with Darwin's first draft of his evolutionary theory. The opening paragraph of *Oliver Twist* leaves no doubt as to the political context: "Among other public buildings in a certain town, which for many reasons it will be prudent to refrain from mentioning, and to which I will assign no fictitious name, there is one anciently common to most towns, great or small: to wit, a workhouse."[10] Dickens uses his novel to critique the poverty of the London of his day, with the workhouse as one of the villains.

The workhouse system was established by the British in colonial Ireland as well, where it contributed to the death toll of the Great Famine of 1847 to 1853. Under British law, the able-bodied poor could receive assistance only if they were residents of a workhouse, but hunger was not considered to be sufficient grounds for admission. Only when people had become too weak and malnourished to work were they admitted to a workhouse and given food, but by then it was often too late.[11]

Whatever its humanitarian limitations, the workhouse is a straight-forward implementation of Victorian social theory. It addresses competition for food, which is the premise of Malthus's Law of Population, while providing an opportunity for advances in social evolution through what Herbert Spencer called "survival of the fittest." The same theory of political economy that inspired the workhouse inspired Darwin's theory of natural selection.

In 1838, when Darwin claims that he first "happened to read for amusement" the *Essay on Population* he was already immersed in Malthusian thought. Four years earlier, while the *Beagle* was anchored off Tierra del Fuego, Darwin received a packet of mail from his sister, which included a copy of *Poor Laws and Paupers Illustrated* by Harriet Martineau, a fierce advocate of Malthus's political program. Martineau "was the darling of the Whigs, a one-woman advertising agency, whose soap-opera novellas popularized and explained the reforms."[12] Then when Charles returned to England, he lived for a time in London with his brother Erasmus, who was smitten with Martineau and invited her frequently as his dinner guest.[13] There were family connections too: Malthus's daughter was a bridesmaid at the wedding of Darwin's sister. As the authors of one well-regarded biography note: "Darwin was becoming enmeshed in a close and personal Malthusian circle."[14]

Darwin's affinity for Malthus and the Whigs also reflected his own economic interests, in that his family's fortune had risen with the incoming tide of industrialism. Charles's paternal grandfather, Erasmus, was physician to the leading merchant families of the Midlands during the formative period of the Industrial Revolution, and he amassed a considerable fortune through investment in their enterprises.[15] Charles grew up in an imposing home with numerous servants, where he associated socially with the families of wealthy landowners and industrialists. Also, Darwin's relatives on his mother's side, the Wedgewoods, were prominent ceramic manufacturers;[16] through his visits to their factory he acquired an owner's perspective on capitalism. Even later in life, when stretched thin by scientific projects and beset by declining health, Charles Darwin still found time to speculate in railroad stocks and acquire income-producing property.[17]

Darwin was raised with the values of the English industrial class—a commitment to the acquisition of wealth, belief in competition as a positive force, confidence in scientific rationalism, and faith in material progress—and they remain among the fundamental values of capitalism today. Nor did Charles Darwin have any motivation to question them. It was his hereditary membership in this class that admitted him to Cambridge University, that gave him a five-year trip around the world, that married him into the family of a wealthy manufacturer, and provided, on his father's death, an inheritance of more than 40,000 pounds in an era when one of his domestic servants would have made fifty pounds a year working a six-day week.[18]

Politically, Darwin supported the Whigs, who represented the interests of the industrialists and the emerging middle class in opposition to the aristocracy. The Whigs began as a political movement in the late seventeenth century to ensure that England would be ruled by a Protestant monarch whose actions would be limited by a strong Parliament, but by Darwin's time they had become a force for modernization,[G] passing legislation that helped to create the world that we live in today. The Whigs were instrumental in obtaining representation for factory towns in parliament, extending the vote to middle class men, instituting free trade, removing legal restrictions against Catholics and Nonconformists,^G abolishing slavery in the British Empire, and replacing church-supported charity for the poor with a system of workhouses. In the year that Darwin published *Origin,* the Whigs merged with another party and ceased to exist by that name, though many of their policies continue to the present day.

Many of the tenets of what later became Darwinism^G are not the findings of natural science but reflect the conventional beliefs of the society in which Charles Darwin was raised, one whose intellectual culture had already been shaped by the interests of the capitalist^G class and the social policies of the Whigs. Just by accepting the conventional wisdom of the educated class of his day, Darwin would have come to believe that societies develop from the simple to the complex, that poor people breed indiscriminately, and that human races can be scientifically classified by means of skin color and ranked on a scale of perfection, with the White* race as the most refined, moral, and intelligent. Darwin uncritically incorporated these social beliefs into his theory of human evolution, giving them a scientific imprimatur that they do not merit.

As one scholar notes, even "Darwin's metaphorical application of the 'survival of the fittest' to society was in fact virtually a commonplace by 1859," the year that *Origin* was published.[19] That same year, Herbert Spencer anticipated natural selection by linking the concept of population pressure and competition for resources to evolutionary change, arguing that population pressure is the cause of evolutionary advance: those with the greatest strength of self-preservation would prevail at the expense of their fellows, a process known as "the survival of the fittest."[20] Spencer was a very successful writer and public speaker who did much to popularize these ideas in the United States and the British Empire before Darwin embraced them.[21]

What was missing from the received wisdom, however, was the concept of organic^G evolution itself. Stripped of the Sturm und Drang, organic evolution is simply the thesis that the species^G alive today are the descendants of different species that lived at an earlier period of geologic time. As we shall see (Chapter 2), the concept of biological evolution was first developed in the late eighteenth century, but it had been suppressed in England on the grounds that it was a radical ideology^G that fostered political revolution and irreligion. Indeed, evolution *is* revolutionary, because it allows even "lower" forms of life, such as peasants and workers, to evolve into more "advanced" species, such as managers and magistrates.

The theory of evolution, in the sense of progressive change over time, began in the eighteenth century as a theory of history, not of biology; and from the beginning it served as a political ideology. In the latter capacity, it had helped to establish the bourgeoisie^G as a political force by discrediting a static, theocratic system of nature supportive of hereditary classes and replacing it with a dynamic, materialist one congenial to progressives.^G Indeed, so successful was this new view of society that by the middle of the nineteenth century industrialists and financiers had wrested the machinery of state from the landed aristocracy, leading to a new ruling class of bankers, brewers, and boiler makers. Thus, by Darwin's day, immutable species created by God no longer supported the economy, which by now promised material progress and opportunity for all

With the publication of *Origin* in 1859, Darwin brought biological phenomena into the evolutionary mainstream, but he gave it a capitalist spin by merging it with Malthus.

The First Darwinians

The theory of natural selection had great appeal to the Victorian intelligentsia because it confirmed their expectations of what a science of life should be: a small number of concise, universally applicable laws of nature similar to those discovered by physics. Alfred Russel Wallace, the nineteenth-century biologist who developed the idea of natural selection in parallel with Charles Darwin, expresses this enthusiasm very succinctly:

> Mr. Darwin's work has for its main object, to show, that all the phenomena of living things,—all their wonderful organs and complicated structures, their infinite variety of form, size, and colour, their intricate and involved relations to each other,—may have been produced by the action of a few general laws of the simplest kind, laws which are in most cases mere statements of admitted facts.[23]

Then Wallace goes on to provide a list of the six laws that constitute the theory of natural selection:

• The Law of Geometrical Progression (Malthus's observation that populations have the potential to increase very rapidly).

• The Law of Limited Populations (populations soon reach a limit to size, leaving no room for the newborn).

• The Law of Heredity (children are like their parents).

• The Law of Variation (no child is exactly like its parents).

• The Law of Unceasing Change (the physical conditions of life are in constant flux).

• The Equilibrium or Harmony of Nature (well-adapted species and individuals survive while the less
adapted die off).

As Wallace summarizes: "It is from these universally admitted
facts, that the origin of all the varied forms of nature may be deduced by a logical chain of reasoning, which, however, is at every
step verified and shown to be in strict accord with facts; and, at
the same time, many curious phenomena which can by no other
means be understood, are explained and accounted for."[24]

There is a strong tendency, even among scientists, to conflate
the observable facts of change over geologic time, what Darwin
called descent[G] with modification, with the mechanism of natural
selection (defined by Wallace's six postulates) to the point that
for many people the two have become synonymous. Evolution,
however, is a description of the history of life, pieced together by
means of the fossil record, the geological record, and the detailed
comparison of organisms from different periods of earth history,
whereas natural selection is a formalism that attempts to explain
these evolutionary changes by means of a small set of abstract
principles.

In Darwin's usage, natural selection is as ubiquitous and as
forceful as gravity, thus making Darwin's theory of biological evolution the peer of Newton's physics—the difference being that every creature on the planet earth has experienced gravity, whereas
natural selection has been experienced by no one.

To Darwinists, the "discovery" of natural selection is Darwin's
original contribution to science (with Wallace often relegated to
a footnote), a discovery that is said to have shaken Victorian culture to its foundations. But far from being perceived as a radical
departure, the theory of natural selection appeared to scientifically
confirm everything that educated Victorians thought they knew
while providing a biological rationale for what they had been
doing already. Natural selection was assimilated to the prevailing

belief in progressive social evolution while changing the theoretical foundation of the latter from history to biology.[25]

In Darwin's day, the capitalist interpretation of the Darwin-Wallace theory had not yet solidified into the dominant ideology, and not even Darwin and Wallace could agree. Wallace thought that "natural selection was more a *product* of evolution than its cause"[26] whereas Darwin thought that it explained all of life and society. Moreover, Darwin was a Whig and a materialist,[G] whereas Wallace was a socialist[G] and a spiritualist,[G] which led them to radically different positions on social issues.[27] Wallace was a forceful critic of capitalism,[28] but Darwin's views on society were more attractive to the capitalist class, which led to the eclipse of Wallace's reputation, which is only now being reassessed.

Although Charles Darwin avoided public life, the social policies implicit in *The Descent of Man* were promulgated by a cohort of supporters, with his knowledge and approval, through their leadership in scientific and academic institutions, as discussed in Chapters 3 and 4. This institutionalization of Darwinism carried his influence far beyond biology, enabling or facilitating a broad range of social changes that are definitive of the twentieth century, among them the professionalization of science, the peripheralization of religion[G] from intellectual life, the emergence of technocratic[G] biomedicine, and a society dominated by corporations.[G]

In Darwin's writings, evolutionary change is so intertwined with natural selection that one would think that they are simply two aspects of the same process. Conceptually, however, the description of evolutionary change and the theory of natural selection are quite distinct—to the point that one can accept the evolution of life while questioning Darwin's explanation of it. Biological evolution is the history of life on earth as documented by genetics, comparative anatomy, and the fossil record, whereas the theory of natural selection is Darwin's interpretation of how the evolutionary process works.

Darwinism vs. Evolution

My first serious exposure to human evolution was as an undergraduate major in anthropology at the University of California at Berkeley in the 1960s, when I took a course in paleoanthropology,ᴳ learning to identify extinct species of primates from fossilized skulls and teeth. Also, while at Berkeley I happened on a course called the History of Paleontology. It was taught by an elderly, soft-spoken man in a gray flannel suit who delivered his lectures in a precise, monochromatic style reminiscent of a corporate accountant. He was on the verge of retirement and had enough seniority to wave away the survey courses and devote his remaining classroom hours to something more outré. His course dealt with everything that had been left out of modern textbooks on the earth sciences. There was nothing in it about radiometric dating or magnetic reversals, much less erosion rates and the art of wielding a pick—indeed, we barely got to the twentieth century by the end of the semester. Rather, it dealt with theories that some of the more science-minded students had never heard of before, such as the universal deluge and the special creation of species. I remember congratulating myself at the time that I managed to find the one course at the university that will never be relevant to anything in the wider world.

In the 1960s, the excavation of human fossils was being supplemented by field studies of nonhuman primate social behavior, exemplified by Jane Goodall's research among chimpanzees in East Africa.[29] Her unexpected findings about the lives of anthropoid apes in their natural habitat led to a surge of interest among anthropologists in the behavior and ecology of nonhuman primates, an enthusiasm largely due to Sherwood Washburn, a professor of physical anthropology at Berkeley. I remember him as a slightly-built, silver-haired man with the energetic self-confidence of an Ivy League dean of chapel.[30] Washburn reasoned that because humans had descended from ape-like primates and that the most diversified array of human-like fossils had been found in Africa, African primates and ecology might hold important clues to the emergence of the human species. Although Washburn had been trained in classical anatomy, not as a fieldworker or behavioral scientist, he motivated a generation of graduate students to head into the bush with notebooks and cameras.

One tangible result was an upper-division course offered by the anthropology department at Berkeley called Primate Behavior, probably the first such course in the world. When I took it, the teacher was Jane Lancaster, a predoctoral student in physical anthropology.[31] She was an articulate woman in her twenties, with waist-length brown hair and sleek knit dresses. Most of the facts were younger than the students, and the readings were chapters from a forthcoming book edited by Irven DeVore, who had studied baboons in Kenya. DeVore had proposed that each of his fellow fieldworkers contribute a chapter on the naturalistic behavior and ecology of the species of nonhuman primate they were studying. It was this compendium that defined the new discipline of primatology when it was published a year later.[32] In addition, every week there was a guest lecturer, usually a young doctoral candidate who had just come back from fieldwork in some tropical country. They told us about their experiences during the previous eighteen months: about primate life cycles and diurnal[G] rhythms, about mutual[G] grooming and agonistic[G] displays, about consort[G] pairs and status[G] hierarchies, about methodology and tape recorders, about diarrhea and the language barrier, about sandstorms and monsoons. I was hooked.

From the mid-1960s through the early 1970s, I did research at several major universities and at important biological laboratories, conversing with evolutionists in their native language, observing what they did, and participating in their activities. While at the time I thought of myself as practicing science, years later I realized that I was also engaged in participant^G observation, a methodology that I learned about in my courses in cultural^G anthropology. This method was first employed by adventurous ethnographers^G in the nineteenth century, but it was popularized in the 1920s by the work of Bronislaw Malinowski, a Polish anthropologist who chronicled the way of life of farmers and fishermen in a remote archipelago in the central Pacific. Malinowski was a keen observer of human activity and a good writer with a flair for attention-getting titles, such as *The Sexual Life of Savages*—titles that propelled social anthropology into fashionable circles, enabling it to reach a wider audience.[33]

By the early 1970s, social scientists were applying the method of participant observation to the process of science itself,[34] but at the time I was more participant than observer. I tape-recorded the vocalizations of macaque monkeys, undertook a laboratory experiment to see if they could hear phonemically,^G established breeding colonies of two species of macaques, observed the social behavior of monkey troops^G in outdoor enclosures, tested juvenile gorillas on latch-box problems, observed social play in small groups of gorillas, did experimental manipulations of play and social attachment in monkeys, communicated with a home-schooled gorilla, served as a teaching assistant in courses on neuropsychology and population^G genetics, attended lectures and symposia, published papers in refereed journals, taught university courses on human evolution, toured excavations with a paleoanthropologist in East Africa, and surveyed field sites with a primatologist in West Africa.[35] These experiences gave me an ethnographer's perspective on the field of human evolution, and in this book I introduce vignettes describing my personal experience so as to better convey the observer's vantage point on the subject matter.

Although I was drawn to primatology because it held the promise of illuminating human evolution, it also invoked Darwin as its putative ancestor, thus privileging a theoretical framework that would grow more influential as the science matured. However, thanks to the course on the history of paleontology, I had learned at a young age that the idea of organic evolution antedates Charles Darwin by at least a generation, so I was effectively inoculated against Darwinist hagiography. Also, being familiar with the twisting road that the theory of evolution had followed historically, I knew that the history of science is not the same as history as presented by scientists. Whereas scientists seem to be content with idealized chronologies of even their own disciplines, arranging discoveries like steps on a ladder that lead inevitably to the priorities of the present, anthropologists, like historians, try to chronicle the often obscure circumstances that enabled the present to emerge from the past.

Although Darwin's theory of natural selection is always presented to the public as natural science, it has evolved in tandem with sociopolitical movements that are anything but scientific. Indeed, history suggests that the idea of natural selection attracts ideologues like bears to bacon: militarists and empire builders, eugenicists and White[G] supremacists, neocons[G] and libertarians, as well as Bible bashers and born-again atheists. Darwinian house historians rarely note this cast of characters, and, even when it is called to their attention, they dismiss such advocacy as distortions of their master's science—thereby ignoring the essential role that Darwinian scientists have played in fostering these movements, beginning with Darwin's own paean to Malthus and his endorsement of Galton (see below, this chapter). I began to wonder if such "distortions" might not be implicit in the intellectual content of Darwinian theory and nurtured by its ideological role in capitalist society.

Fieldwork in the Capitalist Camp

When I first entertained this thesis, I knew very little about capitalism. In the 1960s there was still a firewall between academe and commerce. At most universities, academics who had worked in business were seen as tainting the ivory tower, while tycoons were discouraged from coming on campus unless they were contributing to the building fund. However, Stanford University, in Palo Alto, California, where I did much of my primatological research, was one of the universities most accepting of capitalism; indeed, it began its rise to prominence during World War II by developing technology based on government-funded research and contracting with big business to sell it to the military. So successful was this strategy that by the 1960s high-tech corporations circled the Stanford campus like a fairy ring of money.

By the end of the twentieth century, the barriers between academe and business were gone: new legislation enabled recipients of federal research funding to patent the findings and develop them commercially, thus creating a new stage in the history of academe that I call the corporate[G] academy (Chapter 7).[36] This development was as much political as economic. In the wake of the anti-establishment politics of the Sixties, the capitalist class in the United States set out to create a cultural climate more supportive of big business. Using money from foundations and corporate contributions, capitalists established libertarian think tanks, endowed chairs at universities, lobbied for pro-business judicial appointments, enlisted the support of conservative churches, and ran candidates for public office—an effort that culminated in a massive rightward shift of the American body politic.

These trends were given further impetus by the ascendancy of Reagan and Thatcher in the 1980s. Their rise to power was heralded in the mass media as the liberation of big business from obsolete government regulations, with the promise of increased prosperity for everyone. Although not apparent at the time, this was the beginning of the end of prosperity for the American working class for it coincided with the offshoring of factory jobs and a decline in union membership. As for anthropologists, the effects were felt immediately: funding for social science all but disappeared.

Fortunately, the muse of anthropology guided me to a culture where few ethnographers had ever been: Silicon Valley. At a dinner party in Palo Alto I met an executive recruiter named Joanne Rampelburg. We talked a bit about new developments in technology, and she was surprised to learn that I was familiar with the programming language LISP, which was little known outside of academic computing circles. I told her that while doing research at Stanford I had met many of the people who were creating the field of artificial intelligence and that LISP was being used to simulate human language and tool using. When Joanne learned that I was unemployed, she brightened and said: "I can sell you!" Even though I had no background in business or engineering, she found me a job as a software instructor at the pseudonymous Falcon Computer Company.

At this time the high-tech startup was first entering public awareness. The first portable computers had already been developed (they were about the size and weight of a small microwave oven),[37] and Falcon was making one of the world's first laptop computers—one that could fit in a briefcase.[38] The company was a start-up, which is to say that it had not yet made an initial public offering of stock (an IPO).

During the start-up phase, a company is like an acorn, full of potential but small in size. Whereas mature corporations have facilities all over the world, a start-up is more likely to have all of its employees working in a single building. Also, the corporate hierarchy is much flatter than in a mature company, so the CEO might be dressed in faded blue jeans and working on the same floor as everyone else, with the corner office as the only indicator of rank. Also, there is much more unity of purpose than in a large corporation, as the first employees of a firm are typically motivated by a shared desire to "take the company public," which is to say by the desire to convert their stock options (in my case "warrants" convertible to stock) into shares that can be sold on the stock exchange for many times what they paid for them. Also, functions that constitute entire divisions in a mature company, such as marketing or engineering, are represented by a handful of individuals that one can know by name, as in a village. So startups are ideal for an inquiring anthropologist.

I was fortunate in that my first boss, Sunny Baker, was a skeptical observer of the computer industry in general and of Falcon Computer Company in particular. In start-up corporations, there is considerable social pressure to invest one's own money in the enterprise, but Sunny advised me against it—thus giving my own tenure at Falcon Computer a happier ending than it would otherwise have had. She seemed to sense what an ex-academic needed to know about the social relations of capitalism, and she gave me the time to learn it. Six months after I embarked on my new career, Sunny resigned to take a job with a well-known software company in Redmond, Washington; before she left she recommended me as her successor to the position of department manager.

Sunny's recommendation was accepted, and I reported directly to the vice president of marketing, one of the key positions in any company. I attended the meeting of marketing department managers every Monday morning for a year, where I mostly took notes as if in college. Nearly all of my colleagues had MBAs and considerable experience in computing, business, and industry. At these meetings we discussed most of the issues that companies have to deal with—the features of the new product, the strengths and weaknesses of competitors, the amount of financing needed for development and marketing, the timetable for product release, the theme of the advertising program, and a host of other issues, all of which seemed to require immediate attention.

What is good for anthropologists is not necessarily good for investors. Due to a design flaw in the motherboard, the new computer ultimately failed to meet its manufacturing deadline, so I was able to witness a nearly complete corporate life cycle in the course of only two years: from the heady second round of venture capital financing—a day when employees openly fantasized about what they planned to do with their new wealth after the successful IPO—to that day not long after when the financiers turned off the flow of capital, forcing the company to file for bankruptcy.

Shortly thereafter a long black limousine came to a stop in front of company headquarters. A dark-suited man emerged from the car, accompanied by a uniformed security guard. He ordered the employees to leave the building and then padlocked the door behind them. In retrospect, I could not have found a better platform for viewing the social relations of corporate[G] capitalism had I planned it.

I learned that the belief[G] system of Silicon Valley is not as far from the theory of evolution as one might think. Every new product is claimed to be more advanced than those that preceded it, so the computer industry embodies the idea of Progress[G] in a form that is little changed since Victorian times. Also, Darwinian theory is implicitly embedded in capitalism through the centrality of competition. Employees compete with each other for promotion, departments compete for resources, and the corporation competes with others in the marketplace.

In this book, I explore the relationship between evolutionary theory and capitalism, not to find commonalities between the two but to delineate how they function as complementary belief

systems in contemporary society. Drawing upon historical studies and my own participant observation. I argue that theories
of the biological body as taught in the elite universities and the
body politic of capitalist society are coevolutionary[G] processes.

Evolution as Ideology

Even though I had spent my academic career exploring the relationship between biological and social evolution, I still lacked an
intellectual framework that could explain the long-term association between evolutionary biology and such sociopolitical movements as laissez-faire[G] capitalism and White supremacy. When I
was working in Australia in the 1970s, the first postmodernists[G]
were lecturing in Paris, but I did not read literary criticism, especially when written by Marxists in French. I had grown up
during the McCarthy period in the United States, when Marxism[G] was synonymous with Communism.[G 39]

Senator McCarthy's anti-Communist speeches marked the
beginning of the Cold War,[G] and his supporters thought that
intellectuals, artists, and academics were especially prone to treason.[40] In 1949, the regents of the University of California imposed a loyalty oath on employees, leading to the dismissal of
thirty professors who refused to sign it as a matter of principle.
American universities responded to government pressure as one
would expect of an organization modeled on Prussian bureaucracy (discussed in Chapter 3). In a book published by Oxford
University Press, historian Ellen Schrecker concludes that "The
academy did not fight McCarthyism. It contributed to it."[41]

The United States government had insufficient evidence of
treason or espionage to bring convictions of academics in criminal trials, so it smeared their reputations through subpoenaed
testimony at public hearings, then pressured universities to ter-
minate their employment. The academy almost invariably did.
Moreover, once someone had been fired by one university, it was

almost impossible to get a job at another, thanks to secret liaisons between the academy and the FBI. The firing of Communists and purported fellow travelers was a warning to others, and faculty members responded by adopting a policy of self-censorship. They removed controversial topics from course syllabi and refrained from any criticism of U.S. foreign policy and big business. As Eleanor Leacock, a professor of anthropology reflected, "until the 1960s it was virtually impossible for an [American] academic to discuss Marxism as such."[42]

My professors at Berkeley had mentioned Marx as one of the seminal figures of social science, then quickly moved on to Malinowski, so I had learned that Marxism was somewhat subversive. While working in Australia in the 1970s, I met a young English woman, Hilary Yerbury, who was fluent in French and getting a postgraduate degree in social theory. In spite of my initial resistance, Hilary introduced me to the thought of the Continental postmodernists. Then in 1975 I was invited to a conference in Europe that featured prominent members of the Frankfurt School[G]—a scholarly project after World War I to make available the little-known works of the young Karl Marx. These hitherto unpublished works provide some insight into "Marx before Marxism," to borrow David McLellan's apt phrase, while calling attention to disparities between Marx's thought and Stalin's interpretation of it.[43]

Appropriately, it was in Frankfurt that I first encountered *The Social Construction of Reality* by Peter L. Berger and Thomas Luckmann.[44] From this and other works, it became obvious that the theory of natural selection, irrespective of the biological evidence invoked in its behalf, is also an ideological framework that is superimposed on organic nature, thus merging the science of evolution with the values of the British industrial class. In Darwin's own words, natural selection "is the doctrine of Malthus, applied to the whole animal and vegetable kingdoms."[45]

In the aftermath of the culture wars, *ideology* is a worrisome word that for many people implies misleading facts and deliberate untruths; but when used empirically the term is descriptive, not pejorative, and denotes a system of beliefs that *facilitates the political and economic power of a particular social class, political party, or social group.* The postmodernist critique has been used to debunk the possibility of science, and is often seen by scientists as an attack, but it is more correct to conclude that it debunks science's philosophical claims while leaving the techniques of science largely unaffected.

When applied to science, the concept of ideology typically denotes the shaping of scientific questions and the selection of scientific findings by interest groups and prevailing beliefs. Any science whose subject matter impinges directly on human beings will always have an ideological aspect since its findings will be evaluated by people in the light of their own interests and beliefs, and these in turn feed back, through legislatures and granting agencies, to affect the kinds the research that gets done and the findings that get presented in textbooks—just as Marx's critique of capitalism was edited out of the American social science curriculum.

Science is subject to ideological influences and often performs ideological functions—and evolutionary biology is no exception. The ideological aspect of contemporary evolutionary biology has been recognized in the pages of the journal *Science* itself. Michael Ruse notes that "there is professional evolutionary biology: mathematical, experimental, not laden with value statements," which is published in journals such as *Evolution* and *Animal Behaviour.* "Then, sometimes from the same person, you have evolution as secular religion, generally working from an explicitly materialist background and solving all the world's major problems, from racism to education to conservation."[46]

However, it would be a mistake to conclude that evolutionary biology is easily separated into "good" naturalistic description and "bad" secular religion. In human institutions, ideology and factuality are not mutually exclusive. Think of science as bipolar^G—not manic-depressive but more like a water molecule. At the pole where it interfaces with naturalistic observation, science exemplifies those properties beloved by British philosophers: logic, empiricism, falsifiability, self-correction, peer review, and all the rest, producing those rock-hard facts that anyone can verify, such as the diameter of the hydrogen atom. But where science interfaces with the larger society, it functions as an ideology, using its findings to justify its prerogatives to both itself and outsiders. At this level, certain findings are shoved forward as politically efficacious, while others, less socially acceptable, are left to wither on the vine. Moreover, once scientific concepts, such as stem^G cells and selfish^G genes, are selected for promotion, they become mythologized to the point that their truth or falsity is irrelevant to anyone except scientists working in a particular specialty.

However, it is not the case, as positivists^G might hope, that when scientists are working in their laboratories they are producing unbiased descriptions of nature whereas the ideological distortion is added by deans and publicists further up the food chain. Even though the two poles of science are as conceptually distinct as mass is from gravity, one cannot exist without the other: without funding for research, no scientific findings; without scientific findings, no funding for research.

Thus, the selection of "appropriate" research topics is often made before the scientist even begins to work on them, while culturally-defined standards of success are as central to the belief systems of researchers as to administrators. Scientific findings are factualized at the methodological pole and mythologized at the ideological pole—often, as with Galileo, by the very same person.

The ideological and research components of science are often mutually reinforcing, not contradictory. At the same time, descriptive statements that are not motivated politically can function ideologically when they alter public opinion. For example, the thesis "medical science developed an effective polio vaccine" facilitates the power and prestige of the medical profession; moreover, it helps to create a political climate where scientific medicine is seen in a leadership role, commanding more public funding and higher salaries than the well-meaning family practitioner. Thus, truth can confer political and economic advantage too, and often it is far more effective than lies. Even hardball politics is replete with motivated truths: "Insurance broker says he was pressured to buy ads on vice-president's radio station before winning federal contract."[47]

The study of ideology is further complicated by the fact that not all declarative sentences are to be read as statements of fact. Certainly, when we read a declarative sentence, our first impulse is to assign to it a truth value: "Adolf Hitler is alive in Argentina." But there are many declarative sentences to which the attribution of truth and falsity is irrelevant, even misleading, sentences like "the economic prosperity of Germany requires *Lebensraum* in the east." Even though it is possible to debate this proposition with tables of statistics, such a factual approach fails to recognize that the purpose of the sentence is not descriptive but ideological. The Third Reich did not encourage public debate of its policies, so that if a sentence such as this is promulgated in the Nazi-controlled press, one can be sure that its purpose is to solidify popular support for the war with Russia, not to inform the public about economics.

Moving closer to home, we are all familiar with parallel constructions, sentences like "the continued prosperity of the United States requires control of the oil in the Middle East." Again, this point could be argued on purely economic terms, but as oil companies are no more interested in public debate than was Hitler, it is more illuminating to consider the source than to argue the evidence.

Properly speaking, a statement or belief is ideological when it becomes attached to a specific political and economic interest. In such circumstances it is promulgated not because it is true (or false) but because it is socially efficacious. Any group with special privileges needs to demonstrate that its higher status is deserved, not merely fortuitous, and people in the modern period think science is especially credible. So it is not surprising that nowadays people justify their actions by citing scientific facts, in effect converting science into ideological discourse. At the same time, scientists, being well-socialized members of society, can be expected to share some of these proclivities.

Because ideology is about social effectiveness, not truth or falsity, science can be factual and ideological at the same time. Indeed, science has been so successful because its self-promotion is usually verifiable. What other institution can say: "Here, look through the telescope! Tell me what you see." Now *that* is a foundation for an enduring ideology—there is no way out of science's conceptual embrace except to disbelieve the evidence of one's own eyes!

The ideological use of science is not hidden away in laboratories—you can watch it on TV. In California around the start of the current millennium, there was a well-publicized debate on the merits of embryonic stem^G-cell research, fueled in part by the effort of Christian fundamentalists^G to outlaw such experimentation because it makes use of cells from aborted human fetuses. The biomedical community, in contrast, saw stem-cell research as a portal to scientific progress. According to a scientist at the University of California at San Diego, stem-cell research could contribute to biomedicine by overcoming four technological bottlenecks: grow tissue for transplantation, serve as a test bed for drugs targeted to humans, create cell lines specific to a particular genetic disease, and tailor therapies to individual patients.⁴⁸

President George W. Bush sided with the anti-abortion advocates and denied federal funding for stem-cell research; in response, the biomedical community put a proposition on the California ballot, Proposition 71, to set up an agency (CIRM) supported by the State of California to carry this science forward with the help of a three billion dollar budget.⁴⁹

A Stanford University scientist, Irving Weissman, M.D., emerged as a leading advocate of Proposition 71, giving press conferences, button-holing politicians, and starring in a television commercial.⁵⁰ Weissman also presented his arguments for unrestricted stem-cell research in testimony before the U.S. Congress.⁵¹ With his impeccable credentials (Professor of Cancer Biology at Stanford University, Director of the Institute of Cancer and Stem Cell Biology and Medicine, and founder of several biotech companies commercializing this research), he cannot be dismissed as a naive popularizer of science, yet his presentation to the Congressional committee is a good example of science as ideology.

Weissman starts conventionally enough with a list of the potential medical benefits, such as cures for cancer and genetic diseases, which he dangles before the committee like a piñata. Then he reminds his audience about what happened to the Soviet Union when Stalin banned population^G genetics—it missed the biotech boat, that's what, so don't let that happen to you! Finally, like a fire-and-brimstone preacher, he strikes a tone of moral self-righteousness tinged with threat:

> Those in a position of advice or authority who participate in the banning or enforced delays of biomedical research that could lead to the saving of lives and the amelioration of suffering are directly and morally responsible for the lives made worse or lost due to

the ban, or even of a moratorium that would deny
such treatments in that short window of time when it
could help or save them.[52]

It would be hard to find a use of language further from science
than this: anyone who doubts the hypothetical benefits of yet-to-
be discovered techniques is a murderer!

California voters passed Proposition 71, effectively circum-
venting the federal ban on stem-cell research, and the result was
hailed as a triumph of science over religion. Yet it was justified, by
scientists and public alike, by *faith* in science and *fear* of disease
and *concern* for technological leadership. While understandable
motivations, they are not science in the accepted sense of the
word, certainly not deductions from logico-mathematical models of cause and effect in the natural world. Perhaps someday,
stem cells will perform as advertised, but hope is not a scientific
prediction.

Proposition 71 supports the premise of this book, namely, that
science exists in a social and political context and is affected by
that context, not only in its propaganda but in its research priorities as well. Indeed, as shown by the campaign for Proposition
71, science can be as partisan as a political party and as moralistic
as religion.

Because science is embedded in the Western belief in Progress—that secular mythology of hope created by the Enlightenment—its connection to society is not *logical* but *ideo*logical.[53]
Even when scientific findings are as solid as a crystal lattice,
they are sold to the public as terrifying weapons, medical break-
throughs, and economic bonanzas, the way Weissman sells stem
cells. And it is a congenial sales pitch for modernists of all persuasions, from capitalists to Marxists, from technocrats to libertarians, because all agree that science is the engine of progress,
propelling society from a more primitive stage of development

to a more advanced one, from horse power to steam, from steel to biotechnology—with each successive innovation confirming the theory of material progress for the public and practitioners alike.

Yet even when presented by scientists, such visions of the future are not descriptive but ideological, for no conceivable research program could ever prove such claims: the social consequences of stem-cell research do not depend on laws of nature but on what human beings choose to do with the technology.

Congruent Belief Systems

Any attempt to focus on the ideological use of science, so easily deflected by the futuristic glitter of stem cells, is even more difficult in the glare of Darwin's solar persona. In the late nineteenth century, some prominent industrialists, such as Andrew Carnegie, maintained that the theory of natural selection is directly supportive of capitalist economics.[54] Although Darwin's theory embraces competition, individualism, and materialism,[G] it differs significantly from capitalism in that the former is about organisms while latter is about money. For this reason alone, identification of the two is easy to dismiss.

Propaganda is most effective when it is seen as coming from a reliable source, so it is important to keep the source distinct from whatever one is trying to justify. The Social Darwinism of Victorian times merged evolution with capitalism in the public mind, conflating the source with the referent. It is far better to inculcate a system of nature that is supportive of capitalism while claiming it to be a science that is exclusively engaged in the study of plants and animals. For this reason, the explicit Social Darwinism of the nineteenth century was replaced in the twentieth by what I call *congruent* [G] *systems of belief.*

Nowadays, tycoons no longer justify their rapacity by appealing to the works of Charles Darwin, while evolutionary scientists never discuss anything but biology within the confines of the scientific journal (although they have no such inhibitions outside of it). In this way, Darwinian evolution inculcates habits of mind and standards of behavior that are congruent with the premises of capitalism while creating the impression that they have been arrived at independently by a science far removed from social policy. This ensures that the two endeavors are kept distinct in terms of their manifest content, which helps to create the false impression that Social Darwinism disappeared a century ago.

With congruency, ideological function does not depend on identity of content but on the similarity of the thought processes. Even though capitalism is about money and Darwinism is about organisms, they share a similar conceptual framework and address similar issues, such as competition for scarce resources, strategies to increase one's rank in a status hierarchy, hiding one's intentions from potential rivals, and so on. Anyone trained in one system will feel at home in the other.

Congruency requires the transfer of training from one field to the other, so that familiarity with one facilitates the mental and/or somatic skills needed for the other. For example, the art of origami could be congruent with organic chemistry. Even though organic chemistry and origami have very few concepts, techniques, and applications in common, both require an understanding of three-dimensional shapes. If the artistic folding of paper into three-dimensional shapes improves one's mental manipulation of objects, and if the mental skills so learned facilitate the mental manipulation of organic molecules, then these two activities would be congruent in spite of their dissimilarity.

Traditional biological fieldwork is congruent with capitalism because it promotes habits of predatory acquisition. In Darwin's day field biology was largely the practice of killing wild animals and shipping the carcasses back to England, where they were purchased by prominent museums and wealthy collectors, a prac-

tice that gave Alfred Russel Wallace his livelihood. Significantly, Darwin's own enthusiasm for natural history began with the
Victorian fetish for the competitive display of dead animals. Not
only was he an avid hunter, but as a youth he became fascinated
with collecting beetles.[55] At Cambridge University Darwin participated in an informal network of entomological collectors who
vied with one another for possession of the rarest specimens.[56]
While aboard the *Beagle,* Darwin killed and preserved animals
by the crateful. Field biology in the Victorian tradition reinforces
the predatory and acquisitive practices of capitalism, just as Darwinian theory cultivates competitive habits of mind.

I argue that the social function of Darwinism is to maintain a
congruent relationship between the content of biological science
on one hand and the body politic of capitalism on the other.
Darwinism ensures that the tenets of capitalism are scientifically
supported by the biology of the day (whatever that biology happens to be) and that the content of Darwinian science remains
consistent with the ideological needs of capitalism (however
those may be construed at any particular moment in history). The
empirical content of evolutionary biology changes with new research, as with any science, but Darwinian theory is constrained
by a metatheory with nonscientific content of an explicitly social
nature. The metatheory consists of the four premises of the Darwinist belief system, that is, PHAGe—Progress through genetic
change, hostility to religion, atomistic[G] individualism, and the
genetic inheritance of social behavior.

This metatheory is rarely explicitly taught in courses in evolutionary biology but is embedded in the culture of Darwinist
institutions, where it frames the content of courses, sets research
priorities, and enables funding. For example, in a course called
Human Behavioral Biology taught at Stanford University by
primatologist Robert Sapolsky, a full professor and MacArthur

recipient, two of the four tenets of PHAGe (2 and 4) are introduced anecdotally in the first two minutes of the video.[57]

As the historian of science Jan Sapp has observed, Darwinism cannot be defined by its biological findings but only as the circular process of interpreting organic evolution through the lens of natural selection while justifying social policy in terms of evolutionary biology.[58]

However deficient this circularity may be as science, it is brilliant ideology. Darwin's theory of natural selection can be presented to the public with all the authority of science, because it really is science as methodologically defined, that is, typically built from facts, not fabrications. At the same time, Darwinism is believable because of its latent social beliefs and not because of the facts used to support it. Also, since Darwinists do not want the metatheory falsified, they have no motivation to put its premises to empirical test. As for ideological biases, these can be revealed only by systematic comparison with social facts and cultural premises that lie outside the system, ensuring that no members of Darwin's[G] cohort will ever examine them.

Because Darwinism supports deeply held social beliefs, it is as resistant to contrary facts as any religion. And because Darwinists have no doubts, their presentations to the public are all the more persuasive.

To this day, Darwinism continues to perform an ideological service to captains of industry that is impossible to obtain in any other way: namely, the transformation of predatory practices into scientific laws of nature. So effective is this approach that it has given rise to what has been called the "Darwin industry," a seemingly inexhaustible flow of books, articles, and television documentaries that promulgate a reductionist view of human nature and society.[59] High in the ivory tower, the methods of biological science are used to produce findings that support the naturalness of Darwinian social beliefs, either intentionally or by what Darwin called unconscious selection; then, in step two, they are promulgated to the public in textbooks, mass media, and so-called popularizations as impartial findings about human nature and society, while at the same time preempting alternative views. Even though evolutionary biology and the practice of capitalism remain distinct areas of human endeavor, they are part of a single social process, comparable to the relationship between stem-cell biology and the campaign for Proposition 71.

Darwin the biologist was far from being a neutral bystand-er in this naturalization of capitalism. He not only transposed the intellectual framework of English political economy into the new domain of biological evolution but he did so while preserv-ing the values of the colonial and capitalist elites. In spite of his self-imposed isolation, Darwin developed a theoretical system of nature and society that is consistent with the values and as-pirations of robber barons and empire builders. In his magnum opus *On the Origin of Species* he attributes the emergence of new species to the cumulative effect of continuous struggle for lim-ited resources, while in *The Descent of Man* his mechanism for progressive change is the extinction of one society by another. So even though Darwin never once suggested publicly that his theory of natural selection supports big business and imperial-ism—he didn't need to. He made competition for resources and collective[G] aggression into the basic premises of evolutionary theory itself.

Charles Darwin was a Social Darwinist before anyone had coined the term. For this reason, his major work on human so-ciety, *The Descent of Man,* should not be read as a scientific trea-tise on human evolution. When it was published in 1871 there were scarcely any scientific findings on human evolution at all. As confirmed by Lyell's *The Geological Evidences of the Antiquity of Man*, published eight years before, there were no fossils of ex-tinct humans except some sketchy Neanderthal remains, no understanding of genetics, no methods of absolute dating, no pre-historic archeology outside of Europe, no comparative primate behavior, no fieldwork among gatherer-hunters, and so on.[60] In the absence of any real science, Darwin drew upon the content of English political economy and the social beliefs of the class in which he was raised.

Darwin's biographers Desmond and Moore have captured the fanciful nature of *The Descent of Man*. They describe it as "an arm-chair adventure of the English evolving, clambering up from the apes, struggling to conquer savagery, multiplying and dispersing around the globe,"[61] an adventure in which "the 'intellectually su-perior' out-breed the inferior, the better classes out-distance the 'intemperate, profligate, and criminal classes,' and even the rich tend to leave more offspring than the swelling poor, who are cut down in infancy."[62]

The Descent of Man is an origin[G] myth of modernism[G] —and therein lies its power. Many of the findings of genetics, paleon-tology, geology, and other sciences that are used to support Dar-winian theory today are not in dispute, being science in the strict sense of the term. But once scientific findings are incorporated into a prescientific framework that developed as a political cri-tique of the landed aristocracy and its state[G] religion they become susceptible to strong distorting forces. Think of scientific facts as iron filings. Certainly, iron filings are physical objects that can be weighed and counted by physicists, yet once they are brought into proximity to a magnet they will be collectively reconfigured into a predictable pattern. In human society, political power is a force field comparable to magnetism—and one that resonates strongly with Darwinism itself.

Evolutionist Postscript

If Darwinian theory is primarily a projection of capitalist social relations onto the world of plants and animals, does this not challenge the veracity of organic evolution itself? Organic change over geologic time is a natural phenomenon, whereas natural selection is one possible explanation of how such change occurs.

Although in Darwin's time many still interpreted the massive extinctions in the fossil record as evidence of successive creations, as Cuvier[G] believed, subsequent biologists established the principle of the continuity of life, showing that all organisms alive today are descended from organic precursors. Louis Pasteur proved to every scientist's satisfaction that there is no spontaneous generation of microbes, while German microbiologists established the principle of cellular[G] continuity—that the cells of organisms develop from preexisting cells by division and are not assembled anew each generation out of their chemical constituents.[63]

In the twentieth century, organic chemistry showed that the basic biochemical processes within the cell are shared across the broad spectrum of life. Genetic science, by analyzing the sequences of nucleotides[G] of DNA, extended the concept of homology[G] to the molecular level, showing similarities among very different species of organisms. Also, contemporary paleontology, using more refined methods of analysis, shows that a small number of animal body plans first emerged in Cambrian[G] times almost three billion years ago and have been conserved ever since through a multiplicity of modifications.[64]

These facts are consistent with the conclusion that organisms bridged the gaps in the fossil record and survived the catastrophes chronicled by Cuvier. Yet *none* of the scientific evidence for evolution presumes the veracity of the theory of natural selection. Once one accepts the reality of the fossil record, the cellular continuity of life, and the timeline provided by physics, then organic evolution follows as a necessary consequence.

Notes

* Note on capitalization: In English, the names of nationalities and ethnic groups are normally capitalized (e.g. Irish, English, Hopi). But with the exception of taxonomic names in Latin (e.g. *Homo sapiens)*, the names of biological entities are usually not capitalized (e.g. human, chimpanzee, horse). However, it is now conventional in the United States to write racial names without capitalization (white, black), as if American races were natural categories. Yet in the antebellum South, "one drop of Negro blood" made one a slave, so the category "Negro" included people of pure African descent as well as those with large fractions of European genes. Many thousands of the latter subsequently "passed for white" and brought African genes into mainstream "white" society. Also, Barack Obama is designated as the first black president, not the first half-white one. For these reasons I judge race in the United States to be an ethnic designation, like Italo-American, not a biological fact; thus I capitalize White and Black.

1 Hofstadter (1955: 201)

2 Ruse (1980).

3 Claeys (2000: 237).

4 "Introduction," *On the Origin of Species* (1859). This and Darwin's other works are available, along with some secondary sources, at http://darwin-online.org.uk. I also used the facsimile print edition of the first edition of *Origin* (Darwin 1966).

5 Darwin and Barlow (1958: 120). This and Darwin's notebooks indicate that he read Malthus (the 1826 edition) between Sept. 28 and Oct. 12, 1838 (Robert M. Young, 1985: 42). This was not the first edition of Malthus's book, which was published in 1798, but the much-altered sixth edition (Desmond and Moore 1994: 264). Darwin's oblique reference to "fifteen months" earlier makes his brainchild contemporaneous with the ascendancy of Queen Victoria, who inherited the British throne on June 20, 1837.

6 Petersen (1979: 35).

7 Both the first edition (Malthus, Wrigley, and Souden 1986a: "1798") and the sixth edition (Malthus Wrigley, and Souden 1986b: "1826") have been reprinted. The various editions of Malthus's major work contain substantial additions and deletions.

3 Desmond (1989: 4).

9 Petersen (1979: 117). Lest the reader think this characterization of workhouses is biased toward the left, Petersen is overtly hostile to Marx. See also Desmond and Moore (1994: 196 ff.).

10 *Oliver Twist* is available online: http://www.gutenberg.org.

11 Smyth (2012).

12 Quotation from Desmond and Moore (1994: 153). Huzel (2006) provides a very readable account of Martineau in reference to the Malthus publicity engine in nineteenth-century England.

13 Desmond and Moore (1994: 216).

14 Ibid. 201.

15 King-Hele (1977). Erasmus Darwin's life and work are discussed in Chapter 2.

15 Desmond and Moore (1994: 419–20).

17 Ibid. 396–97.

13 Ibid. 396.

19 Claeys (2000: 235).

20 Spencer (1847). For the context see Kingsland (1988).

21 Spencer's influence is documented by Hofstadter (1955).

22 Dréze and Sen (1990). For concise definitions of this and other terms used in this book, see the Glossary.

23 Wallace (1871: Chapter 8: "Creation by Law," 129–30). For a re-appraisal of Wallace's life and work see Slotten (2004), Smith and Beccaloni (2008).

24 Ibid.

25 Claeys (2000).

25 Smith (2008: 420).

27 Claeys (2008).

23 Wallace (1898).

29 Goodall (1965). Her work was widely popularized at the time in articles published by *National Geographic* magazine and in associated films.

30 Washburn and Wenner-Gren Foundation for Anthropological Research (1961). The film on baboons that Washburn coproduced with DeVore was very influential on nascent primatology (DeVore et al. 1961). Washburn is also remembered for moving physical anthropology beyond racial typology (Washburn 1963).

31 Jane Lancaster's recent work is discussed in a subsequent chapter of this book.

32 DeVore (1965), Devore et al (1961).

33 Michael W. Young (2004). When I was an undergraduate at Berkeley, *The Sexual Life of Savages* was sold in bookstores wrapped in a cellophane jacket that could only be opened after purchase. I suspect many buyers were disappointed.

34 Latour (1979).

35 A complete list of my publications is given at: http://www.sally-glean.org/reynolds/.

36 Schrecker (2010) describes the machinations during this period in "'A Long-range and Difficult Project': The Backlash Against the 1960s." Jennifer Washburn (2005) describes the incorporation of the university into the capitalist product-development cycle. Her article in the *Atlantic* (Press and Washburn 2000) reprises her critique.

37 The book by Kidder (1981) was a best seller.

38 The start-up where I worked is referred to in my publications by a pseudonym: Falcon Computing Corporation (Reynolds 1994).

39 Schrecker (1998).

40 The impact of surveillance and censorship on American universities in general and anthropology in particular is well documented in the works of Lowen (1997), Lewontin (1997), Nader (1997), Price (2004), and Schrecker (1986).

41 Schrecker (1986: 304).

42 Eleanor Leacock, quoted by Price (2004: 30).

43 McLellan (1980).

44 Berger and Luckmann (1966). This work informs my discussion of ideology in the current chapter.

45 Quoted from the introduction to the first edition of *Origin* (Darwin 1859: 5).

46 Ruse (2003: 1523–24).

47 Hersh (1997).

48 Lawrence S. B. Goldstein, quoted by Mooney (2005: 187–88).

49 The agency, founded in 2004, has a website: http://www.cirm.ca.gov.

50 Interview with Irving Weissman by Richard M. Cohen. Date of Publication: 2002; http://www.laskerfoundation.org/news/weis/weissmant.html [page since removed].

51 "Science, Technology, and Space Hearing: Adult Stem Cell Research, Wednesday, July 14 2004 - 2:30 PM - SR - 253, The Testimony of Dr. Irving Weissman, M.D." http://www.lasker-foundation.org/news/weis/weissmant.html. [page since removed] (Accessed Feb. 2006; a digital copy is in my possession).

52 Ibid. p. 7.

53 I have delineated the mythic infrastructure of modern high technology in a previous book (Reynolds 1991).

54 Carnegie (1900).

55 Desmond and Moore (1994: 70–90 passim).

56 Berry (2008).

57 Human Behavioral Biology, YouTube. Recorded in 2010. Accessed December, 2018.

58 Sapp (2003).

59 Ruse's overview (1996) of the Darwin industry captures the breadth and depth of its output.

60 Lyell (1863).

61 Desmond and Moore (1994: 579).

62 Ibid.

63 Especially by Schlieden, Schwann, Virchow, and Hetwig (Sapp 2003: 82–94). Hetwig argued that because biology deals with the organization of life, it is more akin to social science than to physics and chemistry.

64 Davidson and Erwin (2006).

References

Berger, Peter L., and Thomas Luckmann. 1966. *The Social Construction of Reality: A Treatise in the Sociology of Knowledge*. Garden City, NY: Doubleday.

Berry, Andrew. 2008. "Ardent beetle-hunters": Natural History, Collecting, and the Theory of Evolution. In *Natural Selection and beyond: The Intellectual Legacy of Alfred Russel Wallace*, edited by Charles H. Smith and George Beccaloni, Oxford and New York: Oxford University Press, 47-65.

Carnegie, Andrew. 1900. *The Gospel of Wealth and Other Timely Essays*. New York: The Century Company.

Claeys, Gregory. 2000. The "Survival of the fittest" and the origins of Social Darwinism. *Journal of the History of Ideas* 61: 223–40.

_____. 2008. Wallace and Owenism. In *Natural Selection and Beyond: The Intellectual Legacy of Alfred Russel Wallace*, edited by Charles H. Smith and George Beccaloni, Oxford and New York: Oxford University Press, 235–62.

Darwin, Charles. 1966. *On the Origin of Species: A Facsimile of the First Edition with an Introduction by Ernst Mayr*. Cambridge, MA: Harvard University Press.

_____, and Nora Barlow. 1958. *The Autobiography of Charles Darwin, 1809–1882: with Original Omissions Restored*. London: Collins.

Davidson, Eric H., and Douglas H. Erwin. 2006. Gene regulatory networks and the evolution of animal body plans. *Science* 311: 796–800.

Desmond, Adrian. 1989. *The Politics of Evolution: Morphology, Medicine, and Reform in Radical London*. Chicago: University of Chicago Press.

Desmond, Adrian J., and James R. Moore. 1994. *Darwin: The Life of a Tormented Evolutionist*. New York: Norton.

DeVore, Irven, ed. 1965. *Primate Behavior: Field Studies of Monkeys and Apes*. New York: Holt.

_____ et al. 1961. *Baboon Behavior*. [film] Dept. of Anthropology, University of California. Released by Educational Film Sales, University Extension, University of California/Engels, Frederick.

Dréze, Jean, and Amartya Sen, eds. 1990-1991. *The Political Economy of Hunger*. 3 vols. Oxford: Oxford University Press.

Goodall, Jane. 1965. Chimpanzees of the Gombe Stream Reserve. In *Primate Behavior: Field Studies of Monkeys and Apes*, edited by Irven Devore. New York: Holt. 425-473.

Hersh, Seymour M. 1997. *The Dark Side of Camelot*. Boston: Little, Brown.

Hofstadter, Richard. 1955. *Social Darwinism in American Thought*. Boston: Beacon Press. 1st ed. 1944.

Huzel, James P. 2006. *The Popularization of Malthus in Early Nineteenth-Century England: Martineau, Cobbett and the Pauper Press*. Aldershot, England, and Burlington, VT: Ashgate.

Kidder, Tracy. 1981. *The Soul of a New Machine*. Boston: Little, Brown.

King-Hele, Desmond. 1977. *Doctor of Revolution: The Life and Genius of Erasmus Darwin*. London: Faber and Faber.

Kingsland, Sharon. 1988. Evolution and debates over human progress from Darwin to sociobiology. *Population and Development Review* 14: 167–98.

Latour, Bruno. 1979. *Laboratory Life: The Social Construction of Scientific Facts*. Sage Library of Social Research vol. 80. Beverly Hills, CA: Sage Publications.

Lewontin, Richard.C. 1997. The Cold War and the transformation of the academy. In *The Cold War and the University*, edited by Chomsky and et al, 1-34. New York: New Press/ Norton.

Lowen, Rebecca. 1997. *Creating the Cold War University: The Transformation of Stanford.* Berkeley: University of California Press.

Lyell, Charles. 1863. *The Geological Evidences of the Antiquity of Man.* London: John Murray.

Malthus, T. R., E. A. Wrigley, and David Souden. 1986a. *An Essay on the Principle of Population: the First Edition (1798) with Introduction and Bibliography.* London: W. Pickering

————. 1986b. *An Essay on the Principle of Population: The Sixth Edition (1826) with Variant Readings from the Second Edition (1803).* London: W. Pickering.

Mayo, Henry B. 1960. *Introduction to Marxist Theory.* London: Oxford University Press.

McLellan, David. 1980. *Marx Before Marxism.* 2nd ed. London: Macmillan.

Mooney, Chris. 2005. *The Republican War on Science.* New York: Basic Books.

Nader, Laura. 1997. The Phantom Factor: Impact of the Cold War on Anthropology. In *The Cold War and the University,* edited by N. Chomsky et al. New York: New Press/ Norton.

Petersen, William. 1979. *Malthus.* Cambridge, MA: Harvard University Press.

Press, Eyal, and Jennifer Washburn. 2000. The kept university, *Atlantic,* March. https://www.theatlantic.com/magazine/archive/2000/03/the-kept-university/306629/. Accessed June 2019.

Price, David H. 2004. *Threatening Anthropology: McCarthyism and the FBI's Surveillance of Activist Anthropologists.* Durham: Duke University Press.

Reynolds, Peter C. 1991. *Stealing Fire: The Atomic Bomb as Symbolic Body.* Palo Alto, CA: Iconic Anthropology Press.

_____. 1994. Culture on the Rocks. In *Anthropological Perspectives on Organizational Culture.*, edited by Tomoko Hamada and Willis E. Sibley. Lanham, MD: University Presses of America, 301-310.

Ruse, Michael. 1980. Social Darwinism: the two sources. *Albion: A Quarterly Journal Concerned with British Studies* 12 (1): 23–36.

_____. 1996. The Darwin industry: a guide. *Victorian Studies* 39 (2): 217–35.

_____. 2003. Is evolution a secular religion? *Science* 299 (5612): 1523–24.

Sapp, Jan. 2003. *Genesis: The Evolution of Biology*. Oxford and New York: Oxford University Press.

Schrecker, Ellen. 1986. *No Ivory Tower: McCarthyism and the Universities*. New York: Oxford University Press.

_____. 1998. *Many are the Crimes: McCarthyism in America.* Boston; London: Little, Brown.

_____. 2010. *The Lost Soul of Higher Education: Corporatization, the Assault on Academic Freedom, and the End of the American University*. New York: New Press.

Slotten, Ross A. 2004. *The Heretic in Darwin's Court: The Life of Alfred Russel Wallace*. New York: Columbia University Press.

Smith, Charles H. 2008. Wallace, Spiritualism, and beyond "Change" or "No Change." In *Natural Selection and Beyond: The Intellectual Legacy of Alfred Russel Wallace*, edited by Charles H. Smith and George Beccaloni. Oxford: Oxford University Press, 391–423.

_____, and George Beccaloni, eds. 2008. *Natural Selection and Beyond: The Intellectual Legacy of Alfred Russel Wallace*. Oxford and New York: Oxford University Press.

Smyth, William J. 2012. The Creation of the Workhouse System. In *Atlas of the Great Irish Famine, 1845–52*, edited by John Crowley, William J. Smyth, and Mike Murphy. Cork, Ireland: Cork University Press, 120–26.

Spencer, Herbert. 1847. A Theory of Population, Deduced from the General Law of Animal Fertility. London: G. Woodfall. Online at http://www.victorianweb.org/science/science_texts/spencer2.html

Wallace, Alfred Russel. 1871. *Contributions to the Theory of Natural Selection: A Series of Essays*. 2nd edition. New York: Macmillan.

_____. 1898. *The Wonderful Century*. London: Macmillan.

Washburn, Jennifer. 2005. *University, Inc.: The Corporate Corruption of Higher Education*. New York: Basic Books/Perseus.

Washburn, Sherwood L. 1963. *Classification and Human Evolution*. Chicago: Aldine.

_____ and Wenner-Gren Foundation for Anthropological Research. 1961. *Social Life of Early Man. Viking Fund Publications in Anthropology*. Chicago: Aldine.

Young, Michael W. 2004. *Malinowski: Odyssey of an Anthropologist, 1884–1920*. New Haven, CT: Yale University Press.

Young, Robert M. 1985. *Darwin's Metaphor: Nature's Place in Victorian Culture*. Cambridge Cambridge University Press.

Chapter Two

Evo-Revo:

Evolution as Revolution

For many people, the theory of evolution begins with Charles Darwin, but it is his grandfather Erasmus, an eighteenth-century polymath, who was the first evolutionist in the family.[1] A prominent doctor with Quaker roots, Erasmus Darwin invested in the developing industrialization of the Midlands and counted among his friends Joseph Priestly, James Watt, Matthew Boulton, and Josiah Wedgewood—the big names of the industrial elite.[2]

In 1767, Josiah Wedgewood, the pottery tycoon, sent Erasmus Darwin a batch of fossils that had been unearthed by a canal-building project.[3] Erasmus Darwin realized that he was looking at species of mammals that are no longer found in England, even though he had no idea what they were; this event appears to have been a catalyst to his evolutionist intuition—that people have a kinship with lower forms of life. He hypothesized that life first appeared in the sea, then evolved through a succession of improvements. He even added a Latin motto, the words *E. Conchis Omnia* ("everything from shells"), to his family coat of arms, which featured a picture of three scallop shells. He sought to preserve the moment by painting it on his carriage.

Erasmus Darwin's *Zoonomia, or The Laws of Organic Life* was first published in 1794–96, more than a decade before Charles

Darwin was born. Charles never knew his grandfather, who died in 1802; but when Charles went to medical school at the University of Edinburgh, he studied under the anatomist Robert Edmond Grant (1793-1874), a committed republican who espoused the works of Erasmus Darwin and the Continental evolutionists. Charles Darwin worked closely with Grant, helping him to gather marine specimens in the Firth of Forth, as well as presenting a paper before a scientific society under Grant's guidance. The time spent at Edinburgh was essential to Charles Darwin's scientific formation, since Grant taught the young naturalist to look at nature through his grandfather Erasmus's eyes.

As Erasmus writes:[4]

> Beasts of prey have acquired strong jaws or talons. Cattle have acquired a rough tongue and a rough palate to pull off the blades of grass, as cows and sheep. Some birds have acquired harder beaks to crack nuts, as the parrot. Others have acquired beaks adapted to break the harder seeds, as sparrows. Others for the softer seeds of flowers, or the buds of trees, as the finches. Other birds have acquired long beaks to penetrate the moister soils in search of insects or roots, as woodcocks; and others broad ones to filtrate the water of lakes, and to retain aquatic insects, as ducks. All which seem to have been gradually produced during many generations by the perpetual endeavor of the creatures to supply the want of food, and to have been delivered to their posterity with constant improvement of them for the purposes required.[5]

Erasmus Darwin, more than sixty years before his grandson's famous book, summarizes the arguments for the transformation of species in nature, and these are essentially the same that evolutionists give today: that all organisms begin life as a microscopic germ, what he calls a filament and we call a cell; that biological transformation is directly observable in the process of development of an egg into a fetus; that transformation of a species is a gradual process of adaptation^G based on the animal's way of life; that the anatomy of species can be altered by selective breeding by humans; and, most important, that there is a detailed correspondence in the anatomical parts of distinct species, what is known as the argument of homology.^{G} In Erasmus's words:

> In some this filament in its advance to maturity has acquired hands and fingers, with a fine sense of touch, as in mankind. In others it has acquired claws or talons, as in tygers and eagles. In others, toes with an intervening web, or membrane, as in seals and geese. In others it has acquired cloven hoofs, as in cows and swine; and whole hoofs in others, as in the horse. While in the bird kind this original living filament has put forth wings instead of arms and legs, and feathers instead of hair.[6]

In the late eighteenth century, evolution was not simply a scientific theory—it was a radical political stance. In a hereditary class system perpetuated by strategic marriages, those at the top consider themselves "well bred" compared to "lower" forms of humanity such as slaves and peasants. But evolution asserts that lower forms of life can evolve into higher forms; and if this be so, then there are no natural laws preventing the lower social ranks of humans from rising in the political hierarchy until they equal or surpass their superiors. Thus, by presenting human history as a succession of stages, political reformers implicitly repudiated a static hierarchy established by God and made the abolition of monarchy into an attainable goal. Evolution was revolution.

Across the Atlantic, in Britain's North American colonies, there were murmurings of popular discontent. The prominent settlers of New England were descended from radical Calvinists[G] whose coreligionists in the old country had waged a civil war and executed the king of England.[7] In the New World, contempt for aristocratic privilege and hostility to the divine right of kings flourished like a hothouse plant. Less than a decade after Erasmus Darwin had received the shipment of fossils, Thomas Jefferson wrote the manifesto that would topple monarchies and launch the quest for the Rights of Man: that governments[G] rule by the consent of the governed and that mankind is endowed with inalienable rights.

In the 1770s, stung by official hostility to his evolutionist sentiments and fearing for his medical practice, Erasmus Darwin painted over the motto on his coach and confined his theorizing to poetry:

> Organic life beneath the shoreless waves
> Was born and nurs'd in ocean's pearly caves;
> First forms minute, unseen by spheric glass,
> Move on the mud, or pierce the watery mass;
> These, as successive generations bloom,
> New powers acquire and larger limbs assume;
> Whence countless groups of vegetation spring,
> And breathing realms of fin and feet and wing.[8]

A quarter of a century later, Erasmus Darwin added his evolutionist observations to his treatise on medicine, an act of defiance that was seen as such. In 1798, the British government, still smarting from a humiliating defeat by its American colonies and stymied by Napoleon's armies in Europe, resolved to crush revolution at home. England passed sedition laws, hired spies, and arrested radicals. That same year the authorities jailed Erasmus Darwin's publisher for selling seditious literature,[9] and they resolved to silence the literary dissidents themselves, a group that included Erasmus himself. Certainly Charles's grandfather was a religious skeptic and a confirmed materialist. A family acquaintance of Erasmus remembered him telling her as a girl that "man has five gates of knowledge, the five senses; he can know nothing but through them; all else is a vain fancy, and as for the being of a God, the existence of a soul, or a world to come, who can know anything about them?"[10]

A measure of Erasmus Darwin's importance is the caliber of the weapon used against him: he was pilloried in a publication edited by George Canning, undersecretary for foreign affairs and a future prime minister of England.[11] A difference between the Age of Reason and our own is that the government's campaign of character assassination consisted of a parody of Darwin's published poetry. The parody, penned by Canning and two professional writers, was designed to destroy Darwin's literary reputation by painting him as a French sympathizer and a scientific crackpot. The parodists ridiculed three of Erasmus's most preposterous assertions: first, that humans had evolved from lower forms of life; second, that electricity could be made to do useful work; and, third, that mountains were older than six thousand years.

Erasmus Darwin was not the only Englishman to see the possibility of organic evolution or the only one to be silenced for it. His friend, James Hutton, one of the prominent geological theorists of the day, argued that the earth was far older than anyone could imagine, old enough for mountain ranges to have eroded into the sea; in his magnum opus published in 1794 Hutton dealt with organic changes too, devoting a whole chapter to natural selection.[12] Moreover, historians have confirmed at least two more Englishmen who anticipated Darwin and Wallace's idea that nature can produce varieties analogous to those produced intentionally by humans, including a presentation on the subject to the Royal Society in 1813.[13] But these authors subsequently fell into obscurity—more accurately, they were pushed.

Organic evolution prospered in revolutionary France even as it was being suppressed in England. Jean Baptiste Lamarck, whom the French memorialize as the discoverer of organic evolution, was one of the world's first professional biologists, employed by the new Museum of Natural History founded in the wake of the French Revolution.[14] His professional duty was the classification of all those animal specimens not already claimed by his more powerful colleague Georges Cuvier, who had made hefty fossils his specialty. That left Lamarck with animals without backbones as his oyster, for which he coined the term *invertebrate*.

Examining the "first forms minute" with the help of "spheric glass," Lamarck scientifically described and differentiated a number of groups of hitherto little-known organisms, separating spiders from insects while excluding brachiopods and tunicates from Mollusca. He had also done paleontology, showing that different species of fossil snails succeed one another in the sedimentary rocks of the Paris basin. Yet he was skeptical of the concept of extinction. Surmising that organisms change over geologic time, he argued that existing species are transmutations of earlier ones known only from fossils. Furthermore, he argued that as species evolve into more complex forms in the course of evolution new microbes fill in the gaps from below, such that our knowledge of organic nature consists of freeze frames of a process constantly in flux.[15] Lamarck published his theory of organic evolution in 1809, the year that Charles Darwin was born.

The concept of evolution developed within the context of what historians refer to as the great[G] chain of being or *scala naturae*, an idea that can be traced back to classical antiquity. In this view, all of nature is conceived of as a linear hierarchy, with spiritual beings above, humans in the middle (with a range of ranks from kings to serfs), and animals at the bottom (with species ranging from noble to debased).[16] Furthermore, these relative ranks are not changeable by individuals but are determined by the nature of things. In Platonic thought, this ladder of creation is also a scale of perfection: God is the most complete and perfect being, while all creatures reflect God's nature each in its assigned degree. Even though Georges Cuvier, the father of vertebrate paleontology, denounced the *scala naturae* as "one of the most untrue notions ever introduced into natural history,"[17] it rationalized the social order, so it was taught in the universities and supported by the state, while anyone proposing evolution as an alternative was as intellectually suspect as someone questioning Darwinism is now.

Yet the idea of progressive evolutionary change is not the radical intellectual departure that the secular intelligentsia of the Enlightenment believed it to be. Rather, it was the great chain of being laid on its side.[18] Social hierarchy, instead of issuing fully formed from a creative act by God, now unfolds in time, such that the rungs of the ladder become the stages of historical development while the degrees of perfection are replaced by material progress. In both progressive history and cosmic evolution, those that emerge first are necessarily the most primitive, while those that emerge last are those who are most fit to rule.

This temporal unfolding of the *scala naturae* became the modern alternative to the garden of Eden. Once upon a time, humans lived an animal-like existence, close to nature and wandering from place to place in primitive equality, like the "savages" revealed by the voyages of exploration. Then Man developed agriculture and settled into permanent communities, allowing the accumulation of wealth and the development of specialized classes of artisans, scholars, warriors, and priests. These changes led to social hierarchy and class inequality. This theory of history became the premise for social revolution. As many eighteenth-century evolutionists believed, abolishing monarchy and religion will restore social equality and bring about a future golden age of material prosperity for all.

By the early nineteenth century, Nature itself appeared to confirm that history is a succession of stages punctuated by radical
breaks. Georges Cuvier made anatomical reconstructions of fossils from the Paris basin, enhanced by his own meticulous illustra-
tions, and demonstrated that in the course of geologic time whole
faunas had suddenly appeared on earth, continued unchanged for
some long period of time, and then abruptly disappeared from
the geological record, wiped out by what he called catastrophes.[G]
[19] Cuvier had lived through the French Revolution, even setting
up his laboratory in what had been the gardens of the royal family; and he married a widow whose royalist husband had been
dispatched by the guillotine. So he knew as well as anyone how
one group can succeed another through catastrophe. Significantly, even though he worked in the same institution as Lamarck, he
was strongly opposed to the idea of organic evolution: to Cuvier,
life has unbridgeable discontinuities.[20]

As the British aristocracy watched with horror the events unfolding in France, a theologian at Oxford University began writing a multi-volume work that attacked the intellectual premises
of the French Revolution.[21] Although not a naturalist, he sensed
that biological evolution is a serious threat to the hereditary aristocracy. If lower species can evolve into higher ones, then there
are no *natural* aristocrats, only people with the will to rule and
the ability to fight their way to the top.[22] William Paley's book,
called *Natural Theology*,[G] was published in 1802. At the heart of
his critique of revolutionary atheism is what scholars call the argument from design.[G][23]

Imagine that you found a mechanical watch lying on the
ground. You pick it up and examine it. You marvel at its pol-
ished metal case, its precision movement, and transparent crystal.
You open the back of the case and see the tiny gears rotating
one within the other. Would you conclude that the watch had
come together by chance or that it had been made by a skilled

artisan? The question is rhetorical and Paley's artifact carefully chosen. At this time in European history, when people thought of a science of nature, they thought of the "majestic clockwork" of Newton's astronomy. As Paley argues, not just the solar system but all of nature is carefully crafted for its purposes, so when we examine the natural world, we see evidence of design that can be explained only by the hand of an intelligent Creator.

This type of writing is what Christians call apologetics,ᴳ the use of rational argument to justify religious doctrine; and in this case it had an explicitly political purpose as well: countering on an intellectual level the atheism and materialism being promulgated by enemies of the Old Regime. Even though it is an axiom of Christianity that in the beginning God created the world, expressed in the very first sentence of the Bible, Paley's idea of a Divine Watchmaker is very much an eighteenth-century interpretation of how the Creator went about it.

For a time, evolutionism appeared to be as unstoppable as Napoleon's armies, and it swaggered across Europe for more than two decades, only to retreat with the Republican Guard at the battle of Waterloo. With Wellington's victory, the European aristocracy sought to reassert its political dominance under the leadership of the British. The triumph of reaction logically required that the aristocratic hierarchy of pre-revolutionary Europe be reinstated too, not only in politics but in natural philosophy as well, the field of learning that included the study of plants and animals. Even though the political gains of the capitalist class had to be tacitly approved, since the aristocracy was now too dependent on investment, money, and machines, it was still possible for the British intelligentsia to erase the memory of Erasmus Darwin while repudiating Lamarck as a French dilettante.

Expunging early evolutionists from the scientific record is perhaps the one thing on which Anglicanᴳ monarchists and doctrinaire Darwinians agree. As late as 2003 in *Science,* the flagship journal of the American scientific establishment, Michael Ruse tells us that the "serious science" of evolution began with Charles Darwin in 1859, while pre-Darwinian "evolution was little more than a pseudoscience on a par with mesmerism (animal magnetism) or phrenology (brain bumps)."[24]

This interpretation erects insurmountable conceptual barriers between the theories of Darwin and Lamarck. There are differences to be sure. Lamarck emphasized a ladder of progress with successive emergence of higher life forms, whereas Charles Darwin, like his grandfather, combined evolutionary progress with a family tree of descent. Also, Lamarck's new species pull themselves up by their bootstraps by striving to improve their lives, whereas Darwin's species out-compete their rivals in the struggle for existence. But if organic evolution is defined as the thesis that the biological species of today are the modified descendants of species found earlier in geologic time, then there is no doubt that Lamarck was an evolutionist—and Erasmus Darwin too.

Fortunately for organic evolution, the young Charles Darwin did not go directly to a British university. At the time, Oxford and Cambridge were Anglican seminaries that admitted only members of the Church of England; they regarded Protestants from other denominations as second-class citizens, dismissing them as "Nonconformists"[G] and "dissenting sects," while Catholicism was not an option. Charles's father was Anglican, enabling his son to go to Cambridge; but historically the family was Nonconforming, descended from Quakers and Unitarians. However, Charles Darwin, under pressure from his father to have a respectable profession, went first to the University of Edinburgh in Scotland to test the waters of medical school. Edinburgh was nondenominational, and it was supported by student tuition, so the anticlerical bias of the eighteenth century had found sanctuary there.

Darwin's teacher of anatomy, Robert Edmund Grant, personified religious skepticism and progressive evolution, ensuring that
Charles was exposed to the mutability of species early in life.
But when Charles later enrolled at Cambridge University with
the intent of becoming a priest of the Church of England,[25] he
found that Paley's *Natural Theology* had been established as the
definitive text for the study of natural history.

Paley's treatise is quite explicitly a religious work, in that its
purpose was to demonstrate the truth of creationism[G] rather than
explicate natural science; and Paley did not try to square his natural theology with the facts of the life sciences, being content to
frame a logical argument.[26] But his successors were less cautious,
and their merger of natural history with biblical text resonated to
the major themes of the Reformation.

Catholicism interprets the Bible allegorically, but the Reformation in England emphasized the literal and historical interpretation of Scripture. William Tyndale, the sixteenth-century
scholar who first translated the New Testament into English
from the original Greek, adjured his readers that "Thou shalt
understand that scripture hath but one sense, which is the literal sense. And that literal sense is the root and ground of it all,
and the anchor that never faileth, whereunto if thou cleave, thou
canst never err or go out of the way."[27]

Given that English Protestantism gives great weight to the
literal interpretation of Scripture, it is not surprising that such
literalism would carry over to the Bible's passages delineating the
relationship of the human species to nature. Thus, by the early
nineteenth century, the Bible was being used at Oxford as a theory in natural science, which is to say as the narrative framework
for the interpretation and prediction of physical facts, a phase in
the history of science known as the English[G] school of geology.[28]

The Last Catastrophe

No one was more instrumental in putting Genesis on a firm scientific footing than William Buckland, professor of natural philosophy at Oxford University.[29] Born into a clerical family in 1784, he was raised in a literate home and attended Oxford University, where he took Holy Orders[G] and joined the faculty. Initially a teacher of classics, he switched to geology, where he soon became a one-man scientific institution, teaching the geology course every year from 1814 to 1849. A great communicator, he hosted scientific events that drew crowds from surrounding towns, but he was also a solid scientist whose geological atlas of the British Isles included estimated ages of rock formations that made possible a chronology of the ice ages throughout all of Europe.

In July of 1821, in a rerun of history, a group of workmen cutting stone at a quarry in rural England came across a cave filled with animal bones. They collected specimens and took them to a local physician. The doctor in turn sent them on to an anatomist he knew in London for identification, where they came to the attention of the Bishop of Oxford. The bishop told Professor Buckland about the discovery, who arranged for the bones to be sent to the university from London. When they arrived in Oxford in November, Buckland immediately realized that they were the remains of species of animals not found in Europe; and the next month he was off to Kirkdale Cave to see for himself.[30]

Convinced of the authenticity of the finds, Buckland compared them to bones collected in Africa and concluded they were the remains of animals eaten by hyenas. To test his hypothesis, he provided ox limbs to the caged hyena in a traveling circus and compared the tooth marks to those on the bones from Kirkdale Cave. He concluded that hyenas had once been present in England but had become extinct in remote times. He also predicted that a hyena skull would eventually be found at the site, which came to pass. The next year, in 1822, he presented his research on extinct species of mammals to the Royal Society, for which he won a Copley Medal, the first time it was ever given to a geologist.[31]

This is science by anyone's definition, but it is not evolutionist science because the interpretive framework is completely different. Even today, evolution is a hybrid of physical fact and chronological narrative, but in England in the 1820s the narrative was specifically biblical—it accepted the story of Noah as an historical event and used the universal flood to explain the present-day distribution of sedimentary rock. Sedimentary rock, such as sandstone, is deposited by water or is precipitated out of solution, yet it is often found in places where there are no bodies of water today, such as mountain tops and deserts. Buckland, in common with many geologists of the time, hypothesized that all sedimentary rock had been deposited by a universal flood, a thesis that is also consistent with the story of Noah in the book of Genesis. This hypothesis, known as diluvialism,[G] was also consistent with the vertebrate fossil record in France that had been documented by Georges Cuvier. The latter had shown that extinct faunas appear in the fossil record, continue for a long period of time, and then disappear—the victims of catastrophes.

By postulating Noah's flood as the last catastrophe in the fossil record, Buckland could reconcile the biblical account of creation with the most advanced earth science of the day. Significantly, Cuvier himself, although a staunch Protestant, never attempted to reconcile geology with Genesis. As his biographer argues, Cuvier had a strongly empirical approach to science and a faith-based approach to religion, so he could more easily keep the two apart, thus avoiding the trap that snared the English school of geology.[32]

Diluvialism also fit the culture of Oxford and Cambridge, which was literary and aristocratic, not scientific and hands-on. At that time, the core curriculum emphasized the classics of Greece and Rome, and it cultivated an attitude of mind that was more encyclopedic than empirical. Basically, if one wanted to find out about hyenas, one looked up what Pliny the Elder had said about them. And certainly one did not, as Buckland did, feed ox limbs to circus animals in order to study the tooth marks left on the bones—that sort of activity was more appropriate for chamberlains than professors.

This conflict between the classicists and the modernists was *not* a conflict between science and religion. The modernists were ordained priests of the Church of England just as the classicists were, while religion and science, far from being in contention, were thought to be but different paths to the same universal truth. It was primarily a clash of intellectual cultures: between the classical curriculum, based on intimate knowledge of a canon of texts, versus scientific practice, which was observational and experimental—a split that would resurface more than a century later among atheistic modernists as C. P. Snow's concept of the Two Cultures.[33]

Buckland reconciled science and religion by working within the premise of natural theology: that a knowledge of God can be inferred from the study of creation. Some of the finest minds in English science worked within this tradition, which culminated in an eight-volume collection of books, the Bridgewater Treatises. These were published between 1833 and 1836. The series was named for the Eighth Earl of Bridgewater, who had left a generous bequest for a series of works that demonstrated "the power, wisdom, and goodness of God as manifest in his creation." As with Paley's natural theology, the project had a political rationale as well, but one more in keeping with the industrial age. The editor of the series, the Rev. Thomas Chalmers, saw his life work, as do many fundamentalist clergy in the United States today, as the unification of Christian doctrine with laissez-faire economic theory.[34]

Significantly, by the time of his own contribution to the Bridgewater project, Buckland had abandoned diluvialism, in part for scientific reasons. In spite of increased geological field-work, investigators failed to find any human remains or artifacts in the oldest sedimentary rocks of England, even though the Bible is quite clear that human beings were numerous before the universal flood. In short, diluvialism made a prediction that could not be substantiated empirically, and the fact that it could do so indicates that diluvialism was a theory in science, not a pseudo-science, however dissonant such a use of Scripture may seem to us.

Buckland's disaffection from diluvialism did not end Noah's flood as an explanation of geological phenomena, which continues today in conservative Protestant circles, but its demise marked the end of biblical narrative as a theoretical construct in mainstream natural science. Within Christianity the failure of diluvialism helped to discredit the idea that the Bible is a fac-tual narrative of geological and historical events. In the larger intellectual culture, however, the damage had already been done. By positioning allegorical language as description of physical fact, the English school of geology made the Bible susceptible to falsification by the emerging natural sciences. And falsification of religion's empirical claims tarnished its spiritual credibility as well. It was this vacuum that Darwinism and Marxism eventu-ally filled.

In England, evolution had been suppressed, but it had not disappeared.[35] Although invisible to the British intellectual es-tablishment, the views of Erasmus Darwin and Jean Baptiste Lamarck had become the stock in trade of independent medical practitioners. Evolutionist ideas were also reprinted in the penny press, where they became part of the culture of newly literate tradesmen and city dwellers. Also, during this post-Napoleonic period, English medical students from well-to-do families frequently spent a year in Paris, studying anatomy in French laboratories and learning of the work of Etienne Geoffroy St. Hilaire. The latter, a survivor of the Revolution, interpreted the broad spectrum of life as the modification of a small number of primal body plans, what he called *archetype*s. Although Geoffroy St. Hilaire's underlying framework is philosophical idealism, with Platonic essences occupying the intellectual space where genes are now, his framework is consistent with the transmutation of species on the material plane. In Scotland too, the flame of the Enlightenment continued to burn, and Erasmus Darwin's views were taught in the medical school, as his grandson Charles discovered.

After the Napoleonic Wars, Great Britain emerged as the hub of global capitalism, and London mushroomed into the world's largest city, its population soon hitting the two million mark. The militant disestablishment of feudalism had failed on the battlefield, but it was breaking out anew in the British metropolis and the factory towns of the Midlands, as class rivalry, political agitation, labor unrest, and mob violence made the peace imposed at Vienna seem a stopgap measure. Leading the column of homegrown dissidents were independently employed physicians.

Nowadays, the term "radical physician" suggests a doctor who buys a red sports car instead of a somber Mercedes sedan, but in the 1820s physicians were marching in the streets of England, allied with skilled tradesmen and republican firebrands who had supported the French Revolution. The independent physicians (among them Darwin's teacher, the anatomist Robert Edmund Grant) had created their own medical schools and colleges and were opposed to the Royal College of Physicians and the Royal College of Surgeons, which they regarded as corrupt nests of cronyism that needed to be disbanded in the name of progress.

The Lancet, now one of the most distinguished medical journals in the world, was at that time publishing editorials supportive of strikes and protests.[36]

This intense activity eventually led to the incorporation of shopkeepers and capitalists into the system of political power in nineteenth-century Great Britain, bringing with it a wide range of institutional changes, both social and economic, that are definitive of the modern world. The consolidation of power by merchants and financiers also ensured the intellectual triumph of the ideology that had brought them to power, namely the theory of progressive social evolution. Evolution, however, is Janus-faced, with different political implications depending on where one sits relative to the arrow of time. If one is an advanced life form, one can look down on the base levels through which one has ascended, contemptuous of those that history and progress have left behind. Conversely, if one is an aspiring life form, one can scrutinize those in positions of prominence with the confidence that they represent the spent force of history, susceptible to replacement by new, more progressive elements. In short, evolution can justify progress and revolution or stasis and reaction with equally compelling logic.

In the late eighteenth-century, when the bourgeoisie were excluded from power and constrained by the customs of feudalism, they trumpeted the radical side of evolutionist cosmology: universal freedom, political democracy, and social mobility. But by the end of the nineteenth century, as they began to enjoy the privileges of wealth and power while being increasingly dependent on overseas colonial ventures, they came to view the working class in Europe and the inhabitants of the colonies as ignorant, inferior people incapable of governing themselves, just as the aristocracy had once viewed them.

All ideologies of class superiority tend toward the same social result, namely, oppression of the weak by the powerful, but a class that comes to power through anticlericalism and regicide cannot easily justify its position by invoking the divine right of kings. Thus, evolutionism^G is a radical departure in terms of its intellectual content from the rationalizations of feudal Europe and the early stages of Western colonialism. Spain and Portugal justified their conquest of the New World by the number of souls that would be saved through conversion to Christianity, while the Puritans in New England interpreted the die-offs of the native inhabitants by European diseases as a divine mandate to appropriate Indian land. As late as the Civil War, Americans in the South justified slavery in terms of the biblical story of Ham, the putative ancestor of the Black race, whose lineage was cursed by God after he saw his father, Noah, naked.[37] But as modernity advanced, social hierarchy was increasingly justified in scientific and economic terms, as were the political critiques of the left. From the time of the French Revolution, science and pseudoscience increasingly formed the discourse of ideology, until, by the late nineteenth century, if religion was discussed by the intellectual elite at all, it was to condemn it as outmoded superstition. A ruling elite chosen by God had been superseded by one selected by Nature itself.

Significantly, William Buckland adumbrated the transition from a conservative ideology based on Christian Scripture to one based on natural science. In 1845, he left Oxford to accept the position of Dean of Westminster, then the most bully pulpit in the realm. While in London, he used the opportunity to get in step with the new age of commerce and industry, investing in a public utility and becoming an honorary member of the Institution of Civil Engineers. In 1848, a year remembered for its abortive revolutions, Buckland sketched in a sermon how animal life had progressed over geologic time. He then anticipated a thesis of this book, reassuring his audience that "progressive earth history cannot be separated from justification of the class system."[38]

A generation later, Buckland's insight would be given intellectual weight by the establishment of evolution as the dominant ideology in the elite universities of the English-speaking world.

Natural Selection

In 1859, more than two decades after his best-selling account of his scientific adventures, *The Voyage of the Beagle,* Charles Darwin reentered the public arena with a very different kind of book, a thick treatise in the academic style, *On the Origin of Species.* The dry text is counterbalanced by a subtitle carefully chosen to engage the Victorian imagination: *The Preservation of the Favored Races in the Struggle for Life.* I suspect that there were many people at the time who never read the book but who were favorably impressed by it, for the subtitle captures in a short phrase the key ideas that would come to form the ideology of class and empire that characterized colonial capitalism: *favored races* and *struggle.*[39] And no Victorian reader would ever have doubted that when Darwin spoke of "favored races" he meant literate, White, English people such as themselves.

Only eight years earlier, in 1851, London heralded the arrival of the new era by hosting a coming-out party for industrialism: the Crystal Palace Exhibition. Opened by Queen Victoria, its 13,000 exhibits housed in a magnificent hall of glass and iron showed six million visitors the supremacy of British science and technology. Where industry provided the means, Darwin provided the ideology. His theory of natural selection—hegemonic, competitive, mechanistic, and materialist—fit this new era perfectly. Natural selection confirms the "naturalness" of individual struggle while validating the hierarchy that emerges from this competition. Instead of an aristocracy of blood propagated through strategic marriages, Darwin argued that superior bloodlines are selected in a free market of competition of each against all, while society becomes an aggregate of competing individuals motivated by economic and genetic self-interests. Life itself is a struggle for existence in a world of chronic shortages and competitive markets, driven by biological needs and irrational lusts that keep the blood of commerce flowing.

The compatibility of Darwin's theory with capitalism and modernity is not in doubt, but its impact on religion has been as over-sold as its scientific originality. We have all read how Darwin came "into the theological world like a plough into an ant-hill," but historians have found no evidence of the crisis in Christianity that Darwin's book supposedly provoked.[40] In fact, among the Anglo-American intelligentsia, there was no significant conflict between science and religion until the last third of the nineteenth century, when this thesis was promulgated for political reasons in books such as Andrew Dickson White's *A History of the Warfare of Science with Theology in Christendom* (1888). This author was the first president of Cornell University, one of the "nonsectarian" colleges founded to teach industrial arts at the expense of the religiously grounded curriculum of traditional higher education (discussed in Chapter 3), so he stood to benefit personally by discrediting the credentials of clerical educators.[41] In the same vein, Thomas Henry Huxley and Francis Galton (Charles Darwin's cousin and the founder of the eugenics[G] movement) both saw educational reform as the establishment of a scientific priesthood.

In 1859, when *On the Origin of Species* was first published, belief in the literal interpretation of Scripture had already been eroded in theological circles. Not only had diluvialism failed in the 1820s, discrediting the literal interpretation of Genesis, but the historical authenticity of the Bible was being questioned by German philologists.[G] Using linguistic research and textual comparison, these scholars believed that three of the four Gospels derived from a common source—an unsettling idea that undermined the conventional view that the narratives of Jesus's life were written independently by four evangelists.[42] Only three months after Darwin published *Origin*, biblical modernists threw down their gauntlet to orthodox Anglicanism, inciting an internecine conflict on the authenticity of the Bible that eclipsed the controversy over organic evolution. Moreover, Darwin was careful to never attack religion directly, concentrating instead on Paley's eighteenth-century apologetics.

Even more important, by the time that Darwin's *Origin* appeared, progressive theologians had already abandoned biblical[G] Lteralism as scientific theory, while others were rethinking the relationship of science to religion. In the early 1850s, James Mc-Cosh, an evangelical[G] theologian, had set out to prove that there is no conflict between divine providence and the natural origin of species, seeing the relationship between science and revelation as complementary. In the New World, botanist Asa Gray, a Congregationalist minister and professor at Harvard, undertook to ensure that Darwin got a fair hearing in the United States, stating explicitly that the Bible is not a scientific textbook. In the words of one historian, the Christian response to Darwin in Victorian times was "both thoughtful and tolerant,"[43] and by concentrating on Huxley and Tyndale, historians "have failed to see how easily the theory of evolution was accommodated by some of the most sophisticated and subtle thinkers of the period."[44]

The reception of Darwin's thesis was also facilitated by the fact that the anti-evolutionist cause had spent much of its force fifteen years earlier in response to *The Vestiges of the Natural History of Creation*, a book that had been published anonymously in London in 1844. The author of *Vestiges* arranges both paleontological and historical events on the same scale of geologic time, thus ensuring that the evolution of the universe culminates in European civilization. Even though the author is dismissive of Lamarck, his narrative framework is implicitly evolutionary.

Vestiges unleashed a firestorm of criticism, not just from clergymen but from future Darwinists as well. Even Thomas Henry

Huxley, whom history knows as "Darwin's bulldog," contributed a hostile review of the book. Historians have likened *Vestiges* to a lightning rod that diverted negative attention from Darwin's theory of natural selection when it was published less than two decades later.[45]

Although Charles Darwin did not produce the crisis in Christianity with which he is often credited, he *did* repudiate the natural theology of his school days, marshaling numerous facts to show that what Paley thought to be design in organic nature is the culmination of natural processes; and he did it within a materialist framework that was in its way as atheistic as any French revolutionist could have hoped. If the change in species over geologic time is a natural and lawful process of physical cause and effect, then God, if involved at all, becomes at best an absentee landlord.[46] Even though Darwin's theory incorporated the basic premises of capitalism, and has coevolved with the latter, the irreligion implicit in *Origin* made it attractive to many on the political left, including Karl Marx. Even today, Darwinism continues to enjoy the approbation of progressives in spite of its long association with the right.[47]

Significantly, it was contemporary scientists, not clergy, who were the most skeptical of the theory of natural selection.[48] Fleeming Jenkin, an engineer, homed in on Darwin's blending theory of genetics, showing that if favorable variations arose in individuals they would be swamped in a few generations by blending with the rest of the population. Another critic, Lord Kelvin, one of the most famous physicists of the day, doubted there was sufficient time for organic evolution to occur, arguing that the eons assumed by Darwin were not supported by physical science. Others, such as the anatomist St. George Mivart, pointed out that natural selection was insufficient as an evolutionary mechanism because it explained how favorable traits could increase in frequency after they arose but did not explain how they developed in the first place. Even Alfred Russel Wallace, the naturalist and explorer who developed a theory of natural selection independently of Darwin, doubted that the proposed mechanism could account for the evolution of the human brain because, well, humans have far more gray matter than they ever seem to use.[49] Finally, the Russian naturalist Peter Kropotkin, citing the cooperative behavior of animals in Siberian winters, argued that competition was counterbalanced in nature by the equally widespread principle of Mutual Aid.[50]

Darwin Merges Biology with Political Economy

Darwin's theory of evolution was not seen by the Victorian intelligentsia as a radical departure from what came before. Europe had been awash in social evolutionism since the eighteenth century, while Lamarck's views on the transmutation of species were already familiar to many educated people. Evolutionist ideas were also widely circulated in the writings of Herbert Spencer, a member of the Darwinist inner circle.

Nowadays, especially among Darwinists, Spencer's argument is usually dismissed as a contribution to "philosophy," whereas Darwin's work is seen as "science," but in fact both sprout from the same root. Herbert Spencer's father was secretary to the Derby Philosophical Society, an organization founded by Erasmus Darwin; and as an adolescent, the younger Spencer had read the works of both Charles's grandfather and Jean Baptiste Lamarck. Not long after, Spencer became a close friend of Thomas Henry Huxley, well before the latter became Darwin's scientific publicist. Indeed, Spencer's mechanism was close enough to Darwin's intent that the latter incorporated the phrase "survival of the fittest" into later editions of *Origin*.

Because of Darwin's overt deference to Malthus, many intellectuals perceived *On the Origin of Species* to be a work of political advocacy. Certainly, the left's hatred of Malthus was no secret.

Friedrich Engels observed that "the worst open declaration of war of the bourgeoisie on the proletariat is Malthus's Law of Population and the New Poor Law framed upon it."[51] The historian Daniel P. Todes has studied the Russian response to Darwin in the nineteenth century, well before the Communist revolution, by examining the works of a number of authors now forgotten or never known in the English-speaking world. One such critic was the Lamarckian naturalist, N. G. Chernyshevskii, who presented Darwin's work to a progressive Russian audience in 1888. He dubbed natural selection "the theory of the beneficence of struggle" and complained that the "result was the same as if Adam Smith had taken it upon himself to write a course in zoology."[52]

Observers at the other end of the political spectrum, such as the Reverend Professor S. H. Haughton, president of the Royal Geological Society of Ireland (then an English colony), also judged Darwin's work to be a Malthusian tract. On the evening of July 1, 1858, Haughton attended a meeting of the Linnean Society in London, the famous meeting where Alfred Russel Wallace's twenty-page manuscript on natural selection was read into the society's official record along with excerpts from Darwin's forthcoming book on the same subject.

Back in Dublin, Haughton summarized his impression of the meeting for his own society's members: "Mr. Darwin's paper is simply an application of Malthus's doctrine of population to organic species, and a consequent demonstration that none but the healthiest, the most vigorous, and the best provided of a species can survive; and that the weakest must 'go to the wall' . . . To this there can be no objection, except that of want of novelty."[53] However, Darwin drew from Malthus's premises conclusions that the political economist himself would never have drawn.

Thomas Robert Malthus (1766–1834) was a younger contemporary of Lamarck and Erasmus Darwin though quite different from them in intellectual temperament. Thomas Robert's father was an enthusiast of the Enlightenment and a correspondent of Rousseau; but his son, at the age of thirty-two, achieved fame (or notoriety) with an epitaph to the perfectibility of man.[54] In his *Essay on Population*, published anonymously in 1798, Malthus argued that it ultimately did not matter how much one improved the physical conditions of human life, for the poor would respond by having more children; a few generations later, things would be back where one started.

To Malthus, this was a natural law, like gravity, that he called the Law of Population. He even produced a mathematical analogy to illustrate his point. He asserted that population increases geometrically (2, 4, 8, 16, . . .), that is by doubling, while food resources increase arithmetically (1, 2, 3, 4, . . .). Probably everyone who has ever taken a course in history or sociology knows this equation, but it is fiction not fact: no one had ever plotted statistics of population growth against metrics of food availability, least of all Malthus, who at that time was working as a curate in a country parish.

Population growth is kept in check, he argues, by two sorts of processes: negative and positive. (He uses "negative" in the sense of a minus sign, as the absence of something, whereas "positive" processes are active interventions.) Among the negative processes he includes delayed marriage and celibacy, both of which he recommends as the solution to overpopulation, whereas the "positive" mechanisms include famine, war, and pestilence, which weed out the excess population whenever the baby curve gets too far ahead of the food curve. Even though Malthus was an Anglican cleric, he had little use for Christian charity. In a passage that was removed from later editions of his most famous work, the young Malthus writes that "a man who is born into the world already possessed, if he cannot get subsistence from his parents on whom he has a just demand, and if society do not want his labor, has no claim of *right* to the smallest portion of food, and, in fact, has no business to be where he is."[55] As Marx has noted: "What characterizes Malthus is *the fundamental meanness* of his outlook [italics in original]."[56]

Malthus developed his political theory from overt theological premises, explicitly stating that the prod of hunger resulting from overpopulation is established by God as punishment for the lack of "moral restraint," which is to say control of the sexual urge. Thus, the supposedly scientific Law of Population is really crypto-theology, a stand-in for sexual abstinence and a punitive God. Significantly, two chapters on theology were dropped from subsequent editions of the *Essay on Population*, making it read more like descriptive economics and scientific theory.[57] These bowdlerized versions are often used in classrooms today.

Everyone has heard of Malthus's formula, but empirically no equation has ever been more wrong. Rarely is human famine due simply to bad weather and the failure of a single crop—these are usually the most immediate causes. Typically famine is the consequence of malicious politics and flawed economies as well.[58] The social history of human famines is depressing but instructive: the economic decision to plant export crops instead of food crops, inadequate stockpiling of grain, kidnapping farmers to work in the gold mines, enclosures of agricultural land by large landowners, and so on. Even during the Irish potato famine in the mid-nineteenth century, when there really was a disease that destroyed the principal food crop, the famine was caused by the policies of the British colonial administration, not by the potato blight.

The Irish peasantry was dependent on potatoes for sustenance because they had been pushed into marginal agricultural land by the British colonizers, who occupied the rich, grain-growing areas. English landlords operated their farms as capitalist enterprises and exported the bulk of Irish produce to England, where the prices were higher. Even after it became common knowledge that hundreds of thousands of people were dying of hunger, the British continued exporting food from the starving country—to the point that contingents of English soldiers were assigned to guard the wagons carrying food for export. At the same time, tenant farmers who could not pay their rent because their potato crop had been wiped out were evicted from the land by its English owners. To ensure that the tenants never came back, land agents, accompanied by policemen, burned the cottages that the peasants left behind. The eviction policy created a quarter of a million starving beggars overnight.

Official indifference to the suffering of the Irish people was justified in Parliament in terms of laissez-faire capitalism—that the government should never interfere with free trade. Moreover, British policy was inspired at least in part by Malthusian ideology, which attributed the wide-spread starvation to "too many Irish." When a critical world opinion finally goaded the British government into taking action, its solution was to build more workhouses and give those people who were still ambulatory an opportunity to line up for free soup.

Even the free soup had a catch. The Temporary Relief Act of 1847 was based on the premise of "deserving" versus "undeserving" poor, so that people got access to soup kitchens only if they could prove to British authorities that they owned no more than a quarter of an acre of land. Many signed away their land rights for the promise of food. Also, a premise of the legislation was that Ireland should pay for its own relief, which translated into new burdens for landlords in Ireland, who were taxed by the number of tenant farmer households on their property. Thus, the "relief" act further encouraged British landlords to rid themselves of Irish tenant farmers and replace them with high-value export crops.

Thus, the Great Famine, far from being a natural disaster, could never have achieved the magnitude it did without the callousness and connivance of the English ruling class. If government policies are judged by their actual effects, rather than by their proclaimed rationales, then it is noteworthy that Ireland is the only European country to have fewer people at the end of the nineteenth century than at the beginning. This suggests that British policy was formulated with the conscious intent of depopulating Ireland of its native inhabitants through neglect.[59]

Although Malthusians are confident that at some future point any population will hit the limit imposed by the food supply, Malthus's law is a purely logical construct with only two variables, whereas in the real world other causal factors become operative before his theoretical limit is reached. For example, when a nation becomes healthier and infant mortality decreases, people respond by having fewer children, which is exactly what has happened in the developed countries over the past century. Even in China, the food supply has increased faster than the population in every year since 1949, in spite of a famine during the forced collectivization of farms—a famine that was caused not by natural forces but by the misguided policy of the Communist Party.[60]

Yet in the Malthusian tradition, a pseudoscientific law of nature substitutes for critical analysis of the economic decisions and social policies that leave some people malnourished and others obese. Dressed in pin-stripes and wingtips, Malthus could have slipped effortlessly into Thatcher's cabinet or Reagan's White House.

In Malthus's formulation, the poor are essentially animals because they breed without moral restraint, so Darwin needed no leap of imagination to apply the model to all living things. Moreover, the famous economist had already conflated the class system with natural law and politics with mathematical models, making the application even easier. Thus Darwin concluded that where there are insufficient resources there must be competition; if there is competition there must be winners and losers; and if some species go extinct then it is the survivors who are the winners of the evolutionary race.

At this point, the foundation of Darwinian theory is essentially complete: Malthus's model applied to biology, with resource competition, population growth, and survivability all wrapped up in a single package. Darwin's *On the Origin of Species* is really his *Essay on Malthus.*

Yet Darwin's next step, the origin of species through natural selection, does not follow logically from Malthus's theory. In fact, it floats on top like an oil slick. Malthus did *not* say that as food becomes more scarce, competition among the poor will produce a leaner, meaner race of poor who will be more fit than the poor who came before them. To the contrary, for Malthus, those whose sexual restraint was insufficient for their economic means were simply getting their due as God had ordained it—namely, poverty, hunger, war, disease, and ultimately death.

Darwin's embrace of Malthus is even more anomalous when one considers that the famed economist not only repudiated the transmutation of species but used an example of selective breeding to refute the possibility of it:

> In the famous Leicestershire breed of sheep, the object is to procure them with small heads and small legs. Proceeding upon these breeding maxims, it is evident that we might go on till the heads and legs were evanescent quantities, but this is so palpable an absurdity that we may be quite sure that the premises are not just and that there really is a limit, though we cannot see it or say exactly where it is. In this case, the point of the greatest degree of improvement, or the smallest size of the head and legs, may be said to be undefined, but this is very different from unlimited, or from indefinite, in Mr Condorcet's acceptation of the term. Though I may not be able in the present

instance to mark the limit at which further improvement will stop, I can very easily mention a point at
which it will not arrive. I should not scruple to assert
that were the breeding to continue for ever, the head
and legs of these sheep would never be so small as the
head and legs of a rat. It cannot be true, therefore, that
among animals, some of the offspring will possess the
desirable qualities of the parents in a greater degree,
or that animals are indefinitely perfectible.[61]

But Darwin takes the same premises and reasons to exactly the
opposite conclusion—that resource scarcity breeds winners not
losers. With a *species ex machina*, Malthus's four horsemen of the
Apocalypse suddenly vanish, magically replaced by the transformation of species in nature.[62]

Where Malthus was skeptical of the perfectibility of both nature and society, invoking the limitations of selective breeding as
one of his prime examples, Darwin viewed nature through the
eyes of a breeder and saw endless variety waiting to be selected.
As early as 1838, shortly after returning home from the voyage of
the *Beagle*, Darwin read pamphlets on the breeding of domestic
plants and animals, which provided an empirical work-around to
Malthus's pessimistic argument.[63]

The theory of natural selection is almost always interpreted as a
scientific revolution, but that is to fundamentally misunderstand
Darwin's contribution to Western thought. Darwin's merger of
natural selection with political economy did eventually produce
new scientific findings by inspiring the fields of genetics, ecology,
and human evolution. But Darwin's rise to eminence in the 1860s
cannot be explained by developments that did not happen until
after his death. There was something about the theory of natural
selection that immediately inspired Darwin's contemporaries in
spite of the cautionary voices of the scientific community. What's

more, Darwin was not only regarded by contemporaries as an intellectual force—he became to them a symbol of the forces that he set in motion.

Darwin's appeal to his fellow Victorians is that he is *the man who saved Progress.* He used the facts of biological science to remove the conceptual impediments to evolutionary advance. First, natural selection changed the social implications of Malthus's Law of Population. Even if the food supply always lags behind increases in population, as Malthus contended, Darwin's theory implies that those who survive the crunch are better for the experience, being by definition the most fit, while those who are caught short can be confidently dismissed as "poorly adapted" to the future. Darwin made overpopulation and extinction compatible with Progress.

Second, Darwin's theory negated the religious impediments to Progress. By showing that what looks like design in organic nature is really the cumulative effect of natural processes, Darwin naturalized the moral^G order, which had hitherto been the prerogative of religion. Darwin's "natural morality" reinforces the mechanistic nature of laissez-faire economics while removing the values of the predatory corporation from any ethical sanction.

Darwin begins his master work, *On the Origin of Species*, by illustrating varieties of domestic pigeons that have been developed through selective breeding by amateur pigeon fanciers. The birds differ in body shape, size, plumage, and carriage from the wild rock doves from which they are descended, and the casual observer might mistake them for different species. To most of us, the variation of domestic dogs is a more accessible example: a St. Bernard and a hairless chihuahua are both members of the same species, though to the casual observer they appear to be more different than a jaguar is from a tiger. Furthermore, these different varieties of pigeons did not just happen. In the England of Darwin's day, there were competitions for animal breeding, where a panel of judges watched the animals parade before them, selected the "best of breed," and awarded a ribbon to the proud owner, just as with dog shows today.

Next, Darwin summarizes the variation in wild populations of organisms, showing that variety also exists in nature. Finally, in step three of his argument, Darwin theorizes that the multiplicity of causes in the natural world select from the variation of species in nature just as a human breeder selects organisms with the desired traits to use as breed stock for the next generation.

Darwin's argument assumes that selection is a natural phenomenon, one that can be directed by humans but that normally exists independently of them. For example, water runs downhill without the help of hydrological engineers, though it can be channeled and directed by the latter. Even though Darwin did not have the concept of the gene, as he was unaware of Mendel's [G] work, he certainly had a concept of "blood" that was inherited by the child from both parents, although he realized that it was not identical to the red liquid that courses through our veins but a distillation of parental traits that concentrated in the sex organs.[64] Genetic science has replaced blood flow with gene flow, but it is still like water running downhill in that it is thought to happen naturally in the course of reproduction.

Darwin's case for *natural* selection is weakened by the fact that he illustrates his thesis with changes that have been directed by human breeders and not on gene flow as observed in nature.[65] The main problem with using selective breeding by humans as a model for physical processes in nature is that it presumes the equivalent of an "intelligent designer."[66] Breeders already have an idea of the properties they are trying to facilitate, what Aristotle called the final cause; so they select the breed stock with those in mind. The philosopher Daniel Dennett has called design without a designer "Darwin's dangerous idea."[67] I would call it a flawed analogy—flawed because the intentionality of human beings when selecting new strains of plants and animals is deliberately left behind when the concept is transposed to nature. That is, the theory of *natural* selection jettisons the idea of an intelligent agent while claiming that the process will still produce similar results.

Significantly, in *Origin*, Darwin downplays conscious intent, saying that "for our purpose, a form of Selection, which may be called Unconscious" will suffice, as when a dog owner consistently chooses a particular feature each generation without an explicit goal in mind.[68] But making final cause unconscious does not obviate its logical role.

Darwin's argument, that species are formed in nature in the same way that breeds are bred by humans (with the proviso that in nature no one actually intends the effects that are produced), makes no specific predictions about the actual selection pressures that have shaped one species rather than another, so it must be applied retroactively; and since it is consistent with any fossil that paleontology might happen to excavate or any species that naturalists might discover, it can be used to explain anything and everything. Thus, it is more like a logic-tight system of belief than a scientific theory, since it is essentially unfalsifiable.

Darwinians, however, by taking metaphors literally while treating analogies as identities, can claim to not see the problem. Indeed, for many Darwinians, evolution is *defined* as natural selection, so that it becomes impossible to imagine the former without the latter. Adam Gopnik, for example, touts Darwin's work as literature while denying that analogy and metaphor have any place in his oeuvre at all:

> But the remarkable thing about Darwin as a writer is not how skillfully he uses metaphor but how artfully he avoids it. He argues by example, not by analogy; the point of the opening of 'The Origin' is not that something similar happens with domestic breeds and

natural species; the point is that *the very same thing happens* [italics mine], albeit unplanned and over a much longer period.[69]

As with Malthus's Law of Population, a hypothetical process that *could* occur given the right circumstances is elevated into a law of nature that admits of no exceptions.

An even more significant problem for Darwin's theory is the fossil record itself. As Cuvier demonstrated, paleontology shows prolonged periods of stasis rather than gradual, incremental change, yet Darwin predicts "an infinite number of those fine transitional forms, which, on my theory, have assuredly connected all the past and present species of the same group into one long and branching chain of life."[70] He explains their absence in the fossil record by the lessened probability of preservation of less well-adapted forms, which would be expected to have a more restricted distribution and smaller populations. Eventually, in the late twentieth century, Darwinians changed their prediction to something more consistent with the fossil record, now postulating "punctuated equilibrium" instead.[71]

Indeed, from the perspective of the twenty-first century, Darwin's concept of adaptation appears to inform our view of organic evolution far more than does his theory of natural selection. Darwin recognized that evolutionary change is equivalent to adaptation to a particular environment and way of life, such that the anatomy of a species reflects what subsequent biologists would call its ecological niche. For example, a hummingbird's beak is said to be adapted when the length and shape of its beak is related to the length and shape of the nectar sources that it feeds on or maybe by its need for a weapon in territorial display.

Adaptation is a scientific concept, since it is ultimately validated by comparative anatomy, ecology, and the geographical distribution of organisms; but it is logically distinct from the concept of natural selection. Even though bird beaks are adapted to the foods that the birds feed on, facts such as this are not deduced from the theory of natural selection but are inferred from observable relations in nature. Thus, such adaptations would remain facts whether speciation is Lamarckian, Darwinian, or due to something else entirely.

We also credit Darwin with the concept of adaptive[G] radiation, the situation in which an ancestral species diversifies into a number of new niches simultaneously. Reflecting on the Galapagos Islands, Darwin wondered if the different species of finches had all descended from a common ancestor that had arrived there from the mainland: "Seeing this gradation and diversity in one small, intimately related group of birds, one might really fancy that from an original paucity of birds in this archipelago, one species had been taken and modified for different ends," he writes.[72]

But this prediction does not explain Darwin's celebrity because he never showed that different species of finches evolved on different islands of the archipelago: his tags on the bird specimens in question do not record the island of origin, while some of the birds he identified as finches are actually tanagers.[73] Rather, the evidence for the radiation of Galapagos finches was first established in the 1930s, while the term *adaptive radiation* was coined by the paleontologist H. F. Osborn years after Darwin's death.

In addition to divergence and adaptation, Darwin emphasized a number of other evolutionary concepts that are taken for granted today. For example, he argued that competition for mates (sexual selection) is an important locus for evolutionary change that can explain such features as a buck's antlers and a peacock's tail, a theory that has become part and parcel of orthodox Darwinism.[74] However, if one assumes that the animals themselves are making decisions based on the displays of potential mates, then his explanation reintroduces final cause into nature.

Although adaptation, divergence, adaptive radiation, and co-evolution are solid contributions to our understanding of organic evolution, they are not enough to make someone a household name almost two centuries later. Yet in the anglophone world, Darwin is virtually synonymous with evolution to the point that the 200th anniversary of his birth was marked by an international extravaganza funded by corporate donations and accompanied by a drumbeat of adulation in the mass media. There is even an international Darwin Day.

Natural Selection Replaces Natural Theology

In Darwinian house histories, Darwin's rise to intellectual prominence is explained by the scientific power of the mechanism of natural selection as the agency of organic evolution. Yet in 1859, the proposed mechanism was not only conjectural and insufficient but was based on the blending theory of inheritance and was at odds with the fossil record. The science of genetics, which began with the discovery of discrete units of heredity and the process of mutation, was still decades into the future. Moreover, Darwin's key argument, namely analogy with selective breeding by a breeder with unconscious motives, requires a blind eye as well as a blind watchmaker.

In considering Darwin's place in intellectual history, there is, as the scholar Robert M. Young has observed, a discrepancy between "the generality of his influence and the particularity of his theory."[75] The enigmatic nature of Darwin's achievement was also sensed by Charles Degler, a former president of the American Historical Association. In Degler's summation of the history of evolutionary thought, Darwin's role is presented as anticlimactic: "Charles Darwin's work is best seen as the culmination rather than the initiation of a line of thought that saw evolutionary change in man and nature."[76]

The explanation for this discrepancy is that Charles Darwin was not simply a scientist. Indeed, it would be more accurate to call him a theologian of modernity who took the cultural premises of the English capitalist and industrialist classes and reformulated them as laws of organic nature. And for this framework, as noted in Chapter 1, Darwin quite explicitly expresses his debt to Thomas Robert Malthus, the man whose writings inspired the New Poor Law, indicating that natural selection is not simply about biology.

Darwin's book *On the Origin of Species* was written as a critique of Paley's natural theology, so it should not be read as a treatise in evolutionary biology. Darwin entered Cambridge University with the intention of receiving Holy Orders, and he was indoctrinated with the view that divine providence explains the facts of organic nature. In the 1850s, systems of nature were intertwined with religious presuppositions, while the Anglo-American intellectual elite consisted largely of Protestant clergy. Since modernists do not take theology seriously, when they read Darwin, they read him in the only way they can—as science. But in the Victorian period, especially to someone of Darwin's age and background, theology was still the framework of intellectual discourse; anyone who hoped to succeed in the world of ideas needed to address its concerns using the conventions it imposed. Darwin's work needs to be read from the perspective of the theological framework under which it was written.

Is there an intellectual context where empirical evidence is subordinated to the logical structure of an argument in the service of higher principles? From this perspective, Darwin's most famous book is written as a work of natural theology argued from an original premise, namely, one that assumes *the absence of God in an uncreated world.*

Darwin's thesis is a perfect inversion of Paley's—and it is this covert religious skepticism combined with its implicit capitalist values that sustains the uncritical acceptance of his work.[77]

Reflections

Darwin's theory of natural selection was embraced by the progressive intelligentsia of the Victorian era for reasons that had little to do with biology. Because natural selection explained the diversity of life as the byproduct of mechanistic laws modeled on those of physics, it was attractive to the emerging industrial class of businessmen and engineers, as well as to religious skeptics and materialists. And by explaining speciation as the product of competition, Darwin transposed the basic premises of Whig political economy onto the biological world—thus naturalizing capitalism. Just as the invisible hand of Adam Smith was believed to guide the economy, so the invisible hand of natural selection shapes the history of life.

Thus, in spite of the reservations voiced by many in the scientific community at the time, Darwinism became the keystone ideology that enabled human Progress to be redefined as industry, science, and the absence of religion.

Notes

1 King-Hele (1977, 1999, 2003), Smith (2005).

2 E. Darwin was in the circle known as the Lunar Society, an influential group of inventors, scientists, and industrialists (Uglow 2002).

3 King-Hele (2003).

4 Wikert (2009: Chapter 1). Darwin wrote home about his discovery of Erasmus: Desmond and Moore (1994: 40).

5 E. Darwin (1803, vol. 1: 396).

6 E. Darwin (1803, vol.1: 395). Erasmus's understanding of the "filament," however, was different from our own. Initially, he subscribed to the traditional view that the embryo was a product of the male and only nourished in the womb of the female, although by 1801 he had changed his mind on this point and credited both sexes with a role in conception. Nor did his understanding of genetics presage our own. He attributed hereditary disease to the drinking of alcoholic beverages, which he thought should be outlawed, while his views of the selection of marriage partners foreshadow eugenics (Smith and Arnott 2005: 117–30).

7 This regicide had echoes in the New World. In New Haven, Connecticut, adjacent to Yale University, three streets converge that are named for the three judges who condemned King Charles I to death.

8 Erasmus's poetry is discussed by King-Hele (1999).

9 Uglow (2002: 464).

10 King-Hele (1999: 313).

11 Ibid. 315–16. Canning, however, was only prime minister for four months.

12 Hutton (1999).

13 Eiseley (1961, Chapter 5).

14 Corsi (1988), Lamarck (1984). In the latter work, see also Hull's introduction: "Lamarck among the Anglos."

15 In eighteenth-century science, microbes were commonly thought to be created by a hypothetical process called *spontaneous generation* —a hypothesis that was finally laid to rest in the nineteenth cen-

tury by cell biology, which showed that all microbes are descended from preexisting microbes through cell division.

16 A classic study is Lovejoy (1936). In one of the most popular works of natural history in the eighteenth century, Buffon's *Natural History* (Buffon, Smellie, and Chambers 1866), this hierarchical scheme is implicit in the descriptions of the animals.

17 Quoted by Coleman (1964: 148) from *Historie naturelle des poissons* by Cuvier and Valenciennes , 1828. Cuvier, however, did believe in a hierarchy of human races (Coleman 1964: 166), the scheme that succeeded the *scala naturae.*

18 I explore this in a previous book (Reynolds 1981). Becker (1932) points out that the *philosophes* substituted "posterity" for the Christian afterlife.

19 Some of Cuvier's work has been reprinted in English (Cuvier 1980). Rudwick and Cuvier (1997) provide a readable introduction to the man and his science.

20 There is evidence that geological and political revolutions were linked in Cuvier's mind. In his *Discours sur les révolutions de la surface du globe*, he notes that in "political history past events are easily explained when one knows the passions and intrigues of his own day," but this is not the case in geology, where "none of the agents that it employs today would have sufficed to produce the ancient works"; quoted by Coleman (1964: 135).

21 Paley was aware of Hume's critique of religion and the writings of Erasmus Darwin (Shapiro 2009).

22 Thomson (2005: 201).

23 Shapiro (2009) discusses Paley's argument in detail, pointing out that Paley's theology, because it assumes the invariance of natural law, is in this respect more congenial with evolutionism than is the intelligent[G] design school of the late twentieth century.

24 Ruse (2003). This exemplifies Robert M. Young's (1985: 79:80) criticism of the treatment of Darwin by historians, which is to say that his predecessors are dismissed while his contemporaries are downplayed.

25 Desmond (1989: 3-7).

26 Thomson (2005: 195).

27 From "The Obedience of a Christian Man," *Doctrinal Treatises*;
quoted by Davies (1996: 302).

28 Gillispie (1951).

29 Rupke (1983).

30 Gillispie (1951: 107–10).

31 Rupke (1983, Chapter 2).

32 And if Cuvier did see an incompatibility between science and religion, he would be the last person to make it an issue. As a biographer writes: "If in the sciences authority could be fairly questioned, in religion and political affairs authority must be regarded as a source of wisdom and social stability and therefore necessarily beyond the unrestrained probing of the curious. No man, Cuvier believed, could rightfully arrogate to himself the privilege of criticizing the established religious and social powers" (Coleman 1964: 17).

33 Snow (1961).

34 Kruze (2015), Robert M. Young (1985: 33).

35 Desmond (1989).

36 Turner (1978: 365–66).

37 Pleins (2003: Chapter 8) describes the ideological uses of the biblical story of Ham in the antebellum South.

38 Rupke (1983: 255). Additional quotations relevant to this theme are in Gillispie (1951: 202).

39 The argument presented in the balance of the chapter—namely, that natural selection is an ideology of modernism that is scientifically suspect—is also presented by the biologist Stanley N. Salthe in a web page (accessed 2006) that I did not see until after the first draft of this book was written.

40 Livingston (1987).

41 See the discussion in Marsden (1994: 117). The expositor of Darwinism Steven Jay Gould also recognizes that the conflict between science and religion dates from the late nineteenth century (Gould 1999: 99–102).

42 Karl Marx's views on religion were much influenced by these German critics, whose works are briefly summarized in Wolff (2002: 13–18).

43 Livingston (1987: 146). Livingston (2014) shows that the reception of Darwin's work by the clergy reflected local interests and political issues.

44 Young (1985: 146).

45 Eiseley (1961: 132–40).

46 This phrase in in Desmond and Moore (1994: 479).

47 See Chapter 4.

48 For reprints of reviews of Darwin's book by his contemporaries, see Hull (1983). A brief summary of scientific critics is given in Livingston (1987: 52–53).

49 In *Contributions to the Theory of Natural Selection*, published in 1870, Wallace argued that nature could not provide a brain disproportionate to the requirements. Wallace's works are online at http://wallacefund.info and at http://www.wku.edu/~smithch/index1.htm.

50 Kropotkin (1902). Sapp (2003: Chapter 5) discusses Kropotkin's work in reference to Darwinism, as does Todes (1989).

51 From *The Condition of the Working Class in England in 1844*, reprinted in Marx, Engels, and Meek (1954: 69).

52 Todes (1989: 36–37).

53 *Journal of the Geological Society of Dublin* (1857–60) 3: 137; quoted by Brackman (1980: 74).

54 Malthus may have acquired his anti-revolutionary stance by attending to the fate of his teachers. Petersen (1979: 23) points out that all three of his tutors suffered for their refusal to abandon their radical beliefs: one was socially ostracized for marrying beneath his station, another imprisoned for libel, and a third expelled from his university position for refusing to retract his Unitarian views.

55 Malthus, quoted in Meek's introduction to Marx, Engels and Meek (1954: 15).

56 Marx in *Theories of Surplus Value* (1954, Vol. 2: 118). The italics are Marx's own.

57 Pullen (1986), Young (1985: 31).

58 Dréze and Sen (1990–1991), Sen (1981).

59 Crowley, Smythe, and Murphy (2012), Kinealy (2015), and Woodham-Smith (1962).

60 Dréze and Sen (1990–1991), Riskin (1991).

61 Malthus (1826: III.I.19). Darwin probably read the sixth edition of Malthus's work, which had been substantially rewritten since the first edition of 1798 (Malthus, Wrigley and Souden 1986). The passage on Leicestershire sheep is found in both.

62 Gillian Beer (2000: 29) says that Darwin transformed Malthus by interpreting fecundity as "a liberating and creative principle." Certainly Darwin transformed Malthus, but fecundity in his scheme is only liberating and creative for the "chosen races."

63 Ruse (1975).

64 Darwin's theory of pangenesis.^G

65 Alfred Russel Wallace anticipates this criticism in *Contributions to the Theory of Natural Selection,* noting that Darwin's evidence for natural selection is drawn from breeding experiments and not from observations in nature; cited by Brackman (1980: 281).

66 See the critique of natural selection by Fodor and Piattelli-Palmarini (2010).

67 Dennett (1995).

68 C. Darwin, *Origin*, Chapter I: 34. The word "unconscious" also occurs elsewhere in this work for a total of twenty-eight times.

69 Gopnik (2006: 56). See Fodor and Piattelli-Palmarini (2010) for discussion of this point.

70 C. Darwin, *Origin,* Chapter 10 of the sixth edition.

71 Eldredge and Gould (1972).

72 Quoted by Desmond and Moore (1991: 328).

73 Grant (1986).

74 This generalization too has been challenged, especially by Roughgarden (2009), who is a professor biology at Stanford.

75 Young (1985: 80).

76 Degler (1991: 6).

77 The inversion of Paley has been noted by at least two authors, including Livingston (1987: 48) and Thomson (2005: 261).

References

Becker, Carl L. 1932. *The Heavenly City of the Eighteenth-Century Philosophers: Based on the Storrs Lectures Delivered at Yale University.* 33rd printing, 1969 ed. New Haven: Yale University Press.

Beer, Gillian. 2000. *Darwin's Plots: Evolutionary Narrative in Darwin: George Eliot and Nineteenth-Century Fiction.* Second edition. Cambridge: Cambridge University Press.

Brackman, Arnold C. 1980. *A Delicate Arrangement: The Strange Case of Charles Darwin and Alfred Russel Wallace.* New York: Times Books.

Coleman, William. 1964. *Georges Cuvier, Zoologist: A Study in the History of Evolution Theory.* Cambridge, MA: Harvard University Press.

Corsi, Pietro. 1988. *The Age of Lamarck: Evolutionary Theories in France, 1790–1830.* Rev. and updated ed. Berkeley and Los Angeles: University of California Press.

Crowley, John, William J. Smyth, and Mike Murphy, eds. 2012. *Atlas of the Great Irish Famine, 1845–52.* Cork, Ireland: Cork University Press.

Cuvier, Georges. 1980. *Memoirs on Fossil Elephants and on Reconstruction of the Genera Palaeotherium and Anoplotherium.* New York: Arno Press.

Darwin, Charles. 1859. *On the Origin of Species by Means of Natural Selection or the Preservation of Favoured Races in the Struggle for Life.* London: John Murray.

Darwin, Erasmus. 1803. *Zoonomia, or, the Laws of Organic Life. 2 vols.* 2nd American ed. from the 3rd London ed., corrected by the author. Boston: Thomas and Andrews.

Davies, Horton. 1996. *Worship and Theology in England: I. From Cranmer to Hooker, 1534-1603; II. From Andrews to Baxter and Fox, 1603–1690.* Consolidated paperback ed. Grand Rapids, MI and Cambridge, England: William B. Eerdsmans. Original edition, Vol. I Princeton University Press 1970 and Vol. II 1975.

Degler, Carl N. 1991. *In Search of Human Nature: The Decline and Revival of Darwinism in American Social Thought*. Oxford: Oxford University Press.

Dennett, Daniel C. 1995. *Darwin's Dangerous Idea: Evolution and the Meanings of Life*. New York: Simon and Schuster.

Desmond, Adrian. 1989. *The Politics of Evolution: Morphology, Medicine, and Reform in Radical London*. Chicago: University of Chicago Press.

———, and James Moore. 1994. *Darwin: The Life of a Tormented Evolutionist*. Paperback ed. New York: W. W. Norton. Originally published 1991.

Dréze, Jean, and Amartya Sen, eds. 1990–1991. *The Political Economy of Hunger. 3 vols.* Oxford: Oxford University Press.

Eiseley, Loren. 1961. *Darwin's Century: Evolution and the Men Who Discovered It*. Garden City, NY: Anchor Books. Original edition Doubleday 1958.

Eldredge, N., and S. J. Gould. 1972. Punctuated equilibria: an alternative to phyletic gradualism. In *Models in Paleobiology*, edited by Thomas J. M. Schopf. San Francisco: Freeman.

Fodor, Jerry A., and Massimo Piattelli-Palmarini. 2010. *What Darwin Got Wrong*. New York: Farrar, Straus and Giroux.

Gillispie, Charles Coulston. 1951. *Genesis and Geology: A Study in the Relations of Scientific Thought, Natural Theology, and Social Opinion in Great Britain, 1790–1850*. Cambridge: Harvard University Press. Paperback edition 1969.

Gopnik, Adam. 2006. Rewriting nature: Charles Darwin, natural novelist. *The New Yorker*. 26 Oct. 52–59.

Gould, Stephen Jay. 1999. *Rocks of Ages: Science and Religion in the Fullness of Life*. New York: Ballantine.

Grant, Peter R. 1986. *Ecology and Evolution of Darwin's Finches*. Princeton, NJ: Princeton University Press. Paperback edition.

Hull, David L. 1983. *Darwin and His Critics: The Reception of Darwin's Theory of Evolution by the Scientific Community*. Chicago and London: University of Chicago Press. Original edition Harvard 1973.

Hutton, James. 1999. *Investigation of the Principles of Knowledge and of the Progress of Reason, from Sense to Science and Philosophy*. Bristol: Thoemmes.

Kinealy, Catherine. 2015. Saving the Irish poor: charity and the Great Famine, MIMOC 12. https://journals.openedition.org/mimmoc/1845#ftn10

King-Hele, Desmond G. 1977. *Doctor of Revolution: The Life and Genius of Erasmus Darwin*. London: Faber/Maughan Library Humanities Books.

_____. 1999. *Erasmus Darwin: A Life of Unequalled Achievement*. London: Giles de la Mare. Paperback edition.

_____. 2003. The furtive evolutionist. *New Scientist* 178 (2390): 48.

Kropotkin, Petr Alekseevich. 1902. *Mutual Aid: A Factor of Evolution*. London: William Heinemann.

Kruze, Kevin M. 2015. *One Nation under God: How Corporate America Invented Christian America*. New York: Basic Books.

Lamarck, J. B. [Jean Baptiste]. 1984. *Zoological Philosophy: An Exposition with Regard to the Natural History of Animals. With introductory essays by David L. Hull and Richard W. Burkhardt, Jr. Translated by H. Elliot*. Chicago and London: University of Chicago Press.

Livingston, David N. 1987. *Darwin's Forgotten Defenders: The Encounter between Evangelical Theology and Evolutionary Thought*. Grand Rapids, MI, and Edinburgh, Scotland: William B. Eerdmans and Scottish Academic Press.

_____. 2014. *Dealing with Darwin: Place, Politics, and Rhetoric in Religious Engagements with Evolution*. Baltimore, MD: Johns Hopkins University Press. http://muse.jhu.edu/books/9781421413273/

Lovejoy, Arthur O. 1936. *The Great Chain of Being: A Study of the History of an Idea*. Cambridge, MA: Harvard University Press.

Malthus, T. R. 1826. *An Essay on the Principle of Population; Or, a View of Its Past and Present Effects on Human Happiness; With an Inquiry into Our Prospects Respecting the Future Removal or Mitigation of the Evils Which It Occassions [sic]*. London: John Murray.

_____, E. A. Wrigley, and David Souden. 1986. *An Essay on the Principle of Population: The First Edition (1798) with Introduction and Bibliography*. London: W. Pickering.

Marsden, George M. 1994. *The Soul of the American University: From Protestant Establishment to Established Nonbelief*. Oxford and New York: Oxford University Press.

Marx, Karl, Friedrich Engels, and Ronald L. Meek. 1954. *Marx and Engels on Malthus: Selections from the Writings of Marx and Engels Dealing with the Theories of Thomas Robert Malthus. Edited with an introductory essay and notes by Ronald L. Meek. Translations from the German by Dorothea L. Meek and Ronald L. Meek*. New York: International Publishers.

Petersen, William. 1979. *Malthus*. Cambridge, MA: Harvard University Press.

Pleins, J. David. 2003. *When the Great Abyss Opened: Classic and Contemporary Readings of Noah's Flood*. Oxford and New York: Oxford University Press.

Pullen, J. M. 1986. Malthus: theological ideas and their influence on his Principle of Population. In *Thomas Robert Malthus: Critical Assessments*, edited by J. C. Wood. London and Dover, NH:

Croom Helm.

Reynolds, Peter C. 1981. *On the Evolution of Human Behavior: The Argument from Animals to Man*. Berkeley and Los Angeles: University of California Press.

Riskin, Carl. 1991. Feeding China: the experience since 1949. In *The Political Economy of Hunger*, edited by J. Dréze and A. Sen. Oxford: Oxford University Press.

Roughgarden, Joan. 2009. *The Genial Gene: Deconstructing Darwinian Selfishness*. Berkeley University of California Press.

Rudwick, Martin J. S., and Georges Cuvier. 1997. *Georges Cuvier, Fossil Bones, and Geological Catastrophe: New Translations and Interpretations of the Primary Texts*. Chicago: University of Chicago Press.

Rupke, Nicholas A. 1983. *The Great Chain of History: William Buckland and the English School of Geology, 1814–1849*. Oxford: Oxford University Press.

Ruse, Michael. 1975. Charles Darwin and artificial selection. *Journal of the History of Ideas* 36 (2):339-350.

_____. 2003. Is evolution a secular religion? *Science* 299 (5612): 1523-24.

Salthe, Stanley N. Analysis and critique of the concept of Natural Selection http://www.nbi.dk/~natphil/salthe/Critique_of_Natural_Select_.pdf (Accessed 20 April 2016).

Sapp, Jan. 2003. *Genesis: The Evolution of Biology*. Paperback ed. Oxford and New York: Oxford University Press.

Sen, Amartya. 1981. *Poverty and Famines: An Essay on Entitlement and Deprivation*. Oxford and New York: Clarendon/Oxford University Press.

Shapiro, Adam. 2009. William Paley's lost "Intelligent Design." *History and Philosophy of the Life Sciences* 31: 55–78.

Smith, C. U. M., and Robert Arnott, eds. 2005. *The Genius of Erasmus Darwin.* Burlington, VT: Ashgate.

Snow, C. P. 1961. *The Two Cultures and the Scientific Revolution.* New York: Cambridge University Press.

Solnit, Rebecca. 2009. *Paradise Built in Hell: The Extraordinary Communities That Arise in Disasters.* New York: Penguin/Viking.

Thomson, Keith. 2005. *Before Darwin: Reconciling God and Nature.* New Haven, CT, and London: Yale.

Todes, Daniel Philip. 1989. *Darwin without Malthus: The Struggle for Existence in Russian Evolutionary Thought: Monographs on the History and Philosophy of Biology.* New York: Oxford University Press.

Turner, Frank M. 1978. The Victorian conflict between science and religion: a professional dimension. *Isis* 69 (248): 356–76.

Uglow, Jennifer S. 2002. *The Lunar Men: The Friends Who Made the Future, 1730–1810.* London: Faber.

White, Andrew Dickson. 1896. *A History of the Warfare of Science with Theology in Christendom.* New York: D. Appleton. 1st ed. 1888.

Wikert, Benjamin. 2009. *The Darwin Myth.* Washington, D.C.: Regnery.

Wolff, Jonathan. 2002. *Why Read Marx Today?* Oxford: Oxford University Press.

Wood Woodham-Smith, Cecil. 1962. *The Great Hunger, Ireland 1845–9.* London: H. Hamilton.

Young, Robert M. 1985. *Darwin's Metaphor: Nature's Place in Victorian Culture.* Cambridge: Cambridge University Press.

Introduction to Book II

In Darwinian theory, even the moral order evolves through the process of natural selection, so by installing the latter as the dominant view of human nature in the universities, both egocentricity and competition became foundational values of modern society. Thus Christianity, an ideology that professed concern for the poor, yielded place to one congruent with laissez-faire capitalism. Because of its structural role within the academy, natural selection has acquired a sacrosanct status that has forestalled any serious criticism. In the following chapters, I examine the implications of Darwinist ideology for society and social theory.

Chapter Three

The Corporate Moral Order

In 1864, a small group of Charles Darwin's supporters met over dinner in London. Although most of them were in their late thirties and early forties, all were well known in their respective disciplines, and all but one were Fellows of the Royal Society. The mathematician Thomas Archer Hirst (1830–1892) recorded the event in his diary:

> On Thursday evening Nov. 3, an event, probably of some importance, occurred at the St. George's Hotel, Albemarle Street. A new club was formed of eight members; viz: Tyndall, Hooker, Huxley, Busk, Frankland, Spencer, Lubbock and myself. Besides personal friendship, the bond that united us was devotion to science, pure and free, untrammeled by religious dogmas.[1]

The next month, they added a ninth member, a mathematician working as the Queen's Printer.

The gentlemen's club was where business was done in Victorian London, and although there were other clubs devoted to science whose members were as well connected to the Royal Society, this new group, the X Club,ᴳ would prove to be the most significant for the story of evolution.[2] Some of its members, in particular Thomas Henry Huxley and Herbert Spencer, are pivotal figures in the history of evolution, and they were shapers of public opinion in both the British Empire and the United States.

The X Club served as the inner circle of British science for more than thirty years at a time when science was transitioning from a gentleman's hobby to a modern profession. The X Club was instrumental, in some cases pivotal, in establishing an effective institutional framework for science that persists to the present day. First of all, the X Club was a de facto executive committee for the Royal Society, helping to set the agenda for meetings, recommending nominees for society offices, and providing three of its presidents. X Club members were also active in the British Association for the Advancement of Science, lecturing in its sessions on specific research topics while providing five of its presidents. The biologists in the X Club were also examiners for the Army, Navy, and Indian Army, with the job of assessing the knowledge of candidates seeking employment in their respective medical services, a role they used to set up technical schools and initiate more scientific training of doctors.[3] By 1869, they had founded the journal *Nature*, for which Huxley contributed the lead article of the first issue. *Nature* is now the most prestigious scientific publication in the world.

The X Club was essential to the establishment of science as a profession, helping to provide career opportunities independent of fortuitous sinecures, such as Queen's Printer, while establishing its own standards of performance and reward outside the elite universities, which were run by the Church of England. Significantly, the careers of the majority of the X Club members mirror the growing importance of science in this period of rapid industrialization when technically trained people were increasingly in demand. As Ruth Barton points out, the club formed from two preexisting social networks: "Tyndall, Hirst, and Edward Frankland, artisans who became physical scientists; and Huxley, George Busk, and Hooker, surgeons who became naturalists."[4] Some scientists, such as Darwin, came from well-to-do families that provided financial support; but those entering

science from the artisanal class found that the profession conferred few privileges and very little money. As science burgeoned,
its practitioners sought to differentiate it from related activities
such as medicine, surveying, and mechanics while establishing
salaried, full-time positions that were independent of the church
and aristocracy.

Yet the X Club was not just about science. The members were
united, for example, in their opposition to home rule for Ireland,
to the point that they considered drafting a public statement
condemning prime minister Gladstone's proposal to grant the
Irish political freedom. Adamantly opposed to what they considered religious superstition and idolatry, they were incensed by the
prospect of an independent Catholic nation almost on England's
shore. This heartfelt belief also facilitated their other goals, for as
Turner points out: "Linking the advance of science to anticathol-
icism allowed the cause of the professional scientists to benefit
from the widespread popular antipapist sentiment in Britain."[5]

The club had a position on the state religion too. Although two
members belonged to the Church of England, all were united in
their opposition to the ecclesiastical establishment, which they
saw as an obstacle to a free and independent science. Yet disdain
for religion did not prevent them from taking sides in a contemporary theological controversy, agreeing with the modernists that
the Bible should be read and interpreted using scientific methods
of scholarship.

To Thomas Henry Huxley, the most outspoken member of the
group, religion was more than an obstacle to be removed: it was
a model for what science should be. Huxley's understanding of
professionalization went well beyond achieving parity with law
and medicine. He saw science as the ultimate source of moral and
intellectual authority in society—the successor to the Church of
England. One month after the founding of the X Club in 1864,
Huxley published an editorial called "Science and Church Poli-

cy," which asserts that science has "uncontrolled domination over the whole realm of intellect."[6]

Huxley's imperial ambition is still at the heart of Darwinism. More than a century later, the cofounder of sociobiology,[G] Harvard biologist E. O. Wilson, unequivocally staked a claim on the social sciences:

> Cognition will be translated into circuitry. Learning and creativeness will be defined as the alteration of specific portions of the cognitive machinery regulated by input from the emotive centers. Having cannibalized psychology, the new neurobiology will yield an enduring set of first principles for sociology.[7]

E. O. Wilson's ideological forebear, Thomas Henry Huxley, was born in 1825 above a butcher shop in a village outside London, the son of a poorly paid mathematics teacher.[8] While Thomas was still a boy, the school suddenly shut its doors, laying off his father at the age of 55; in desperation the family moved to Coventry, a silk-spinning town in the north of England, where his father had relatives. The arrival of the Huxleys coincided with the installation of the first steam-powered looms, which were turning small, independent producers into industrial proletariat.

Too poor to attend school, Thomas was apprenticed to a surgeon. In England at that time, the rich and well born were usually attended by college-educated physicians, whereas the poor used the services of surgeons who had learned their craft by assisting established practitioners.

It was in this circle of provincial apothecaries and surgeons that Huxley acquired a quasi-religious faith that would last him the rest of his life, an amalgamation of Unitarian rationalism, Continental evolutionism, Calvinist self-righteousness, and vocal dissent from religious orthodoxy, which for Huxley meant the Church of England. In short, he perfectly embodied the age that was about to be born.

Both of Huxley's sisters had married independent medical practitioners; in January of 1841, Huxley followed his sisters and their husbands to London, becoming an apprentice to a surgeon in a grimy working class district. Dressed in a frock coat and stovepipe hat, as befit his new profession, he stood out among the destitute as a man of means and learning; but Huxley wanted the esteem of his social superiors as well. In the grim East End surgery, he set out to give himself the education he had never received, studying an hour of German each day and reading late into the night while the other young men were relaxing in public houses and pool halls.

Through paid courses in a diploma mill, financial support from his sisters and their husbands, and a scholarship to Charing Cross Hospital, by 1846 Huxley had learned enough science and medicine to apply for the position of ship's surgeon with Her Majesty's Navy. His scientific talents were recognized, and the Admiralty assigned him to a ship that was being readied to survey and explore the coasts of New Guinea and Australia, *HMS Rattlesnake*. This four-year voyage would give Huxley the scientific credentials of a Darwin and prepare the way for the founding of the X Club.

After the publication of Darwin's *On the Origin of Species* in 1859, Huxley became the acknowledged bearer of the evolutionist standard, presenting Darwin's theory to the public in such clear, compelling words that all London was clamoring for tickets to hear him speak. Karl Marx probably attended Huxley's lectures,[9] and even a London cab driver refused payment from Huxley when he learned that his passenger was the celebrated evolutionist.[10] Huxley's well-received book, *Man's Place in Nature*, continues to inspire more than a century later.[11]

Significantly, Huxley was more than an anatomist—he was a religious reformer in scientific guise. One of his biographers calls him a "Manichaean Calvinist,"[12] and his contemporaries recognized an evangelical preacher when they saw one. As one Victorian journalist wrote:

> His nature is essentially Puritanic, if not Calvinistic. He has the moral earnestness, the volitional energy, the absolute confidence in his own convictions, the desire and determination to impress them upon all mankind, which are the essential marks of Puritan character . . . and he might fairly be described as a Roundhead who had lost his faith.[13]

Even though Huxley always spoke as if there were no God, in 1869 he coined the term *agnosticism* in order to distance his own brand of rationalism from the revolutionary atheism being trumpeted by Marxists and the like, while recognizing that a public stance of metaphysical uncertainty is more compatible with the purported open-mindedness of science.[14] For a similar reason, he insisted that his own program to make science the successor to religion was in no way influenced by Auguste Comte.[15]

More than half a century earlier, Auguste Comte had formulated what he called the Law of Three Stages, which asserts that human thought progresses from a religious stage through a metaphysical stage to a last and final "positive" stage (that is, certain knowledge based on science).[16] The underlying goal was to dethrone theology as the queen of the sciences by making empiricism definitive of the intellectual life; but Comte went further, envisioning a new "religion of humanity," complete with secular rituals, that would be the successor to the Catholic Church. Huxley dismissed Comte's proposed religion as the "hocus-pocus of Catholicism minus the Christianity," though he did promulgate Comte's major premise that science is the culmination of human thought.

Far from advocating godless rituals to replace those of Christianity, Huxley imagined the successor to religion to be as liturgically spartan as a Unitarian church. Yet his conflation of science with religion is nonetheless consistent with Comte's third stage of history. Also, like Comte's positivism, Huxley's belief in science was overtly imperialistic, being in no way restricted to the study of the natural world, much less to his own scientific specialty, anatomy. As Huxley saw it, even Christian Scripture was the subject matter of biology.

In the early 1860s, the X Club took the side of biblical revisionists, who, inspired by German scholarship, had undertaken to determine the accuracy of biblical accounts of ancient history and to analyze the book's authorship in the light of comparative philology.[G] Subsequently, Huxley himself waded into biblical criticism, expounding Bruno Bauer's thesis that the Synoptic Gospels, namely the gospels of Matthew, Mark, and Luke, cannot be authoritative accounts of Jesus's life because textual comparison shows that all derive from a hypothetical earlier text whose author is unknown. As the scholar of religion Matthew Day has noted:

> By extending the discourse of natural history to include the scientific study of the Bible and religion, Huxley not only transformed a once literary enterprise into a biological one—a small-scale academic transformation that exemplified the sort of grand cultural transformation that he desired. He simultaneously appropriated the text that inspired so many of the religiously motivated creationist[G] critics of evolutionary thought.[17]

The appropriation of religion's ideological role by biology, implicit in Darwin's critique of Paley, was an essential stratagem in the modernization of the university. Until Darwin's day, higher education in the United Kingdom was the responsibility of the Church of England, so any reform of the academic curriculum by outsiders was an implicit challenge to religious authority. After King Henry VIII made religion answerable to him alone, theologians codified the religious beliefs incumbent on the faithful as the Thirty Nine Articles, which were established by an act of Parliament in 1571. Prospective students at Oxford and Cambridge universities were required to affirm their loyalty to this creed, which effectively restricted higher education to members of the Church of England.

Protestant clergy had control of higher education in the United States as well.[18] In the New England colonies, Puritans established their own version of orthodox Christianity modeled on Calvin's government in Geneva, and they founded the colleges of Harvard (1636) and Yale (1701) to educate their clergy. However, in Virginia and the English colonies farther south, the official Church of England prevailed, and higher education was the responsibility of Anglican clergymen.

After the American Revolution, when the former British colonies merged to form the United States, the new constitution guaranteed the independence of church and state on the federal level; but individual state governments continued to appropriate funds for church schools such as Harvard College, just as their colonial predecessors had done. Protestantism commanded the loyalty of a majority of the population; and the descendants of the New England Puritans were firmly entrenched as the religious, cultural, and seafaring elite of the new nation. In Massachusetts, the established church lasted longest, until 1833; but as the nation expanded westward, many new states were founded that had no colonial traditions of established religion to preserve. So Americans founded private institutions of higher education with the same boundless enthusiasm they brought to sawmills and railroads, establishing over 500 colleges in the years before the Civil War. The spiritual descendants of the Calvinists, namely the Presbyterians and Congregationalists, dominated this educational effort. Even today, street names, such as those in Berkeley and Palo Alto, California, bear witness to forgotten New England ministers instrumental in the westward movement of higher education.

Although each college promulgated the doctrine of a specific religious tradition and was staffed primarily by clergymen of that denomination, schools were dependent on local communities for fund-raising and student tuition, giving them a measure of independence from ruling bodies in far-off capitals. In aggregate they represented a pluralist concept of religion in which each group was free to pursue its own vision of the spiritual life while unable to impose it on others as an officially established church. Although "a college education" continued to confer access to elite positions in government, the church, and the professions as before, neither national nor local government had much control over the educational content. Even culturally disenfranchised groups, such as Catholics and Mormons, were able to found colleges of their own.

But about the time of the American Civil War, when the United States began to rapidly industrialize, the independent college was superseded by a new institution, the nonsectarian university, which reestablished state-supported higher education with a more scientific and professional curriculum. For this change to take place, the power of local communities to control their own colleges had to be sharply curtailed and replaced by new standards of professional certification controlled or enforced by governments. In this process of professionalization, American educators looked to Prussia for inspiration. Prussia was not only a staunchly Protestant country but it had developed a new educational bureaucracy with a new standard of academic certification, the Ph.D. degree, which was soon adopted by American universities. Yale University, for example, conferred its first doctoral degree in 1860.

Moreover, the New England intelligentsia had long been attracted to the German tradition of philosophical idealism as expounded in the works of Hegel and Kant. Philosophical idealism is the thesis that knowledge of the material world is to some extent a reflection of preformed ideas in the mind, and it is a hard sell outside the academy, especially in a boisterous, capitalist country addicted to mining, commerce, and machines. Yet in the New England of the early nineteenth century, philosophical idealism swept the intelligentsia, inspiring new religions such as Christian Science, influencing literature through the Transcendentalist movement, and setting the stage for new institutions of higher education modeled on the Prussian university.

The triumph of nonsectarian Mind over Christian soul was largely a Unitarian achievement.[19] Two centuries ago, Erasmus Darwin cynically observed that Unitarianism is "a net to catch a falling Christian"; today the Unitarian Universalist Church attracts Christians who are transitioning to atheism and people who were raised without any spiritual tradition at all who are experimenting with religion. But in the 1700s Unitarians and Universalists (they merged in 1961) had a clear and unambiguous agenda: the repudiation of orthodox Calvinism,[G] although the two churches emphasized different aspects of this process.

John Calvin taught that salvation was God's to give and not humans to merit. Although eternal damnation and the redemptive power of grace have long been part of Christian teaching, Calvin concluded that God reserves salvation to the small minority of humans that had been predestined to receive the gift of grace through the sacrifice of Jesus on the cross. And the rest? Well, they are to be damned in hell for all eternity, having inherited original sin from Adam. Calvinism was meticulous in its attention to Scripture, but it emphasized a punitive God fundamentally at odds with the spirit of compassion that permeates the Gospels. Even within the Calvinist camp, there were those who embraced a less punitive deity, but their response was an inversion of the original doctrine. Where Calvin's God predestined people to hell for the hell of it, Universalists argued that salvation is universal, given to all human beings whether they sinned or not. Once sin is without eternal consequence, there is no need for God's son to mediate redemption, so the Trinity becomes superfluous. In a parallel development, Unitarians maintained that God is not three distinct persons but a single universal spirit.

In the mid-1700s, even as the American public was caught up in an unprecedented wave of religious fervor known as the Great Awakening,ᴳ when Methodists and Baptists held enthusiastic revival meetings up and down the eastern seaboard, the established religion of the New England colonies began to move in a Unitarian direction, affirming rationalism and logic as the foundation of theology. While Unitarians remained committed to Protestantism as a social identity, they rejected such core beliefs of Christianity as the Last Judgment, the Trinity, and, by implication, the divinity of Christ. Although conforming in outward dress and demeanor to the traditions of Calvinist clergy, doctrinally they were worlds away, reinterpreting religion as a kind of moralistic rationalism, as emotionally far removed from the polemics of the Reformation as from the stigmata of Francis of Assisi. In 1805 the Unitarian faction wrested control of Harvard College from the more orthodox Calvinists. Although they retained for a generation or more an overt commitment to Scripture and the external forms of Christianity, they substituted an intellectualized curriculum based on German idealism for the heritage of Calvinist orthodoxy.

By the end of the nineteenth century, the change at Harvard was palpable. As historian George M. Marsden writes:

Harvard in 1850 was in many ways closer to the Middle Ages than to the Harvard of 1900. At midcentury
many of the forms of seventeenth-century Harvard
—the tutors, the recitations, the discipline, the strong
clerical presence, daily chapel, classical curriculum —
were still in place. The professoriat[G] was largely Unitarian, drawn predominantly from the local eastern
Massachusetts aristocracy. By the final decade of the
century, only a fifth of the professoriat were Unitarian.[20]

The eclipse of Unitarianism coincided with the transformation
of the clerical college into a secular university inspired by Prussian bureaucracy, driven by professionalization, and beholden to
the new industrial elite.

Paradoxically, the power of Christian churches and local communities to control the content of higher education was broken
not by atheists but by advocates of "nonsectarian Christianity."
Since a sect is a group of people with a shared religious outlook, the word *nonsectarian* suggests a religious outlook held by
no one—and this in fact is a good description. Religion is like
language: it is lived by some community in some historically specific form, such as the Catholic Mass or the rites of Dionysius,
whereas generic religion, like generic language, is an academic
abstraction without reality in the lives of people. Moreover, "nonsectarian" is the colonizer's terminology, for it implies that the
independent colleges were not real schools run by real communities but merely "sectarian" in nature, that is broken-off sections of
a greater and presumably more noble whole. Although nonsectarian Christianity is as conceptually flawed as Esperanto, it was
the political strategy needed to sideline the pluralist system of
colleges and to reestablish state-supported orthodoxy in higher
education.

One of the key figures in this historical development is Henry P. Tappan, chancellor of the University of Michigan from 1852 to 1863. Like many upper-class Americans of the nineteenth century, Tappan had studied in Germany, which was at the forefront of intellectual and cultural life in Europe during his lifetime. Tappan was a Presbyterian minister with impeccable East Coast theological credentials, but his pedagogical mission was formed in Germany. Tappan took home to the United States a vision of state bureaucracy as the unique spirit of a people, a kind of nationalist reinterpretation of Augustine's *City of God*. For him, the University of Berlin, founded in 1810, was the prototype for American higher education. In Berlin, professors were civil servants, enjoying the prestige befitting representatives of the government, with lifetime job security and immunity from popular pressure.

The state of Michigan, inspired by Jeffersonian anticlericalism, had never given religious colleges the right to grant degrees. Instead, it had established a state-supported college that under Tappan's leadership became a model for what nonsectarian education should be. When Tappan first arrived as the college's new president, he was appalled to find not a state bureaucracy as in Prussia but a blatant example of American pluralism—a multi-religious curriculum organized on democratic principles. The faculty, as with other colleges at the time, were nearly all clergymen; and the leading Protestant denominations had informally agreed to allocate professorships in proportion to the denomination's share of the student body. Tappan convinced the faculty to abolish the quota system in favor of nonsectarian Christianity, in part by pointing out that Unitarians, Universalists, and Catholics would soon be wanting chairs as well. Christianity, he assured them, would continue to be a strong cultural force at the university through compulsory daily attendance at chapel and Sunday lectures on morals and theology. The nonsectarian University of Michigan became one of the largest schools in the nation; four of its faculty went on to become university presidents, making the Michigan model a national presence.

"We want a seminary," newsman Horace Greeley declared in 1858, "which provides as fitly and thoroughly for the education of Captains of Industry as Yale and Harvard does to those dedicated to either of the Professions."[21] This wish would come to pass with the help of the U.S. federal government, which ushered in an era of new state-supported universities that were still culturally Protestant but officially nonsectarian. In 1862, during the Civil War, Congress passed the Morrill Land Grant Act to speed settlement of the western territories by antislavery farmers, and this legislation included substantial grants of land for new colleges, which the state legislatures were to establish.

Although the existing colleges attempted to divert some of this largesse to their own institutions, they were seriously handicapped by the epithet "sectarian" and outmaneuvered by the advocates of autonomous rationality and science. The new state colleges insisted in their public proclamations that they were "Christian" institutions, even in some cases to the point of requiring students to attend daily chapel, but there were few requirements for courses on religion, ethics, classical philosophy, or any of the other subjects that hitherto had constituted the core of the curriculum of Western higher education; nor were faculty any longer identified as members of any specific religious tradition.

The movement toward "nonsectarian Christian" higher education was further enhanced by the establishment of new private universities by rich industrialists. These were intended to give degrees in science the prestige of a diploma from Harvard and Yale. Ezra Cornell, for example, was a self-made millionaire who had abandoned the Quaker beliefs of his youth to embrace moral progress through technology. As he expressed it: "The steam engine, the railroad and the electric telegraph are the great engines of reformation that will supersede the dead and putrid carcass of the Church."[22]

Seeing the possibilities of the Morrill Land Grant Act, Cornell teamed up with a Presbyterian educator and opened Cornell University in 1868 as a nonsectarian "Christian" college, even though the bulk of the curriculum was devoted to practical subjects such as agriculture, mining, engineering, and medicine. Indeed, the traditional curriculum of Western higher education was now sidelined as a "general track," roughly equivalent to liberal arts, that could be taken with or without classical languages. Also, chapel and religious courses were no longer compulsory; but, as Cornell's president was quick to point out, lectures were often held on edifying and moral subjects.

In 1867, across the bay from San Francisco, a group of Congregationalists and Presbyterians met to found a new institution of higher education that they envisioned as the future Yale of the West. They named their new school after the Anglo-Irish philosopher and clergyman George Berkeley, whose project to create an English-speaking university in Bermuda collapsed in the early 1730s, although his phrase-making—"Westward the course of empire takes its way"—continued to inspire the American public.[23] The new town of Berkeley was laid out as a monument to scientific leadership and the westward expansion of Protestantism. The north-south streets were named for secular worthies, such as scientists and inventors, and the east-west ones for pioneering New England clergymen and theologians. When the project became stalled by internal politics, the founders approached the State of California, which agreed to help finance the new university provided that the governor could appoint trustees. As it happened, none of the trustees appointed by the governor were Calvinist clergymen, so with the scratch of a pen, the people of California had a new state university with no religious pretensions whatsoever.

Thirty miles south of San Francisco, a railroad tycoon, Leland Stanford, Jr., created a new university on the 8,000 acre horse ranch he kept for weekend getaways. Although the university proclaimed its commitment to Christianity by its Spanish mission architecture and a commodious chapel decorated with Byzantine murals, the new school's religious culture was, in Marsden's words, "vaguely Christian nontheological, nonsectarian, theistic, romantic, moral idealism."[24] Moreover, Stanford University's first president was a zoologist whose interest in religion was confined to occasional attendance at meetings of the local Unitarian church.

In the aftermath of Appomattox, American higher education fundamentally altered its culture, transitioning from Christian to agnostic and from aristocratic to capitalist without so much as re-decorating. Enormous chapels in the Gothic style, complete with flying buttresses, proclaimed continuity with the past, even as a new class of professional educators reinvented the curriculum to bypass Christianity. Knowledge was reconstituted as a collection of technical specialties, while expertise became divorced from any pretense to spiritual insight and the development of moral character. The college of bachelor professors, with its clubby congeniality and meals taken together in the refectory, gave way to a new institutional form, the academic department composed of people whose only bond was knowledge of a particular intellectual craft. The clergyman-scholar was superseded by the Ph.D., a purely secular character who lived off campus and wore a suit.

As Christianity and moral philosophy were eliminated from the mainstream college curriculum and religious practice was reduced to voluntary participation in campus ministries, their place was taken by a world view that was compatible with the goal of establishing a scientific and rational basis for all human knowledge and experience—the theory of progressive evolution.

To progressive evolutionists, human history is a never-ending drama of accelerating change, provided that a radical break is made with the institutions of the past. In art and architecture, it took the form of repudiating classical and Renaissance models in favor of "experimental" art forms that often were deemed of higher value simply because they were new. In politics, it engendered ideologies of revolution that sought to sweep away the institutions of the past and create the social conditions for the perfectibility of the human species. In science and philosophy, it emerged as a radical materialist skepticism, dismissing the possibility of anything that could not be explained in terms of physics and chemistry.

The transition from religious to capitalist values is reflected in the composition of governing boards of colleges. As George M. Marsden summarizes: "In 1860–1861 nearly 40 percent of the board members of private colleges were clergymen, and these were often the most prominent, the best educated, and the most influential trustees. By 1900–1901 less than a quarter of board members were clergy, and for the first time they were outnumbered by businessmen and lawyers. The percentage of clergy representatives continued to drop precipitously, especially at schools without church ties."[25]

The change in American higher education was heralded by the first generation of university presidents to be recruited from the sciences.[26] In 1869, Harvard chose the first layman in its history as president: Charles W. Eliot, a chemist. This choice was part of a trend: Gilman of Johns Hopkins was a geographer; Jordan of Stanford, a biologist; Woodrow Wilson of Princeton, a political scientist; and Hadley of Yale, an economist (and the first layman).

Secularization was made possible by peripheralizing religion from intellectual life and by privileging scientific knowledge. One contemporary observer of this process was James Ward, professor of moral philosophy at Cambridge University, who was professionally active in the 1880s, the period when mind was replacing soul. In the Gifford Lectures of 1896 and 1898, he was one of the first to characterize the concept of human nature implicit in the new intellectual culture. He presented his observations as a system of three axioms. Premise one, nature is ultimately resolvable into a single vast mechanism.[27] Two, the theory of evolution is the working of that mechanism. Three, the subjectivity of mind may accompany physical processes, but it never determines physical processes, a doctrine called psycho-physical parallelism.

Based on my own experience with the technocratic culture at Berkeley, Yale, and Stanford, I would add (premise four) that natural science, especially physics, is the intellectual method of choice for explicating this vast mechanism and (premise five) that mind (if it exists as a distinct level of organization at all) is located inside the individual brain and has no intrinsic social dimension.

This is not to say that these premises are accepted uncritically by all academics. In any university, one can usually find a few faculty members who disagree with key premises of the dominant ideology, and there may even be departments, such as cultural anthropology, that are poorly socialized into the prevailing system of belief. Ideologies are best understood by examining the decisions of the institution as a whole, such as the courses that are typically taught and the projects that are most generously funded.

In the modernist university, this five-point characterization of nature and society dovetailed with an implicit hierarchy of fields of knowledge based on positivist criteria that marginalized any humanistic viewpoint. Gross and Levitt, authors of the provocatively titled *Higher Superstition*, have captured this culture exactly:

> For decades certain assumptions about the episte-
> mological ranking of various fields have prevailed,

though rarely explicitly, among academic intellectuals. The rule of thumb has been that the hard scientists produce reliable knowledge, assembled into coherent theories. Historians, it is conceded, generate
reliable factual knowledge (as long as they keep their
methodological noses clean)... Economics has rigor
of method, but its assumptions are serious, often fatal, oversimplifications of the real world. In the other
social sciences impressionistic description and subjective hermeneutics rule, though they may come dressed
in elaborate statistical costumes... Literary criticism,
finally, had been looked upon as a species of highly
elaborate connoisseurship, interesting and valuable,
perhaps, but subjective beyond redemption.[28]

This implicit hierarchy of knowledge was the framework that
prevailed at Berkeley when I was an undergraduate there, and it
was this system that was targeted by the student activists of the
Sixties and the postmodernists of subsequent decades.

Darwin's theory of evolution was central to the modernist
program because it established scientific materialism as academic orthodoxy while discrediting religion. But because Charles
Darwin never publicly criticized God, his work can be read as
pure science, as scientists read him today.[29] To his Victorian contemporaries, however, he was critiquing the religious interpretation of life on earth as established by the Church of England.
Moreover, by explicitly acknowledging his intellectual debt to
Malthus, a man whom educated Englishmen of the time would
recognize as the theoretician of the Whigs, Darwin was putting
his readers on notice that *Origin* was to be interpreted politically
as well. Even though Darwin's treatise touches on the subject
matter of both religion and politics, and has clear implications
for both, neither subject is discussed within the work, leaving the

reader to connect the dots. In effect, *Origin* is a kind of Trojan horse that can easily be slipped into the academy because it conforms to the strictures of natural theology while appearing to be natural science.

The Rise of the Corporation

The replacement of the clerical college by the secular university complemented the transition from familial to corporate capitalism. Before the mid-nineteenth century businesses were typically owned by families and partnerships, whereas corporations were quasi-governmental entities, exemplified by the East India Company which had received a charter from the English crown. In the new United States, legislators were suspicious of enterprises chartered by the state, which they remembered as the legal form favored by royal monopolies. The few corporations that existed in the new republic had been chartered by legislatures to carry out specific tasks that served a demonstrable public need, such as construction of a canal from one town to another. After the Civil War, however, corporations began a life of their own.[30]

In traditional English law only persons could sue or be sued, but this rule proved impractical when businesses became large industrial enterprises owned by stockholders. So during the second half of the nineteenth century, the law was changed so that businesses could become legal persons by registering with the government as corporations, thus giving them the right to enter into contracts, earn money, pay taxes, and so on. An added advantage of corporate status is that it provides limited liability for its owners and managers, who are not held responsible for any debts that the corporation incurs, on the grounds that the latter is a separate person.

At the same time, the process of establishing a corporation was streamlined so that it was no longer necessary to petition a legislature and demonstrate a public need for the project; one simply paid a fee and filed a form with the appropriate government agency. In the United States, state governments chartered corporations to undertake "any legal purpose" and that "in perpetuity." Financed by the anonymity of the stock market, managed by professionals, and increasingly national and international in scale, the corporation made the family factory largely a thing of the past.

Even though American capitalism has successfully fostered a perceived community of interests between Main Street and Wall Street—between the sole proprietorship and the capitalist corporation—the fact remains that these are socially different species. A small business may conduct its affairs as avariciously as any robber baron and strive to become a colossus, as Sam Walton succeeded in doing with Walmart; but so long as a business is built to a human scale and managed by its individual owners, it remains vulnerable to community pressure and moral persuasion. The corporation, however, is a fictive individual that is typically administered by members of a professional managerial class with ownership parceled out among multiple shareholders, which greatly reduces accountability and the power of local communities to influence its decisions. Also, the bureaucratic structure of the corporation enables it to use the latest technologies to give itself a global reach, which in turn gives it the power to dominate communities, local governments, and regulatory agencies.

For real human beings, social life and community have great motivating power—to the point that we judge solitary confinement to be one of the worst of punishments. But a corporation, although legally a person, has no such motivations. Even when a corporation does publicly-spirited things, such as sponsoring runners in a marathon to raise money for cancer research, such pro bono efforts are, from a corporate point of view, justified as tax deductions and public relations: they are not taken into account in the valuation and performance of the business itself.

Moreover, such social concerns are the first to go when sales head south.

Since the second decade of the twenty-first century, the rapacious for-profit corporation has been supplemented in the United States by the option of a more socially-conscious one. Now a majority of states of the United States give businesses the option of incorporating as a benefit^G corporation or "B corp," which is an entity that is legally committed to providing a social or environmental good in addition to earning a profit. Well known B corporations are Patagonia, the wilderness outfitter, and Ben & Jerry's, the ice cream manufacturer.

This legal innovation holds the potential of moving corporate capitalism in a more socially-responsible direction and getting social values reflected in the valuation of the business itself. Even so, the benefit corporation in no way addresses the class system that prevails within a corporation or the concentration of wealth in the hands of its owners, though it does provide a legal framework within which such concerns could be addressed. It remains to be seen whether the good intentions of the corporate founders or the values of the capital markets will prevail.

For most of its history, with the exception of the recent B corp, a corporation's sole reasons for existence have been the acquisition of wealth and the provision of limited liability to its owners and employees. Thus, the corporation, although legally a person, is by nature a sociopath, as it recognizes no moral restraints or social obligations beyond the coercive power of the law and the proclivities of its owners.

The modern corporation emerged historically in conjunction with industrialism, but it does not need iron mines and steel mills in order to thrive and prosper. Nowadays, the corporation perpetuates itself as effectively in finance, mass media, and Big Data as it did in heavy industry. For this reason, the capitalist corporation cannot be defined by its products or techniques but only by its legal status and social objectives: it is an entity chartered by the state that has as its highest measure of performance the acquisition of wealth for its owners.

A Moral Charter for the Corporation

In the predatory context of nineteenth-century capitalism, the curriculum of traditional higher education, with its classical languages, great books, and emphasis on moral character, began to look as dated as ox carts. The corporation needed bureaucrats and technocrats, not moralists and philosopher kings. And the universities responded with a new kind of graduate—one unencumbered by traditional religious notions such as charity, contemplation, and the virtues of simple living. Darwinism was essential to this transition from Christian seminary to technocratic graduate school, for it provides the ideology that underlies both modern corporate capitalism and the secular university. In this transition, Darwinism was greatly helped by its congruency with Calvinism.

Early in the twentieth century, the social theorist Max Weber argued that the theology of John Calvin promulgated a value system consistent with capitalism that enabled the transition to economic modernity.[31] He based his argument on historical sources. In 1618 to 1619, the Synod of Dort convened in the Netherlands to define the key doctrines of Calvinism in response to heretical interpretations.[32] The synod defined the Five Points of Calvinism that formed the doctrinal basis of the sect for subsequent centuries, and it was attended by representatives from Calvinist communities all over Europe, including some from England. A short time later, these doctrines were taken to the New World by the Puritans, who landed in Massachusetts in 1620, where their church became the orthodox religion of the new colony. Calvinist clerics founded the colleges of Harvard and Yale, whose graduates became the intellectual elite of the

United States.

Significantly, both Darwinian biology and industrial capitalism grew from the same root—from those Protestants who had
challenged the temporal authority of the English crown and the
doctrinal authority of the Church of England. Since adherents of
these sects departed from the official teachings of the Church of
England, in the Great Britain of Darwin's time they were known
as Nonconformists, and their descendants in the United States
form the core of today's evangelical Christianity. *Evangelical* is
not a church or organization but a descriptive term for Christians who believe in "personal conversion and a rigorous moral
life, on the one hand, and concentrated attention on the Bible as
a guide to conviction and behavior, on the other, with a special
zeal for the dissemination of Christian faith so conceived (evan-
gelism)."[33] Churches and movements in the evangelical tradition
include Anabaptism, Puritanism,G Wesleyism, Continental pi-
etism, and converts of the Great Awakenings.

While there is no point-to-point correspondence between the
tenets of Darwinian theory and the Five Points of Calvinism,
there is enough overlap to establish a congruency between Darwinist and Calvinist assumptions about human nature and society. Indeed, three of the concepts implicit in Darwin's theory,
namely, cosmic destiny, geneticG determinism, and the derivative
nature of altruism,G have unambiguous Calvinist roots. These
ideas constitute what I call the *CalvinistG substrate* of Darwinian
theory. The points of correspondence are as follows:

Cosmic destiny. The key concept in Calvinism is the doctrine
of predestination:G that all people are guilty through original sin
inherited from Adam, but God has chosen some to be rewarded
with eternal life and others to be damned for all eternity, irrespective of people's actions here on earth. Darwinism retains the
concept of cosmic winners and losers based on inheritance but

substitutes the inheritance of genes for the inheritance of sin. Divine election becomes natural selection.

The irrelevance of good works. The Calvinist doctrine of total depravity of human nature asserts that human beings cannot seek God on their own and that even altruism and generosity are motivated by self-interest, so good works merit one nothing. This belief has an almost exact equivalent in the Darwinian interpretation of altruism, which is explained in terms of competitive advantage and self-interest.

The demotion of community. In Calvinism, the social dimension of religion is much reduced compared to Catholicism. Bible reading and preaching take the place of the Mass and the celebration of feast days of the Virgin and the saints, while communities of monks and nuns were abolished, replacing the communitarian aspect of religion with individual piety and church membership. In Darwinism, with the exception of intergroup competition (that is, group selection), the individual is the basic unit of evolution, while society is a mere aggregation of phenotypes.[G]

This is not to say that the tenets of Darwinian theory are religious in nature or that evolutionist ideas are directly beholden to religion. Certainly, the idea of descent with modification is an original thesis inspired by comparative anatomy, while the concepts of adaptive radiation and isolating mechanisms are the contributions of biogeography.[G] However, some key assumptions about human nature and society ultimately derive from the Calvinist school of theology, and these were transmitted to Darwin through the community in which he was raised. Indeed, even the relationship between population growth and competition for limited resources was originally introduced by Malthus as divine punishment for lack of sexual restraint (discussed in Chapter 2), although the theological origins have been obscured through the use of later editions of his work.

This congruency between the premises of Darwinism and those of a secularized Puritan culture no doubt contributed to the former's uncritical acceptance in Great Britain and the United States. Indeed, Darwinism is attractive to anyone raised as an evangelical Protestant who wants to dispense with the Bible reading while keeping the moral absolutism. Significantly, some of the most vocal proponents of evolutionary materialism, such as E. O. Wilson, are fallen-away fundamentalist Christians who have described their first encounter with Darwinism in terms comparable to a conversion experience.[34]

The affinity between Protestantism and Darwinism was recognized by Victorian evangelicals themselves. As Adrian Desmond notes in his biography of Thomas Henry Huxley: "The Nonconformist motor had carried Huxley to power. And Nonconformist money kept him there—bequests from Quaker manufacturers, Cobden's free-traders and Congregationalist steel barons, all of whom understood his *Lay Sermons*."[35]

The Moral Trojan Horse

In the nineteenth century, the religious subtext of Darwinism was more accessible than it is today. Not only was Charles Darwin educated for the Anglican priesthood, but Anglo-American intellectual life was still dominated by Protestant clergymen, so intellectual controversies reflected clerical concerns. Far from being publicly opposed to the Bible, Huxley touted its ethical efficacy, while both Huxley and Darwin assured their clerical readers that morality had nothing to fear from natural selection. Indeed, Loye laments that Darwin's moralistic view of evolution was "lost" in twentieth-century Darwinism, noting that the author of *The Descent of Man* mentions "love" ninety-five times and "moral sensitivity" and "moral evolution" ninety-two times.[36]

The evolution of morality was not original with Darwin but is implicit in the Enlightenment's belief that all of history is tending towards perfection, be it political, technical, or moral. This belief was succinctly expressed by the eighteenth-century botanist Linnaeus,ᴳ whom Darwin read and admired:

> That in an uncultivated stage you [mankind] are foolish, lascivious, imitative, ambitious, prodigal, anxious, cunning, austere, envious, avaricious, and get *transformed* so as to be attentive, chaste, considerate, modest, sober, tranquil, sincere, soft, beneficent, content.[37]

In other words, the formation of moral character, which in the preceding Christian centuries involved both ethical precepts and sustained religious practice, now unfolds as a natural process on an evolutionary timescale, with "savages" being judged to be as morally backward as they are technically deficient.

The purported moral primitiveness of savages is consistent with the Darwinian thesis that a strong moral code is essential for evolutionary progress. In Huxley's words: "The tribeᴳ of savages in which order is best maintained; in which there was most security within the tribe and the most loyal and mutual support outside it, would be the survivors."[38] In a similar vein, Darwin argues that groups in which the "social instincts" and the "moral sense" are most developed will out-compete those with less solidarity.ᴳ [39] Thus, for Darwinians, morality not only enables and validates competition, both individual and collective, but it is just another tool in the struggle for existence.

This emphasis on morality as a winning strategy is consistent with Huxley's evangelical roots, as is his belief that it is the Bible, and the Bible alone, that is the foundation of the moral order— not moral consciousness, not ethical philosophy, not religious practice, not social tradition, not social consensus, not enlightened self-interest, and certainly not a personal encounter with

God on a mountaintop. In Huxley's words:

> On the whole, then, I am in favour of reading the
> Bible, with such grammatical, geographical, and his-
> torical explanations by a lay-teacher as may be need-
> ful, with rigid exclusion of any further theological
> teaching than that contained in the Bible itself.[40]

Thus, Huxley, who coined the word *agnostic* and was a de facto religious skeptic, has the incongruous role of biblical fundamentalist, though not a creationist fundamentalist[G]—an agnostic
one! Moreover, Huxley argues that the Bible should be taught by
laity, not clergy, who would purge it of its "legend and theology."
No wonder that Darwinism has been called the last act of the
Reformation.[41]

To this end, Huxley the lay preacher devoted many pages to
reinterpreting biblical myth as history and debunking any purported miracles so that the perennial ethical wisdom of Christian
Scripture would stand more fully revealed. Indeed, he noted that
"the human race is not yet, possibly may never be, in a position to
dispense with it."[42] Yet one wonders if even Huxley believed that
the way to make the Bible more enduring is to debunk much of
its content while discrediting those to whom it is sacred.

Even so, Huxley never abandoned the Calvinist belief in righ-
teousness manifested through ethically rigorous conduct. To the
contrary, he presumed that evolution and ethics are companions
on the same journey, although with manifestly different, even an-
tithetical, goals:

> For his successful progress, throughout the savage
> state, man has been largely indebted to those qualities
> which he shares with the ape and the tiger; his excep-
> tional physical organization; his cunning; his sociabil-
> ity, his curiosity, and his imitativeness; his ruthless and

ferocious destructiveness when his anger is aroused by opposition.[43]

At the same time, Huxley maintained that ethics "repudiates the gladiatorial theory of existence," because it "involves a course of conduct which, in all respects, is opposed to that which leads to success in the cosmic struggle for existence" by demanding self-restraint and assistance to others.[44]

Huxley argued that as evolution advanced the struggle for existence would recede, in effect transforming savagery into civilization:

> when the ethical process has advanced so far as to secure every member of the society in the possession of the means of existence, the struggle for existence, as between man and man, within that society is, ipso facto, at an end. And, as it is undeniable that the most highly civilized societies have substantially reached this position, it follows that, so far as they are concerned, the struggle for existence can play no important part within them.[45]

The selective advantage of moral progress is a point of difference between Darwin and Huxley. Where Huxley saw compassion as the culmination of progressive evolution, Darwin worried that the reputedly high moral standards of Victorian Englishmen were a drag on the health of the breed stock, for compassionate social policies allowed the poor, the infirm, and the indolent to survive to reproduce. Also, Darwin indicates that artificial selection is needed to redress the effects of well-meaning but misguided charity (Chapter 5), whereas Huxley judged eugenics to be impractical and at odds with individualism, writing that: "I do not see how such selection could be practiced without a serious weakening, it may be the destruction, of the bonds which hold society together."[46]

In *The Descent of Man*, Darwin devotes a chapter to the evolution of morality and fellow feeling; but, as with everything else, he makes no distinction between biological and social evolution.[47] This enables him to explain something as intrinsically social as the moral order as if it were present within the individual brain in the form of "instincts" and "sentiments." As Darwin writes in an oft-cited passage:

> any animal whatever endowed with well-marked social instincts, the parental and filial affections being here included, would inevitably acquire a moral sense or conscience as soon as its intellectual powers had been as well, or nearly as well developed as in man.[48]

As defined by ethology,[G] an instinct[G] is an innate motivational system with inborn perceptual triggers and a distinctive consummatory[G] act.[49] Certainly there are innate behaviors in primates, such as facial expression, and innate social motivations, such as the sex drive; but as Darwin himself states, humans have few instincts compared to lower animals. As documented by ethologists, animals such as insects have complex linkages among innate behaviors and innate perceptions; in humans, by contrast, these instinct chains are replaced by emotion, learned contextual cues, and skilled behavior. So innate *feeling* rather than "instinct" perhaps comes closer to Darwin's meaning in the above quotation.

Darwin believed in the power of reason to improve the human species; but as shown by the above quotation, he pairs it with the social instincts to explain how fellow feeling evolves from the level of ants and wasps to that of a human being. Feeling and intellect, however, are quite different mental states. The intellect is a system for formulating logical propositions and making correct deductions from premises, whereas feelings monitor the state of somatic well being.

The above quotation gives the impression that the Sage of Down had treated the evolution of ethics with the diligence that he devoted to the evolution of barnacles (about eight years and more than a thousand pages), but in fact Darwin had first acquired his moral theory, like his Malthusianism, within the family circle. His wife's brother's father-in-law, Sir James Macintosh, was a Whig theoretician and a colleague of Malthus, who had written a book titled *Dissertation on the Progress of Ethical Philosophy*, which the young Charles Darwin read, possibly while aboard the *Beagle*, certainly upon returning from his trip around the world.

Macintosh, who "thought the moral faculties inborn, and the knowledge of right and wrong instinctive," [50] was on this point a Darwinian before Darwin. The influence of Macintosh on the young Darwin is indicated by the latter's 10-page, unpublished commentary on the former's ethical theory. In the end, Darwin sidelined his in-law's explanation of morality in favor of his own view of morality as a product of natural selection.

In his writings Darwin gives instances of sympathy and altruistic action drawn from the animal world, such as monkeys coming to the defense of group members that are under attack or pelicans feeding a blind member of the flock. But instead of presenting a case for the biological evolution of the moral sense, he simply expresses the received wisdom of the Whigs in a handful of lines, claiming that the moral sense develops "inevitably" from "intellectual powers" in interaction with the "social instincts." *Inevitable* is a word that writers use when they cannot formulate a convincing demonstration; and by postulating social *instincts*, Darwin presumes the biological nature of the phenomena that he claims to explain biologically.

The moral order—"the surrounding climate of ideas about how to live,"[51] especially our behavior towards others—is at the heart of the human condition, but Darwin's characterization of it is little more than a caricature. To participate in the moral order, a creature must have the capacity for intentional action, voluntary control of behavior, knowledge of right and wrong, and the conscious assessment of the effects of one's action on others. Although partly motivated and sustained by emotions such as guilt and shame, the moral order also requires such abstract concepts as repentance, fairness, forgiveness, and restitution.

In Darwinian biology, instinct and intelligence are inborn psychological processes that are located inside of the individual brain, but from an anthropological perspective the moral order is an intrinsically social phenomenon, requiring awareness of the effects of one's own action on other people and knowledge of culturally-appropriate actions.

Darwin does acknowledge the importance of social validation of altruistic acts, but his emphasis is on the instinctive nature of the feelings expressed and their selective benefits to the group as a whole. Also, social instincts would seem to preclude the need for a moral order at all. Huxley at least recognizes that terms such as morality and ethics are meaningful only if there is a domain of human action that is independent of genetic control, namely, an area of volition and intent.

Darwinian luminaries such as Pinker and Wilson often grace the pages of the *New York Times* with edifying articles on the biological nature of human morality.[52] This is more than self-indulgence. As the historian of science Robert J. Richards notes:

> From the beginning of his speculations about the changes in species, Darwin fully understood that his theory would require a reconceptualization of human nature, one that would naturalize man's moral behavior. For had he allowed an exception to a naturalistic

explanation of that very defining trait of man—moral behavior—then he would have left an opening for a return of the Creator.[53]

Charles Sedgwick, Darwin's former mentor at Cambridge University, was also keenly aware of the ethical implications of his most famous student's theory. Writing in the Victorian periodical *The Spectator*, Sedgwick notes that Darwin's theory

> utterly repudiates final causes, and thereby indicates a demoralized understanding on the part of its advocates. By the word demoralized, I mean a want of capacity for comprehending the force of moral evidence, which is dependent on the highest faculties of our nature. What is it that gives us our sense of right and wrong, of law, of duty, of cause and effect?[54]

Sedgwick's question was never answered. So successful was the X Club's effort to replace the Christian worldview with one of its own that subsequent generations of intellectuals, raised as materialists and evolutionists, did not share the Victorians' concern for morality with a capital M. In fact, many modernist intellectuals saw no need for a moral framework at all. The generation of the 1890s believed in progress through science and technology, and many assumed that evolutionary Progress was a law of history as inevitable as the law of gravity, making ethics of any sort superfluous. Indeed, in the "evolutionary ethics" of biologist Julian Huxley (Thomas Henry's grandson), non-interference with progress is one of the maxims; another is to act in a manner that is consistent with the direction that evolution is heading.[55]

During the Enlightenment, evolution was bundled with demands for equality and democracy, so that it justified not only material Progress but moral Progress as well. The political left that emerged during the French Revolution still maintains that the poor need our help and that the state is in the best position to help them; but the theory of natural selection implies that the poor are losers of the evolutionary race, which makes Darwinism more congenial to the political right.

Even though Darwin emphasized in his writings the importance of morality and sociality, while postulating social instincts, these ideas do not make his system of thought more congruent with the political left. To the contrary, an instinct is an automaton whose behavior requires neither moral consciousness nor political activism, so Darwin's theory of moral sentiments simply reinforces the "hands off" premise of laissez-faire capitalism.

Until the legalization of the benefit corporation in the twenty-first century (a legal form that still charters only a minority of for-profit corporations), the definitive activity of the capitalist corporation has been the pursuit of profit unencumbered by any concern for its social and ecological effects. Thus, the corporation needs a morality that never interferes with technical and business decisions, much less raises doubts about the moral legitimacy of capitalism itself.

In *The Descent of Man*, Darwin provides a moral order that evolves through the "natural" process of natural selection—which is to say, a moral order that no scientist nor CEO need ever concern himself with.

Reflections

By assimilating human nature to biological evolution while reducing the latter to the struggle for existence, Darwin precluded any possibility of justifying moral action by appeals to the supernatural, thus eliminating the moral authority of religion with a single decisive stroke.

Concurrently, Darwinism became the sustaining ideology of the modern university, transforming it from an institution that formally espoused a Christian system of values to one that privileges naturalistic discourse and empirical research. Like any human community, the modernist university has a moral order, but its values are those of modernism itself: rationalism, factuality, individual upward mobility, and a dismissive attitude towards religion. These philosophical beliefs provide little moral guidance for interpersonal conduct and little incentive for cooperation. Moreover, they are so congruent with corporate capitalism that the values of the marketplace have to a large extent superseded humanistic values in American universities (Chapter 4).

Once Christianity was out of the way, science and capitalism were free to develop without moral restraint of any kind. The modernist university, instead of providing a critical lens and a moral voice, promotes a middle class agenda of individual careerism within an institutional framework established by capitalism.

It also de-democratizes society. As Bledstein notes: "Universities quietly took devisive issues such as race, capitalism, labor, and deviant behavior out of the public domain and located these problems within the sphere of professionals..." [56]

By refusing to constrain knowledge with any system of values beyond factuality, the new class of technical professionals put knowledge and thought in the unrestricted service of the powerful.

Notes

1 Barton (1998: 415). See also Jensen (1970–1971: 689).

2 Barton (1998: 412).

3 Barton (1998: 427).

4 Barton (1998: 417).

5 Turner (1978: 373).

6 Quoted by Barton (1998: 440). Huxley was writing in *The Reader*.

7 Quoted from an excerpt in Appleman (1979: 458).

8 The biographical material is from Desmond (1997). Paradis provides a readable account of the intellectual context of Huxley's thought (Paradis, Huxley, and Williams 1989).

9 Colp (1974: 329).

10 Desmond (1997: 629).

11 Also, according to the biography of Donald C. Johanson, the finder of the famous fossil Lucy, his interest in the field of paleoanthropology "was sparked as a young teenager growing up in Hartford, Connecticut, when he first read Thomas Henry Huxley's book, *Man's Place in Nature*" (web page of the Institute of Human Origins, accessed 2009). When I first read Huxley's *Man's Place in Nature* in my teens, I was inspired to storm the citadels of anti-evolutionists—had I known any.

12 Desmond (1997: 407).

13 Quoted by Desmond (1997: 624).

14 Later in life, Huxley wrote an essay with the title "Agnosticism." Huxley's essays have been widely reprinted, and I refer to them by their titles.

15 Huxley discusses this subject in "The Scientific Aspects of Positivism," published in 1869 in the *Fortnightly Review*. Another member of the X Club, Herbert Spencer, was equally vociferous in denying any influence by positivists (Eisen 1967).

16 I have used English translations: Comte and Thompson (1975), Comte and Lenzer (1998).

17 Day (2005: 556).

18 I have relied on Marsden (1994) for the history of the American university in the late nineteenth and early twentieth centuries, es-

pecially its transformation from a religious institution to a secular one. Schrecker (1989) complements Marsden, presenting an overview of the history of the American university with an emphasis on the twentieth century.

19 I have drawn on Robinson (1985) for a history of American Calvinism. The tenets of Calvinism are summarized by Marsden (1994: 224) and discussed in detail by Weber (1958).

20 Marsden (1994: 181).

21 Quoted by Marsden (1994: 115).

22 Quoted by Marsden (1994: 114).

23 Mead (1929 : 421–30).

24 Marsden (1994: 254)

25 Marsden (1994: 300).

26 Hofstadter and Metzger (1955: Chapter 7, "Darwinism and the New Regime").

27 Turner chronicles the transition from a religious to a scientific ideology through the thought of key intellectuals, such as James Ward (Turner 1974, Chapter 8). Ward is often described as a psychologist, but he was a good friend of the classicist James George Frazer and introduced the latter to anthropology (Kuklick 1991: 15). Frazer went on to write *The Golden Bough*, the multi-volume work of armchair anthropology that inspired Malinowski. See Bledstein (1976) for the emergence of the university-educated middle class.

28 Gross and Levitt (1994: 12).

29 God, however, is mentioned figuratively in *Origin*, to the annoyance of Harriet Martineau, the Malthusian publicist and translator of Comte, who wrote to Fanny Wedgewood that "I rather regret that C. D. [that is Charles Darwin] went out of his way two or three times … to speak of 'the Creator' in the popular sense of the First Cause"; quoted by Desmond and Moore (1991: 486–87).

30 My assessment of corporations is based on my fieldwork in Silicon Valley and my experience as an owner of a corporation. For the history of the institution in the United States, I have drawn on the lectures of David Cobb, an American lawyer and co-founder of Move to Amend: "David Cobb from Move To Amend speaking

against corporate personhood - May 15, 2012," https://www.youtube.com/watch?v=HkyfBg0kGFI (last accessed August 2016). .

31 Weber (1958).

32 Hanko, Herman, and Van Baren (1976). Also, the Westminster Confession of 1647 makes predestination and the uselessness of good works very explicit (Weber 1958).

33 Fackre (1983).

34 This is in Wilson's (1998) *Consilience*, cited by Haught (2000) in his excellent discussion of the atheistic evolutionists.

35 Desmond (1997: 625).

36 Loye (2004: 30). Lest anyone doubt that Darwin's work has become secular Scripture that is mined for scientific authority on any subject, Loye claims that Darwin anticipates transpersonal psychology and "the new scientific interest in spirituality by more than a hundred years" (p. 31). It is true that Darwin was once dragged along to a spiritualist session, but his interest ended there.

37 Quoted by Bendyshe (1865: 428). Sloan (1999) provides a good introduction to the ethical theories prevalent in the eighteenth century and their relationship to theories in biology, showing that Darwin's evolutionist ethics were anticipated by Lamarck. See also Crook (1994) for the social uses of Darwinian theory.

38 Huxley, "Prolegomena." Unless otherwise indicated, all citations of Huxley's works are from the online source The Huxley File at http://aleph0.clarku.edu/huxley/ (last accessed September 10, 2016).

39 Darwin (1871).

40 Huxley, "The School Boards."

41 Desmond (1997: 625).

42 Huxley, "The School Boards."

43 Huxley, "Evolution and Ethics."

44 Ibid.

45 Huxley, "Prolegomena."

46 Ibid.

47 Ridley (1997) and Ruse and Wilson (1985) set forth Darwin's evolutionary ethics in its contemporary form, namely as sociobiol-

ogy. For an antidote to the evolutionary ethics literature, see Clark (2000).

48 Darwin (1871: Chap. 4). Also Desmond and Moore (1994: 262, 283).

49 Thorpe (1979) won a Nobel prize for his experiments on instinctive behavior in animals. See Leyhausen's (1979) monograph for the application of the instinct concept to an intelligent mammal.

50 Richards (1999: 283). Richards discusses Macintosh's role in the making of Darwin's theory of morals. Manier (1978: 141-146) documents the importance of Macintosh (spelled Mackintosh) to the young Darwin as indicated by the latter's notebooks.

51 Blackburn (2001:1), "Introduction."

52 Pinker (2008), Wilson (2013).

53 Richards (1999: 137).

54 Quoted by Clark (2000: 5). Charles Kingsley, the author of *Water Babies* and one of Darwin's early supporters, began distancing himself from Darwinism because of this issue (Hale 2013).

55 J. Huxley (1943). For an overview of Julian Huxley's work in its intellectual context see Phillips (2007).

56 Bledstein (1976:327).

References

Appleman, Philip. 1979. *Darwin: A Norton Critical Edition*. 2nd paperback edition. New York and London: Norton.

Barton, Ruth. 1998. "Huxley, Lubbock, and half a dozen others": professionals and gentlemen in the formation of the X Club, 1851–1864. *Isis* 89 (3): 410–44.

Bendyshe, T. 1865. The history of anthropology. *Memoirs of the Anthropological Society of London*, no. 1: 335–458.

Blackburn, Simon. 2001. *Being Good: An Introduction to Ethics*. Oxford and New York: Oxford University Press.

Bledstein, Burton J. 1976. *The Culture of Professionalism: The Middle Class and the Development of Higher Education in America*. New York: Norton.

Clark, Stephen R. L. 2000. *Biology and Christian Ethics*. Cambridge and New York: Cambridge University Press.

Colp, Ralph, Jr. 1974. The contacts between Karl Marx and Charles Darwin. *Journal of the History of Ideas* 35: 329–38.

Comte, Auguste, and Gertrud Lenzer. 1998. *Auguste Comte and Positivism: The Essential Writings*. New Brunswick and London: Transaction Publishers.

Crook, Paul. 1994. *Darwinism, War and History: The Debate over the Biology of War from the "Origin of Species" to the First World War*. Cambridge and New York: Cambridge University Press.

Darwin, Charles. 1871. *The Descent of Man*. 1st ed. 2 vols. London: John Murray.

Day, Matthew. 2005. Reading the fossils of faith: Thomas Henry Huxley and the evolutionary subtext of the Synoptic problem. *Church History* 74 (3): 534–56.

Desmond, Adrian. 1997. *Huxley: From Devil's Disciple to Evolution's High Priest*. Reading, MA: Perseus/Helix.

_____, and James Moore. 1991. *Darwin: The Life of a Tormented Evolutionist*. Paperback ed. New York: W. W. Norton.

Eisen, Sydney. 1967. Herbert Spencer and the spectre of Comte. *Journal of British Studies* 7 (1): 48–67.

Fackre, Gabriel. 1983. Evangelical, Evangelicalism. In *The Westminster Dictionary of Christian Theology*, edited by A. Richardson and J. Bowden. Philadelphia: Westminster Press.

Gross, Paul R., and Norman Levitt. 1994. *Higher Superstition: The Academic Left and Its Quarrels with Science*. Baltimore: Johns Hopkins University Press.

Hale, Piers J. 2013. Monkeys into men and men into monkeys: chance and contingency in the evolution of man, mind and morals in Charles Kingsley's "Water Babies." *Journal of the History of Biology* 46 (4 winter): 551–97.

Hanko, Herman, Homer Hoeksema, and Gise J. Van Baren. 1976. *The Five Points of Calvinism*. Jenison, MI: Reformed Free Publishing Association.

Haught, John F. 2000. *God after Darwin: A Theology of Evolution*. Boulder, CO: Westview Press.

Hofstadter, Richard, and Walter P. Metzger. 1955. *The Development of Academic Freedom in the United States*. New York: Columbia University Press.

Huxley, Julian. 1943. Evolutionary Ethics: The Romanes Lecture for 1943. In *Darwin: A Norton Critical Edition*, edited by P. Appleman. New York: Norton.

Huxley, Thomas Henry. 1948. *Selections from the Essays of T. H. Huxley*. Edited by A. Castell. New York: Appleton-Century-Crofts.

_____. 1959. *Man's Place in Nature*. Ann Arbor: University of Michigan.

Jensen, J. Vernon. 1970–1971. The X Club: fraternity of Victorian scientists. *British Journal for the History of Science* 5: 63–72.

Johanson, Donald J. "Donald J. Johanson, Biography." http://iho.asu. edu (Accessed Feb. 2006).

Kuklick, Henrika. 1991. *The Savage Within: The Social History of British Anthropology, 1885-1945*. Cambridge; New York: Cambridge University Press.

Leyhausen, Paul. 1979. *Cat Behavior: The Predatory and Social Behavior of Domestic and Wild Cats*. New York: Garland STPM Press

Loye, David. 2004. *The Great Adventure: Toward a Fully Human Theory of Evolution*. Albany: State University of New York Press.

Manier, Edward. 1978 *The Young Darwin and His Cultural Circle*. Boston: D. Reidel.

Marsden, George M. 1994. *The Soul of the American University: From Protestant Establishment to Established Nonbelief*. Oxford and New York: Oxford University Press.

Mead, George Herbert. 1929. Bishop Berkeley and his message. *Journal of Philosophy* 26 421-430.

Paradis, James G., Thomas Henry Huxley, and George C. Williams. 1989. *Evolution and Ethics: T. H. Huxley's Evolution and Ethics with New Essays on Its Victorian and Sociobiological Context*. Princeton, NJ: Princeton University Press.

Phillips, Paul T. 2007. One world, one faith: the quest for unity in Julian Huxley's religion of evolutionary humanism. *Journal of the History of Ideas* 68 (4): 613–33.

Pinker, Steven. 2008. The moral instinct. *New York Times Magazine*, 13 Jan.

Richards, Robert J. 1999. Darwin's romantic biology: the foundation of his evolutionary ethics. In *Biology and the Foundation of Ethics*, edited by Jane Maienschein and Michael Ruse, 113–53. Cambridge and New York: Cambridge University Press.

Ridley, M. 1997. *The Origins of Virtue: Human Instincts and the Evolu-*

tion of Cooperation. New York: Viking/Penguin.

Robinson, David. 1985. *The Unitarians and the Universalists.* Westport, CT: Greenwood Press.

Ruse, Michael, and Edward O. Wilson. 1985. The Evolution of ethics. *New Scientist* 108: 50–52.

Schrecker, Ellen. 2010. *The Lost Soul of Higher Education: Corporatization, the Assault on Academic Freedom, and the End of the American University.* New York: New Press.

Sloan, Phillip R. 1999. From Natural Law to Evolutionary Ethics in Enlightenment French Natural History. In *Biology and the Foundation of Ethics,* edited by Jane Maienschein and Michael Ruse. Cambridge and New York: Cambridge University Press.

Thorpe, W. H. 1979. *The Origins and Rise of Ethology: The Science of the Natural Behaviour of Animals.* London and New York: Heinemann Educational Books/Praeger.

Turner, Frank Miller. 1974. *Between Science and Religion: The Reaction to Scientific Naturalism in the Late Victorian Period.* New Haven, CT, and London: Yale University.

———. 1978. The Victorian conflict between science and religion: a professional dimension. *Isis* 69 (248): 356–76.

Weber, Max. 1958. *The Protestant Ethic and the Spirit of Capitalism.* Translated by T. Parsons. New York: Scribners. Original edition, 1904–1905, *Archiv für Sozialwissenschaft und Sozialpolitik,* vols. 20 and 21.

Wilson, Edward O. 1998. *Consilience.* New York: Knopf.

———. 2013. The riddle of the human species. *New York Times.* 26 Feb.

Chapter Four

The Takeover

The Coevolution of Darwinism and Capitalism

As the economic historian Marc Flandreau advises: "think less of the relevance of Darwinism as a dematerialized system of ideas and more of its institutions, powers, and forms of exploitation."[1]

Between 1860 and 1880, as the capitalist corporation was taking over the economy, scientific societies dominated by Darwinists forged alliances with the state, the university, and the financial community in order to create a new center of power—a biomedical technocracy. Such long-term collaboration requires an ideology that bridges multiple institutions and harnesses them to a common purpose, what I call a keystone[G] ideology. The latter usage is analogous to a keystone species in ecology, which is a species that is essential to the maintenance of an ecosystem. Darwinism is the keystone ideology that enables collaboration among science, academe, the military, and capitalism.

Charles Darwin was not the public face of the takeover; he was more its éminence grise. Once Darwin got the wanderlust out of his system, he rarely traveled far from home; and he depended on visits by his colleagues and on his extensive web of correspondents for information about the state of science and the wider world. Nonetheless, through his personal connections with members of the X Club, Darwin had considerable indirect control of the course of English science. The X Club was more a cabal than a scientific society, since it was not open to the public, and it retained the same small membership (allowing for attrition) from its founding in 1864 until its last meeting in 1893.[2]

One of the key people in the Darwinist consolidation of power was Sir John Lubbock, a wealthy banker and literary archeologist whose family's estate of 3,000 acres adjoined Darwin's home in the county of Kent.[3] Lubbock met Charles Darwin shortly after Darwin moved to Down House and Lubbock was still a youth. Lubbock loved ants and wasps, which no doubt endeared the boy to the beetle collector. Lubbock subsequently sought the scientist's advice on entomological matters and contributed original drawings to one of Darwin's monographs. Darwin in turn introduced Lubbock to his inner circle of acquaintances. When the X Club was formed, Lubbock was a founding member.

Lubbock had a capacity for work that rivaled Darwin's. After leaving Eton at the age of fourteen to help run the family bank, he leapfrogged from one achievement to the next, scoring successes in a variety of endeavors. In his early twenties, Lubbock streamlined the English system for processing bank checks; in his early thirties, he was elected to Parliament as a Liberal. Working two jobs, as politician and banker, he still found the time to write tomes in prehistory and entomology, helped to preserve the ancient stone circles of Avebury, and served for twenty-five years as secretary of the London Bankers.

It was Lubbock's practice to make an extensive trip abroad once a year, giving him familiarity with a variety of culturally significant destinations, from newly-excavated Paleolithic sites in France to ancient Middle Eastern ruins. He used these trips to gather data for his book *Pre-historic Times* (1865). This book gave him the reputation of an anthropological savant and earned him a place in academic histories as a founder of archeology. However, it is now recognized that much of Lubbock's treatise is derived from a prior book by a Scottish archeologist who lived obscurely in a distant province of the British Empire (Canada).[4]

Lubbock's chosen bailiwick was the Ethnological Society of London. *Ethnology* is Greek for "study of nations," and the society had been founded in 1843 in order to better arrange and classify races, artifacts, and societies as one would specimens in natural history.[5] The year before, the French had founded a similar society in Paris. Even though organic evolution had been kept out of British universities for more than half a century, social evolutionism was acceptable, provided it was confined to documenting the backwardness of savages. Naturalists on Royal Navy expeditions, such as the *Beagle* and the *Rattlesnake*, were charged with observing the natives as well as collecting flora and fauna; and colonial officials sent home collections of "primitive" artifacts that needed to be labeled and maintained. Even Charles Darwin in 1842 helped to compile a handbook on *Queries respecting the Human Race to be addressed to Travellers and Others.*[6]

Lubbock's interest in anthropology was consistent with the British banking industry's penchant for foreign investment. Railroads, canals, mines, and plantations had long been financial fodder for the City of London, but the rush to industrialize gave British bankers an even bigger playing field and more opportunities to profit.[7] As in the past, investment followed exploration. All the great exploratory sagas of the Victorian era, from the discovery of the source of the Nile to the race for the south pole, heralded potential investment opportunities, as new resources were discovered and new territories brought into the capitalist orbit.

Great fortunes could be made by lending money to foreign countries to build infrastructure such as railroads. If the foreign government paid the loans back in full, the bank made a tidy profit from the interest. If the government defaulted, then the bank took the lands, mines, and forests that had been used as collateral. But success was predicated on effective control of the local legal system, both to ensure the terms of the contract and to lay claim to the collateral in the event of default. The European colonial infrastructure provided this sort of reassurance, while the Royal Navy ensured compliance outside the boundaries of official crown colonies.

Even so, there was still a credibility problem. It is one thing to float a bond issue for a new railroad from Chicago to Saint Louis, quite another to get the public to invest in a railroad from the Mosquito Coast to Managua. Most London investors were vaguely familiar with the geography of the United States, but the Mosquito Coast sounds as unpleasant as it is obscure.

Prudent speculators prefer to invest other people's money, but this requires a confident and optimistic investor community that can be tapped in time of need. The Ethnological Society of London was ideally positioned to put the Mosquito Coasts of the world quite literally on the map. Their experts in ethnology and geography could independently confirm the stability of a country's government and the wealth of its resources. Scientific data such as this reassured potential investors.

However, creating a working relationship between such different undertakings as finance and ethnology is not easy, because every institution comes with a culture that is resistant to change. An institution is a community of people that performs a critical function in society and commands sufficient resources to perpetuate itself from one generation to the next. Many human groups are short-lived, such as a jury in a criminal trial or the attendees at a wedding, but an institution inculcates the values and tasks needed to perform its function to new members, such that the group and its activity endure longer than a lifetime.

Each institution has an ideology that justifies its role to its members and outsiders (Chapter 1), but collaboration among institutions requires a shared belief system that subsumes parochial ideologies into a grander vision—a keystone ideology. For cooperation to happen, there must be people who can promote the integrative ideology by means of their social contacts in multiple institutions. Such people I call *straddlers* because they straddle disparate social sectors so as to better enable collaboration.[8]

In the 1860s, the situation confronting the Darwinists can be represented by the following one-line diagram, which shows three institutions: (1) Lubbock's own profession (banking), typified by the financial sector known as the City of London; (2) the Ethnological Society of London, a scientific society favored by evolutionists; and (3) the Church of England (abbreviated C of E), which the evolutionists considered to be an obstacle to Progress. These institutions are shown below as items on a list separated by commas, indicating distinct entities with little overlap in their charters and activities:

City of London, Ethnological Society, C of E

The Church of England had a monopoly on higher education, which did not sit well with people from a Nonconformist background, such as Quakers and Presbyterians, denominations that included many merchants and industrialists. As for the Darwinians, they read the Bible literally, so they judged the creation stories of Genesis to be in conflict with evolutionary science. The Darwinians led the call for a new class of professional educators without ties to any religion.

In the early 1870s, the government of Great Britain reformed the civil service, replacing candidates chosen from the aristocracy with ones selected by merit, while at the same time establishing a system of publicly-funded education.[9] A similar program of modernization was taking place in the United States, but there it marched under the banner of nonsectarian Christianity (Chapter 3). The X Club used its influence to establish more scientific training for medical doctors entering military service. Also, Huxley wrote and lectured in favor of public education, while he and Lubbock served on the new school boards.

The English-speaking countries retained many schools staffed by clerical educators, so Huxley's vision (Chapter 3) of a scientific priesthood supplanting that of Christianity was never fully realized. Even so, secular schools funded by government were added to the mix of institutions, while the Christian ideology of class and empire taught at the universities yielded to an evolutionist one. In the schematic below, the peripheralization of religion from mainstream education is indicated by a slash mark separating the Church of England from the other institutions:

City of London, Ethnological Society, secular schools /C of E

Secular schools imply a secular curriculum, and Darwin's hegemonic materialism was waiting in the wings, ready to step in and fill the need. But in Victorian times, when people thought of evolution they thought of human Progress, and they did not make much distinction between the theory of natural selection and the unilinear evolution of the Enlightenment. Both were avenues to the better future so dramatically presented at the Crystal Palace Exhibition. It was widely believed that the rising tide of industrial capitalism would lift all boats, including the leaky vessels of the barely buoyant poor.

In the late nineteenth century, the Enlightenment's vision of human progress fused with the productive potential of scientific industrialism. Nowadays, "progress" is almost always presented in material terms, but in previous centuries it had a moral and spiritual dimension as well. The latter sense is conveyed by the title of that perennial Protestant allegory *The Pilgrim's Progress,* a book first published in 1678 that has been in print ever since. It tells the story of a Christian pilgrim progressing through life, encountering challenges to moral rectitude that he must deftly avoid for the sake of his soul.

In the late nineteenth century, the pilgrim set off in a different direction. As Steve Fraser points out, during the Gilded Age the word *progress* took on "its overriding singular attachment to industry, science, technological innovation, economic development, material abundance, and private capital accumulation," a definition that conflates "the metaphysics of freedom with the mechanics of material abundance."[10]

In spite of its philosophical shortcomings, this new definition of progress dispensed with the eighteenth-century baggage that had long worried the ruling elite—democracy, regicide, and the Rights of Man. Where Progress had once implied moral improvement, now it came to mean industrial capitalism operating independently of the moral order. This new sort of Progress fit quite well with the territorial ambitions of the British Empire, the intellectual aspirations of science, and the financial sector's quest for money.

Significantly, in the 1870s, the British banking industry was changing, moving from reckless speculation in the colonies to an investment strategy more attuned to the foreign policy needs of the British Empire. In Flandreau's words: "The art of bankrupting foreign countries, formerly a business left to vulture investors, had become a policy tool, made legitimate by science, in the hands of the government."[11]

Thus, it is not a coincidence that in 1871 John Lubbock was simultaneously the president of two dissimilar organizations: the newly reconstituted Ethnological Society (now renamed the Anthropological Institute) and the Corporation of Foreign Bondholders, a trade association that kept watch over debtor countries.[12] Lubbock was the daddy longlegs of straddlers, with one foot in the City of London and the other in a learned society where perceptions of race, culture, and history were formed. In a stock and bond market attuned to foreign investments, the perceptions of the savants could influence the investing public, so the findings of anthropology could not be left to chance.

Lubbock helped to create a scientific technocracy congruent with capitalism by forging enduring collaborative links among the financial community, the political shapers of empire, the new secular school system, and the professionalizing sciences.

As discussed in Chapters 1 and 3, Darwin himself was far from being a neutral bystander in these events. Not only did he exercise a measure of control through his influence on members of the X Club, but it was Darwin who married biology to capitalism in the first place by transposing the political economy of the Whigs to organic nature.

The Darwinist takeover began in the 1870s, but the institutional configuration it created has lasted 150 years. During this time, the relationship between Darwinism and the technocracy has remained stable, but the ideology and the institutional configuration have coevolved in response to geopolitical developments and new ideological requirements.

Darwin's Cohort

The coevolution of Darwinism and capitalism presumes personal and professional contacts between wealthy members of the capitalist class and academic practitioners of Darwinian science. Chapter 5 documents the historical role of corporate foundations in funding the development of genetic science and evolutionary biology. Since then, venture capitalists have become involved to the point that scientists now function as both academics and entrepreneurs. Such commercial relationships require the cultivation of common interests and shared perceptions among scientists, academic administrators, business executives, and financiers. The development of Big Science^G during World War II provided the initial financial incentive.

In addition to these economic relationships, Darwinist ideology is embodied in a community of believers, what I call Darwin's cohort, that makes possible personal relationships between academic celebrities and capitalist entrepreneurs. Steven Pinker, Harvard's top promoter of evolutionary psychology, and Microsoft founder Bill Gates have such a close personal relationship that *The New York Times* has characterized it as a "mind meld."[13] Pinker is an expert on the evolution of morality—and in his personal pantheon of inspirational moral leaders, Bill Gates outshines Mother Teresa.[14]

Members of Darwin's cohort play together too. A published photograph shows three top-tier Darwinists— Pinker, Dawkins, and Dennett—relaxing on the private jet of Jeffrey Epstein, a half-billionaire who gave millions of dollars to Harvard for an evolutionist institute.[15] Epstein envisioned seeding his own master race, but these plans went awry in 2019 when Epstein reputedly hanged himself in prison after being charged with sex trafficking of underage girls.[16] Some years earlier, in 2008, Epstein had been convicted in Florida of procuring an under-age girl for prostitution. At that time, Robert Trivers, the doyen of reciprocal altruism (Chapter 6), provided the public with a biological perspective on Epstein's case. As quoted by Reuters news service: "Trivers also said he believes girls mature earlier than in the past. 'By the time they're 14 or 15, they're like grown women were 60 years ago, so I don't see these acts as so heinous,' he said."[17]

Personally supportive relationships among elites enable a dynamic and flexible coevolution between Darwinism and capitalism, one which has spanned more than a century. This history can be conveniently divided into four phases, which are summarized in Table 1.[18]

The Four Phases of Darwinism

The first column of Table I shows the development of policies and programs within the institutions of state capitalism; the second column shows how evolutionary biology and Darwinist ideology mirror the ideological needs of capitalism and the institutional environment.

The four phases are arranged in rough chronological order, though the characteristic activities of one phase may continue into future phases as well. Racial typology, for example, was part of the scientific mainstream in the nineteenth century and has since waned in importance, but it has not entirely disappeared.[18]

Phase I Darwinism begins in the 1860s and lasts until the Second World War. During this period, Darwinism took over the Christian university and replaced the ruling ideology with evolutionism and materialism; Darwinists also played a key role in the strategic alliance between an emerging corporate capitalism and a professionalizing science.

During this time European colonialism was changing from a system of economic exploitation justified in terms of the religious and moral superiority of Europeans to one that was rationalized in terms of the innate inferiority of the colonized people. When people are colonized in the name of Christianity, it implies that the exploited can become the conqueror's peers after being baptized; but the attribution of innate inferiority has no such fortuitous loopholes. Racial inferiority is forever.

Biologists did not invent the concept of racial inferiority, but they actively assisted in its ideological development. In the nineteenth century, they drew up charts of cranial capacity to demonstrate the mental superiority of the White race and the inferiority of the Black. At the turn of the twentieth century, as immigrants from southern and eastern Europe flooded into the United States, biologists helped to develop immigration quotas based on putative racial characteristics. Also during this period, evolutionary biology developed population genetics,[G] which naturalizes a free market of competitive individuals.

At the same time, Darwinists carried out the logic implicit in *The Descent of Man* and made eugenics into government

Table 1. Major changes in the corporate body politic (left column) are mirrored by developments in Darwinist ideology (right column). They are arranged in approximate order of historical emergence, though some continue into the present.

STATE + CAPITALISM	DARWINISM
Race-based Colonialism	
Colonize, enslave, and suppress any peoples deemed racially inferior.	Postulate a hierarchy of "advanced" vs. "primitive" races based on anatomical differences;[2]
	Stigmatize people based on putative innate characteristics.[2]
Laissez Faire Capitalism	
Charter for-profit corporations; Establish a social order based on greed and competition among fictive individuals (corporations);	Reduce evolution to competition among individuals;[1]
	Replace the moral order with social "instincts";[2]
Eliminate local communities and kin groups and replace them with populations of atomistic individuals by means of enslavement, migration, and the factory system.	Replace social solidarity with group selection;[2]
	Conflate kinship with gene flow;
	Replace affection with reproductive strategies.
"Racial Hygiene"	
Establish eugenics as government policy;	Repudiate epigenetic inheritance as "Lamarckian";
Mandate eugenic practices.	Identify putatively innate traits for eugenic intervention;
	Develop and implement eugenic techniques.
1. See Charles Darwin, *On the Origin of Species.*	
2. See Charles Darwin, *The Descent of Man.*	

Cold War/Neocolonialism	
Replace European colonies with client states governed by westernized elites recruited from hitherto "primitive" races; Suppress political movements that advocate social equality; Forcibly establish pro-capitalist regimes.	Remove "primitive races" from the biological curriculum; Suppress Darwin's concept of group selection as "socialist"; Blame eugenics on Nazis; Replace overtly racist genetics with studies of identical vs. fraternal twins and covert sterilization of minorities.
Reagan/Thatcher Neoliberalism	
Replace welfare-state capitalism with laissez-faire capitalism; Promote capitalist individualism.	Emphasize "selfish genes"; Imply that altruism outside the family is "unnatural"; Replace the social sciences with genetics (e.g. sociobiology, evolutionary psychology).
Bio-immortality and Commercialized Eugenics	
Turn life into a manufactured product; Make eugenics commercially available; Sell biotech products that promise eternal life.	Develop synthetic genes and designer pesticides; Develop cloning, implanted embryos, and gestational surrogacy; Develop synthetic genomes and artificial life; Promote bio-immortality.
The Global Neocon Empire	
Establish a class of super rich; Impose laissez-faire capitalism worldwide via economic "restructuring" and the U.S. military. Impose a "solidary" homeland.	Implement a genetic class system ("naturals" vs. "gen-rich"). Develop a genetically-engineered race of "genius" entrepreneurs; Propose genes for "cooperation."

policy, especially in affluent, progressive states, such as California and the industrial midwest.[20]

Phase II Darwinism began with the rise of Nazism and lasted until the mid-1970s. It is characterized in England and the United States by ideological differentiation from the Nazis on one hand and the development of molecular biology on the other. Differentiation from the Nazis was accomplished by the public repudiation of eugenics and the downplaying of racist theories of human behavior (Chapter 5). So-called primitive races disappeared from the academic curriculum, but the spirit of such research was kept alive through genetic studies of the heritability of IQ in identical versus fraternal twins.[21]

The public repudiation of Nazi policies did not eliminate eugenics in the United States but changed its focus from the culling of "inferior" phenotypes to the manufacture of "superior" genotypes. Molecular biology and genetic engineering follow directly from this research priority. Where Nazi-style eugenics presumes the coercive power of an autocratic state, the manufacture of "superior" genes is an inherently capitalist project.

After World War II, as the Western powers replaced their colonies with client states governed by Westernized indigenous elites, White supremacy became an ideological liability. Local elites had always been part of the European system of colonial control, but now they were needed as allies in the fight against Communism. One of the major figures in the formation of the American postwar world, Dean Acheson, secretary of state in the Truman administration, complained in 1946 that America's racial caste system "has an adverse effect on our relations with other countries."[22]

In response to the Communist threat, Anglo-American internationalists began presenting their own countries as color-blind democracies that offered political freedom and equal opportunity for all—and to some extent they acted on it. The White House desegregated the military, the U.S. Supreme Court integrated public schools, and major sports teams hired Black athletes for the first time. In the 1960s, the quest for racial equality mushroomed into a mass movement.

Racial integration and counter-Apartheid policies have been successful in part because they are consistent with global capitalism, which needs to sell to everyone not just to White people. Moreover, ascribed statuses, such as race and gender, are premodern, and therefore part of the past, whereas the capitalist future will have no social distinctions except those made possible by differences in wealth. In a world where White people are a shrinking minority, the capitalist elite sees its financial future in the United Colors of Benetton.

The push for racial equality developed in concert with an emphasis on higher education as a pathway for racial integration and upward mobility. After World War II, the U.S. government passed legislation providing financial assistance to war veterans seeking higher education. Hitherto, a college degree was the prerogative of children of the well-to-do or the rare achievement of a poor person awarded a scholarship. Many working class Americans used the "GI Bill" to make themselves nominally middle class—a demographic shift that benefitted institutions of higher education in particular.

The now more widely-opened doors of elite institutions are often pointed to as evidence of social equality and democratization, but such a characterization is at best a half truth. The American meritocracy[G] facilitates individual careerism within an institutional framework established by corporate capitalism.[23] Upward mobility takes the most ambitious people from the subordinate classes while leaving the system of social stratification intact.

Phase III Darwinism is characterized by the incorporation of academic biology into the institutions of state[G] capitalism.[24]

Although there is a long history of commercialization of bio-medical innovations, epitomized by X-rays and penicillin, the latter biomedical techniques were developed within an institutional context that maintained a firewall between pure research and commerce (Chapter 1). This firewall began to erode during World War II, when the university was enlisted into developing technology for the war effort in exchange for research funding from the military. This arrangement became known as Big Science, and it has continued into the present. In the decades after World War II, the academic/military/industrial complex became the economic strategy for all major American institutions of higher learning.[25]

As the Silicon Valley start-up caught the popular imagination (Chapter 1), there was a parallel effort to commercialize molecular biology.[26] In 1976, the Genentech corporation was founded to manufacture drugs with the aid of human genes transplanted into bacteria. When the company went public in 1980, its stock went from $35 a share on opening to more than $71 at the close of the day. Genentech's IPO was one of Wall Street's great success stories, and it validated a business model for biotech that endures to the present day.

The direct linking of academic science with commercial product development began a new stage in the history of academe. I use the term *corporate academy* for this transformation. Socially, there is a big difference between commercializing the products of biological research and doing biological research *in order to produce* commercial products. Where traditional medical research serves the values of medicine, research driven by the profit motive serves the values of capitalism.

The commercialization of biotech was facilitated by new Congressional legislation in 1980 that enabled universities and research organizations to claim ownership of the technology developed through federally-funded research. With this mandate in hand, universities were free to launch their own start-up corporations, thereby transforming the university into the corporate academy of today. Bioscience and capitalism are now so tightly intertwined that faculty members serve as corporate CEOs.

The increased penetration of capitalism into the academy reflected the rejuvenation of laissez-faire economics during the Reagan/Thatcher years. The societal shift towards neoliberalism that began in the early 1970s was marked in evolutionary biology by the promotion of sociobiology and the publication of *The Selfish Gene*, indicating that Darwinism was still playing an important ideological role (Chapter 6) in the development of corporate capitalism.

For almost two generations, the American university has operated on the premise that there is no contradiction between biomedical science and the commercialization of scientific findings, just as the promoters of stem cells see no contradiction between doing lab work in the morning and serving as CEOs in the afternoon. Proponents of this system point to the rapid commercialization of biomedical innovation.

Yet the value systems of medicine and capitalism are profoundly divergent. Where a biomedical researcher might be inspired to develop a "cure for cancer," an entrepreneur might conclude that it is more profitable to keep cancer patients alive with a drug that prolongs their life instead of selling them a drug that cures them.

There are many real-life situations analogous to this where the values of commerce have preempted those of medicine. Take, for example, the case where a public university laboratory developed an effective drug at taxpayer expense and licensed it to a commercial company, only to have it sold at a price that is beyond the reach of many sick people to pay.[27] Is this medicine? And while we are on the subject, why don't the American taxpayers get the medicine at cost?

Phase IV Darwinism is marked by a strategic change in Darwinism's approach to religion. Hostility to religion is one of the axioms of Darwinism, required by its academic role as the foil to Christianity. Also, the denigration of religion is implicit in any progressive view of history in which religion is thought to be part of the past and science part of the future. Thus modernists of all persuasions, from Darwinists to Communists, from progressives to futurists, are united in the belief that religion will soon be left behind by the forward march of history. However, the gears of progressive history have been grinding since the late eighteenth century, yet religion is still here.

Harvard biologist E. O. Wilson explains what went wrong with the modernist prediction: "Religion cannot be defeated by those who merely cast it down" he writes, because "the evolutionary epic" denies immortality to the individual. "Does a way exist," Wilson asks rhetorically, "to divert the power of religion into the great new enterprise [genetic biology] that lays bare the sources of that power?"[28]

In 2009, Nicholas Wade, a science writer for *The New York Times,* signaled the change in strategy by his book *The Faith Instinct,* which argues that religion can be explained in Darwinian terms.[29] That same year, Darwinian theorists in Germany published a thick volume in the academic style that conveys a similar thesis.[30] Significantly, Wade's book was endorsed by top-tier Darwinists, including James Watson and E. O. Wilson, and it serves as a podium for the latter's ideas. Wade's book marks the transition of religion from pariah to subject matter.

Even though prominent Darwinists such as Dennett and Dawkins continue to attack religion directly,[31] this strategy is being supplemented by a technocratic effort to steal religion's fire by promising eternal life through biological science. To this end, bioscience and corporate capitalism have allied to implement what I call bio-immortality.[G]

Bio-immortality is the belief that science will enable you to live forever, thus creating a new blend of science and religion that defies conventional definition.[32] As Jeff Lyon and Peter Gorner note in their book on gene therapy:

> Are aging and death themselves forms of 'genetic disease'? Are there longevity genes that determine life span and mortality genes programmed to switch off at a certain time, resulting in the eventual demise of an organism? A growing number of scientists think so.[33]

And not only scientists. As Dara Horn observes, this movement includes "tech billionaire Peter Thiel, the TED talk darling Aubrey de Gray, Google's billion-dollar Calico longevity lab and investment by Amazon's Jeff Bezos."[34] It would not be an exaggeration to call bio-immortality the cutting edge of biotech.

As cultural anthropologist Nicole Sault explains:

> Resurrection is needed only if you die. But biotechnology promises you immortality as a bionic chimaera, genetically enriched through man-made genes and augmented by digital downloads, which together confer superpowers, all immortalized through successive cloning.[35]

As with eugenics, bio-immortality presumes a biomedical context. But where racial hygiene was presented as hard science by surgeons in white coats, the new interventionism appropriates religious symbols and metaphors while giving them a materialist interpretation. Indeed, to biological literalists, even every-day metaphors such as "his eyes popped out when she walked into the room" get reimagined as a scene from a horror movie. So if the New Jerusalem descends from the sky as imagined in the book of Revelation, then it must mean a physical event like the descent of the flying saucer in Steven Spielberg's *Close Encounters of the Third Kind*.[36] Also, since moral character and social justice have no place in Darwinist notions of progress, the "fittest" are reinterpreted as those who best exemplify materialist measures of superior humanity, such as good looks, high intelligence, and athletic ability—creating a market for eugenics.

Bio-immortality is still in the realm of science fiction and is likely to remain there. To be happy as an immortal I will need to preserve my social environment and my personal living situation as well as my genome. Also, for this agenda to be faithfully carried out from one generation to the next, one must first institute an unchanging social order that accepts bio-immortality for the rich as a matter of faith. Such belief is not implausible—for millennia, the ancient Egyptians provided tombs fully-equipped for the pharoah's rebirth. Yet it might be harder to convince a capitalist populace that keeping billionaires alive forever is the best use of increasingly scarce resources. Even in ancient Egypt, tomb robbing was as venerable an industry as pyramid building.

On the symbolic level, however, even the promise of eternal life is very powerful ideology as religion itself proves, and futuristic visions are not contingent on a realistic assessment of extant technology as the debate on stem cells confirms. The main product of bio-immortality is not eternal life but the hope that it inspires and the prestige that it confers. Although scientifically flawed and spiritually debased, bio-immortality would have widespread appeal to materialist consumers while receiving considerable support in the technocracy itself.

Bio-immortality is also synergistic with biotech. Indeed, the manufacture of eternal life is in many respects the logical culmination of Progress through genetics. Bio-immortality is a spin-off of the eugenics program described in Chapter 5. With the help of genetic science, corporations can intentionally alter the human genome, introducing manufactured products that use the human host to propagate themselves, with royalties due on every replication—thus establishing a literally parasitic stage of capitalism!

And since bio-immortality is only for the few with the money to avail themselves of the latest biotechnology to extend human life (the GenRich envisioned by Silver),[37] it is consistent with the premises of a secularized Puritan culture as well: only the elected are selected. By offering an alternative to death, the technocracy can better occupy the shelf space of traditional religion and make Thomas Henry Huxley's dream of a scientific priesthood a reality.

The Triumph of Consumption

Both Marxism and Darwinism are ideologies that occupy the space of a state religion and redefine the moral order in the light of material progress and philosophical[G] materialism. This serves a dual role: first, it keeps Christianity at bay; second, in the case of Darwinism, it reinforces capitalism's own virtues of individualism, competition, and self-interest.

Since the Darwinist takeover in the 1870s, these values have percolated from the intellectual elite to the rank and file, leading to a major reorientation of American culture known as consumer capitalism. In the last decades of the nineteenth century, industrial production was taking off, the corporation was taking over, and Darwinism was taking hold in academe.[38] Yet industry was producing more than the public was buying, leading to falling prices and a poor return on capital investment. The obvious solution was to increase consumption, but the working class lacked the money to buy more than they already had.

The solution that emerged in the United States was as unpredicted as it was effective—what historian William Leach calls the culture of consumer^G capitalism. As Leach explains:

> American capitalism began to produce a distinct culture, unconnected to traditional family or community values, to religion in any conventional sense, or to political democracy. It was a secular and market-oriented culture, with the exchange and circulation of money and goods at the foundation of its aesthetic life and of its moral sensibility.[39]

This new ethical and cultural regime requires that the majority of people believe in "acquisition and consumption as the means of achieving happiness; the cult of the new; the democratization of desire; and money value as the predominant measure of all value in society."[40] Thus, the culture of consumer capitalism requires a revolution of the moral order: that is, the replacement of Christianity with a hegemonic materialist philosophy—with the only proviso that the latter not be socialist.

The idea that acquisition and consumption are the means to happiness has appealed to the rich of all eras, from pagan Rome to the court of Versailles; but it was rarely an option for the common people and is at odds with the official teaching of any previous version of Christianity, be it Catholic or Protestant. In the late Victorian period, however, Christianity was being displaced by materialism in the universities, while Darwinist ideology was especially well suited for providing a new moral order congruent with both corporate and consumer capitalism.

In addition to this ideological charter, consumer capitalism was enabled by technical innovations in advertising and mass media.[3] With the steam-powered press and the Linotype machine, a newspaper could print a million copies overnight, making possible the full-page ad and the one-day sale. Advances in photography produced the slick magazine filled with seductive ads, while the mail order catalog and an expanded postal service ensured that the latest products could be bought and delivered anywhere. The department store, itself an innovation, displayed the latest fashions on mannequins so women could imagine the same garments on themselves. On the furniture floor, families could walk through life-like rooms, imagining the transformation of their own homes. And the cost? Not a problem.

The democratization of desire was achieved through the invention of consumer credit. Progressive department stores opened charge accounts for women for the first time, while the first credit bureaus kept track of consumer indebtedness. The working class of the nineteenth century honored Polonius's injunction (neither a borrower nor a lender be), but twentieth-century workers aspired to a millionaire's life style purchased on the installment plan. By 1906 America had become, in the words of retailing magnate John Wanamaker, the Land of Desire.[41]

Consumer capitalism also dealt a body blow to religion. The traditional moral order embraces the common good, but in Darwinism the latter is nothing more than the aggregate of individual interests, making it equivalent to the economist's aggregate demand. Instead of a process of personal sanctification that leads to eternal unity with the divine, consumer capitalism offers a cornucopia of material goods that elevate one's temporal status in the eyes of the world.

Not coincidentally, consumer capitalism also marked the beginning of the end of socialism as a mass movement in the United States. Darwinian theory redefined groups as coalitions of individuals based on common interests ("group selection"), just as in capitalism. Once groups become shifting alliances of individuals, there is no group solidarity, while individual upward mobility makes class conciousness impossible. Most important, to participate in the status hierarchy of capitalism, even as a wannabe, is to accept its value system and to identify with its luminaries, even to the point of thinking that their interests and yours are the same. In the United States, billionaires can run for public office as champions of the common man.

By implicitly redefining Progress as *genetic selection through competition in the absence of the moral order,* Darwin simultaneously hamstrung socialism while giving capitalism the aura of science. The collective effect was the perpetuation of the premodern class system in a new guise. Instead of paying a share of one's agricultural production to the lord of the manor, as did the premodern peasant, the worker now pays a portion of his paycheck to creditors. People who do not own their own homes also pay a portion of their wages to a property owner for a place to live. So great was the class continuity that the English language did not even need to invent a new word for the social relations of consumer capitalism: the word *landlord* seamlessly transitioned from hereditary titles to purchased ones, from feudal lords to slum lords. While the rich still accumulate wealth, everyone else now accumulates debt.

Reflections

Darwinism is to state capitalism as Marxism is to state socialism. In the next two chapters, I deal with the history of genetics and sociobiology, highlighting their ideological biases and showing how these unconscious premises facilitate their political utility within state capitalism. Finally, in the last chapter, I explore the path not taken by explicating social and moral alternatives to both capitalism and Darwinism.

Notes

1 Flandreau (2016: 274).

2 The year of the last meeting is given in Hutchinson (1914, vol.1: 64).

3 For biographical information about Lubbock I have relied primarily on Hutchinson (1914) and Patton (2007).

4 Lubbock's book is derivative of Daniel Wilson's *Prehistoric Man* published three years earlier, in 1862 (Kehoe 1999).

5 Ethnology had a long prior history in central and eastern Europe, especially in those countries that were confronted with the problem of codifying law that would applicable to a wide variety of indigenous ethnic groups (Vermeulen 2015).

6 Sera-Shriar (2013: 153). I also use this source for my description of the transition from the Aboriginal Protection Society to the Ethnological Society of London.

7 Flandreau (2016) is my source for the interaction of finance and ethnology.

8 Flandreau (2016: 277) calls Lubbock "the ultimate invisible hand of science and finance."

9 Kuklick (1991: 20) recognizes the importance of meritocracy and civil service reform to the success of evolutionism and early anthropology.

10 Fraser (2015: 27-28).

11 Flandreau (2016: 269).

12 Flandreau (2016: 268-69).

13 Galanes (2018),

14 Pinker (2008).

15 See the photo by the *Daily Mail* in the entry "Brockman, John," a catalog of Epstein's contacts compiled by *New York Magazine* : http://nymag.com/intelligencer/2019/07/jeffrey-epstein-high-society-contacts.html Accessed July 2019.

16 See: James B. Stewart; M. Goldstein, M.; J. Silver-Greenberg. 2019. Jeffrey Epstein hoped to seed human race with his DNA. *New York Times,* 31 July.

17 The quote from Trivers is at: https://www.reuters.com/article/
us-epstein-charity/exclusive-some-charities-to-refuse-mon-
ey-from-u-s-financier-accused-in-sex-case-idUSKBN-
0L51G720150201 Accessed Sept. 2019.

18 The information in Table I on the history of biology is found in
Sapp (2003) and in the references to Chapter 5.

19 For example, in the 21st century, there was a scientific controversy
about whether Samuel George Morton's (1799-1851) measure-
ments of the cranial capacity of the skulls of different races were
factually correct.

20 See the data in Kevles (1985).

21 Books such as *The Bell Curve* that provide data on racial differences
in IQ tests are a perennial favorite of the conservative media.

22 Quoted by Kendi (2016: 352). All of Kendi's Chapter 28 is dedicated to this period.

23 The university's transformative role in American society is described in historical detail by Bledstein (1976).

24 My usage of the term state capitalism is taken from Chomsky
(1979).

25 Washburn (2005) describes the incorporation of the university into
the capitalist product-development cycle, including the federal legislation that made it possible.

26 Rasmussen (2014).

27 Lazano (2018). In 2019, Novartis released a drug that will sell to
patients for more than US$ 2,000,000 per treatment: *The Guard-
ian*, 25 May 2019.

28 Wilson (1979).

29 Wade (2009a). For Wade, the science of primatology might as well
not exist: "in the societies of our apelike forebears, coordination
was achieved relatively simply, through a strict hierarchy dominated by an alpha male" (Wade 2009a: 39). Compare this statement
with the information on primate societies presented in Chapter 6.

30 Vaas (2009), Voland and Schiefenhövel (2009).

31 Dawkins (1996), Dennett (1995).

32 The imagery of immortality has been commonplace in the American technocracy since World War II. I discuss this at length in *Stealing Fire* (Reynolds 1991).

33 Lyon and Gormer (1995: 28).

34 Horn (2018). For more on Thiel see Packer (2011).

35 Personal communication. See also Sault (1994).

36 Reynolds (1993, 1997).).

37 Silver (2002). Kimbrell (1993) documented the commercialization of the human body decades ago.

38 Trachtenberg (2007).

39 Leach (1993: 1).

40 Ibid.

41 Leach (1993: 1).

References

Bledstein, Burton J. 1976. *The Culture of Professionalism: The Middle Class and the Development of Higher Education In America*. New York: Norton.

Chomsky, Noam. 1979. *Language and Responsibility: Based on Conversations with Mitsou Ronat*. Translated by from the French by John Viertel. New York: Pantheon Books/Random House.

Dawkins, Richard. 1996. *The Blind Watchmaker: Why the Evidence of Evolution Reveals a Universe without Design*. New York: Norton.

Dennett, Daniel C. 1995. *Darwin's Dangerous Idea: Evolution and the Meanings of Life*. New York: Simon and Schuster.

Flandreau, Marc. 2016. *Anthropologists in the Stock Exchange: a Financial History of Victorian Science*. Chicago: University of Chicago Press.

Fraser, Steve. 2015. *The Age of Acquiescence: The Life and Death of American Resistance to Organized Wealth and Power*. New York: Little, Brown.

Galanes, Philip. 2018. The mind meld of Bill Gates and Steven Pinker, *New York Times*. 27 Jan.

Horn, Dara. 2018. The men who want to live forever, *New York Times, Sunday Review*, 25 Jan.

Hutchinson, Horace G. 1914. *Life of Sir John Lubbock, Lord Avebury in Two Volumes*. London: Macmillan. Also available through HathiTrust Digital Library. http://catalog.hathitrust.org/Record/001489916

Kehoe, Alice Beck. 1999. Recognizing the Foundation of Prehistory. In Alice Beth Kehoe and and Mary Beth Emmerichs, eds. 1999. *Assembling the Past: Studies in the Professionalization of Archaeology*. Albuquerque: University of New Mexico Press.

Kendi, Haram X. 2016. *Stamped from the Beginning: The Definitive History of Racist Ideas in America*. New York: Nation Books.

Kevles, Daniel J. 1985. *In the Name of Eugenics: Genetics and the Uses of Human Heredity*. New York: Knopf.

Kimbrell, Andrew. 1993. *The Human Body Shop: The Engineering and Marketing of Life*. New York: Harper Collins.

Kuklick, Henrika. 1991. *The Savage Within: The Social History of British Anthropology, 1885-1945*. Cambridge; New York: Cambridge University Press.

Leach, William. 1993. *The Land of Desire*. New York: Pantheon Books.

Leah Salzano. 2018. UCLA's patent war in India prevents access to prostate cancer treatment worldwide. *truthout.org*, 5 Sept.

Lewis, Jason E. et al. 2011.The mismeasure of science: Stephen Jay Gould versus Samuel George Morton on skulls and bias. *PLoS Biology* 9 (6). doi: doi:10.1371/journal.pbio.1001071

Lyon, Jeff, and Peter Gorner. 1995. *Altered Fates: Gene Therapy and the Retooling of Human Life*. New York: Norton.

Packer, George. 2011. No death, no taxes: the libertarian futurism of a Silicon Valley billionaire. *The New Yorker*, 11 Nov.

Patton, Mark. 2007. *Science, Politics, and Business in the Work of Sir John Lubbock: A Man of Universal Mind*. Aldershot, Hampshire, England ; Burlington, VT: Ashgate.

Pinker, Steven. 2008. The moral instinct. *New York Times Magazine*, 13 Jan.

Rasmussen, Nicolas. 2014. *"Gene Jockeys," Life Science and the Making of the First Biotech Drugs*. Baltimore: Johns Hopkins University Press.

Reynolds, Peter C. 1991. *Stealing Fire: The Atomic Bomb as Symbolic Body*. Palo Alto, CA: Iconic Anthropology Press.

_____. 1993. The Priests of cyborg. *The Month* (July): 257–66. https://www.sallyglean.org/reynolds/.

_____. 1997. Abandoned bodies. *The Month* (November): 421–26. https://www.sallyglean.org/reynolds/.

Sapp, Jan. 2003. *Genesis: The Evolution of Biology*. Oxford and New York: Oxford University Press.

Sault, Nicole L., ed. 1994. *Many Mirrors: Body Image and Social Relations*. New Brunswick, NJ: Rutgers University Press.

Sera-Shriar, Efram. 2013. *The Making of British Anthropology, 1813-1871, Science and Culture in the Nineteenth Century*. London: Pickering & Chatto.

Silver, Lee. 2002. *Remaking Eden: Cloning and Beyond in a Brave New World.* New York: Perennial/ Harper-Collins.

Smith, Richard. 2013. Time for science to be about truth rather than careers. https://blogs.bmj.com/bmj/2013/09/09/richard-smith-time-fo... (Accessed Aug. 2018).

_____. 2014. Medical research: still a scandal. https://blogs.bmj.com/bmj/2014/01/31/richard-smith-medical (Accessed Aug. 2018).

Trachtenberg, Alan. 2007. *The Incorporation of America: Culture and Society in the Gilded Age*. 2nd ed. New York: Hill & Wang.

Vaas, Rüdiger. 2009. Gods, gains, and genes: on the natural origin of religiosity by means of bio-cultural selection. In *The Biological Evolution of Religious Mind and Behaviour*, [electronic resource] The Frontiers Collection, edited by Eckart Voland and Wulf Schiefenhövel. Berlin and London: Springer.

Vermeulen, Han F. 2015. *Before Boas: The Genesis of Ethnography and Ethnology in the German Enlightenment.* Omaha: University of Nebraska Press.

Voland, Eckart, and Wulf Schiefenhövel, eds. 2009. *The Biological Evolution of Religious Mind and Behaviour,* [electronic resource] The Frontiers Collection. Berlin and London: Springer.

Wade, Nicholas. 2009a. *The Faith Instinct: How Religion Evolved and Why It Endures.* London: Penguin Press.

———. 2009b. The evolution of the God gene. *New York Times.* 15 Nov.

Washburn, Jennifer. 2005. *University, Inc.: The Corporate Corruption of Higher Education.* New York: Basic Books/Perseus.

Wilson, E. O. 1979. *On Human Nature.* Cambridge, MA: Harvard University Press.

Chapter Five

The Tree of Life Needs Pruning

In the early 1950s, James Watson and Francis Crick, inspired by a surreptitious preview of Rosalind Franklin's X-rays of the DNA molecule, determined that a key building block of life consisted of two strands of nucleic acid coiled around each other, a configuration that they dubbed the double helix.[1] This effort to explicate the chemistry of inheritance and cell formation became known as molecular biology.

The nascent field of molecular biology adopted one-way genetic causation as its founding premise. That is, it assumed that genes make the body but that the latter never affects the chemisry of inheritance. Francis Crick expressed this as the Central Dogma[G] of genetics, which asserts that DNA, which is transmitted in the germ cells of the species, determines complementary strands of RNA found in the body of the cell and that these RNA molecules in turn determine the sequence of amino acids within a protein molecule, thus giving the protein its chemical structure and characteristics. Proteins are a class of chemical compounds, composed of amino acid molecules, from which much of a living body is built, including the skin, muscle, nerves, and internal organs. The process of making protein from instructions encoded in DNA is rendered schematically as

$$DNA \rightarrow RNA \rightarrow protein$$

As Watson notes in his classic monograph, *Molecular Biology of the Gene*, published in 1965: "Most importantly, both of these latter arrows are unidirectional, that is, RNA sequences are never copied on protein templates; likewise, RNA never acts as a template for DNA."[2]

Also, around this same time, Weismann's[G] barrier was given a new lease on life. In the 1890s, a German anatomist, August Weismann, described in detail the development of jellyfish, showing that the germ cells (eggs and sperm) develop from precursor cells that are distinct from the other cells of the body. Weismann concluded that the germ cells are impervious to modification during the life of the individual, so that feedback from the body does not occur, making impossible the genetic transmission of acquired characteristics.[3]

Weismann conceptualized growth and development of the organism as the hierarchical unfolding of units already present in the germ plasm, like workers building from a blueprint that admitted no deviation. Molecular biologists casually referred to organisms as "read-outs" of genes. In 1972, Richard Dawkins took this principle even further and asserted that organisms are robots that do the will of genes.[4]

In his first publication of the Central Dogma in 1958, Crick was careful to keep the door open for additional pathways, including RNA → DNA, although he considered them not very likely; but over the next decade these caveats were forgotten, even by Watson, to the point that the Central Dogma came to mean the sequence DNA → RNA → protein to biologists and public alike. As the journal *Science* noted in 1972: "The majority of molecular biologists have generally been propelled by the 'central dogma,' as propounded by Watson and Crick, namely that the flow of genetic information is unidirectional, from DNA to RNA to protein."[5]

In 1970, in two separate laboratories, scientists working with viruses discovered an enzyme called reverse[G] transcriptase which enables RNA molecules to produce complementary strands of DNA, reversing the normal process. Reverse transcriptase is not a laboratory curiosity but an essential component of a class of disease-causing agents called retroviruses[G] —"backward viruses," as, for example, HIV, the pathogen involved in AIDS. Retroviruses are strands of RNA with a protein case that infect an organism's cells, taking over the DNA of the cell nucleus[G] in order to produce copies of the virus. It is now known that a significant fraction of the human genome, around 8 percent, is composed of DNA sequences derived from retroviruses, which are remnants of viral infections at an earlier time in human history, while almost half of the DNA in the human genome is derived from mobile genetic elements of parasitic origin.[6]

Subsequently, there have been detailed studies of the penetration of the germ cells of multicellular organisms by bacterial DNA. For example, in the adzuki bean beetle (*Callosobruchus chinensis*), an insect normally subject to disease caused by bacteria of the *Wolbachia* species, a portion of the bacterial genome has been found in the beetle's germ cells, where it is inherited on the X chromosome.[7] In a case closer to home, the infectious agent in Chagas disease, a malady that kills thousands of people each year in Latin America—a disease that some historians think killed Charles Darwin— can transfer portions of its DNA into human chromosomes.[8]

In other words, Weismann's barrier, the doctrine that there is a complete separation of the genetic content of a species from its environment (except for whatever causes mutations) and the isolation of the germ cells from the body, can no longer be assumed to be a universal principle of biology. In fact, molecular biology has now established so many instances of what is called horizontal[G] gene transfer that an introduction to the subject requires a thick book.[9]

Even before Watson published *Molecular Biology of the Gene* in 1965, the one-way causality set forth in the Central Dogma was known to be an oversimplification of molecular genetics. In 1961, Francois Jacob and Jacques Monod at the Pasteur Institute in Paris published the first description of how a gene functions in a single-celled organism to do actual biological work. They experimented with a bacterium that lives in the human gut, *E. coli*. This organism has genes (segments of DNA) that produce the enzymes needed to break down lactose, the sugar found in milk. As the Central Dogma predicts, segments of bacterial DNA (genes) serve as a templates for RNA molecules, which in turn enable sequences of amino acids to be linked together into a chain, making specific proteins, in this case the molecules needed to metabolize lactose. But the genes that encode the required molecules are themselves part of a regulatory mechanism that Jacob and Monod named the *lac operon*.[G] [10] Their research was hailed as a breakthrough at the time, and its authors subsequently won a Nobel Prize.

In Jacob and Monod's terminology, (1) the sugar lactose functions as an environmental trigger or *inducer*, initiating the metabolic process; (2) then genes they call structural genes produce the enzymes that metabolize the milk in a manner consistent with the Central Dogma while (3) additional genes (what they call regulatory genes) modulate the output of the structural genes. In other words, protein synthesis in even a single-celled organism requires an environmental trigger as well as control processes for its normal functioning, but feedback loops such as this are not represented in the Central Dogma. Instead, the latter presents genetics as a straight line from DNA → RNA → protein. In Watson's *Molecular Biology of the Gene*, Jacob and Monod's model is relegated to the tail end of genetic science, being discussed in Chapter 14 under the rubric "regulation of protein synthesis and function."

In the 1970s, even as sociobiology (Chapter 6) was reaffirming genetic determinism as the cornerstone of evolution, this Darwinian dogma was being increasingly undermined by the findings of molecular biology. The discovery of reverse transcriptase was bad enough, but when molecular biologists turned their attention from bacteria to organisms whose DNA is located in the cell nucleus, which includes all the organisms one can see without a microscope (as well some species one cannot), the one-way causality of the Central Dogma became increasingly harder to maintain.

Bacteria reproduce by dividing, but multicellular organisms reproduce by building a whole new body from a single cell, that is, from a fertilized egg. In this process, there are genes that control the embryonic development of specific organs just as genetic determinism predicts, but the genes that build each organ also require specific proteins called transcription factors that alter the rate and timing of the gene expression.[11] As summarized by a modern textbook on genetics: "DNA sequences, in and of themselves, just exist. For genes to be actively transcribed, proteins must recognize particular DNA sequences and act on them in a way that affects the transcription process."[12]

The finding of alternative[G] splicing complicated the picture even further.[13] In the original formulation of the Central Dogma, each segment of DNA, or gene, encodes for one protein; but molecular biology discovered the phenomenon of alternative splicing, which is nature's way of making many different proteins from the same DNA sequence. To use a verbal analogy, if the DNA sequence spells the protein CARRIAGE, then additional cellular mechanisms come into play during the RNA transcription stage that use the same code to produce the proteins CAR and AGE. These rearrangements are handled by RNA molecules working in conjunction with many specialized proteins. Far from being a curiosity, alternative splicing enables an organism to do more with the same genes, and it is essential to fundamental biological processes, such as the production of antibodies.[14]

Even as the linearity of genetic determinism was losing ground in the laboratory, the Central Dogma became the rationale for one of the largest and most expensive projects in the history of science. Molecular biologists proposed a new "Manhattan Project" to sequence the human genome,[15] and they publicly promoted it with a degree of hyperbole that would make a carnival barker blush. They called the proposed project to sequence the human genome a "'Delphic Oracle,' a 'time machine,' a 'trip into the future,' a 'medical crystal ball.'"[16] Even James Watson, the first director of the United States Human Genome Project, solemnly informed *Time* magazine that "our fate is in our genes."

The sequencing project was also marketed in medical terms, promising miracle cures for some of the very same diseases that the proponents of stem cells are promising to cure today. It was based on the principle of "one gene, one disease, one treatment"[17] —and retrospectively: one wrong idea. As biologist Barry Commoner has observed: "By 1989, when the Human Genome Project was still being debated among molecular biologists, its champions were surely aware that more than 200 scientific papers on alternative splicing of human genes had already been published."[18]

Even as bio-engineering was being trumpeted as the next industrial revolution, geneticists knew that the Central Dogma applied to less than 2 percent of the genome, because only a small percentage of the DNA in a cell nucleus is ever transcribed into protein at all. Instead of concluding that they were 98 percent ignorant, geneticists dismissed the noncoding portion of the genome as "junk DNA," implying that it had no function. However, as it is now known, the cell is constantly transcribing "junk DNA" into RNA molecules that play important roles in the metabolism of the cell, including gene expression itself.[19]

In 1990, James Watson assumed command of the U.S. government's Human Genome Initiative, which was tasked to make a complete list of the three billion nucleotides in a sample human genome.[20] Three billion dollars and twenty years later, the Human Genome Initiative proved even to geneticists that the doctrine of genetic determinism is problematical. Single-cell organisms have thousands of genes, as, for example, yeast with about 6,300 and *E. coli* with about 4,300.[21] Since the prevailing theory asserted that the complexity of the organism reflects the complexity of the genome, which in turn is reducible to the number of genes and the sequence of nucleotides in the DNA, geneticists expected that human beings would have many more genes than simpler organisms. Initial estimates were between 100,000 and 140,000. But when sequencing of the human genome was completed twenty years later, it showed that human beings have around 25,000 genes that code for proteins, which is comparable to many other multicellular organisms, such as the mouse, while the protein-coding genes of mice and men are almost identical, within about 1 percent.

Barry Commoner, professor of biology at Harvard, noted that

> it is difficult to avoid the conclusion—troublesome as it is—that the project's planners knew in advance that the mismatch between the numbers of genes and proteins in the human genome was to be expected, and that the $3 billion project could not be justified by the extravagant claims.[22]

Even Craig Venter, the venture capitalist turned gene sequencer, had second thoughts: "I made a million dollars in biotech. I started with a billion dollars and worked my way down."[23]

To celebrate the fortieth anniversary of the publication of the Central Dogma, two molecular biologists interviewed Francis

Crick himself, and they record a startling admission: "Still, according to Crick, simplifications of the Central Dogma in terms such as 'DNA makes RNA, and RNA makes protein' were clearly inadequate from the beginning."[24]

One could argue that Watson and Crick needed to keep the Central Dogma as simple as possible for maximal generality, but Mae-Wan Ho, a molecular biologist, suggests a different motivation.[25] The Central Dogma was promulgated as it was in order to preserve genetic determinism. And this was done not only to preserve the Darwinian superstructure for all the ideological reasons previously discussed but, more important, to smooth the way for genetic engineering. The "simplicity" of genetics as presented by the Central Dogma argues for its feasibility as an industrial process, whereas feedback loops, regulatory genes, and environmental triggers might raise questions in the minds of investors. Since industrialists already believe that they have achieved their wealth through a Darwinian process of survival of the fittest, while geneticists believe that their own scientific achievements are due to superior genes, the Central Dogma simply confirms what many financiers and technocrats already think they know.

More important, the linear causality of the Central Dogma maps perfectly to the industrial chain of command, whereas feedback from proteins does not. In 1999, when the president of the National Agricultural Biotechnology Council testified before the U.S. Senate, he informed his audience that "DNA (top management molecules) directs RNA (middle management molecules) directs protein formation (worker molecules)."[26] What better illustration could one have of the synergy between the dogma of genetic determinism and the hierarchy of corporate capitalism?

The Dark Side of Genetic Determinism

To anyone with a knowledge of history, the ideological use of partial and erroneous theories of genetics evokes a tragic moment of déjà vu. Even today few people know that during the twentieth century genetics in England and the United States was as politicized as that of the Soviet Union and the Third Reich. In the decade before the First World War, the plutocratic elite of the United States, through their charities and foundations, funded eugenically-inspired social programs and genetic research, an agenda that developed pari passu with restrictive immigration policy and anti-miscegenation laws. These eugenic policies reflected the concerns of Charles Darwin himself. [27]

In *The Descent of Man* Darwin argues that the progress of the human species is due to natural selection operating on both individuals and races, while in the fifth chapter of that work ("On the Development of the Intellectual and Moral Faculties during Primeval and Civilized Times"), he pinpoints an obstacle that interferes with the proper functioning of his evolutionary mechanism:

> But some remarks on the agency of natural selection on civilised nations may be here worth adding. This subject has been ably discussed by Mr. W. R. Greg, and previously by Mr. Wallace and Mr. Galton. Most of my remarks are taken from these three authors. [8]

Mr. Greg, one of Darwin's school chums, was a mill owner turned political commentator, whereas Mr. Galton, Darwin's cousin, is commonly regarded as the founder of the eugenics movement.

Darwin continues:

> With savages, the weak in body or mind are soon eliminated; and those that survive commonly exhibit a vigorous state of health. We civilised men, on the other hand, do our utmost to check the process of elimination; we build asylums for the imbecile, the

maimed, and the sick; we institute poor-laws; and our medical men exert their utmost skill to save the life of every one to the last moment. There is reason to believe that vaccination has preserved thousands, who from a weak constitution would formerly have succumbed to small-pox. Thus the weak members of civilised societies propagate their kind.[29]

Alfred Russel Wallace would subsequently challenge Darwin's premise of the callousness of savages based on his years of field research in the Malay Archipelago, but let us for the moment assume that Darwin's anthropology is correct. Having noted this incompatibility between natural selection and civilized standards of conduct, Darwin raises the issue again a few pages further on:

A most important obstacle in civilised countries to an increase in the number of men of a superior class has been strongly insisted on by Mr. Greg and Mr. Galton, namely, the fact that the very poor and reckless, who are often degraded by vice, almost invariably marry early, whilst the careful and frugal, who are generally otherwise virtuous, marry late in life, so that they may be able to support themselves and their children in comfort.[30]

One of Darwin's favored literary devices is to express his own controversial opinions in the form of quotations from other authors, just as he relied on his disciples to fight his battles in the lecture hall. Darwin quotes Greg approvingly:

Or as Mr. Greg puts the case: "The careless, squalid, unaspiring Irishman multiplies like rabbits: the frugal, foreseeing, self-respecting, ambitious Scot, stern in his morality, spiritual in his faith, sagacious and disciplined in his intelligence, passes his best years in struggle and in celibacy, marries late, and leaves few behind him. Given a land originally peopled by a thousand Saxons and a thousand Celts—and in a dozen generations five-sixths of the population would be Celts, but five-sixths of the property, of the power, of the intellect, would belong to the one-sixth of Saxons that remained. In the eternal 'struggle for existence,' it would be the inferior and less favoured race that had prevailed—and prevailed by virtue not of its good qualities but of its faults."[31]

Significantly, Darwin does not dispute this argument; he merely adds a caveat, noting that "there are, however, some checks to this downward tendency," specifically a high death rate among the poor, which given the context is clearly seen as felicitous. Considering that Darwin is writing less than twenty years after the Great Famine in Ireland, it is hard to believe that he is not reassuring his English readers that the massive die-off of the Celts exemplifies Progress through natural selection.

Since Mr. Greg and Mr. Galton occupy such a prominent place in the argument, it is also hard to believe that Mr. Darwin is not advocating selective breeding of the human species as the scientific answer to the problem delineated by Mr. Malthus, namely, the "unrestrained" breeding by the poor. Of course, given the standards of the time, Mr. Darwin does not say this in so many words. Rather, he points the reader toward certain biological conclusions, which because of their source—Darwin himself—are to be taken as authoritative:

Thus the weak members of civilised societies propagate their kind. No one who has attended to the breeding of domestic animals will doubt that this must be highly injurious to the race of man. It is sur-

> prising how soon a want of care, or care wrongly di-
> rected, leads to the degeneration of a domestic race;
> but excepting in the case of man himself, hardly any
> one is so ignorant as to allow his worst animals to
> breed.[32]

Darwin also merges the heritability of social traits with the
need for genetic hygiene:

> we now know through the admirable labours of Mr.
> Galton that genius, which implies a wonderfully
> complex combination of high faculties, tends to be
> inherited; and, on the other hand, it is too certain that
> insanity and deteriorated mental powers likewise run
> in the same families.[33]

This passage is in the section on the process of domestication,
and, even though the connection between human breeding and
animal breeding is only hinted at in the text, it is logically implicit in the argument. As Darwin notes:

> Domesticated animals vary more than those in a state
> of nature; and this is apparently due to the diversified
> and changing nature of their conditions. The different
> races of man resemble in this respect domesticated
> animals.[34]

Once one accepts the world view of a pigeon breeder, then it
follows logically that humans are self-domesticated animals, that
domesticated animals are breed stock, and that breed stock needs
to be improved through selective breeding.[35]

Writing in *Popular Science Monthly* in 1890, Wallace confirms
that Darwin was personally concerned with this issue:

In one of my last conversations with Darwin he expressed himself very gloomily on the future of humanity, on the ground that in our modern civilization
natural selection had no play, and the fittest did not
survive. Those who succeeded in the race for wealth
are by no means the best or the most intelligent, and
it is notorious that our population is more largely renewed in each generation from the lower than from
the middle and upper classes.[36]

Darwin's contemporary audience had been formed in a Christian culture, with the belief that human beings have both an animal nature and an immortal soul that together enable a distinctly
human consciousness, whereas selective breeding of mental qualities only makes sense from the perspective of philosophical materialism and genetic determinism. But to the generation of the
1890s, formed by the materialist culture that Darwin helped to
create, eugenics is the obvious conclusion to draw. In the words
of Stanford biologist Vernon Kellogg, author of a book on evolution widely read in the interwar years, eugenics is simply the
"application of scientific knowledge and common sense."[37]

Inspired by Darwin's writings, evolutionary biologists in the
late nineteenth and early twentieth centuries began to transform
the value system of Western society. They raised public concern
about the dangers of racial degeneration; classified criminals on
the basis of body type; developed racial typologies based on comparative anatomy; sterilized those deemed genetically inferior;
and advocated involuntary euthanasia of the handicapped and
the mentally ill.[38]

Until World War II, this merger of eugenics with evolutionary science was part of the academic mainstream. Key figures in
the formation of the science of genetics, such as Ronald Fisher
(1890–1962), whose book *The Genetical Theory of Natural Selection*
(1930) crystallized neo-Darwinism,[G] and Karl Pearson, whose

statistics of gene pools inspired Fisher, advocated social policies that prefigured the Nazis.[39] The First International Congress of Eugenics held in London in 1912 was presided over by Charles Darwin's son Leonard; far from being marginal, it was attended by Winston Churchill and the president of Stanford University.[40] The Second International Congress of Eugenics, held in 1924, was sponsored by the administrative arm of the U.S. National Academy of Sciences and held at the American Museum of Natural History in New York City.[41]

The Eugenics Society included in its membership many prominent evolutionary biologists, including Ronald Fisher and Huxley's grandson Julian, as well as at least one Nobel laureate in genetics. Even Jewish geneticists, who were later to suffer at the hands of the Nazis, initially embraced the eugenics cause.[42] As for its public presence, in the 1920s over 90 percent of biology textbooks used in American high schools endorsed eugenic policies.[43]

Geneticists did not repudiate these policies but were deeply involved in carrying them out. Charles B. Davenport, who held a doctorate in biology from Harvard University, founded the Eugenics Records Office in 1910 at the evolution laboratory in Cold Spring Harbor, New York. Initially funded by the Harriman family (who made a fortune in railroads) and supported for many years by the Carnegie Institute (funded by U.S. Steel), it created the first mass database on genetically "inferior" individuals.[44] Subsequently it advised the federal government on the immigration act of 1924, which set quotas for ethnic groups based on their putative genetic contributions. Indeed, until after World War, II, there was no hard and fast dividing line between genetics and eugenics, which were thought to be analogous to the relationship between medical research and clinical practice.

As the scholar Frank Dikötter has pointed out, eugenics, far from being the exclusive property of the political right, is primarily a "modern" and "scientific" way of viewing such issues as race, population, and reproduction; it was part of the ideological stance of every Anglo-American progressive movement between the world wars, attracting not only scientists but Marxists, Protestant clergy, and rabbis as well.[45] Only the Catholic Church and the British Labour Party repudiated it.[46]

In 1929, a wealthy agriculturalist, Ezra S. Gosney, established a not-for-profit organization in San Marino, California.[47] Called the Human Betterment Foundation (HBF), its goal was to promote sterilization of the genetically disadvantaged and to advocate eugenics at public forums. It had the backing of many prominent members of Southern California's wealthy elite: White Anglo-Saxon Protestants who saw themselves as racially superior to the Spanish speakers that their forebears had displaced in the aftermath of the U.S.-Mexican War.

An important corollary of their racism was their support of eugenics. The powerful publisher of *The Los Angeles Times*, Harry Chandler, was a charter member of the Human Betterment Foundation, and the society's membership included four members of the prestigious Huntington Library board of trustees. The president of the California Institute of Technology, Robert Millikan, joined in 1937. Significantly, when the HBF was dissolved in 1942, Cal Tech erected a memorial to its founder, Ezra S. Gosney, in the biology department.

The Human Betterment Foundation was international in scope, and it kept in close correspondence with like-minded people in Germany. Adolf Hitler had written that Germany needed to catch up with the advances in "racial hygiene" pioneered by the United States; when he became chancellor in 1933, he put the full force of the totalitarian state behind an ambitious eugenics program. One of his first acts was the German Law for the Prevention of Genetically Diseased Offspring, enacted in July of 1933, which legalized eugenic sterilization. Some months later, when the law was disseminated in official legal circles, the Reich Minister of Justice appended to his proclamation a German translation of one of the pamphlets from the Human Betterment Foundation in California.[48]

The historian Richard Weikart has argued that Darwin's theory of evolution enabled the eugenics programs of the Nazis, with its concomitant extermination of the Jews and other groups deemed racially inferior.[49] Weikart's thesis has been dismissed by some as unilinear history and caricatured as "Darwin caused the Holocaust,"[50] while others have pointed out that there is nothing in Darwin's oeuvre that prefigures the Nazi's distinctive merger of eugenics, militarism, and anti-Semitism.[51]

However, as I argue in this book, it is important to distinguish between the theory of evolution and the theory of natural selection. Evolution is the history of life on earth as documented by natural science, whereas Darwin's theory of natural selection was inspired by the artificial selection of genetic traits by breeders of plants and animals. Also, when Darwin applied the concept of natural selection to human evolution in *The Descent of Man*, he presented it in conjunction with explicit statements affirming racial superiority and the need for improving the breed stock. Thus, the "necessity" of eugenics for human health and progress follows logically from Darwin's own writings.

Significantly, the eugenics program of the Nazis would not have been possible without widespread support from the German biomedical community. One measure of that support is that a quarter of German doctors joined the Nazi "Brown Shirt" movement (the SA), while half of German biologists joined the Nazi Party.[53] Moreover, social policies that are now seen as quintessentially Nazi—policies such as state-sponsored genocide, sterilization of the intellectually subnormal, killing the physically handicapped and the mentally ill, prevention of marriage between "superior and inferior" races, and arranged marriages based on supposed genetic superiority—were all derived from putatively scientific research that had been given the approbation of evolutionary biology a generation earlier. As Weikart notes: "Hitler was drawing on ideas that were circulating widely among the educated elites... These were not dominant in German society, but they were reputable and mainstream in scholarly circles, especially among the medical and scientific elites."[54]

The historian Aristotle A. Kallis argues that the Nazi era is best understood as the merger of an autocratic German nationalism with eugenic beliefs that were already well entrenched in the biomedical community:

> The vision of biomedical totalitarianism rested on the idea that biomedical science alone could promote and guarantee the idea of infinite individual and social perfectibility through eliminating all forms of perceived pathology; and that its practitioners could make the most authoritative and effective decision about all matters relating to the life and 'health' of the individual and society alike.[55]

Kallis goes on to note that this vision required "jettisoning deep-seated cultural and moral convictions as well as overcoming the strength of common wisdom about the role and scope of scientific intervention in life."[56]

The Nazis are the bad guys of choice in contemporary ideology, but genocide, slavery, and imperialism are as least as old as civilization, while the genocide of American Indians and the mass enslavement of Africans began centuries before Hitler, at a time when European nations were still officially Christian. In the American South, slavery even had an explicitly biblical rationale in the story of Ham, the son of Noah, whose descendants (Black Africans) were cursed by God.[57]

Far from being the inventors of eugenics, the Nazis were fa-
cilitators who provided the legislative and bureaucratic means
needed to implement a preexisting biomedical vision; once they
got involved, "racial progress" was far faster than the Californians
had been able to imagine. As Charles M. Goethe, a tireless promoter and benefactor of eugenics, noted in his 1936 presidential
address to the Eugenics Research Association (which he founded), California "has led all the world in sterilization operations.
Today even California's quarter-century record has, in two years,
been outdistanced by Germany."[58]

Therefore, the question is not whether Hitler read Darwin
but whether the latter's writings facilitated the eugenics policies
of the Nazis. The answer is unequivocal: it was not Hitler but
Darwin who created the intellectual framework that made the
selective breeding of the human species seem both "scientific"
and "modern."

Some Darwinian scientists who identified with the political
left, such as Julian Huxley and J. B. S. Haldane in Great Britain,
wrote popular books to express their concerns with Nazi policies, though neither man was opposed to eugenics per se. Julian
Huxley was, at various times, both vice president and president
of the British Eugenics Society. In the United States, an Ameri-
can-born geneticist Hermann J. Muller, an alumnus of Morgan's
laboratory and a future Nobel laureate, emerged as the leading
critic of sterilization. He too was a Marxist who pointed out that
much of the social pathology attributed to bad genes was due
to the oppressive nature of the capitalist class system—yet he
remained an enthusiastic promoter of "socialist" eugenics that
would breed the new socialist man.

The shift in American opinion was signaled at a meeting of
the American Eugenics Society in New York City, when Muller
pronounced eugenics to be scientifically flawed. Not long after the Rockefeller Foundation ceased all support of anything

with the word *eugenics* in it. The Carnegie Institute followed suit in 1934, phasing out its director of many years, the eugenicist Charles B. Davenport, while terminating support for eugenics programs. At the University of Chicago, a course in the biology department that had been taught for more than twenty years, entitled Evolution, Genetics, and Eugenics, had its name changed to Human Genetics.[59]

Much of the repudiation of eugenics in the United States was cosmetic. Even the geneticist Hermann J. Muller, who led the reform movement, was himself an advocate of selective breeding of the human species, but he saw eugenics as the prerogative of serious scientists such as himself, not as something that could be entrusted to scalpel-wielding surgeons in prisons and mental hospitals. Also, it is perhaps relevant that Muller's denunciation of sterilization had the effect of diverting foundation funding from eugenics into his own scientific specialty of genetic research.

Even as eugenics was being publicly repudiated in the United States, the liaison between German and American eugenicists continued as before. During the 1930s, as historian Stefan Kühl notes: "The Rockefeller Foundation played a central role in establishing and sponsoring major eugenic institutes in Germany, including the Kaiser Wilhelm Institute for Psychiatry and the Kaiser Wilhelm Institute for Anthropology, Eugenics, and Human Heredity"—organizations that carried out the Nazi policy of racial hygiene.[60] Also, in the United States members of the medical profession continued to sterilize women without their consent, especially the poor, the mentally ill, and those from ethnic minorities.[61] As Kühl points out, the British and Americans repudiated the Nazis because of the authoritarian and brutal nature of the regime, not because they disagreed with eugenic goals per se.[62]

Following the defeat of Germany in the Second World War, there was an effort to put as much distance between Hitler and

Darwin as possible. The eugenics movement adopted the stratagem that one of its leaders dubbed "crypto-eugenics," which is
the support of mainstream causes consistent with eugenic goals.[63]
During the Sixties, as the push for racial equality became a mass
movement in the United States, eugenics advocacy organizations
repositioned themselves as pure science. In 1969, the *Eugenics Quarterly* was renamed *Social Biology* (note the similarity to
sociobiology, the term promoted by E. O. Wilson three years later), and in 1973 the American Eugenics Society renamed itself
the Society for the Study of Social Biology.[64]

The sanitization of Darwin was facilitated by the mass media.
For example, in a popular BBC television series "The Day the
Universe Changed" (1985), Social Darwinism is presented as an
American distortion of Darwin's thought (Herbert Spencer is
not even mentioned) while the German biologist Ernst Haeckel
is fingered as the inventor of eugenics. The implication is that
Charles Darwin had nothing to do with these "aberrations" of
Darwinism, a thesis that is now presented as historical fact.[65]

By the time I first became conversant in evolutionary biology
in the late 1960s, sanitization had been so effective that unless
one did some diligent digging in academic journals one would
never know that eugenics had not been invented by Nazis.

Also, it would be decades before I learned that Nazi-style eugenics continued to be practiced in the postwar United States,
albeit underground. Between the late 1960s and 1974, when
President Nixon left office, about 100,000 sterilizations were
carried out annually, with funding provided by the federal government through the Office of Economic Opportunity. Between
1973 and 1976 the Indian Health Service sterilized more than
3,400 American Indian women, usually with the backing of the
department of Health, Education and Welfare.[66]

Nonetheless, there are important differences between Nazi
and American notions of racial hygiene. Where the Nazis had

emphasized eliminating the genetically "unfit" by the ruthless culling of phenotypes, the Americans promoted a new eugenic strategy more in keeping with progressive private enterprise— the building of bigger and better bodies through biotechnology. As early as 1931, Warren Weaver, head of the scientific funding programs for the Rockefeller Foundation, wrote an internal memo to the board of directors: "Can we develop so sound and extensive a genetics that we can hope to breed, in the future, superior men?" he asked rhetorically.[67]

Apparently, the answer is yes, because the Rockefeller Foundation funded the work of eighteen of the twenty-five Nobel laureates who created the field of molecular biology, which took only a generation to accomplish. In the 1960s, the irrepressible Muller addressed the Third International Congress of Genetics (note the name change—*not* the Third International Congress of *Eugenics*!) and announced that the improvement of the human species would finally be accomplished by means of artificial insemination, man-made genes, and implanted embryos.[68] In the twenty-first century, all of these techniques are commercially available.

Neoliberal Eugenics

In 1968, James Watson, the co-discoverer of the molecular structure of DNA, became director of Cold Spring Harbor Laboratory, the very same institution that had hosted the Eugenics Record Office (ERO) and its files on putatively degenerate phenotypes. The ERO closed in 1944, and its collection of file cards was shipped to an archive at the University of Minnesota, but institutional memory was not so easily effaced.

As the director of the Cold Spring Harbor Laboratory, Watson undertook the rehabilitation of the laboratory's founder, Charles B. Davenport. Under Watson's guidance, the laboratory reissued Davenport's 1911 book, *Heredity in Relation to Eugenics*, antiseptically bound with a collection of scholarly essays.[69] Lest there be any doubt as to its intention, the forward to the volume states unequivocally that "eugenics is back but in individual, not state-sponsored form."[70]

In 2018, Harvard geneticist David Reich confirmed Watson's racist thinking:

> Dr. Watson said to me and my fellow geneticist Beth Shapiro something to the effect of 'When are you guys going to figure out why it is that you Jews are so much smarter than everyone else?' He asserted that Jews were high achievers because of genetic advantages conferred by thousands of years of natural selection to be scholars, and that East Asian students tended to be conformist because of selection for conformity in ancient Chinese society. (Contacted recently, Dr. Watson denied having made these statements, maintaining that they do not represent his views; Dr. Shapiro said that her recollection matched mine.)"[71]

With backers at such a high level in the biomedical technocracy as Watson, it is not surprising that the eugenics movement, which had gone underground with the collapse of the Third Reich, suddenly re-emerged in the 1990s in the guise of medical therapy to insert bio-engineered genes into "defective" human genomes. These advocates of genetic perfection reject the term "eugenics," pointing out that since the genetic intervention is purchased voluntarily by parents for the benefit of their children, it is quite different from sterilization enforced by the state.

While no one denies there is a difference between surgeons sterilizing people against their will in the back rooms of mental hospitals and prospective parents browsing through a glossy catalog of genetic traits they desire in their offspring, the latter nonetheless replicates all the key features of Galton's original program: providing a genetic basis to the class system, eliminating supposedly inferior phenotypes, and artificially inducing genetic change to improve the human species. As Davenport defined it in his treatise of 1911: "Eugenics is the science of the human species by better breeding or, as the late Francis Galton expressed it: 'The science which deals with all influences that improve the inborn qualities of a race.'"[72]

In the 1990s, when critics were warning that man-made embryos were the "back door to eugenics,"[73] the prospect of designer babies was already emerging into the light of day. In 1997, Lee M. Silver, a professor of genetics and evolutionary biology at Princeton University, published a book with an unequivocally provocative title: *Remaking Eden: How Genetic Engineering and Cloning Will Transform the American Family*. It is an ironic contribution in an era when the phrase "family values" became a campaign slogan, but it does present the biotechnology in a readable and accurate manner while exemplifying the politically neutered naturalism of modern biological science. The author appears to be unaware that the technology he describes did not just happen but was specifically developed to improve the human species through genetic manipulation, so by describing it naturalistically, he forecloses the possibility of understanding its social context and political motivation. But that, of course, might be his intent.

Silver notes that since in capitalist economies the rich have greater access to medicine of any kind, one can anticipate that genetic engineering will lead to the evolutionary divergence of two hereditary classes, what he calls the "GenRich" and the "Naturals."[74] The GenRich are those people who can afford to be genetically enhanced, while those who cannot will become a permanent underclass of servants and manual laborers. In Silver's scenario, as biotech advances, these two classes will increasingly diverge, eventually evolving into separate species, incapable of interbreeding. As Darnovsky notes, proposals such as Silver's are not socially marginal but are endorsed by the writings of Nobel laureates, economists, and journalists of science.[75]

Moreover, eugenics has been blessed by James Watson of DNA fame:

> Yet anyone who proclaims that we are now perfect as human beings has to be a silly crank. If we could honestly promise young couples that we knew how to give them offspring with superior character, why should we assume they would decline? Those at the top of today's societies might not see the need. But if your life is going nowhere, shouldn't you seize the chance of jump-starting your children's future?[76]

Maybe even Blacks could be raised to the level of Whites?

The Man Who Saved Progress

Eugenics is not optional in Darwinism. It is needed to address a logical lapse in the ideology. Darwin replaced Lamarck's ladder of organic evolution with the tree of natural selection—a tree that sprouts from microbial roots and diversifies into a plethora of organic forms, most of which go extinct. Significantly, a dendrogram of hypothetical speciation is the *only* illustration in *Origin*. But the family tree came at a cost.

The unilinear evolution of the Enlightenment provided an upward path for progressive social change through social revolution and the Rights of Man, but natural selection ensures only struggle and continuous change. From a Darwinian perspective, human evolution is simply natural selection acting on apes; it is not the operation of some natural law that inevitably produces improvements, much less a social revolution that challenges the powers that be. Progress, however, has an implicit moral dimension in that things are supposed to get better as the human species evolves, not just change in some haphazard way. Faced with this implicit incompatibility between the tree of natural selection and the ladder of progressive evolution, Darwin concluded that the evolutionary tree needs pruning by human beings. Instead of abandoning Progress, Darwin tried to save it.

Darwin sketched the theoretical case for eugenics in *The Descent of Man,* but he left direct advocacy to disciples such as Galton, just as he left the popularization of natural selection to Huxley (Chapter 3) and the institutionalization of Darwinism to Lubbock (Chapter 4).

The pruning of the tree of life by biological science follows from Darwin's own premises. He assumes that society consists of individuals who are busy competing with members of their own species and with other species, while sometimes joining together in temporary alliances so as to better compete against a common enemy. The premise of atomistic individualism unites Darwinian theory with the social organization of capitalism, which consists of either fictive individuals (the corporation) or "visionary" individuals (entrepreneurs). The entrepreneur is still a flesh-and-blood human but one who assumes the right to "move fast and break things," amassing a personal fortune while leaving to others the task of repairing the torn social fabric and cleaning up the environmental damage that follow in the wake of his schemes.[77]

Since there are only individuals in Darwin's system, the properties of society must necessarily exist as social traits inside of the bodies of the individuals themselves, either as genes (sociobiology) or as instincts in the brain (evolutionary psychology). Given this assumption, then the only way to ensure social progress is to eliminate those "unprogressive" individuals who carry the undesired social traits, either by preventing them for breeding or by repairing their defective genes. If Progress is not assured by natural selection, then it must be helped along by artificial selection.

Darwinism and capitalism confuse a population with a society. A population is a statistical concept in which all the individuals comprising it are considered to be identical to one another, like the atoms of a chemical element or ball bearings in a barrel. Human society, in contrast, is composed of groups, not individuals; and each group interacts with its neighbors. Moreover, far from acting identically to its neighbors, an individual of the human kind usually performs actions that are complementary to the actions of others. In human society, social participation consists largely of collective activities that no individual can do alone, such as team sports, conversations, work groups, political rallies, religious rituals—the list goes on. Even though *Homo sapiens* has a genome very similar to that of apes, human beings produce very different societies because many of the social processes that distinguish them from other animals only operate on the group level of organization.

There is nothing metaphysical about levels of organization. A simple example is provided by a molecule of table sugar. The sugar molecule is composed of carbon, oxygen, and hydrogen atoms, but the constituent atoms do not taste sweet. For sweetness, one needs a particular configuration of the constituent atoms and a receptor organ such as a tongue. Sweetness is an emergent property of atoms grouped in a sugarlike way and interacting with organisms that can taste the molecule.

In an analogous way, groups require multiple individuals arranged into specific configurations and interacting by means of psychosocial processes, but the properties of the group are not the properties of the individuals that comprise it. Only an individual can have gastritis, pattern baldness, or perfect pitch. Conversely, only a group can have a social hierarchy, male members, or multiple generations. Darwinism flattens levels of organization and confuses essential components of a system with the system itself—an intellectual error known as reductionism.[G]

Primatology confirms that it is a mistake to attribute the properties of a social system to the individuals that live in it. Just as rhesus monkeys normally inherit the social rank of their mother through social learning (Chapter 6), so individual human beings are born into social systems that they are largely powerless to change.

Because there are only individuals in Darwin's system, Darwinists conclude that flawed societies are necessarily the product of flawed individuals. Eugenics operates on the biological level of organization while ignoring the properties of groups, so it cannot deliver the social benefits that Darwinists hope; yet it still remains an essential part of the Darwinist/capitalist complex because it unites capitalism with Progress on an ideological level. Since Darwin believed in both natural selection and evolutionary Progress, he tried to reconcile these two incompatible concepts by suggesting that artificial selection could be used to eliminate unprogressive social traits.

The belief that social problems can be remedied by genetic assessment and intervention is now mainstream American science. In a recent op ed piece in *The New York Times* that is explicitly directed at "progressives," a professor of psychology at the University of Texas informs the reader that there are genes that predict poor performance in school and that if we are serious about social equality then we need to give these kids a leg up.[78]

One should worry when a biomedical professional tells you to get your genes checked. Real progressives address the differential resources, values, and life situations that result in poor school performance, whereas proposals inspired by Darwinism stigmatize your child as genetically deficient. Even worse, such diagnoses are usually a prelude to some pseudoscientific genetic intervention, one based on correlations, not causality.

In spite of Darwin's seminal role as the inspiration of eugenics, he is still accorded deniability. If we look up the word *eugenics* in the *New Oxford American Dictionary*, for example, we learn that it was "Developed largely by Francis Galton as a method of improving the human race, it fell into disfavor only after the perversion of its doctrines by the Nazis."[79]

Significantly, the definition of eugenics in the Oxford dictionary leaves out the most relevant historical information: namely, that the English invented it, the Americans implemented it, and the Nazis subsequently adopted it. Genetic Progress and racial hygiene were not created by the Nazis, nor did they disappear with the Third Reich.

The Emergence of Epigenetic[G] Inheritance

Eugenics is based on two complementary assumptions that were so obvious to Darwin and his cohort that they were never subjected to any serious scientific critique: the principle of genetic determinism and the genetic inheritance of social behavior. The doctrine of genetic determinism asserts that the phenotype is simply an expression of the genotype. No one doubts that there are measurable genetic influences on the development of organisms, but genetic determinism is a philosophy that privileges genes at the expense of other, well-documented psychobiological processes such as phenotypic plasticity, imprinting, sensory deprivation, the effects of malnutrition, a supportive family, the opportunity to practice motor skills, and so on. The second thesis, namely the genetic inheritance of social traits, asserts that socially valued attributes, such as musical talent and athletic ability, or socially disparaged ones, such as laziness and kleptomania, are the result of specific genes.

As a point of fact, science has never established the existence of such genes nor measured their effects on the social development of individuals (though much has been claimed)—so the theory is on no firmer empirical footing than is social causation by sprites. But in Anglo-American culture the burden of proof is on those who question conjectural explanations by Darwinists.

From a cultural anthropological perspective, the key question is not whether genes for talent exist but why it is so important for people to believe that they do; the answer is that such genes follow logically from a system of power rationalized by Darwinist ideology. If natural selection enables upward mobility by the best and the brightest, then it follows that those in power must be the most naturally talented and intelligent, which is to say they must have superior genes. Conversely, if I want my children to rise in the class system, I will need to enhance my modest genetic contribution with the best genes money can buy, as James Watson has recommended.

But in spite of the claims of geneticists, talent is not a property of individuals that can be measured independently of the social situations in which the traits are normally expressed. For example, even if there were a gene for musical ability, it can influence development only if it is activated by the appropriate social situations—by having a mother who sings to her baby, by living with musicians who play at family gatherings, being taught by tutors who are themselves accomplished musicians, living in a society that supports careers in music, and so on. Thus, in a normal human community, a putative gene for musical ability cannot be empirically distinguished from the social life that expresses it and the musical culture that informs it, thereby making the genetic explanation of social traits logically tautologous and empirically vacuous.

In Darwinian theory, genetics and learning have traditionally been seen as opposites, like the two pans of a balance scale, so that if learning increases then genetics decreases, and vice versa. This premise is built into the methodology of twin studies, in which identical twins raised apart are compared to each other and to fraternal twins. In the 1960s, such research constituted a significant fraction of the content in college courses on genetics, such as the one taught by Theodosius Dobzhansky at Yale University, in which I served as his teaching assistant.[80] In these studies, any similarities between the twins are attributed to genetic inheritance, while any disparity between them is attributed to environmental factors, which assumes that genes and environment are mutually exclusive. But biological experiments show that the normal development of even species-typical behaviors in mammals and birds requires the *interaction* of genetic factors with specific environmental stimuli.

For a male white-crowned sparrow to sing its species-typical song during the mating season, it needs to hear a song from a male of its *own* species at a particular stage of its development. If the critical period is missed, then the song never becomes typical, even when the bird is given subsequent opportunities for learning. On the other hand, even if the bird hears the right song at the right time, it still needs to practice what it has heard during its first breeding season a year later in order to sing like a normal bird. If it is exposed to an atypical song during the critical period of development, and practices it subsequently, then it learns the atypical song.[81] In songbird species, genes and learning are not in opposition: they are essential components of a single developmental process.

The limitations of genetic determinism are apparent in the development of species-typical anatomy as well. *Euprymna scolopes* is a species of squid that lives in the ocean off Hawaii. When this animal emerges from the egg it is already equipped with a little pouch suitable for holding light-emitting bacteria.[82] However, the organ becomes functional only if the squid encounters the appropriate species of bacteria in the seawater within twelve hours after hatching. If it does, then cilia on the squid's body sweep the microorganisms into the pouch, which metamorphoses into a light organ, consisting of translucent stomach muscle with a reflector behind it, with the live bacteria providing the light source. Subsequently, the squid flushes out the old bacteria every day and refills its pouch with new.

Such intricate interaction between two very different species fits the Darwinian concepts of local adaptation and coevolution very well, but one cannot explain it by a theory of genetic determinism. Unless the squid encounters an appropriate environmental input during a specific stage of development, the genes for the light organ remain functionless. So even if one had a complete knowledge of the genome and the role of all the genes in it, one would still not have a blueprint of the normal adult animal.

When two different species become dependent on each other, the process is known as symbiosis. Margulis and Sagan theorize that new species *normally* arise in the history of life by borrowing genomes through prolonged symbiosis, and they illustrate this thesis with a large number of instances from the biological literature too extensive to review here.[83]

Even during the heyday of the neo-Darwinian synthesis, biologists knew, or should have known, that there are some traits that are inherited independently of gene change and are successfully propagated during reproduction to successive generations, a process now known as epigenetic inheritance—"above the gene."[84] For example, a type of single-celled organism, the ciliates, are named for the hair-like appendages called cilia that they use to propel themselves through the water.[85] These microscopic creatures differ from bacteria in having their DNA enclosed in a cell nucleus, and for this reason biologists classify them as eukaryotes,[G] a category that includes all multicellular organisms. They differ from you and me, however, in having two genomes in two distinct nuclei, one for the germline[G] DNA and another for everyday use.

The microbiologist Tracy Sonneborn began working on the genetics of ciliates in the 1930s, and his experiments showed that it was possible to make alterations in the cytoplasm of the cell that are inherited by subsequent generations. (The cytoplasm is the part of the cell that lies outside the nucleus, whereas the nucleus is the part of the cell that contains the DNA.) Thus, Sonneborn demonstrated that not all inherited changes require changes to the genes in the nucleus of the cell, as the genetic theory of the day maintained. Sonneborn became a professor of zoology at the University of Indiana in 1939, doing research there until his death in 1981, a period when Indiana was formative in the history of molecular biology.[86] He was a member of prestigious scientific societies and knew the important people in genetics, but his findings never generated much enthusiasm among his scientific peers. Although Sonneborn's work is cited in textbooks, his eulogist notes that "it is located in optional chapters with other phenomena that the instructor usually chooses to ignore."[87] James Watson was in regular contact with Sonneborn when he was studying genetics at Indiana, even attending the Friday night seminar held in Sonneborn's home,[88] but Watson does not mention him in *The Double Helix*.

Since Sonneborn did not work in obscurity as Mendel did, his historical anonymity must be due in large measure to the fact that he defined genetics in a perverse (though accurate) way, as "the interaction of genes, cytoplasm and the environment in the control of cellular heredity."[89] Moreover, his findings contradicted the major premise of Darwinian orthodoxy, namely, that genes, and only genes, determine what is transmitted to the next generation.

To take ciliates seriously is to admit that the inheritance of acquired characteristics has been confirmed by biological science and that Lamarck has a legitimate claim to be the discoverer of organic evolution. Sonneborn did much of his work during the Cold War, a time when Lamarckism[G] was Communist Party dogma, so it is not surprising that the American scientific establishment chose to endorse genetic determinism while dismissing ciliates as the exception that proves the rule.

Over the past two decades, epigenetic inheritance has moved from microbes to mammals. Where Darwinism postulates a top-down model of ontogeny, best expressed by Dawkins' metaphor that genes are like a recipe and the organism the baked cake, building a living creature with billions of cells from a single fertilized egg turns out to be far more complicated than the Betty Crocker model implies.[90] Since all the cells of the body usually contain the same genes, the differentiation of the fertilized egg into hundreds of different cell types suitable for a multiplicity of organs requires that only a subset of genes be active in any particular cell. Thus, there are complex biochemical mechanisms that turn genes off and on, mechanisms that are susceptible to environmental influence and the biological context imposed by the developing body itself.

Some environmental factors that alter the readout of genes in a parental generation continue to have effects on gene expression in subsequent generations.[91] Methylation,[G] for example, is a chemical process that adds methyl groups (the organic radical -$CH3$) to a DNA molecule while leaving the sequence of nucleotides (the genes) unchanged. The methyl groups block access to the DNA by other molecules, thereby preventing genes from being expressed; and methylated DNA can be passed on to subsequent generations. Moreover, biologists have shown that the process of methylation can be influenced by both environmental and social factors.

Psychologists have long known that when rat pups receive little affection from their mothers in the form of licking and grooming, they grow up to be more excitable (stress prone) than their well-groomed peers.[92] In the past decade, molecular biologists have shown that maternal grooming in rats affects the methylation process, thus altering the expression of the underlying genes (but not the sequence of nucleotides in the genes themselves). In the case of rat pups who are licked and groomed during their first week of life, methylation affects the gene that produces the receptors for glucocorticoids, which is the hormone that triggers the stress response, thereby reducing the reactiveness of the latter.[93] That is, a rat pup's experience with its mother affects the functional properties of its DNA, even though there is no change in the sequence of nucleotides that make up the genes. Moreover, the effect is due to the mother's behavior, not to the genes that the pups inherit from its mother, since the effect can be induced in unrelated pups that the mothers cross-foster. Further confirmation is that the process is reversible even in adult rats by drugs that remove methyl groups from the genome.

The effect of maternal behavior in rats is perhaps the most dramatic case of epigenetic inheritance, but it is not an isolated instance. As one authority has summarized: "Transgenerational epigenetic inheritance has now been documented or suggested to occur in many eukaryotes, from plants to yeast, flies, rodents, and possibly in humans."[94]

The evidence of epigenetic inheritance in humans is based on historical and statistical data. For example, in an isolated Swedish town near the Arctic circle that is subject to frequent crop failures, historical records over several centuries document the fact that food shortages during a grandparent's childhood have predictable effects on the diseases that occur in the grandchildren, even though the descendants have not suffered from famine themselves.[95]

This finding is supported by experiments in rodents, which show both the effects of the mother's nutrition on gene expression in the fetus and the epigenetic inheritance of such effects. For example, one author notes that the protein genistein, "the major phytoestrogen in soy, is linked to diminished female reproductive performance and to cancer chemoprevention and decreased adipose deposition."[96] When pregnant mice are fed genistein in levels consistent with a high-soy diet in humans, the pups are born with an altered coat color and a reduced tendency to obesity, both characteristics traceable to the altered expression of a specific gene. In a similar way, exposure of pregnant rats to certain pesticides and fungicides not only induces diseases in the fetus, including prostate disease, kidney disease, and immune system abnormalities; but these maladies *are also inherited by subsequent generations which have never been exposed.*[97]

Epigenetic inheritance is similar to Lamarckian evolution in that some acquired characteristics are inherited, but it differs from the latter in one very important respect. Because the science of the early nineteenth century had no concept of genotype versus phenotype, Lamarck's "transformist hypothesis" (as evolution was called then) is necessarily based on the unrestricted malleability of protoplasm, in which organs and species change their morphology as a function of use and disuse. For many of his colleagues, however, a species, even when acknowledged to be anatomically variable, was conceptualized as an immutable type that bred true when mated with others of similar morphology. Moreover, the mutability of any individual was constrained by its constituent anatomical parts, which in turn are constrained during development by the functions for which they are used.

As a promulgator of the naturalness of species, Georges Cuvier was dismissive of Lamarckian evolution: "A system founded on a similar basis might amuse the imagination of a poet; a metaphysician might derive from it a wholly new generation of systems; but it cannot for a moment hold the attention of anyone who has dissected a hand, a visceral organ, or even a feather."[98] Could a quadruped, he asks, become a snake by frequently escaping through narrow openings?

In Cuvier's critique, as in the writings of Lamarck himself, the behavioral level of organization is being confounded with the genetic level of organization, and the phenotype with both; it is the achievement of the twentieth century to show that all these levels are conceptually distinct, each with processes of its own. Even so, they are not isolated in nature, only in our academic departments; normally, they interact during the development of each individual organism. Moreover, in primates, they develop within a social context.

Even though some Darwinian biologists now talk about the coevolution of genes, culture, and society, for many culture and evolution remain two distinct tracks, one of genetic information and the other of cultural information—genes and memes. Nor does this phrasing significantly affect Darwinian theory because culture is hypothesized to select for "social instincts," thereby keeping genetic determinism and competition intact.[99] Moreover, sociobiologists consider culture to be a second-class citizen that does the will of the genome, a thesis expressed by E. O. Wilson's phrase of "genes having culture on a leash."[100]

As for their understanding of culture, Darwinians typically see it as an analog of population genetics, composed of discrete particles of meaning—"memes"—that propagate independently of mind among atomistic individuals.[101] Even when Darwinians tout the importance of culture, defining the relationship between genes and culture as one of "obligate mutualism,"[102] and even when they explicitly reject the term meme as too atomistic, they still get mired in the atomistic individualism that underlies all Darwinian theory. For example, in their frequently-cited book, Richerson and Boyd write: "Thinking about culture as something that is acquired, stored, and transmitted by a population of *individuals* [emphasis in the original] enables us to explore interactions between culture and other aspects of human biology."[103]

But human culture is not primarily a process of information transmission between individuals. Even though cultural content is learned, and even though once learned some of the content will be communicated to others, a human level of cultural^G adaptation rests on the interplay of a number of factors, all of which are inherently social: inference of intentionality in others, complementary role relations among two or more individuals, observational learning from the behavior of others, verbal instruction, reciprocal exchange, generalized altruism, cooperative parenting, and language—not on social transmission per se.[104] But to do justice to these topics one would need a whole book.

To pour new science into old bottles ensures that the findings will have no effects beyond those already approved and institutionalized by the prevailing system of power. To embrace Darwin is to embrace the X Club, and to embrace the X Club is to embrace its journal *Nature*, which every practicing scientist wants to be embraced by. Yet reciprocating *Nature*'s embrace requires at least tacit acceptance of its institutional values: a firm commitment to genetic engineering, a reductionist account of human origins, religious skepticism, and perhaps repudiation of home rule for Ireland as well (see Chapter 3). Rather than perpetuate the values of the X Club uncritically for yet another century, it would be more scientific to explore the implications of a genetics without genetic determinism.

Geneticists are fond of pointing out that humans and chimpanzees have much of their DNA in common, some 98 percent or more,[105] and they argue that only a small number of genetic changes are needed to evolve a chimpanzee into a human. But there is an alternative explanation that is rarely mentioned: that there is so little genetic difference between humans and chimpanzees because genes, at least as they are understood by Darwinians, are not very important in human evolution.[106]

The epigenetic approach to human evolution considers it normal for some genes to interact with psychosocial information during development, even as many now recognize that the significant discontinuities between humans and other primates evolve in the cultural and cognitive context created by human society itself. In this view, human and simian genomes are almost identical because genes provide a stable biological foundation on which the human system of cultural adaptation is erected.

Reflections

For all of the TV documentaries about the fall of the Third Reich, evolutionary biology has never repudiated eugenics. Even though state-sponsored programs to sterilize the supposedly genetically unfit have fallen into disfavor, the complementary effort to build bigger and better bodies through biotechnology is now mainstream science.

In 1902, that apostle of modernism, H. G. Wells, defined what he called "the future-looking person" as someone who "sees the world as one great workshop, and the present as no more than material for the future, for the thing that is destined to be."[107] This is a good description of the mindset that underlies biomedical technocracy generally and genetic engineering in particular.

In Darwinist ideology, eugenics is not optional, for intentional genetic change by human beings bridges the gap between random natural selection in nature and the directional evolution needed for human Progress. As Galton expresses it: "The creed of eugenics is founded upon the idea of evolution; not on a passive form of it [that is, as found in nature], but on one that can to some extent direct its own course."[108]

In his 1932 novel *Brave New World*, Aldous Huxley imagined a future society in which human embryos are developed in artificial wombs on assembly lines and biologically altered so as to better adapt them to their adult roles in society.[109]

It is often forgotten that Aldous Huxley was not simply a novelist but was born into the top tier of Darwin's cohort. His grandfather was Thomas Henry Huxley while his brother Julian was one of England's most distinguished eugenicists. Aldous did not share his brother's views on this subject, but no doubt he was aware of them.

Although often consigned to the genre of dystopian fiction, Huxley's novel is better interpreted as an accurate description of the values of Darwin's cohort and the aspirations that shape the biomedical technocracy of today.

Notes

1 Sayre (1975).

2 Watson (1965: 298).

3 Weismann (1902). For a modern critique of Weismann, see Jablonka and Lamb (1995).

4 Dawkins (1976).

5 Culliton, (1971: 928).

6 Bannert and Kurth (2004), Griffiths (2001).

7 Kondo et al. (2002).

8 Lock (2004), Teixeira et al. (2000).

9 Bushman (2002).

10 Stent (1970: 932–33). The lac operon was subsequently confirmed by other laboratories; see Brooker (2012: chapter 14) for a contemporary account of gene regulation in bacteria.

11 These developmental processes are clearly illustrated in the article by Carroll (2005) and by Carroll, Prud'homme, and Gompel (2008). Kirschner and Gerhart (2005) give a readable overview of the chemical and biological processes that make life possible.

12 Brooker (2012: 300).

13 Commoner (2002) reviews this and other challenges to the Central Dogma.

14 Ho (2003: 44–45).

15 Sapp reviews the Human Genome Initiative in Chapter 17 (Sapp 2003: 201–22).

16 Quoted by Nelkin (2001: 51).

17 Ibid. 203.

18 Commoner (2002).

19 Yu (2008).

20 Ibid.

21 Kirschner and Gerhart (2005: 53).

22 Commoner (2002).

23 Quoted by Sapp (2003: 203).

24 Thieffrya and Sarkarb (1998).

25 Ho (2001).

26 Ibid. 8.

27 Black (2003), Kevles (1986), Paul (1995), Stern (2005), and elsewhere in this chapter.

28 Darwin (1871: 167–68).

29 Ibid. 168.

30 Ibid. 173–74.

31 Ibid. 174. The choice of ethnicities by Darwin and Greg is not arbitrary. The Scots are Presbyterian whereas the Irish are Catholic, which is consistent with the Calvinist substrate of Darwinian theory discussed in Chapter 4; it is also consistent with the X Club's prejudice against the Irish noted in Chapter 3.

32 Ibid. 168.

33 Darwin (1871: 111).

34 Ibid.

35 Thomas Henry Huxley was adamantly opposed to eugenics: "Direct selection, after the fashion of the horticulturalist and the breeder, neither has played, nor can play, any important part in the evolution of society; apart from other reasons, because I do not see how such selection could be practiced without a serious weakening, it may be the destruction, of the bonds which hold society together" ("Prologue").

36 Quoted by Caudill (1997: 97).

37 Kellogg (1922: 88–93).

38 Black (2003), Kevles (1986), Paul (1995), Stern (2005), and elsewhere in this chapter.

39 Fisher (1930).

40 Black (2003: 213).

41 Ibid. 236.

42 Paul and Falk (1999: 271).

43 Paul (1995: 11).

44 Ibid. 8–9.

45 Dikötter (1998).

46 In the United States, eugenics was part of the reforming effort of the Progressive Era:[G] Bozeman (2004), Paul (1995), Rosen (2004).

For the position of British Labour and the Catholic Church, see Black (2003), Dikötter (1998).

47 Platt and O'Leary (2006), Stern (2005). Stern's detailed treatment of eugenics in California illuminates the present as much as the past.

48 Platt and O'Leary (2006: 57-58).

49 Weikart (2004).

50 Richards (2013).

51 Bowler (2009).

52 Kallis (2007: 389).

53 Paul and Falk (1999: 258).

54 Weikart (2004).

55 Kallis (2007: 90).

56 Ibid.

57 Pleins (2003: Chapter 8) documents the ideological use of the story of Ham in the antebellum South.

58 Note 94 from the Eugenical News; quoted by Platt and O'Leary (2006: 69).

59 Mitman (1992: 97, 101). Weiss (2010: Chapter 6) devotes a chapter to the reaction of the international eugenics movement to Nazi Germany.

60 Kühl (1994: 20).

61 Stern (2005: 201 ff) provides the statistics on postwar sterilization in the United States. Johnson (2014) documents a contemporary instance.

62 Kühl (1994: 83).

63 Paul (1995: 132).

64 Kevles (1986) reviews postwar eugenics in Chapter 17, "A New Eugenics." Paul and Falk (1999) document how many of perpetrators of the Nazi's racial hygiene policies moved into respectable scientific positions after the war, no questions asked.

65 For example Hofstadter (1955: 201).

66 Stern (2005: 202).

67 Jonas (1989: 210), Weaver (1970).

68 Reprinted in Muller (1973).

69 Witkowski and Inglis (2008).

70 Ibid. "Forward" by Matt Ridley: xi.

71 See Reich (2018) for the quotation from Watson.

72 Davenport (1911: 1) reprinted in Witkowski and Inglis (2008).

73 Duster (1990).

74 Silver (2002). This evolutionary scenario of scientifically altered humans has a precursor in science fiction, being first presented by H. G. Wells in The Time Machine.

75 Darnovsky (2000), Duster (1990)

76 Witkowski and Inglis (2008).

77 Taplin (2017).

78 Harden (2018). The genetic inheritance of social traits is being revived yet again, but this time the whole genome is used to explain social traits instead of individual genes (Ward 2018).

79 Preinstalled on Apple Macintosh computers, Mac OS 10.11 (Accessed April 2018).

80 Dobzhansky (1937, 1963) is well known to biologists as a founder of population^G genetics.

81 Zeigler and Marler (2004).

82 Margulis and Sagan (2002: 176–78), Visick and McFall-Ngai (2000).

83 Margulis and Sagan (2002).

84 Robertson (2005). Epigenetics has since become a scientific fact, as evidenced by two Cambridge University geneticists trying to explain it in the journal Science (Miska and Ferguson-Smith 2016).

85 Meyer and Chalker (2007). Margulis, Chase, and To (1979) recognized the significance of Sonneborn's work in the 1970s.

86 For biographical information I have used the eulogy by Nanney (1981).

87 Ibid. 3.

88 McElheny (2003: 18).

89 Nanney (1981: 6).

90 Discussed by West-Eberhard (2003: 15).

91 Lane, Robker, and Robertson (2014); Paulsen, Tierling, and Jörn (2008).

92 The interaction between genes and social learning in the development of rats and mice, along with myriad examples from other species, is described in the book by Avital and Jablonka (2000).

93 Szyf and Meaney (2008), Weaver, Meaney, and Szyf (2006).

94 Sandovici et al. (2008: 358).

95 Kaati et al. (2007).

96 Dolinoy et al. (2006).

97 Sandovici et al. (2008).

98 Quoted by Coleman (1964: 158) from Recueil des éloges historiques, III: 200.

99 Durham (1991), Lumsden and Wilson (1983a, 1983b).

100 From the 1981 edition of Lumsden and Wilson, Genes, Mind, and Culture: 303; quoted by Richerson and Boyd (2005: 194).

101 The term meme was coined by Dawkins (1976).

102 For the term "obligate mutualists" see Richerson & Boyd (2005: 194); they eschew memes on page 63.

103 Quotation from Richerson and Boyd (2005: 8).

104 Reynolds (1993), Tomasello (2009).

105 For the anthropological perspective on genetics, see Marks (2002).

106 Ho and Saunders (1984: Intro. p. 4).

107 In a speech before the Royal Institute in 1902. Quoted by Gunn (1992).

108 Galton (1909: 68). Online version at: http://www.galton.org/books/essays-on-eugenics/galton-1909-essays-eugenics-1up.pdf

109 Aldous Huxley (1932).

References

Avital, Eytan, and Eva Jablonka. 2000. *Animal Traditions: Behavioural Inheritance in Evolution*. Cambridge and New York: Cambridge University Press.

Bannert, Norbert, and Reinhard Kurth. 2004. Retroelements and the human genome: new perspectives on an old relation. *Proceedings of the National Academy of Sciences of the USA* 101: 14572–79.

Black, Edwin. 2003. *War against the Weak: Eugenics and America's Campaign to Create a Master Race*. New York: Four Walls Eight Windows.

Bowler, Peter J. 2009. Do we need a non-Darwinian industry? *Notes and Records of the Royal Society*. April 15. http://rsnr.royalsocietypublishing.org/content/63/4/393.short.

Bozeman, John M. 2004. Eugenics and the clergy in the early twentieth-century United States. *Journal of American Culture* 27 (4): 422–31.

Brooker, Robert J. 2012. *Genetics: Analysis and Principles*. 4th edition. New York: McGraw-Hill.

Bushman, Frederic. 2002. *Lateral DNA Transfer: Mechanisms and Consequences*. Cold Spring Harbor, NY: Cold Spring Harbor Laboratory Press.

Carroll, Sean B. 2005. The origins of form. *Natural History* 114 (9): 58–63.

———, Benjamin Prud'homme, and Nicolas Gompel. 2008. Regulating evolution. *Scientific American*, May, 61–67.

Caudill, Edward. 1997. *Darwinian Myths: The Legends and Misuses of a Theory*. Knoxville: University of Tennessee Press.

Coleman, William. 1964. *Georges Cuvier, Zoologist: A Study in the History of Evolution Theory*. Cambridge, MA: Harvard University Press.

Commoner, Barry. 2002. Unraveling the DNA myth: the spurious foundation of genetic engineering. *Harpers* 304 (1821): 39–47.

Culliton, Barbara J. 1971. Reverse transcription: one year later. *Science, New Series* 172 (3986): 926–28.

Darnovsky, Marcy. 2000. The new eugenics: the case against genetically modified humans. *CGS Publications.* http://www.geneticsand-society.org.

Darwin, Charles. 1871. *The Descent of Man.* 2 vols. London: John Murray.

Dawkins, Richard. 1976. *The Selfish Gene. Oxford and New York*: Oxford University Press.

Dikötter, Frank. 1998. Race culture: recent perspectives on the history of eugenics. *The American Historical Review* 103 (2): 467–78.

Dobzhansky, Theodosius. 1937. *Genetics and the Origin of Species. Columbia Biological Series.* New York: Columbia University Press.

———. 1963. *Mankind Evolving: The Evolution of the Human Species.* New Haven, CT, and London: Yale University Press.

Dolinoy, Dana C., et al. 2006. Maternal genistein alters coat color and protects Avy mouse offspring from obesity by modifying the fetal epigenome. *Environmental Health Perspectives* 114 (4): 567–72.

Durham, William H. 1991. *Coevolution: Genes, Culture, and Human Diversity.* Stanford, CA: Stanford University Press.

Duster, Troy. 1990. *Backdoor to Eugenics.* New York: Routledge.

Fisher, Ronald Aylmer. 1930. *The Genetical Theory of Natural Selection.* Oxford: The Clarendon Press.

Galton, Francis. 1909. *Essays in Eugenics.* London: London: The Eugenics Education Society.

Griffiths, David J. 2001. Endogenous retroviruses in the human genome sequence. *Genome Biology* 2 (6).

Gunn, James. 1992. "Introduction." In *The Time Machine* by H. G. Wells. New York: Tor Book/Tom Doherty Assoc Associates..

Harden, Kathryn Paige. 2018. Why progressives should embrace the genetics of education. *New York Times* 24 July.

Ho, Mae-Wan. 2001. Human genome sell-out. http://www.ctheory.net/text_file.asp?pick=30 (Accessed May 2005).

_____. 2003. *Living with the Fluid Genome*. Paperback ed. Penang: Institute of Science and Society/Third World Network.

_____. and Peter Saunders, eds. 1984. *Beyond Neo-Darwinism: An Introduction to the New Evolutionary Paradigm*. London: Academic Press.

Hofstadter, Richard. 1955. *Social Darwinism in American Thought*. Boston: Beacon Press. Original edition 1944.

Huxley, Aldous. 1932. *Brave New World*. London: Chatto & Windus.

Huxley, Thomas Henry. 1948. *Selections from the Essays of T. H. Huxley*. Edited by A. Castell. New York: Appleton.

Jablonka, Eva, and Marion J. Lamb. 1995. *Epigenetic Inheritance and Evolution: The Lamarckian Dimension*. Oxford and New York: Oxford University Press.

Johnson, Cory. 2014. California finds illegal sterilizations of female inmates. *San Francisco Chronicle*. 20 June.

Jonas, Gerald. 1989. *The Circuit Riders: Rockefeller Money and the Rise of Modern Science*. New York and London: W. W. Norton.

Kaati, Gunnar, Lars Olov Bygren, Marcus Pembrey, and Michael Sjöström. 2007. Transgenerational response to nutrition, early life circumstances and longevity. *European Journal of Human*

Genetics 15: 784–90.

Kallis, Aristotle A. 2007. Racial politics and biomedical totalitarianism in interwar Europe. In *"Blood and Homeland": Eugenics and Racial Nationalism in Central and Southeast Europe, 1900–1940*, edited by M. Turda and P. J. Weindling. Budapest and New York: Central European University Press.

Kellogg, Vernon. 1922. *Human Life as the Biologist Sees It*. New York: Henry Holt and Company.

Kevles, Daniel J. 1986. *In the Name of Eugenics: Genetics and the Uses of Human Heredity*. Berkeley and Los Angeles: University of California Press.

Kirschner, Marc W., and John C. Gerhart. 2005. *The Plausibility of Life*. New Haven, CT, and London: Yale University Press.

Kondo, Natsuko, Naruo Nikoh, Nobuyuki Ijichi, Masakazu Shimada, and Takema Fukatsu. 2002. Genome fragment of *Wolbachia endosymbiont* transferred to X chromosome of host insect. *Proceedings of the National Academy of Sciences, US* 99 (22).

Kühl, Stefan. 1994. *The Nazi Connection: Eugenics, American Racism, and German National Socialism*. Oxford and New York: Oxford University Press.

Lane, Michelle, Rebecca L. Robker, and Sarah A. Robertson. 2014. Parenting from before conception. *Science* 345 (6198):756-60.

Lock, C. 2004. Invasive genes: humans incorporate DNA from parasite. *Science News* 166: 70.

Lumsden, Charles J., and Edward O. Wilson. 1983a. *Genes, Mind, and Culture*. Cambridge, MA: Harvard University Press.

_____, and Edward Osborne Wilson. 1983b. *Promethean Fire: Reflections on the Origin of the Mind*. Cambridge, MA: Harvard University Press.

Margulis, Lynn, D. Chase, and L. P. To. 1979. Possible evolutionary significance of Spirochaete. *Proceedings of the Royal Society of*

London (2004): 189–98.

_____, and Dorion Sagan. 2002. *Acquiring Genomes: A Theory of the Origins of Species.* New York: Basic Books/Perseus.

Marks, Jonathan. 2002. *What It Means to Be 98% Chimpanzee: Apes, People, and Their Genes.* Berkeley and Los Angeles, London: University of California Press.

McEleheny, Victor K. 2003. *Watson and DNA: Making a Scientific Revolution.* Cambridge, MA: Perseus/Merloyd Lawrence.

Meyer, Eric, and Douglas L. Chalker. 2007. Epigenetics of ciliates. In *Epigenetics*, edited by C. D. Allis, T. Jenuwein, and D. Reinberg. Cold Spring Harbor, NY: Cold Spring Harbor Laboratory Press.

Miska, Eric A., and Anne C. Ferguson-Smith. 2016. Transgenerational inheritance: models and mechanisms of non-DNA sequence-based inheritance. *Science* 354 (6308):59-63.

Mitman, Gregg. 1992. *The State of Nature: Ecology, Community, and American Social Thought.* Chicago: University of Chicago Press.

Muller, Hermann. 1973. *Man's Future Birthright: Essays on Science and Humanity.* Albany: State University of New York Press.

Nanney, D. L. 1981. T. M. Sonneborn: an interpretation. *Annual Review of Genetics* 15: 1–9.

Nelkin, Dorothy. 2001. Genetic predisposition and the politics of prediction. In *New Dimensions in Bioethics: Science, Ethics, and the Formulation of Public Policy,* edited by A. W. Galston and E. G. Shurr. Boston: Kluwer Academic Publishers.

Paul, Diane B. 1995. *Controlling Human Heredity, 1865 to the Present.* Atlantic Highlands, NJ: Humanities Press.

_____, and Raphael Falk. 1999. Scientific responsibility in a political context: the case of genetics under the swastika. In *Biology and the Foundation of Ethics: Cambridge Studies in Philosophy and*

Biology, edited by Jane Maienschein and Michael Ruse. Cambridge and New York: Cambridge University Press.

Paulsen, Martina, Sascha Tierling, and Walter Jörn. 2008. DNA Methylation and the mammalian genome. In *Epigenetics,* edited by J. Tost. Norfolk, England: Caister Academic Press.

Pearson, Karl, ed. 1930. *The Life and Letters of Francis Galton,* 4 vols. Cambridge: Cambridge University Press.

Platt, Anthony M., and Cecilia Elizabeth O'Leary. 2006. *Bloodlines: Recovering Hitler's Nuremberg Laws, from Patton's Trophy to Public Memorial.* Boulder, CO: Paradigm Publishers.

Pleins, J. David. 2003. *When the Great Abyss Opened: Classic and Contemporary Readings of Noah's Flood.* Oxford and New York: Oxford University Press.

Reich, David. 2018. How genetics is changing our understanding of race. *New York Times.* 23 Mar.

Reynolds, Peter C. 1993. The complementation theory of language and tool use. In *Tools, Language, and Cognition in Human Evolution,* edited by K. Gibson and T. Ingold. Cambridge: Cambridge University Press.

Richards, Robert J. 2013. *Was Hitler a Darwinian?* Chicago: University of Chicago Press.

Richerson, Peter J., and Robert Boyd. 2005. *Not by Genes Alone: How Culture Transformed Human Evolution.* Chicago: University of Chicago Press.

Robertson, Keith D. 2005. Epigenetic mechanisms of gene regulation: relationship between DNA methylation, histone modification, and chromatin structure. In *DNA Methylation and Cancer Therapy,* edited by M. Szyf. Georgetown, TX, and New York: Landes Bioscience/Eurekah.com ; Kluwer Academic/Plenum.

Rosen, Christine. 2004. *Preaching Eugenics: Religious Leaders and the American Eugenics Movement.* Oxford and New York: Oxford

University Press.

Sandovici, Ionel, Noel H. Smith, Susan E. Ozanne, and Miguel Constancia. 2008. The dynamic epigenome: the impact of the environment on epigenetic regulation of gene expression and developmental programming. In *Epigenetics*, edited by J. Tost. Norfolk, England: Caister Academic Press.

Sapp, Jan. 2003. *Genesis: The Evolution of Biology*. Paperback ed. Oxford and New York: Oxford University Press.

Sayre, Anne. 1975. *Rosalind Franklin and DNA*. New York: Norton.

Silver, Lee. 2002. *Remaking Eden: Cloning and beyond in a Brave New World*. New York: Perennial/Harper-Collins. Hardback edition 1997.

Stent, Gunther S. 1970. DNA. *Daedalus: The Making of Modern Science: Biographical Studies* 99 (4): 909–37.

Stern, Alexandra. 2005. *Eugenic Nation: Faults and Frontiers of Better Breeding in Modern America, American Crossroads*. Berkeley: University of California Press.

Taplin, Jonathan. 2017. *Move Fast and Break Things*. New York: Little, Brown.

Szyf, Moshe, and Michael Meaney. 2008. Epigenetics, behavior, and health. *Allergy, Asthma, and Clinical Immunology* 4 (1): 37–49.

Teixeira, Antonio R. L., et al. 2000. Emerging Chagas disease: trophic network and cycle of transmission of *Trypanosoma cruzi* from palm trees in the Amazon. *Emerging Infectious Diseases* 7 (1).

Thieffrya, Denis, and Sahotra Sarkarb. 1998. Forty years under the Central Dogma. *Trends in Biochemical Sciences* 23 (8): 312–16.

Tomasello, Michael. 2009. *Why We Cooperate*. Cambridge, MA: MIT Press.

Visick, Karen L., and Margaret J. McFall-Ngai. 2000. An exclusive contract: specificity in the *Vibrio fischeri-Euprymna scolopes* partnership. *Journal of Bacteriology* 182 (7): 1779–87.

Ward, Jacob. 2018. The "geno-economists" say DNA can predict our chances of success. *New York Times*, 16 Nov.

Watson, James D. 1965. *Molecular Biology of the Gene*. New York and Amsterdam: W.A. Benjamin.

Weaver, C. G., Michael Meaney, and Moshe Szyf. 2006. Maternal care effects on the hippocampal transcriptome and anxiety-mediated behaviors in the offspring that are reversible in adulthood. *Proceedings of the National Academy of Sciences* 103 (9): 3480–85.

Weaver, Warren. 1970. *Scene of Change: A Lifetime in American Science*. New York: Charles Scribners and Sons.

Weikart, Richard. 2004. *From Darwin to Hitler: Evolutionary Ethics, Eugenics, and Racism in Germany*. New York: Palgrave Macmillan.

Weiss, Sheila Faith. 2010. *The Nazi Symbiosis: Human Genetics and Politics in the Third Reich*. Chicago and London: University of Chicago Press.

Weismann, August. 1902. *The Germ-Plasm Theory of Heredity*. New York: Charles Scribner's Sons.

West-Eberhard, Mary Jane. 2003. *Developmental Plasticity and Evolution*. Oxford and New York: Oxford University Press.

Wilkins, Adam. 2011. Why did the Modern Synthesis give short shrift to "soft inheritance"? In *Transformations of Lamarckism: From Subtle Fluids to Molecular Biology*, edited by Snait Gissis and Eva Jablonka. Cambridge, MA, and London: MIT Press.

Witkowski, J. A., and J. R. Inglis, eds. 2008. *Davenport's Dream: 21st Century Reflections on Heredity and Eugenics, with a Facsimile Edition of Charles Benedict Davenport's Heredity in Relation to Eugenics, 1911*. Cold Spring Harbor, NY: Cold Spring Harbor Laboratory Press.

Young, Robert M. 1985. *Darwin's Metaphor: Nature's Place in Victorian Culture*. Cambridge and New York: Cambridge University Press.

Yu, Zhenbao. 2008. Non-coding RNAs in gene regulation. In *Epigenetics*, edited by J. Tost. Norfolk, England: Caister Academic Press.

Zeigler, H. Philip, and Peter Marler, eds. 2004. *Behavioral Neurobiology of Birdsong, Annals of the New York Academy of Sciences,* vol. 1016. Chapter Six. New York: New York Academy of Sciences.

Chapter Six

Social Darwinism, The Sequel

In the early 1970s, after a long sleep through decades of the New Deal,^G Social Darwinism sat up and rubbed its eyes.[1] It had a new name (sociobiology) and promulgated a new flavor of selection theory, but its basic premise was still genetic determination of social behavior. But unlike the Social Darwinists of more than a century ago, sociobiologists disavow any connection to capitalist economics and imperialism, just as they blame racial hygiene on Nazis. Nonetheless, the underlying capitalist metaphors sometimes slip through. For example, the geneticist William Hamilton, one of the founders of sociobiology, records in his memoirs that:

> There had come the realization that the genome wasn't the monolithic data bank plus executive team devoted to one project—keeping himself alive having babies [*his* babies!]—that I had hitherto imagined it to be. Instead it was beginning to seem more like a company boardroom, a theatre for a power struggle of egotists and factions.[2]

The merger of the genome with the corporate board room was spearheaded by Harvard University biologist E. O. Wilson. He purged Social Darwinism of its overt White supremacy, added two Amazing New Ingredients (inclusive^G fitness and kin^G selection), and repackaged it as "sociobiology—the new synthesis."[3] Then, as the geneticist Richard Lewontin notes, in a rare and perhaps unprecedented undertaking for an academic press, Wilson's book was introduced with "full-page advertisements in the *New York Times*, author-publisher cocktail parties, prepublication reviews and interviews on television, radio and in popular magazines"—all for a book by an expert on ants.[4]

The New Synthesis had little in it that was new. Even though inclusive fitness is a departure from the more conventional definition of genetic fitness, it was not original with Wilson, while the concept of kin selection had been introduced in the 1950s by J. B. S. Haldane. Reciprocal[G] altruism has a long history in social anthropology under the name of reciprocal exchange. All the other key ideas in sociobiology had been introduced a century earlier in Darwin's *The Descent of Man*, such as competition within a species for mates and the biological inheritance of social behavior.[5]

But to my dismay, few in biology seemed to know or care that this purportedly new scientific synthesis reinstated the major premise of Social Darwinism—that society is just a pool of selfish, atomistic individuals competing with one another for control of limited resources, in this case the opportunity to pass on their genes. Indeed, as the anthropologist Marshall Sahlins pointed out at the time, sociobiology is so closely related to the theory of the Chicago School[G] of economics that one can be converted into the other by substituting *utility* for *genetic fitness*.[6]

Significantly, the rebirth of Social Darwinism at Harvard University was exactly contemporaneous with the renaissance of laissez-faire capitalism at the University of Chicago. In a history of neoliberalism[G] written from the perspective of mainstream economics, Jones characterizes the years from 1971 to 1984 as "the neoliberal breakthrough," indicating that Darwinism and capitalist economics are still fellow travelers that complement one another as congruent ideologies.[7]

Within the academy, sociobiology became dogma overnight. Although there were a few dissenting voices, critics never got E. O. Wilson's access to the mass media.[8] For example, when Richard Lewontin, one of Theodosius Dobzhansky's students and a respected geneticist at Harvard University, publicly challenged the concept of genetic determinism, he was heard only on Canadian radio.[9] As Philip J. Darlington, a distinguished biogeographer in the Darwinian tradition, noted in an article in the *Proceedings of the National Academy of Sciences* at that time: "It follows that the current theory of inclusive fitness ... is ... mathematically elegant but with no basis in reality—although I do not like to think what might happen to a Ph.D. candidate who tried to tell his genetics professor so!"[10]

This resurgence of Social Darwinism put me on the wrong side of scientific progress. Since the single most important factor for advancement in any bureaucratic organization is unquestioning commitment to the prevailing system of belief, I doubted there would be much of a future for an evolutionary anthropologist who judged natural selection to be capitalism in disguise. At this juncture, in 1974, Roger Keesing, the son of a respected social anthropologist from New Zealand, offered me a research fellowship in Australia. He was developing an interdisciplinary program at Australian National University on human ethology, which sounded vague enough to be interesting. I accepted, hoping that the antipodes would provide some intellectual perspective and give me time to write my reflections on evolutionary theory, which some lingering sense of obligation still prompted me to do. Although I still loved evolution, I could no longer recognize her face.

Universities in Australia take direction from Oxford and Cambridge, not Harvard and Yale, but distance was not as effective a barrier to American ideology as I had hoped. Even in the outback, Milton Friedman's free-market fetishes reproduced like rabbits. Thus, my first duty in my new position was to attend a symposium on the relevance of sociobiology for social anthropology—as if there were points in common between the two.

Not long before, a copy of *The Selfish Gene* by Richard Dawkins arrived by post from Blackwell's bookshop in England.[11] Written by a British biologist and published by Oxford University Press, it appeared to be an explication of the genetic theory of evolution, but with the exception of a few references to DNA it could have been written decades earlier. There was no treatment of molecular biology, the focus of research since the late fifties, and its facts about evolution had been textbook fodder for more than a generation.

Also, there is a slippery use of language throughout the book that is more characteristic of propaganda than of science. We understand the word *selfish* through everyday human experience and the phrase *selfish gene* by metaphorical extension, yet a segment of a DNA molecule can no more be selfish than it can be musical or frumpy. While the word *selfish* is introduced as a rhetorical device, it is soon employed in other contexts as a real motivation, such as the purported breeding strategies of territorial birds and the relationship of welfare cheats to the commonweal, indicating that the usage is not simply rhetorical but putatively empirical. Yet instead of providing evidence that birds really do genetically strategize and that welfare cheats are genetically motivated, albeit rather daunting tasks scientifically, Dawkins simply assumes that these organisms are carrying out the dictates of the selfish gene. Sociobiological theory is intellectual bait-and-switch: it promises scientific facts but delivers culturally resonant metaphors.

Even Dawkins's purportedly radical innovation—meme theory—was a retread. The idea of culture as a collection of traits to be "explained" by tracing each to its historical prototype, usually to some previous Mediterranean civilization, was the received wisdom in the Victorian era; but it was abandoned by anthropology in the twentieth century because it has no explanatory power.[12] As with cultural diffusion, meme theory does not tell you what sort of content is propagated or under what circumstances, so it amounts to little more than a laundry list of historical connections. In fact, since memes can be recognized only by their propagation, they are tautologous as well. Even though *The Selfish Gene* was glib, self-assured, and seemingly authoritative, I was mystified as to why it was being treated as an intellectual event by otherwise intelligent people.

It is at the margins of empire where the emperor's clothes are most visible, and it was the work of an Australian, David Stove, a professor of philosophy at the University of Sydney, that first clarified for me the attraction of sociobiology. Stove maintains that the work of Dawkins is not to be read as biological science but as "scientized" Calvinism.[13] In *The Selfish Gene* animals are helpless to escape their genetic destiny just as human souls in Calvinist theology can do nothing to facilitate their own salvation. In Dawkins's own words, stated in the first paragraph of the Preface to the first edition of his book: "We are survival machines—robot vehicles blindly programmed to preserve the selfish molecules known as genes."

Just as Darwin's *On the Origin of Species* is a materialist inversion of Paley's natural theology (discussed in Chapter 2), so Dawkins's book *The Selfish Gene* is a religious skeptic's appeal to the latent premises of a secularized Puritan culture. The theological premises are obscured by scientific terminology, which uses genes in place of souls and fitness as the substitute for divine caprice, but its effect is to replace a theology of divine election with a pseudoscience of natural selection.

The Search for Dominance

This refurbished Social Darwinism spilled over into primatology as well. The study of monkeys and apes is historically beholden to Charles Darwin because he studied the facial expressions of primates in a London zoo with the aim of establishing behavioral continuity with humans. Also, it was his theory of evolution that made apes into putative ancestors, an idea that inspired much of the early research into nonhuman primates. But the primatological renaissance that emerged in the 1960s was largely an empirical discipline that owed little to Darwinian theory per se, relying on the systematic observation of the activities of nonhuman primates in their natural habitat for months at a time, with the goal of gathering accurate information about a species' way of life.

However, by the early 1970s, the field observations of primatologists were being increasingly viewed through the lens of Darwinian theory. For example, at Gombe Stream Reserve in East Africa, where Jane Goodall had begun her field research, the population of feral chimpanzees that she had described in the 1960s as peaceful frugivores had been transformed by the 1980s into "Machiavellian" "hunters" who were "waging war" on other groups of chimps.[14] Observations from other chimpanzee field sites as well indicated a much higher level of hunting, violence, and status seeking than had initially been observed. Indeed, chimpanzees in their natural habitat were beginning to conform to the stereotype long held by zoo keepers, namely, that chimps are cunning, mercurial animals given to outbursts of violence.

However, early in the history of primatology, psychologist Robert Yerkes provided some insight into why zoo-housed chimpanzees might behave the way they do:

> For a study of auditory acuity, James H. Elder, in the
> then current [mid-1930s] tradition of the laborato-
> ries, attempted to place his subjects [chimpanzees] in

a specially constructed restraint chair, on the design
of which Henry W. Nissen [the experimenter] and
the writer [Yerkes] had spent considerable time. The
animals objected strenuously, and their adaptation to
this apparatus was so slow and uncertain that the experimenter finally decided to try treating them as he
would human subjects, by seating them in a chair before the response key, placing the stimulus-delivering
earphones on the head, and proceeding with the rou-
tine of experimentation. Success was almost immediate, and the restraint chair was never again used in
the investigation. This experience naturally gave Dr.
Elder confidence in the ability of the chimpanzee to
understand the requirements of the experiment also
in its readiness to cooperate with him under reasonably favorable conditions.[15]

Significantly, "reasonably favorable conditions" had been
steadily eroding at Gombe Stream Reserve since Goodall began
her research there, as the surrounding forest was logged to make
farmland. This situation, combined with provisioning of the animals and daily disturbance by troops of human observers, made
the life of these "wild" chimpanzees more like those in a zoo.
Indeed, in 1964, when Goodall began feeding bananas to the
chimpanzees at Gombe she noted the changes in their behavior:

The constant feeding was having a marked effect on
the behavior of the chimps. They were beginning to
move about in large groups more often than they had
ever done in the old days. They were sleeping near
camp and arriving in noisy hordes early in the morning. Worst of all, the adult males were becoming increasingly aggressive.[16]

Yet instead of asking what had happened to the social environment and habitat of African apes to make their aggressive side easier to elicit and what considerations had prompted the observations farther afield that documented instances of simian murder, sociobiologists concluded that science had finally discovered what chimpanzees are *really* like. Dispensing with any pretense to scientific objectivity, a professor at Harvard University dubbed chimpanzees *demonic males*![17]

This characterization of primates as aggressive, competitive animals with a penchant to fight over food and mates was a throwback to the science of the 1930s. For much of the twentieth century, science taught that the societies of monkeys and apes are organized around dominance[G] hierarchies in which one high-ranking male aggressively takes the food and monopolizes sexually receptive females, as in a caveman cartoon.[18] As luck would have it, there really is a species of primate where a single male, huge and hairy, maintains a group of females for exclusive sexual access by chasing them back into the center of the troop whenever they stray too far from him. This species is *Papio hamadrayas*, the hamadryas baboon from Ethiopia—the species chosen in the early 1930s for the first intensive scientific study of a nonhuman primate society, using a zoo-housed troop in England.[19]

However, in the 1960s, field research in Africa subsequently showed that hamadryas behavior is atypical even for baboons, while the complexity of its social organization is not observable in captivity.[20] In its natural habitat, the "harems" of hamadryas society are not isolated units but are part of a larger society in which male/female units are combined into several levels of social aggregation, so the harem is not the primary unit of social life as was initially thought. In fact, because of this change in perspective, the word harem is no longer used in descriptions of this species. In effect, hamadryas are like other baboon species in that they live in a troop containing multiple breeding adult males and breeding adult females—though they differ from other species of *Papio* in that exclusive mating and prolonged male-female relationships are embedded within this larger social structure.

Also, long-term studies of hamadryas in their natural habitat show that troop males do not fight with other males or poach the mates of another, as the cave man model would predict. Instead, a young adult male separates an immature but weaned female from her mother, prevents the child from returning, and then assumes a protective, motherly role toward the young female until she becomes sexually mature, at which time she becomes his mate. Alternatively, a young adult male may follow an established group until its resident male dies, thus inheriting the adult females. Yet the view of nonhuman primate society as a "harem" of females controlled by a single "dominant male" shaped the scientific understanding of monkeys and apes for a generation.

Psychologists even devised a way of "objectively" measuring dominance in primates, namely, the pair test.[21] They would put a pair of monkeys together—usually rhesus monkeys, the species most commonly used in laboratory research—and then put a peanut between them: the one who grabbed the peanut most often was judged to be the "dominant" animal. But when scientists began to study rhesus monkeys in naturalistic social groups in their native habitats, they found that competition for food was not much in evidence.

Although rhesus monkeys are highly competitive and aggressive in both captivity and the wild, in their natural habitat they forage alone in social proximity, so they are unlikely to be competing for the same peanut. If one throws a handful of peanuts into a cage of rhesus monkeys, each animal grabs the peanut nearest to it, and little or no aggression is seen. If one puts a bowl of peanuts into the cage, there is no aggression either: the alpha[G] male will station himself next to it until he eats his fill.

However, the other high-ranking animals soon approach and sit down next to him, making appropriate appeasement gestures as they wait for a chance to reach into the bowl. Meanwhile, as the dominant male gets sated, the low-ranking animals sneak in, grab a handful, and run off. Certainly, social rank is much in evidence in this situation, but there is no aggressive control of resources. Significantly, in times of chronic food shortage, such as famine, a situation in which dominance theory would lead one to expect fighting over food, experiments show that free-ranging rhesus monkeys become *less* aggressive rather than more, because they concentrate on foraging while reducing social activities to a minimum.[22]

Also, the more that primatologists studied status interactions in nonhuman primates, the more apparent it became that rank or status is more frequently expressed through gesture, vocalization, and whole-body movements than by biting and attack. In rhesus monkeys, for example, the typical status interactions consist of threat displays (such as a stare directed at the subordinate animal), submissive gestures (avoiding eye contact with the dominant or moving away), and affiliative behavior (such as grooming). Physical aggression sometimes occurs, but it is normally restricted to situations that can potentially alter the social rank of the protagonists, such as an encounter between individuals who are strangers to one other or when a subordinate attempts to rise in the hierarchy by challenging a superior.

Darwinian theories of dominance and sexual selection predict that the most intimidating and aggressive individual will get the most rewards, especially monopolization of receptive females by aggressive males; but studies of free-ranging primates indicate that their normal social life is far more complicated than dominance theory would predict. Certainly there are primate species, such as the hamadryas baboon, that approximate winner-take-all in the arena of sex. But even species closely related to hamadryas, such as the olive baboon, do not live in "harems" but rather in large, permanent social groups where both males and females have multiple sexual partners.

However, there are many species of primates in which the basic social unit consists of a single breeding male and multiple breeding females (the unimale troop), and this type of society best exemplifies the Darwinian thesis of male monopolization of females and male-to-male competition for mates. In unimale troops, the resident male must defend against unmated males who attempt to usurp his position. If defeated, the resident male leaves the troop, and the incoming male mates with the females. In many cases, the incoming male attacks and kills the infants in the troop as well.[23] However, in primates that live in communities containing multiple breeding adults of both sexes, such as macaques, chimpanzees, and most species of baboons, the relationship among social rank, aggression, and sexual access is far harder to interpret.

Robert Sapolsky undertook a field study of baboons in Africa to measure the reproductive success of high-ranking males, even capturing adult males to take blood samples and measure hormone levels. As is normally the case with mammals, non-human primate females have a periodic state of physiologically-controlled sexual receptivity called estrus.[G] In some species, such as baboons and chimpanzees, it is marked by changes in appearance such as swelling of the genitalia and reddening of the skin. Sapolsky found that the average female baboon mated with five or six males in one estrus period but that higher status gives males an edge: the alpha male mated with her at the time of maximal fertility.[24] However, in Strum's study of savannah baboons, a male's copulatory success was not predicted by his social rank at all but by the length of time he had lived in the troop: residents of two to five years did best, whereas males who had cultivated friendships with females did even better.[25]

In primate species that live in groups with multiple breeding adults of both sexes, an ardent male and a sexually receptive female will often separate themselves from the group to spend time alone together, what primatologists call a consort pair. Strum discovered that sometimes male baboons do try to displace the guy with the gal, resulting in what are called consort turnovers, but the outcome is not simply a function of aggressiveness. Rather, in Strum's words, "older males employ a variety of tactics in competition over oestrous females. They try very hard to avoid aggression by diverting it, seeking out coalitions with male allies, using infants and female friends as agonistic buffers and other social manipulations."[26] In a study of the mating behavior of chimpanzees at Gombe Stream Reserve, Caroline Tutin found that opportunistic, noncompetitive mating with multiple sexual partners produces most of the copulations (72%) but that consort pairs produce most of the pregnancies.[27]

High-ranking primates living in multimale groups do generally receive more social grooming, have greater choice of sexual partners (especially at the time of maximal fertility), and get priority at a concentrated food resource; but these individuals are not necessarily the most aggressive animals in the troop when measured by bites, threats, and chases. Long-term studies of free-ranging macaque troops show that social rank in these species is strongly influenced by an individual's genealogical relationship to others in the troop and is maintained by coalitions of multiple individuals, a phenomenon well documented in both rhesus (*Macaca mulatta*) and Japanese macaques (*Macaca fuscata*).[28]

Since social rank cannot be reduced to the level of aggressiveness of the individuals involved, while its social functions go far beyond what the hypothesis of monopolization of resources would lead one to expect, primatologists abandoned the term "dominance hierarchy" entirely, replacing it with *social rank* or *status hierarchy* to better convey the importance of psychosocial processes that are distinct from the aggressive control of material goods.[29] Also, as more species of nonhuman primates were studied, it became apparent that primate social organization is highly diverse, varying even among closely related species,[30] or even within a species,[31] and systems of rank are not universal. Status hierarchies are characteristic of nonhuman primate species in which multiple breeding males live in the same community with sexually mature females, as with macaques, chimpanzees, and baboons.[32] Thus, status hierarchies are behaviorally distinct from dominance hierarchies, even though they have some attributes in common; and both may coexist in the same society.

A half century ago, the primatologist M.R.A. Chance suggested that status hierarchies in primates be called *attention structures* because high-ranking individuals are constantly being monitored by all the other animals in the troop, who notice what they do and where they go, whereas the alpha animals themselves are free to ignore the others and go where they please.[33] Human observers are susceptible to the same attention biases, and the first field studies of primates focused on high-ranking males almost to the exclusion of everyone else.[34] This source of bias has been corrected by randomized observation intervals, but the finding that high-ranking animals are very attention-getting to other monkeys as well as to humans has stood the test of time.

Yet Darwinian theory has never come to terms with the difference between social status and dominance. It is possible for humans to admire someone else of the same sex, imitate that person's behavior, and seek out that person's company without the prestigious individual physically attacking them and taking what they have. In fact, in humans, and to some extent among chimpanzees, high-status individuals often *give* goods to their admirers instead of taking them away.

At the same time, the concept of a status hierarchy is not simply a projection of the concerns of rank-obsessed humans on to socially egalitarian monkeys, nor is it a consequence of captivity. Status-based interactions are scientific facts, which is to say they have been recorded by multiple observers using objective sampling procedures in a variety of habitats and settings over five decades, among animals living in the wild as well as in those in captivity. The reality of social rank is further confirmed by the fact that these same methods of observation reveal that many species of nonhuman primates do not form status hierarchies at all.

The Social Reality of Rank

In a book on baboons, the authors Cheney and Seyfarth begin with a disclaimer: "Baboons are a politically incorrect species."[35] In fact, the ranking systems of nonhuman primate species are bound to offend social theorists of left, right, and center. They will be disliked by materialists who think that the social dimension of life is measured by the number of calories consumed; by biologists who think it is determined by genes; by Marxists who attribute disparities in social rank to private ownership of the means of production; by capitalists who think that wealth naturally accumulates in the hands of the few who most deserve it; and by authoritarians who think that the violent monopolization of resources is justified by our primate past.

My knowledge of primate status hierarchies is based to a large extent on observations during a three-year period of a troop of rhesus macaques housed in an outdoor cage at Stanford University.[36] Rhesus monkeys (*Macaca mulatta*) have dark eyes, bare faces, a tail shorter than their legs, and yellowish-brown fur on top fading to gray and beige below. When mature, the males are about the size of a medium-sized dog, whereas females are a little smaller.[37] Native to the Indian subcontinent, they are a highly adaptable species, stealing crops from farmers and successfully colonizing big cities. They are active, highly social animals that usually forage on the ground, walking on all fours, although they are excellent climbers as well. Usually they sleep in high, inaccessible places, such as a rooftop or a tall tree. The babies are usually born one at a time and ride upside down on their mother's stomach, clasping the fur with all four limbs. Later, when the babies grow larger, they ride on top of their mothers until they are able to keep up with adults on their own.

Rhesus monkeys live in large aggregations of dozens of animals, all of which normally move and sleep as a spatially coherent unit, what primatologists have traditionally called the troop; but within this spatially coherent population there are subgroups organized around kinship, play, friendship, preferred sex partners, and political alliances.[38] The males leave the natal troop after they become socially mature (around four years of age) and migrate to neighboring troops, whereas the females remain in their natal troop for life, forming family groups consisting of multiple generations of individuals descended from the same female, what are called matrilines[G] (not to be confused with the matrilineages[G] of cultural anthropology). In addition, each troop contains adult males who have moved in from somewhere else.

As is typical of mammals, rhesus females have periodic sexual receptivity, an estrus period that occurs only when they are not pregnant. In the rhesus, a female's sexual readiness is indicated by the appearance of red skin in the perineal area and often on the face. During her sexually receptive period, a single female may have sex with multiple males, and they initiate it by standing on all fours and presenting their red rumps as inducements. Male rhesus do not fight over mates, although they fight other males for status in the male hierarchy.

After watching rhesus social interactions for a few weeks, a human observer begins to notice a pattern in the chases and approaches that can be summarized by the concept of a status hierarchy or rank order, a system in which each individual stands in a social position above or below that of others. The positions are most obvious at the top and bottom, whereas intermediate ranks are often more changeable and contextual. But, generally speaking, there is an alpha male recognized by the way other animals treat him: they defer to him and strive to be associated with him. There is usually an alpha female as well, who has social precedence over other troop members except adult males.

Rhesus are very status oriented, engaging in frequent social interactions that reaffirm the relative rank of individuals, such as averting one's eyes to indicate subordinate status or staring at another to indicate social superiority. Fights do happen, especially among monkeys of roughly equivalent rank, but even these are usually more vocal than violent, with a lot of screaming and chasing. They sound worse than they are. The most common way of expressing social rank among rhesus is by social communication, such as vocalization, body language, and facial expression, not by violence. However, when a subordinate animal is challenging the status of a higher-ranking one, or when strangers are put together in a cage for the first time, violent fights do occur, resulting in nasty wounds and sometimes death.

Normally in macaques one's social rank is inherited from one's mother.[39] That is to say, all members of one's matriline (children descended from the same female) are subordinate to individuals that their mother is subordinate to while outranking those individuals that their mother outranks. In the course of social interactions with other members of the troop, young animals learn that their mothers will back them up in squabbles with other juveniles if she outranks the mother of the latter. Otherwise, a young monkey will lose, especially if higher-ranking allies of the targeted individual also join the fray. Because rank is socially inherited, de facto if not by statute, it is not innate, but neither is it changeable by individuals who remain in their natal troop. Rather, it is what sociologists call an ascribed^G status, that is one that is imposed by society that an individual is powerless to change, such as exconvict or Dalai Lama. But when male rhesus monkeys leave their natal troop, which is normally the case, they leave their natal rank behind and need to achieve their status in their new troop. For this reason, social status among rhesus is ascribed in females and immature males but achieved^G in mature males.

There is, however, an exception to this rule: a female can rise above her birth rank (or fall below it) when the matriline to which she belongs changes rank relative to others. In one troop of rhesus housed in a large outdoor cage, primatologists documented four rank reversals of the highest-ranking matriline over a seven-year period.[40] In these instances, females from lower-ranking matrilines joined forces to attack the adult and adolescent females of the highest-ranking matriline, which fell to the bottom of the hierarchy, while the second-ranking matriline usually advanced to the first position. In these status disputes among matrilines, violence does occur, with females inflicting potentially deadly wounds on each other. The adult males had little effect on these events; in one case when the alpha male tried to intervene, the females in the troop ignored him. Nor did those adolescent males still resident in their natal matrilines try to help their female relatives.

Even though females inherit their social rank from their matriline whereas adult males achieve it after joining a new troop, this situation does not indicate an innate difference between the sexes, as genetic determinists might think. If one forms a rhesus social group in captivity by introducing a number of monkeys of both sexes who do not know one another into the same cage at the same time, there will instantly be an enormous donnybrook, with blood-curdling vocalizations and often physical attacks; and both males and females will participate.[41] Within an hour or two, the aggression will abate, to be succeeded by a stable hierarchy that will endure for months or years. The next day, animals will be quietly grooming one another and jockeying for position with individuals of high rank. In a week or two, any chewed ears and raw tails will heal, and the babies born in the next birth cohort will inherit the social position of their mothers, never suspecting that their mothers had achieved it. It is this process of social rank communicatively conveyed that is normal in rhesus, not the violent formation of hierarchies by means of a Hobbesian[G] war of each against all, which is a laboratory artifact.

Contrary to the American belief in rugged individualism, whereby one's social position is said to be a measure of one's talent, perseverance, and competitive spirit, among rhesus monkeys fortuitous circumstances can make a big difference in the rank that an individual ultimately achieves. In one experiment, female rhesus monkeys from different troops who had approximately the same social rank (that is, they were from middle-ranking matrilines) and who did not know one another were introduced into a new cage one at a time, with twenty-four hours elapsing between each introduction. As each monkey was introduced, those who were already there attacked it, as previous experiments would lead one to predict. In this experimental situation, the order of introduction to the group, *which is arbitrarily chosen by the experimenter,* is a big predictor of future rank, accounting for 43 percent of the variance in one case.[42] So, while rhesus social hierarchy allows for some individual achievement, it also presents social situations beyond an individual's control.

At the same time, experimental troop formation tells us that social hierarchy is the default social organization in this species because it is formed by normally socialized monkeys who have never met one another before. But this social organization, although natural in the sense that it forms without special effort, is not innate, as genetic determinists might think, because it re-

quires normal socialization, which in turn requires social interaction with other normal monkeys. The need for social interaction is confirmed by raising rhesus monkeys in social isolation.[43]
Socially deprived rhesus have so little control over their fear and
aggression that they curl up into terrified balls when confronted by a stronger animal, and they violently attack weaker ones,
precluding the possibility of a status hierarchy of any kind, much
less one conveyed by gesture, vocalization, and facial expression.
Socialization enables aggressive animals such as rhesus monkeys
to live together in society by minimizing violent encounters and
replacing them with the social communication of status differences.

In primates, even innate motivational systems such as aggression and fear, far from expressing themselves in a highly stereo-
typed manner, develop normally only through frequent social interaction with other group members. Moreover, in humans, they
develop in a cultural context. As a consequence of such socialization, aggression and fear in primates are exquisitely nuanced
forms of behavior: aggression in a socialized individual can range
from a raised eyebrow to a slash with one's canines; fear can
range from a furtive sideways glance to a sprint to the treetops.
Furthermore, in primates, the aggregate expression of aggression
and fear defines the boundaries of altruism: who can be abused
and who cannot, who is to be ignored and who is to be attended
to. Yet Darwinists continue to mine the data of primatology for
confirmation of dominance, competition, and aggression while
ignoring the social contexts in which these behavioral proclivities
are normally channeled, inhibited, and expressed. Sociobiology,
for example, explains away infant killing by adult males as a male
"reproductive strategy," whereas a primatology informed by social
theory would study it as an animal model of domestic violence.[44]

Status Hierarchy vs. Dominance Hierarchy

In Victorian social theory, social hierarchy functions to allocate material resources, such as food and territory; but rhesus monkeys have conspicuous social hierarchies by both sexes yet almost no allocation of material goods. Except for nursing infants, individual rhesus monkeys forage on their own within a troop that moves as a unit, and each animal eats whatever food it finds or stuffs it into its cheek pouches for consumption later. Mothers do not even feed babies except by nursing. Although rhesus monkeys resemble the atomistic individuals of classical economics, they differ from humans in that they have no inclination to truck, barter, or exchange one thing for another. In fact, unless one defines an economy as feeding oneself on a daily basis, then these animals have no material economy at all—yet they do have a system of hierarchical social status.

Because rhesus monkeys have prominent status systems but no exchange of material goods, then social hierarchy does not develop from the monopolization of material resources as Victorian theorists assumed. Conversely, in a hierarchical species, social equality cannot be achieved by simply providing enough food to go around. In captivity, where rhesus receive ample food on a daily basis, there is no diminution of status-related activity. To the contrary, it increases, probably because the monkeys have more time to get into squabbles and fewer opportunities to get away.

Interpersonal hierarchy emerges in the face-to-face interactions of primates behaving aggressively or submissively. These social processes function in a similar way in the face-to-face groups of both rhesus monkeys and humans. Yet contrary to what economic conservatives have argued for centuries, interpersonal social hierarchies are not intrinsically linked to the control and distribution of material goods because they are present in species that have no economy at all in a human sense of that term.

Perhaps dominance requires *scarce* resources? For the first half of the twentieth century science taught that all nonhuman primates are vegetarians, but by the 1960s it became apparent that many species of monkeys and apes occasionally kill and eat vertebrates, while some monkey species are primarily insectivorous.[45] Also, field studies in Africa provided well-documented instances of hunting by the best-known species of chimpanzees (*Pan troglodytes*), usually involving the killing of immature red colobus monkeys (*Colobus badius*), which share the same habitat.[46] The hunting of small animals is now known to be a common activity of chimpanzees, observed at field sites in both East and West Africa, although research confirms that plants form the bulk of the chimpanzee diet. As with rhesus monkeys, chimpanzees forage as individuals; but when hunting, several adult males usually chase prey together (although the extent to which this is true cooperation, in which the chimps perform complementary roles, as opposed to parallel[G] activity is still controversial).[47]

Male chimpanzees, like male rhesus, form linear status hierarchies—that is, the alpha individual outranks the beta who outranks the gamma, and so on. But female chimps, unlike female rhesus, do not form hierarchies in the wild, although they do so in zoos.[48] However, when male chimpanzees kill other species of animals, such as juvenile colobus monkeys (their favorite prey), they do not always eat all the meat themselves. Sometimes, they allow other chimpanzees to take some of the kill, or they give portions of it away to male companions, favored females, and females in estrus.

Chimpanzees are unique among nonhuman primates because they not only hunt in a group but share some of the meat with others, giving this species a transitional status between the self-sufficient foraging of monkeys and the economic activity of human beings. At the same time, the subsistence economy of chimpanzees, because it is based on individualistic foraging of plant food, is not part of this hierarchical system of distribution. Rather, it is as if two different economies coexisted: the subsistence base, which is done by individuals foraging for themselves, and the status-based distribution of meat by males.

A Dominance Model of Early Human Society

Sociobiologist Craig B. Stanford, who studied the hunting of colobus monkeys by chimpanzees (*Pan troglodytes*) in Africa, developed a model of human evolution in which a male-dominated political system evolves from the meat exchange of chimpanzees.[49] The theory is pertinent because it is representative of the science of human origins: it is written by a well-known primatologist who is a tenured professor at a major university and is published by Harvard University Press, so it can be taken as scientifically respectable. At the same time, it is a good example of how scientific facts become incorporated into an ideological framework supportive of a particular system of power without politics ever being mentioned.

The facts are not in dispute. There are two extant species of chimpanzees in Africa, *Pan troglodytes* (the common chimp) and *Pan paniscus* (the bonobo), but only *troglodytes* provides good examples of violence and competition, so it is the one that figures prominently in sociobiological texts, even though humans are equally related genetically to both.[50] Unlike macaques and baboons, chimpanzees do not live in cohesive troops that forage as a unit but have what is called a *fission/fusion* society. That is, individuals live in a community whose members know one another; but instead of always traveling and foraging together as monkeys usually do, chimpanzees will associate with others in a small group for some period of time and then leave to form new groups with other members of the same community.

Unlike male rhesus, who must leave the troop to find mates, male *Pan troglodytes* remain in their natal community, where they gradually rise in a male-only status hierarchy. In this species, hunting is common and is usually done only by males. For this reason, in *troglodytes* high-ranking males usually control the meat of any animals that are killed. Also, aggressive encounters with neighboring communities are common, and strangers are often killed or wounded. *Pan paniscus*, on the other hand, does not live in societies with exclusively all-male hierarchies; the males have much less interest in hunting; and there is not one documented instance of fatal violence in this species. Also, bonobo females frequently have sex with other females, which is another characteristic that makes them unique among monkeys and apes.

Stanford specifically states that he will ignore bonobos (*Pan paniscus*), because they do less hunting and the meat is often controlled by females.[51] Even worse, bonobo females have been observed "to take meat from males with impunity," behavior that would be "unimaginable in chimpanzees." Since he already knows where science should end up, he chooses the primate species that will get him there by the most direct route. In a revealing passage he tells us that chimpanzees do not hunt to increase their protein supply, as he originally thought, since they spend hours chasing down troops of colobus monkeys for a 1-kilogram baby when they could get far more protein by eating palm nuts, which they could gather for a fraction of the time and effort.[52]

Stanford discusses various explanations, looks favorably on the status display hypothesis (men hunt to show their hunting prowess to women), and then comes down on the side of a dominance model. Even though the meat "may not be objectively worth its value" when measured in calories or fat, it can function in a dynamic of exchange and power provided that "the resource is accorded high status by both possessor and potential recipients."[53]

Any anthropologist would agree that the exchange value of objects is psychosocial and has nothing to do with their "objective" worth as computed in calories, but there is a serious problem when a biological reductionist thinks this. Once one admits that the exchange value of meat is not materially determined by its protein content but by the demand for it, then one has exited biology and entered the social sciences. At the same time, by focusing on the psychosocial exchange value of meat, as Stanford does, one is in effect ignoring all the other psychosocial rewards, such as grooming and attention, which are common not only to chimpanzees but to all other species of monkeys and apes as well.

Nonhuman primates do not exchange material goods (except for the chimpanzees just mentioned and some South American monkeys discussed in this chapter), but their status hierarchies are very much involved in the distribution of *psychosocial* rewards such as social attention and grooming. Grooming, a form of social behavior found in almost all nonhuman primate species, is often misunderstood by casual observers, who think the animals are "looking for lice." But in terms of its social function grooming is more like getting a massage.

When I managed colonies of macaque monkeys, I would let them know I had no bad intentions by sticking my bare arm through the bars and letting it hang motionless (caution: professional stuntperson —do not try this at your local zoo!). Before long, a juvenile would come up and begin grooming me, rubbing my skin with deft, alternating strokes of its fingers. It was always a juvenile, which shows where I ranked. Adult male rhesus do not groom one another, and the adult females were too busy grooming each other and important adult males to groom me. Grooming is a reward because it feels good to the recipient while inducing a relaxing state of body and mind, as has been shown experimentally by physiologists. The groomer gets additional psychosocial rewards as well, such as access to a VIP (very important primate) or reciprocation by the recipient. In rhesus, up to 20 percent of waking life can be spent in social grooming.

Status hierarchies in primates distribute psychosocial punishments as well as rewards: actions that hurt feelings and leave scars, both physical and psychological, such as scapegoating, social peripheralization, insufficient grooming, furtive sex, chronic stress, and reduced immune function.[54] And when the available food is insufficient and concentrated in one small space, which is sometimes the effect of human intervention, the lowest-ranking individuals can suffer malnutrition too.

A social hierarchy that distributes goods and services to high-ranking males, giving them sexual access to nubile wenches while keeping low-ranking individuals away from bananas, is not a theoretical problem for Darwinism. Darwin is for Darwinners. However, a social hierarchy that distributes psychosocial rewards and punishments while failing to monopolize physical resources is theoretically unsettling.

The major ideological role of Darwinian theory is to demonstrate the material basis of social life. So from an ideological perspective, apes and monkeys *ought* to compete to ensure that the material goods essential for life concentrate at the top of the pyramid—yet they don't. A hierarchy that distributes social rewards and punishments while everyone gets enough to eat is an implicit critique of the naturalness of the class system, and it undercuts the widely held belief that hierarchical control of *material* resources is a biological fact of life rooted in our primate past.

Sociobiology interprets meat sharing by chimpanzees as a stage in the development of human society, but there is an alternative interpretation that focuses on the widespread distribution of psychosocial rewards in primate societies. In the latter analysis, the unusual carnal economy of chimpanzees reflects the unusual level of object-using skills in this species. Where monkeys use their hands to groom one another, chimpanzees can use objects held in the hand as a substitute for the hand itself, as when they use a stick to reach a banana. Primatologists have also documented young chimpanzees using leaves to groom others.

Even when no physical exchange of objects is involved, the physical movements needed in social grooming use the same parts of the brain that are involved in other types of object manipulation, as when peeling fruit and opening nuts: namely, voluntary motor control, dexterous finger movements, visually guided reaching, and tactile feedback. Also, neurological research shows that in rhesus monkeys the same part of the cerebral cortex is active when employing a joy stick to guide a robot arm as when reaching with their own arms. So it is not a stretch to imagine that as object-manipulation skills become socially more complex, as when handing something to someone else, they get plugged into the preexisting grooming network as supplemental psychosocial rewards.[55] In other words, meat exchange is not a new system that emerges first in chimpanzees but a more objectified use of a preexisting psychosocial exchange system found in all monkeys and apes.

If the distribution of desirable material objects conforms to the social dynamics of psychosocial rewards such as grooming, then control of material goods has no special explanatory role for human social organization, nor can red meat be singled out as a unique historical force. I suggest a simple thought experiment: if rhesus monkeys had the chimpanzee's ability to exchange material objects for social rewards, one would predict that desired material goods such as Purina Monkey Chow would follow the same pathways as grooming does now. Female monkeys would pass Monkey Chow to related females and juveniles within their own matriline, and from there it would work its way upward to unrelated high-ranking females. There would also be some mutual feeding of Monkey Chow by sexually consorting male-female pairs, while high-ranking males would receive a disproportionate share from high-ranking females.

Bear in mind that this thought experiment postulates rhesus monkeys with chimp-like abilities to use food instrumentally, whereas a normal rhesus would try to keep all the Purina Monkey Chow for itself, just like a Social Darwinist. But by assuming that the sharing of meat is independent of other shared activities such as grooming (that is to say independent of the extant psychosocial reward economy), Stanford can make hunting, meat, and the all-male hierarchy into the primary forces in human social evolution at the expense of gathering, vegetables, and the family.

Stanford warns the reader against being "excessively swayed" by modern notions of gender equality (thereby conflating a social ideal with the scientific study of cause and effect) while asserting that males and females value meat for different reasons: males hunt because they need meat for "tactical socializing," whereas females value it for "its amino acids while they are gestating or lactating."[56] Apparently, the wheedling female brain is still fixated on protein content, whereas the adult male brain, like the brain of Stanford himself, has moved on to psychosocial exchange value. Not surprisingly, he contends that this physiological dependency in females leads to the evolution of sex differences in the social brain, which explains the "near-universality of patriarchy"[G] in modern humans.

But, significantly, this thesis does not explain why females should become dependent on the amino acids they get from male-dominated meat instead of from vegetable sources they can get themselves, such as nuts. Nor does it consider the possibility that females might be capable of producing items of high exchange value that set males panting with desire. For example, termite fishing and dipping for ants are more frequent in female chimpanzees, while in West Africa, females are more adept than males at cracking the harder varieties of nuts with hammer stones.[57]

To a cultural anthropologist, Stanford's putative sex difference in the brain is nothing more than a conversion of prescientific cultural categories into conjectural neuroscience. By interpreting chimpanzee society as patriarchy, Stanford deflects our attention from the one theoretically relevant conclusion implicit in the chimpanzee data he presents. Patriarchy is a class society in which legal authority is vested in adult males, but chimpanzees have a lot to learn on this score. Although it is true that chimps may kill foreign females and their infants, they also try to kill foreign adult males as well, being gender-blind in their xenophobia, whereas the power they exercise over females within the community is rather limited. They do not restrict a female's sexual access to other males, do not limit her geographical mobility, do not make her work at a menial job for less pay, or insist on controlling the TV remote. The reference to patriarchy deflects our attention from the fact that high-ranking chimpanzees do not just *monopolize* meat as Darwinian dominance theory predicts but *redistribute* it to other chimpanzees in exchange for their political support. That's not patriarchy— that's cronyism!

I have singled out Stanford's article because it is such a concise illustration of the sociobiological mind at work, not because it falls below the intellectual standards of the field in which he works. In virtually all of this literature, authors cherry-pick primatological facts to fit their preconceptions, merge them with hypothetical genes and conjectural selection pressures, fold in some unexamined cultural premises, add a dash of putative instinct, and then feed this fallacious mix to biologically uninformed audiences as purportedly scientific descriptions of human origins and behavior.

In forcing the facts of human evolution into the Procrustean bed of Darwinian ideology, primatologists have foreclosed the possibility of making real contributions to social theory. One theoretical possibility, for example, is that nonhuman primates, in spite of foraging alone, really do have "property." All species of nonhuman primates live in core areas to which a group has exclusive or consistent access, while rhesus monkey troops are hierarchically ranked, displacing one another in areas of home range overlap. A number of primate species aggressively defend territorial boundaries. Male chimpanzees of the species *troglodytes* provide one of the most dramatic examples of the defense of the group's range, even killing individuals from adjacent communities, whether male or female, who wander into their territory.[58]

Not so long ago, such facts would have been published in the popular press as prima facie evidence for the naturalness of ethnic boundaries, with a call for legislation to keep out immigrants; but today's imperialism is global and financial, which requires the repudiation of "natural" boundaries of any kind, especially aggressive defense of traditional homelands by assertive locals. Yet if one argues that a group's home range is its "property," this is tantamount to saying that nonhuman primates have collective "ownership" of the material resources needed to sustain life — that pesky socialism again!

Chimpanzees now dominate the discussion of human origins, because genetic research has shown that humans are more closely related to this genus of simians than to other species of apes, such as the gorilla; but *Pan troglodytes* has emerged as the first among equals because only this species combines an all-male hierarchy, collective aggression, and political control of material resources into a single functioning system. The other species of chimpanzee, *Pan paniscus*, which is more inclined to make love than war, is perennially sidelined in Darwinian literature, even though human beings are as closely related genetically to *paniscus* as to *troglodytes*. But it is the troglodytes, or "cave dwellers," that best reflect the values of corporate capitalism.

The Hunting Hypothesis

Stanford's model has much in common with what has become known as the hunting hypothesis, which was advocated by Sherwood Washburn and his colleagues at the University of California at Berkeley in the 1960s.[59] This hypothesis identifies male hunting as the stimulus that moved bipedal apes in a more sapient direction. According to this formulation, once upon a time—the late Pliocene[G] to be exact—climate change reduced the forest cover, necessitating a shift in diet from vegetables to meat. The need to pursue prey put a premium on intelligence, which selected for increased brain size. Big heads, however, required females to give birth to babies at an earlier stage of development, resulting in babies that needed more care and mothers who were less mobile. This conflict was resolved by more restrictive mating—the prototype of marriage—that gave males incentive to feed females, because they had confidence in the paternity of the children produced by their consorts.

An underlying premise of the hunting hypothesis is that males strive to propagate their genes at the expense of other males: hence the emphasis on restrictive mating—a premise that reappeared a few years later as a cornerstone of sociobiology. This interrelationship among hunting, sharing, male-female social bonding, identification of paternity, and the establishment of a home base in turn selected for males who were willing to assume a more economic role in society by providing meat to females and their offspring, thus producing the nuclear family as we know it. This theory was also given an archeological interpretation in the 1970s by Glynn Isaac, a colleague of Washburn at Berkeley.[60]

Being a product of the Berkeley anthropology department, I taught the hunting hypothesis in my maiden voyage as instructor of physical[G] anthropology in the 1960s; but it has not stood up well to the feminist critique or to anthropological fieldwork.[61] However, it did initiate considerable theoretical interest in extant human foraging societies, an endeavor that bore ethnographic fruit. In the 1960s, field research among the !Kung San ("Bushmen") in the Kalahari Desert of Africa by two separate research teams demonstrated the primacy of vegetable foods gathered by women in a society that lives by "male hunting."[62] Also, contrary to what the theory of inclusive fitness predicts, this research underscored the fact that among the !Kung meat is shared by everyone within the local band,[G] irrespective of the degree of genetic relationship with the hunter.

Since that time, there have been many subsequent studies in a variety of extant gathering-and-hunting[G] societies by indefatigable field workers who track the number of hours spent each day in food acquisition, weigh each animal killed, and keep detailed accounts of how much meat in each carcass goes to whom, in habitats as diverse as the savannahs of East Africa and the rainforest of the Amazon. These data show that human hunting societies are organized quite differently from the carnal politics of male chimpanzees. As one group of fieldworkers (Hawkes, O'Connell, and Blurton Jones) summarizes:

> The distribution procedures among the Ache [in the Amazon], !Kung [South Africa], and Hadza [East Africa] differ, but in none of them can the hunter, or anyone else, exclude others from shares of the animal. This is the common pattern among ethnographically known foragers. The hunter has no opportunity to control the size or final destination of shares, let alone obligate recipients to repay him in future meat or anything else.[63]

However one characterizes the societies of contemporary gatherer-hunters, dominance hierarchies they are not.

The anthropological research on extant foraging societies also underscores the divergence between the findings of social science and the "hunter" of Darwinian discourse. In evolutionist theory, from the eighteenth century to the present, hunting is synonymous with the most primitive stage of human society, a hypothetical past when people ranged over the landscape like animals gathering wild plants and hunting game. Darwin himself believed that gathering-and-hunting societies are remnants of the earliest stage of human history; and his successors to the present day have uncritically promulgated the same premise, blissfully untouched by a century of anthropological fieldwork. E. O. Wilson, for example, tells us that: "For at least a million years—probably more—Man engaged in a hunting-gathering way of life, giving up the practice a mere 10,000 years ago. We can be sure that our innate social responses have been fashioned largely through this life style."[64]

If this be so, then the study of contemporary gathering-and-hunting societies, such as the Inuit of the Arctic, the !Kung of Africa, and the Batek De' of Asia, indicates that our "innate" proclivities incline us more toward sharing than toward dominance.

Anthropologists, however, have gone beyond the living fossil premise. Instead of postulating hunting as the primal stage of human social development, anthropologists now commonly regard it as one subsistence[G] strategy among many. Although the "primitive" hunter and the "subsistence" hunter are superficially similar, these two interpretations have different theoretical implications. If hunting is a subsistence strategy, then it can coexist with other such strategies such as cultivating seasonal vegetables, gathering acorns, and selling wood carvings to tourists, even while allowing for the possibility that the people might give up their nomadic life entirely and take a job at Walmart.

Empirically, contemporary gatherers and hunters, as well as those known archeologically, do in fact combine subsistence strategies in a flexible and adaptive manner. For example, among the Batek De', a nomadic gathering-and-hunting society in the Malaysian rainforest that I know first-hand, people spend most of their work day hunting wild game and digging wild tubers; but they also gather wild rattan and medicinal plants that they trade to Malays for such valued items as tobacco and machetes.[65] Thus, "hunters" such as the Batek De' are not a stage of social development but exemplify a mixed economic strategy of gathering, hunting, fishing, and trading.

Darwin's "primitive hunter" is really a theory of economic determinism disguised as a stage of history, for it implies that the primary subsistence strategy determines the social organization of the larger society. But even in chimpanzees the subsistence economy (which is based on individualist foraging) is socially distinct from the hunting economy (which in *Pan troglodytes* is composed exclusively of adult males).

In human society, the economic determination of social organization is even more implausible. To consider a familiar example, both the Soviet Union and the United States had a comparable subsistence economy based on mechanized agriculture, a factory system of manufacturing, and machines powered by fossil fuels, yet the political organization and the distribution of goods and services in these two societies were quite different. Moreover, in pre-Columbian times the Indians of the northwest coast of North America were technically gatherer-hunters, since fishing, whaling, and gathering wild plants formed the subsistence base of their societies, yet they lived in permanent settlements with hierarchically-ranked lineages and complex ceremonies of status display.

Evolutionists, however, especially those committed to biological explanations of human social life, like to think of "hunting and gathering" as a stage of societal development to which humans are "naturally" adapted. Indeed, to the school that calls itself evolutionary[G] psychology, the social behavior of contemporary human beings is "explained" in terms of hypothetical genes that are adapted to the hypothetical social organization of prehistoric hunters.[66]

Even "Man" the Hunter is problematical. Hunters kill animals, which is consistent with interspecific competition, and the killing is usually done by men, which is consistent with sexism,ᴳ but this sexual division of labor reflects risk assessment more than a biological imperative. Among the Batek De', most hunting is done by men, but women are free to hunt if they want to; and anthropologists have observed instances of it.[67] Female hunters have also been documented in other nomadic Asian societies.[68] Among the Martu people in the Australian desert, women not only hunt but they bring in half of the bush meat that the community consumes.[69]

But no matter who kills the game, human hunters do not monopolize kills as dominance theory would predict nor do they share the meat with only blood relatives, as sociobiological theory would predict. To the contrary, people in hunting societies *invariably share* what they have with *everyone* in the band—not just with those to whom they are genetically related.

Contrary to dominance models, contemporary gathering-and-hunting societies also show very little aggression. One evolutionary biologist, Irenäus Eibl-Eibesfeldt, was so skeptical of this fact that he traveled to the Kalahari Desert to prove anthropology wrong; he returned in triumph, proclaiming that the !Kung are not "unaggressive" as anthropologists had said, because he had taken photographs of angry facial expressions and aggressive postures in !Kung children.[70] This ethologist has missed the point. People in hunting societies on occasion raise their voices and clench their fists as do people anywhere—indeed, there are even cases of murder—but aggressive display is not encouraged while physical aggression is not tolerated. Instead, there are strong social norms that reinforce cooperation, the peaceful resolution of conflicts, and consensual leadership. Also, aggression can never escalate to the level of intergroup warfare because no one has the right to command another, much less the right to use deadly force against other people.

Significantly, at the end of Eibl-Eibesfeldt's article in which he "refutes" the anthropological findings about the !Kung, he writes that "friendly bonding behavior predominates in the interaction of adults, and these people spend many hours a day grooming each other, chatting, sharing a pipe, and playing with their children, to mention but a few of these social interactions."[71]

Reflecting on anthropological studies of contemporary gatherer-hunters, the biologists Erdal and Whiten have come away with a very different interpretation of the "primitive hunter" from that promulgated by E. O. Wilson. They have concluded that the human mind must have been shaped by *psychological dispositions supporting egalitarianism, vigilant food sharing, informal leadership, and counter-dominant behavior*" [my emphasis].[72]

Darwinian Altruism: Self-Interest in Disguise

Darwinian theory has adapted to the fact of the egalitarian hunter by explaining altruism as self-interest in disguise. We all know that mammalian mothers defend their babies, at least when they themselves have had nurturing mothers, but humans also exhibit *generalized* [G] *altruism*, which is self-sacrifice for the benefit of strangers to whom we are not closely related.[73] When we call the fire department we expect that the firefighter will rush into the burning building and save the injured child regardless of the degree of genetic relationship between the two. In *The Descent of Man*, Darwin remarks on this phenomenon, noting how selfless regard for others exemplifies the highest standards of civilized society, as his Victorian audience would expect him to say; but he downplays the significance of selflessness by claiming that it is restricted to "civilized" societies, by explaining its evolution in terms of competition, and by attributing its motivation to unspecified "social instincts."[74]

Altruism can only be explained within a Darwinian framework by a kind of contrived psychology known as kin selection and reciprocal altruism.[75] Kin selection asserts that altruism can occur in nature only if the act of saving someone else has the effect of propagating one's own genes, so that altruism is a function of genetic relatedness. Reciprocal altruism asserts that I will be altruistic to you only if there is an equal probability that you will be altruistic to me—"You scratch my back and I'll scratch yours." Since both parties expect to get something back, reciprocal altruism is not altruism at all; it is motivated by self-interest and fails to address the issue of self-sacrificing action.

For almost a century, cultural anthropologists have discussed the reciprocation of beneficial actions under the more appropriate name of *reciprocal exchange* and have interpreted it as a type of economic behavior.[76] Although there is no doubt that reciprocal social behavior is a force to be reckoned with in nonhuman primate societies—where it frequently occurs as mutual grooming, and even more so in humans, where it underlies much economic activity—its relevance to *generalized* altruism is less apparent. Exactly how do genetic relatedness and reciprocal exchange explain the case of the firefighter running into a burning building? Or the act of adopting an orphaned child? Or a Christmas campaign to feed the homeless? The significant feature of all these activities is that the benefactors have *no* reasonable expectation that they will ever be reciprocated for their contribution, either financially or genetically, so it is a bad deal from the viewpoint of an economic maximizer.

Moreover, the mechanisms of inclusive fitness and reciprocal altruism cannot explain all cases of altruism even in monkeys. When I was doing my doctoral research, I set up two monkey colonies in large outdoor cages, one of rhesus (*Macaca mulatta*) and another of long-tailed macaques (*Macaca fascicularis*). All macaques reproduce well in captivity, and soon I had two birth cohorts of about half a dozen infants of each species. Unfortunately, one of the *fascicularis* mothers died in childbirth, leaving behind a healthy infant, while one of the rhesus mothers gave birth to a dead baby. Macaque infants need mothers' milk, but mothers with their own infants do not allow others to suckle, which is consistent with Darwinism—but what happened next is not.

I went into the *fascicularis* cage and retrieved the orphaned baby, while a colleague restrained the alpha male who tried to protect it. Then I carried the infant to the rhesus cage and unlocked the gate. When a human enters the cage, the animals suspect the worst and try to get as far away as possible, crowding into the rain shelter in back. But when I came into the cage carrying the *fascicularis* baby, the mother whose infant had died came bounding out of the shelter. While the others watched from the shadows, she ran right up to me, took the infant out of my hands, and clasped it to her chest—not caring that the baby was from a different species. Then she raced back to rejoin the others. The *fascicularis* infant grew to adulthood in the care of its foster mother, becoming a functional member of the troop, grooming and being groomed like a well-socialized rhesus.

There is enough scientific literature on cross-fostering in mammals, such as dogs raising monkeys—even a dog raising Bengal tiger cubs—to establish it as a reliable phenomenon.[77] Also, the adoption of orphans from one's own species has been documented in a wide range of primate species experimentally, by introducing infants to free-ranging troops.[78] Everyone has heard of the theory of "man the hunter"; but why is killing across species boundaries "theoretically significant" while parenting across species boundaries is not?

When you adopt a puppy, it becomes a member of your pack, following family members about, displaying affection, and barking at intruders.[79] Like puppies, young primates are willing to be children for primates who are willing to be parents, but there is no reason to believe that such relationships are motivated by gene propagation or explained by a theory of genetic relatedness. If anything, adoption and cross-fostering indicate the opposite: that once maternal motivation is activated it seeks to find appropriate situations in which to express itself, even to the point of foregoing the possibility of a genetic payoff entirely. Once a capacity for parenting behavior becomes biologically established in a species, as it is in all mammals and nearly all birds, then the motivational systems that sustain it are facilitated hormonally and triggered by the appropriate stimuli, which are phenomena that are explained scientifically by physiology and psychology, not by the presumed genetic benefits to the parent.

Sociobiology postulates conjectural motivations inside the primate brain that on the face of it are implausible: "Whether the genes rhesus females are trying to propagate happen to be in their own bodies or in those of their relatives and their offspring doesn't make much difference,"[80] one theorist informs us. But why suppose that monkeys are propagating genes at all? Gene propagation is a theoretical construct in mechanistic biology whose psychological reality to anyone except sociobiologists remains to be scientifically established. Indeed, the idea that female animals choose males for their "good genes" has been challenged by biologists in the pages of *Science* itself.[81]

Rather than presume that rhesus monkeys discovered genes before biologists did, it is easier to explain maternal behavior in terms of such biological processes as the release of hormones by the pituitary gland and neural activity in the hypothalamus. Moreover, in humans, these psychobiological processes are also influenced by social expectations about what is appropriate and moral to do.

Once one accepts the fact that the bond between caregiver and infant is based on psychosocial activation that can occur independently of the genetic relationship between them,[82] then the whole superstructure of inclusive fitness with its implicit genetic determinism loses its logical force. If parental behavior "evolved" to propagate one's own genes, then adoption of a stranger's child and fostering babies across species boundaries ought not to be possible at all.[83]

The Human Meaning of Kinship

Sociobiology, by reducing the social to the biological, invariably muddles any discussion of human social organization by confounding kinship[G] with genetic relatedness. Anthropologists and Darwinians do agree on aspects of primate biology: that females give birth, that about half the babies born are girls, and that mothers produce milk. Also, both disciplines agree that social relationships among brothers and sisters born from the same womb are fundamental to primate social life. Nonetheless, these two disciplines understand kinship relationships quite differently.

Darwinians maintain that social relationships based on kinship are the same in all primates because they reflect the family tree of genetic relationship, whereas anthropologists have discovered that different human societies conceptualize kinship in different ways, even such basic relationships as paternity and descent. Moreover, these culturally defined differences affect all aspects of human life, including such fundamental Darwinian concerns as who achieves high rank and who inherits the property.

Some Darwinian biologists now at least acknowledge that there is an anthropological viewpoint on the subject of kinship (a point that took over a century to concede), but there is still little recognition among Darwinians that the cultural construction of kinship requires them to think differently about the subject matter. For example, biologist Robin Dunbar writes:

> The claim that our behavior is underpinned by the
> implications of biological relatedness does not mean
> that we do not use social rules to guide our behavior.
> Social and biological kinship rules are not mutually
> exclusive kinds of explanations, but, rather, different
> ways of viewing the same thing. . . If you use social
> kinship to structure your behavior, that will have the
> effect most of the time of allowing you to invest in
> kin.[84]

But genetic transmission and cultural construction are not "different ways of viewing the same thing": they denote *fundamentally different processes*—one biological and the other social—that often produce distinctly different maps of a community. Where genetic relatedness is a function of mating, and is similar in all mammals, human kinship relations are the product of at least three distinct processes that form the social environment in which human mating occurs. These processes include psychobiological attachment (e.g. mother-child bonding); linguistically-encoded concepts of kinship roles (e.g. mother's elder brother as the male authority figure rather than the biological father); and cultural definitions of parenthood (e.g. one's adopted child as the legal equivalent of one's biological children).

The Darwinian approach to kinship begins with genes but the anthropological approach begins with language. Human kinship is encoded in language in the form of kinship terminology. This terminology is not simply a list of names for genetic relationships—brother, sister, mother—but a logically constructed system of contrasting alternatives that defines those relationships within an abstract system of descent.

For example, one can convey the concept of a flower or a toaster by pointing to physical exemplars of these categories. One can even take photographs of many different flowers in case someone is unclear about the range of variation. But one cannot learn the concept of an uncle by pointing to instances of uncles. Flowers and toasters are instances of generic categories that are denoted by the same words for all speakers of a language, but kinship terms are egocentric because the words denote different individuals depending on the speaker. That is to say, unless you and I are siblings, my uncles will be different people from your uncles, which makes pointing to exemplars of the concept unhelpful for understanding the meaning.

Also, in human language, some words denote abstractions that are not reducible to perception, and kinship falls firmly in the category of abstract terminology. Even though both Uncle George and Uncle Bernie have the perceptual properties of maleness, this property is found as well in brothers, fathers, and grandfathers, so maleness is not definitive of uncledom. The word *uncle* is defined (in English) as a male sibling of one's parent or the husband of one's aunt. Try photographing that.

Other kinship relationships are equally abstract. Even though you may never have known your great-grandfather, you can still define the relationship quite explicitly: a lineal male ancestor of the third ascending generation from you. Human kinship is a cognitive process, not a perceptual one, in that it depends on an abstract system of social relationships that is not directly observable.

In this respect, kinship is similar to other abstract systems that define social roles in human societies. For example, try describing the job of a real estate agent without using language. A real estate agent needs detailed knowledge of sales and purchases that unfold over long periods of time, often across generations. The transactions have to be done in a prescribed manner in accordance with culturally defined rules, which are themselves encoded in language. Furthermore, real estate transactions are confirmed by means of purely symbolic constructions, such as deeds, signatures, and money, that have no biological equivalent at all. Yet even genetic determinists think that real estate exists.

A symbolic marker might be as fleeting as a handshake or as physically insignificant as the words "Keep Out" painted on a wall, but in human society, symbols can be the difference between life and death.

In 1914, a Polish student of anthropology, Bronislaw Malinowski, who had been educated as a physicist, became stranded in Australia by the outbreak of the First World War, unable to return to England. Over the four-year duration of the war he made three field trips to a remote archipelago off the coast of New Guinea, where he lived among traditional farmers and seafarers, eventually publishing a detailed monograph on their culture, *Argonauts of the Western Pacific*, that caught the popular imagination and inspired a generation of students.[85]

The method that Malinowski popularized, called participant observation, is the art of learning about a people by living among them, becoming fluent in their language, and observing their activities on a daily basis. Even though Malinowski used the term *savage* and did his fieldwork when unilinear[G] evolution was still widely accepted in anthropology, in his books "savages" are not so much exemplars of a stage of history as real people with a human level of beliefs and practices who are living in contemporary societies, not prehistoric ones.

Had you been born in the Trobriand Islands, where Malinowski did his fieldwork, you would probably live with both of your biological parents— a very common pattern among human beings. But unlike the suburban nuclear[G] family, you would belong to your mother's descent group. In matrilineal[G] societies, a child is regarded as a descendant of its mother, and that child's primary rights and responsibilities are traced through its mother's descent group. Even though there are secondary rights and responsibilities that the child receives from the father, it is the mother's line of descent that is primary. That is, in matrilineal societies, a woman transmits her property to her *own* children, whereas the father transmits his property to his *sister's* children—because he and his sister are descended from the same mother: property must be kept within the matrilineage.

Aha! the sociobiologist would exclaim: note that one's own children and one's sister's children both have 50 percent of their genes in common, so they are equivalent from a genetic point of view! This is true but irrelevant. Anthropological fieldwork shows that human kinship roles and sexual taboos are not simply an expression of degrees of genetic relatedness as determined by biology, nor can the behavior that society prescribes toward categories of kin be predicted from the genetic relationship.

One day Malinowski heard wailing in the village which indicated that someone had died. He was initially told that a sixteen-year-old boy of his acquaintance had fallen from a coconut palm. Through subsequent inquiries, Malinowski learned that the dead boy had been having a sexual relationship with the daughter of his mother's sister. In the English language, any children born to one's aunts and uncles are called *first cousins*, but many languages make additional distinctions in the naming of cousin relationships. In anthropological terminology, children born to same-sex siblings (e.g., to your mother and her sister) are called *parallel*[G] cousins whereas children born to opposite-sex siblings (e.g., to your mother and her brother) are called *cross*[G] cousins.

In American kinship reckoning, a boy's mother's sister's daughter (a first cousin in English) is generally considered to be a close relative, perhaps too close for sex. In Trobriand society, this relationship is even closer. Individuals who are parallel cousins are considered to be the *equivalent* of brother and sister, and they use these sibling terms to address one another.

Although many people knew of the sexual relationship of the boy with his sister (the daughter of his mother's sister) and disapproved of it, Malinowski notes that:

> nothing was done until the girl's discarded lover, who had wanted to marry her and felt personally injured, took the initiative. The rival threatened first to use black magic against the guilty youth, but this had not had much effect. Then one evening he insulted the culprit in public—accusing him in the hearing of the whole community of incest and hurling at him certain expressions intolerable to a native.

In Trobriand society, there is only one socially acceptable response by a person thus publicly accused and humiliated in this way: suicide. The next morning the accused boy put on

> festive attire and ornamentation, climbed a coca-nut palm and addressed the community, speaking from among the palm leaves and bidding them farewell. He explained the reasons for his desperate deed and also launched a veiled accusation against the man who had driven him to his death, upon which it became the duty of his clansmen to avenge him. Then he wailed aloud, as is the custom, jumped from a palm some sixty feet high and was killed on the spot.

Exactly where are the biologically determined outcomes in this event? There are certainly emotions that have some psychobiological basis, such as jealousy, revenge, and anger; but any theory that claims scientific status must predict the observed outcomes of the events to which it is applied. Darwinism explains human social behavior by means of the genetic family tree and instincts for morality. But these concepts cannot even in principle explain why in the Trobriand Islands sex between a boy and his mother's sister's daughter may become the equivalent of a capital offense while in Victorian England Charles Darwin could freely marry his mother's brother's daughter—even though both relationships are equally close from a genetic point of view.

By ignoring the rules laid down by Darwinists, human beings, with their linguistically encoded systems of kinship and descent, are able to form social groups and relationships that have no equivalent in nonhuman primate societies. These cognitive systems of descent and marriage create extended networks of people that have a collective commitment to children and to one another while providing for the orderly transmission of property needed for survival. Like rhesus monkeys, humans have matrilines because they have mothers to whom they are connected by psychobiological processes of social attachment; but rhesus monkeys do not have matrilineages because they cannot organize their social life in relation to a putative female ancestor that no living monkey has known.

Darwinians have got it backward: in human societies, it is *the social relationship of generalized altruism*—not the genetic relationship—that makes people into kinfolk. The most universal expression of this understanding is marriage, in which the culturally-constructed union of a couple makes relatives out of groups of people who have hitherto been either distantly related genetically or not related at all. In human society, intermarriage is a common way of building bridges between groups that had hitherto been enemies.

In human society, altruism and marriage go hand in hand. In English, the noun *kin* and the adjective *kind* play on the same sounds, reinforcing the social dictum that once people become relatives, altruistic standards of conduct apply. Under modernism and individualism, much of the social dimension of kinship has been lost, but traditionally the relationship between kinship and kindness was enforced by custom and community standards of correct behavior. Whether you are genetically related to them or not, once people are defined as kinfolk, you are supposed to help them when they are in need and socialize with them on important occasions. In traditional societies, kin solidarity is further maintained by obligatory food sharing and gift giving among relatives on ceremonial occasions such as feast days, funerals, and weddings.

In English, one expresses the kinship relationships created by marriage with the terms *father-in-law, mother-in-law, step-child,* and so on. Far from being an expression of biology, the terminology is used irrespective of whether or not there are children born to the union—even childless married couples have in-laws. In addition to marriage, all societies have other ways of making unrelated people into kin, such as adoption, in which a person acquires the same rights as the biological child born in a wedded union, and godparents, who publicly commit to care for the child as its biological parents would.

As I pointed out decades ago, the human concept of kinfolk does not develop from genetic relatedness but draws its motivations from systems of psychobiological attachment similar to those of nonhuman primates.[86] Attachment theory makes very different predictions from the inclusive fitness of sociobiology. The psychosocial theory predicts that children raised in the same family group will form attachments to parental figures whether or not they are genetically related, and it predicts that children raised by caring foster parents will be as strongly attached to their caregivers and to their functional siblings as children raised by their biological parents.

Now, however, thanks to Darwinism, kin and kindness have been completely severed conceptually. While the development of the fetus in the womb is clearly a biological process, in human societies there are ceremonies and procedures that define who will be recognized as the parents of the child, as well as rituals such as baptism that publicly announce that the community has a new member. These ties are then reinforced through social relationships of altruism and reciprocity. Darwinian science, by reducing sex to the union between a sperm and an ovum, manages to miss almost everything that distinguishes human reproduction from that of animals—indeed, much of what distinguishes rhesus monkeys from codfish. Even in baboons, as long-term field studies show, sex and friendship are intimately connected.[87]

The genetic reductionist view of childbirth, while at odds with the rest of the human race, is completely consistent with capitalism, which recognizes no social or moral framework beyond a contractual relationship between buyer and seller. When joined to corporate capitalism, Darwinist ideology takes the social alienation of sex and childbirth a step further by inventing gestational surrogacy, the process of using one woman's womb to bring someone else's implanted embryo to term, with no legal rights for the woman who bore the child, the gestational mother.[88]

Such transactions among women who are not kin to one another almost invariably involve economic inequality between the contracting parties. Clearly, only someone who thinks that genes define parenthood could conclude that nurturing a fetus for nine months is without legal, moral, or psychological significance. Indeed, under United States law, not even the *biological* contributions of the gestational mother, such as maternal antibodies, are recognized as having value.

Darwinism imposes a profoundly alienating system of values: it makes the uterine connection and sexual intercourse obsolete by means of reproductive technology; defines kinship as procreation while ignoring parenting; has failed to notice that parenting has no intrinsic connection to genetic relationship; and has replaced a human level of kinship defined by obligatory kindness with one of genetic continuity.

Genes by Other Means

In the mid-1980s, Darwinian theory, having failed to explain primate social organization by dominance hierarchies and genetic determinism, abandoned behavior for psychology.[89] The term social intelligence denotes those mental processes and neural structures that process information about our relationship to others, anticipate the actions of others, and organize appropriate responses.

The social brain is not a physically distinct part of the brain but a functional system that draws on more general capacities, such as perception, motor ability, and memory, as well on such socially specialized abilities as facial recognition and facial expression. Social brain function, like any neural function, includes innate components, but it is not primitive or instinctive because it also requires a neocortical level of function, such as anticipating when a child is about to run in front of a car and choosing exactly the right gift for an anniversary. But because Darwinism explains altruism and kindness as self-interest in disguise, it postulates as the driving force of the social brain something called Machiavellian intelligence.

The hypothesis of Machiavellian intelligence asserts that primates use intelligent thinking to manipulate others for their own advantage. To the historical Machiavelli, power was instrumental to statecraft, a process that had as its goal the security of an entire country, but Darwinists conflate collective security with individual self-interest. Even so, as human beings often use power to their own advantage, we can look to see if this ability occurs in nonhuman primates as well. Consider, for example, a hypothetical scenario called tactical deception, the situation where there are two monkeys (Bruiser and Tiny) and one banana, which Bruiser has claimed.[90] It is an instance of tactical deception if Tiny gives a predator warning call when there is no predator present, causing Bruiser to drop the banana and run away in fright, giving Tiny a chance to take possession of it.

By thinking through this gambit and acting on it, Tiny is exemplifying behavior that is theorized to be a function of the Machiavellian mind. Primatologists have argued that Machiavellian intelligence is not just a collection of circus tricks, as a behaviorist would have interpreted this example, but true intelligence—namely, the ability to mentally anticipate what another primate will do in certain circumstances based on one's own social experience and to use that knowledge to one's own advantage, such as getting access to resources and raising one's rank in a hierarchy.

The hypothesis of Machiavellian intelligence is relevant to human evolution too, because most human beings live in social hierarchies and can certainly manipulate and deceive, often with far more ingenuity than a monkey. However, the concept merges into Darwinian ideology when all social phenomena are to be either explained by it or explained away. First, the expansion of the neocortex in the course of primate evolution is explained as selection *for* Machiavellian intelligence, thereby foreclosing any possibility of the social brain mentally anticipating and carrying out actions that are not rank-related and economic, much less actions to someone else's advantage. Second, as in all Darwinism, biological function is conflated with mental abilities and psychological motivations. Machiavellian intelligence is often treated as if were an actual psychological motive that is represented in the brain, as Dawkins seems to believe,[91] even though it is better psychology to assume that primates just want to get ahead and get laid.

The concept of Machiavellian intelligence enables Darwinian ideology to reaffirm genetic determinism in a psychological guise. Since primates supposedly have been selected to propagate their genes through the social manipulation of others, then it is no longer necessary to find empirical cases of violent monopolization of resources to prove the "naturalness" of dominance hierarchies. Now dominance and competition are built into the definition of primate intelligence itself, just as Charles Darwin built these concepts into his theory of speciation.

Yet in every primate species that has been studied over long periods of time, intergenerational processes (such as attachment) and peer-to-peer processes (such as play groups and coalition building) have proved to be every bit as important to understanding social behavior as competition; but there is no way of falsifying the premise that human beings have been genetically selected in the course of evolution to think only Darwinist thoughts.

From Selfish Genes to Selfless Instincts

Since the beginning of the twenty-first century, Darwinism has been evolving with remarkable rapidity into an ideology that endorses altruism and cooperation. Scientists who have walked faithfully for a quarter of a century in the footsteps of Wilson and Dawkins, uncritically accepting selfish genes and Machiavellian minds, are now writing books on the evolutionary imperative of social cooperation.

Sarah Blaffer Hrdy, for example, is an acclaimed primatologist who made her reputation initially by a vivid depiction of sexual selection in her book *The Woman That Never Evolved*:

> Sex, it is now thought, began as a simple act of hijacking when, some several billion years ago, a small cell waylaid and merged with a bigger one, richer in substance and nutrient. . . . Competition among small cells for access to larger ones favored faster, smaller, and more manoeuverable cells, analogous to sperm. The hostages we might as well call ova.[92]

The historian of science Jan Sapp observes that Hrdy's "biological" account, with its hijackers and waylaid hostages, "is an egregious illustration of how assumptions about the universal nature of human social relationships are used to explain nature, and then, coming full circle, this version of nature is used to explain human social inequalities."[93]

Significantly, thirty years later, this same Hrdy tells us that we are "'wired' to cooperate"[94]—a stunning conclusion from a person who spent decades rationalizing competition. Even Hrdy feels compelled to explain her change in direction:

> Such generosity at first seems irrational, especially to economists who are accustomed to celebrating individualism and economic models that assume a self-interested "rational actors," or to a sociobiologist like me who has devoted much of her professional life researching competition between primate males for access to fertile females, between females in the same group for resources, and even between offspring of the same family for access to nourishment and care.[95]

Hrdy attributes her change of mind to scientific progress: "New discoveries by evolutionarily minded psychologists, economists, and neuroscientists are propelling the cooperative side of human nature to center stage."[96] The problem with this textbook explanation is that much of the evidence was available decades ago, had sociobiologists bothered to look at it. For example, in one of my own papers, published in the twentieth century, I argued that the social organization of human cooperation is the critical factor in a human level of tool use and technology, a level of cooperation not found in apes.[97]

Non-Machiavellian Monkeys

In recent years, field primatology has tossed a monkey wrench into Darwinian theory. There are species of South American monkeys, the tamarins and marmosets, collectively termed callitrichids, that live in small groups consisting of a breeding pair plus a few other adults of both sexes and immature offspring.[98] Among callitrichid monkeys, the adults share food with one another, give food calls that benefit others, and help to care for the children of others by carrying and feeding them. Moreover, primatologists have eliminated kin selection as a sufficient explanation by showing experimentally that callitrichids also share food with unrelated strangers,[99] and they share food even when the act is not reciprocated by a specific individual.

Among chimpanzees, in contrast, food is usually given only in response to solicitations by others and is instrumental in maintaining coalitions in the ranking system, making it more akin to politics than to altruism. Callitrichids, however, distinguish between selfish and unselfish acts of giving; they are more likely to give unsolicited food to individuals who give altruistically, a strategy consistent with a culture of sharing.[100]

Significantly, humans and callitrichid monkeys are the only primates known to have both cooperative[G] parenting and generalized altruism, leading primatologists to speculate that these two phenomena are interdependent. In cooperative parenting, both sexes care for the young, such as by carrying the infant and feeding it, while generalized altruism is the act of giving to others even if there is no possibility of payback. If one expands the definition of "cooperative parenting" from biological parents to culturally constructed groups of kinfolk, then cultural anthropology has recognized the theoretical importance of this type of social system for more than a century.

Jane Lancaster, the physical anthropologist who introduced me to nonhuman primates when I was an undergraduate at the

University of California at Berkeley, has been revising theories of the evolution of the human family in the light of male-female cooperation.[101]

Jane Lancaster and Hilliard Kaplan point out that it is not the total amount of sustenance provided by males to females that is the critical factor in human biological evolution but the male contribution to females during gestation and lactation. Provisioning during this period enables the mother to get high-energy food without a corresponding expenditure of energy and risk to the child.

These authors see human society as diverging from the simian condition when exchange relationships make it possible for males to provision females and their dependent offspring with high-quality foods at critical times during growth and development, thus facilitating higher reproductive success for *both* sexes. Male participation in turn makes possible a longer maturation time for the offspring, which facilitates cultural development by providing more time for learning, thus creating a feedback loop that reinforces the cross-sex relationships.

In what Lancaster and Kaplan call the human adaptive complex, a number of factors, both biological and social, come to reinforce one another:

- The life history of development, aging, and longevity;

- Diet and dietary physiology;

- Energetics of reproduction;

- Social relationships among men and women;

- Intergenerational resource transfers;

- Cooperation among related and unrelated people.

The Lancaster-Kaplan model does not preclude the possibility that some males may give meat to females with the hope of receiving sexual favors in return, but it differs from Stanford's formulation in important ways. Where the latter assumes the primacy of the all-male hierarchy as in *Pan troglodytes*, Lancaster and Kaplan see men and women as engaged in cooperative child-rearing, a shared goal that may take different though complementary forms in the two sexes, as when women gather plant foods and breast-feed young children while men concentrate on fishing and plowing.

In many species of nonhuman primates, the basic social unit is either a male-female pair with dependent offspring or a larger group composed of only a single adult male with females and immatures (the unimale troop). Even in species in which multiple adult males and females do live together, such as macaques and baboons, the members of the female matrilines and the male hierarchy lead largely parallel lives.

In the human case, however, cross-cultural observation underscores the fact that human societies always have *social integration of adult males into groups composed of females and their children*. Male/female integration can be accomplished in a variety of ways: through marriage, godparents, foster parents, male relatives other than the father of the child, reciprocal exchange, and descent groups based on kinship terminology—but in all human societies it is accomplished in one way or another. There is enormous variation in the types of behavior considered to be gender-appropriate, but in all human societies adult males are part of the child-rearing process, whether it be changing diapers or financing a college education.

Beyond Sociobiology: A Post-Darwinist Moral Order

In the 1990s, the primatologist Frans de Waal, drawing upon his life-long familiarity with the societies of chimpanzees and macaques, provided many compelling examples of nonhuman primate altruism, cooperation, and reciprocity. He then for-mulated an evolutionist theory of the moral sense, concisely summarized in a single table, that explains the primate data.[102]

De Waal's model complements that of Lancaster and Kaplan in that both theories require a society in which adult primates are dependent upon other group members for survival, such as finding food, defending against predators, and assisting with the child-rearing process. Reciprocal exchange and social coopera-tion are economically risky behaviors, since there is always the possibility that the individual who gives to another will not get anything back. Life-long relationships provide an opportunity for trust to develop among individuals and allow sufficient time for gifts to be reciprocated.

In spite of increased solidarity, the most highly social primates do not lose their individuality. Reliance on the group, mutual aid, cooperation, and reciprocal exchange evolve within groups where individuals recognize one another and have conflicting interests and desires, often to the point of aggression: thus, primates need to forge alliances with others in order to get what they want.

This social situation provides the context for the development of techniques of conflict resolution by what De Waal terms "a balancing of individual and collective interests." This can be done by individuals vis-a-vis one another by means of "recipro-cation of aid and reconciliation following fights."[103] There is also a community level of conflict resolution in which third parties mediate disputes, support altruistic behavior, and encourage con-tributions to collective well being. Although rare in studies of animal behavior, such concepts have long been part of the social sciences and the moral order.

De Waal's book signaled the end of sociobiology as the dom-inant theory in evolutionary biology. The author employs all the usual signals to affirm his Darwinian group affiliation (quota-tions from the Sage of Down, reflexive obeisance to natural selection, even an adulatory interview with Trivers), but in the first chapter of his book he cites Mary Midgely's objections to sociobiology while criticizing Richard Dawkins for his gene-centric individualism.[104]

Significantly, De Waal's theory of moral evolution has no biological variables at all. The key processes are cognitive and psychological, such as understanding the mental state of another and tallying acts of quid pro quo. De Waal notes that some may regard his theory as "a watering down of the evolutionary approach," but when "faced with a mountain as intimidating as morality," science must "acquire the theoretical gear to climb all the way to the top."[105]

De Waal's "Darwinian" theory of the moral order is essentially evolutionist anthropology whose only connection to natural selection is historical.

Reflections

In the twenty-first century, the long reign of genetic determinism and reductionist explanations of social behavior may be coming to an end. Faced with increased evidence of social learning, even sociobiologists now admit that genetics does not explain the variation in societies of nonhuman primates.[106] In a review of hundreds of studies of the development of behavior across a broad spectrum of animal species, Mary Jane West-Eberhard reflects on three decades of sociobiology: "The result was not massive documentation of genetic determinism in behavior, but rather the opposite—massive documentation of a heretofore widely underestimated capacity for adaptive condition-sensitive behavior and development."[107]

And a little more than a quarter of a century after E. O. Wilson predicted the takeover of the social sciences by his own brand of reductionist biology, West-Eberhard concludes that: "Anthropologists . . . have good reason to question the explanations of a strongly gene-centered sociobiology."[108]

Notes

1 Dawkins (1976); Wilson (1975).

2 W. D. Hamilton, *Narrow Roads of Gene Land. vol. 1. Evolution and Social Behaviour.* Oxford: W. H. Freeman/Spektrum, 1996. Quoted by Ridley (1997: 19).

3 Wilson (1975).

4 Lewontin, Rose, and Kamin (1984: 233). This book is still a relevant critique of the genetic inheritance of social traits.

5 Crook (1994) gives an extensive review of the literature on human nature and society between 1859 and 1914.

6 Sahlins (1976).

7 The Chicago School, associated with the names of Milton Friedman (Friedman and Friedman 1962, Friedman and Selden 1975) and his colleagues, was instrumental in making neoliberal economics the policy of the U.S. federal government. Friedman himself advised the Chilean dictator Pinochet. For the rise of neoliberalism see Jones (2012: Chapter 6).

8 Lewontin, Rose, and Kamin (1984); Midgley (1979, 1983.)

9 Lewontin (1993). I discuss Dobzhnansky in Chapter 5.

10 P. Darlington (1981). Not to be confused with the British geneticist C. D. Darlington, who thinks social class and racism are innate.

11 Dawkins (1976).

12 The work of Grafton Elliott Smith (1933) is often cited as exemplary of the diffusionist school. It was Thomas Henry Huxley's theory of culture as well, and Smith quotes Huxley (1933: 162–64).

13 Stove (1995, 2006, n.d.). Midgley (1983) anticipates Stove's thesis. Stove's book (1995) was not available in the United States, but it was reprinted in 2006 and has since enjoyed a wider readership. For biographical material on Stove see Franklin (1994).

14 Sussman (1999).

15 Yerkes (1937: 255–56).

16 Goodall (1971: 143).

17 The title of Wrangham and Peterson's book (1996), *Demonic Males*, conveys the essentialism of "the killer ape."

18 The dominance concept was initially adopted by primatologists from studies of the pecking order in chickens. See Lewis (2002).

19 Zuckerman (1932).

20 Zuckerman's observation of possessive "herding" of females by the alpha male was confirmed, but the "harem" (unimale group) that he described was shown to be part of larger social aggregation of unimale groups that move as a unit, whereas the relationship between the sexes has a complex ontogenetic development not explicable solely in terms of aggressive male domination of females: Kummer (1968 a "Two Variations "; 1968 b "Social Organization . . .").

21 Maslow (1936). Abraham Maslow is better known as the influential humanistic psychologist who coined the term *self-esteem*.

22 Loy (1970); Southwick et al. (1974).

23 Studies of species with unimale groups (Dolhinow 1968) began contemporaneously with the first field studies of macaques, baboons, and chimpanzees, but it took the discovery of infanticide to make them attractive to the mass media. There is an ongoing debate about the causes of infanticide among primatologists; from the beginning, sociobiological interpretations have dominated the discussion (Hrdy 1977; Hausfater and Hrdy 1984).

24 Sapolsky (2001: 20).

25 Strum, Forster, and Hutchins (1988: 56).

26 Ibid. 64. For a more recent treatment of these issues, see Smuts (1999); Soltis (2004).

27 Tutin (1979). This researcher also recognizes a third category of mating that she calls possessiveness, in which a male tries to keep an estrus female to himself by driving off lower-ranking males; consort relationships, in contrast, require some cooperation on the part of the female.

28 Researchers at Kyoto University have studied troops of Japanese macaques *(Macaca fuscata)* at the same field site continuously since 1949 (Imanishi 1960), and much of this research is published in the journal *Primates*. The social inheritance of rank can be found in Kawamura (1958) and Koyama (1967).

29 Bernstein (1970).

30 Many of the field studies that defined modern primatology are available in DeVore (1965), Dolhinow (1968, 1972), and Smuts et al. (1987). See Strum and Fedigan (2000) for interesting essays on the history of the field.

31 Wrangham et al. (1996).

32 For sources on rhesus *(Macaca mulatta)* see the next section of this chapter. For savannah baboons (*Papio anubis* and *Papio papio*), see Altmann and Altmann (1973), Cheney and Seyfarth (2007), De-Vore et al. (1961), and Smuts (1999). Chimpanzees are discussed in more detail below in this chapter.

33 Chance and Jolly (1970); Chance and Larsen (1976); Virgo and Waterhouse (1969). This terminology was never widely adopted.

34 Female primatologists have noticed this (Strum and Fedigan 2000).

35 Cheney and Seyfarth (2007).

36 My research on rhesus monkeys was made possible by Professor Karl H. Pribram, M.D., the Department of Psychiatry at the Stanford University Medical School, and the National Institutes of Health of the U.S. government.

37 Male rhesus monkeys weigh from 3,500 to 18,000 grams, females from 2,500 to 16,300 grams (Napier and Napier 1967: 412).

38 There are literally hundreds of observational studies involving rhesus monkeys, and this literature indicates that the social inter-actions of this species in captivity do not differ significantly from those in its natural habitat. Important studies include Agar and Mitchell (1975), Altmann (1962), Bernstein and Mason (1963b "Activity Patterns ..."), Kaufmann (1967), Lindburg (1971, 1980), Rawlins and Kessler (1986), Rowell and Hinde (1962), and Sade (1967).

39 Kinship effects on rhesus rank are described by Koford (1963), Marsden (1968), Missakian (1972), and Sade (1967).

40 Ehardt and Bernstein (1986).

41 My own group-formation experiments (unpublished) confirm those of Bernstein and his colleagues: Bernstein (1964, 1974); Bernstein, Gordon , and Rose (1974); Bernstein and Mason

(1963a "Group Formation . . ."). Artificial group formation does not always result in physical wounds: Gust et al. (1991); Jarrell et al. (2008).

42 Jarrell et al. (2008).

43 Harlow (1971).

44 Maestripieri (2007: 100) asserts that rhesus adult males kill infants, yet a search of the primate literature produces no unequivocal examples. To the contrary, it has been shown that when rhesus infants are taken from one free-ranging troop and introduced to another, they are not attacked—they are usually adopted (Southwick et al. 1974).

45 Butynski (1982).

46 Goodall (1965), Teleki (1973).

47 Boesch (1996, 2002), Tomasello (2008, 2009).

48 De Waal (1982). A linear hierarchy is one in which the alpha individual outranks all those below him, the second in rank is dominant over all but the alpha, and so on, until the omega individual is reached, who is subordinate to all and dominant to none.

49 Stanford (1995 , 2001). There is a huge literature on the social life of *Pan troglodytes*. Two excellent scientific sources are Goodall (1986) and Wrangham et al. (1996).

50 Stanford (1998) provides a detailed comparison *of Pan paniscus* and *troglodytes*. The different ideological positioning of the two species of chimpanzees is recognized by Frans de Waal (2009), who is a respected primatologist, a Darwinian, and one of the foremost authorities on *Pan*.

51 Stanford (2001).

52. Ibid. 109–10.

53 Ibid. 115.

54 Stress is indicated by elevated cortisol in the blood, whereas reduced immune function is measured by lowered counts of T cells and lymphocytes. The relationship of these variables to social rank has been documented in a number of mammalian species, including rhesus monkeys (Gust et al. 1991).

55 Carmena et al. (2005); Nicolelis (2006).

56 Stanford (2001: 116).

57 Toth and Schick (2009).

58 Watts et al. (2006).

59 Washburn and C. Lancaster (1968). See also Washburn and Wenner-Gren Foundation (1961). The hunting hypothesis has been critiqued from an explicitly Darwinian perspective by Bird and O'Connell (2006).

60 Isaac (1978, 1989).

61 Slocum (1975), Zihlman (1981).

62 Lee (1979), Lee, DeVore, and Wenner-Gren Foundation (1969), Marshall (1976).

63 Hawkes, O'Connell, and Blurton Jones (2001: 132).

64 Quoted by Sussman (1999: 458) in an anthropological critique of the hunting hypothesis.

65 Endicott and Endicott (2008).

66 Wright (1994), whose book is lauded by Pinker himself, introduces "the new science of evolutionary psychology" in more than 400 pages of Darwinian hagiography.

67 For a summary of the ethnographic evidence on contemporary gatherers and hunters, with sources, see Erdal and Whiten (1996).

68 Estioko-Griffin and Griffin (1981).

69 Bird et al. (2012).

70 Eibl-Eibesfeldt (1974).

71 Ibid. 455–56.

72 Erdal and Whiten (1996).

73 I give examples and sources of altruistic action in humans in Chapter 7.

74 Darwin (1871).

75 Axelrod and Hamilton (1981). This theoretical formulation is still going strong thirty years later, as shown, for example, in Kappeler and van Schaik (2006).

76 The social science of reciprocal exchange is attributed to Marcel Mauss, who wrote in French in the early years of the twentieth century. Mauss's work is available in two English translations, the first published in 1954. For the documentation of reciprocal

exchange in societies studied by subsequent anthropologists, see Sahlins (1965, 1972).

77 Primatologist Frans de Waal (2001) summarizes some of this evidence and reproduces a photograph of a female dog sharing a cage with three adult Bengal tigers that she raised from cubs. For a more complete discussion of this phenomenon see Avital and Jablonka (2000).

78 Thierry and Anderson (1986) summarize adoption by primates, which is usually within the same troop, so it is possible that the animals are related. For evidence of adoption of unrelated individuals by primates, see Deets and Harlow (1974); Southwick et al. (1974).

79 Dogs observe humans for cues as to how to behave in a way more similar to human infants than to wild canines such as wolves: Tomasello and Kaminski (2009).

80 Maestripieri (2007).

81 Roughgarden, Oishi, and Akçay (2006).

82 Bowlby (1969); Harlow (1971). I did some of this research: Patterson et al. (1975); Reynolds (1976).

83 Examples and possible biological explanations for "alloparental behavior" (caring for the child of another) are provided by Avital and Jablonka (2000: Chapter 7). These authors see it as intrinsically related to social learning.

84 Dunbar (2008: 139-40). In the formative period of sociobiology, in the 1970s, the anthropological understanding of kinship was readily accessible in books commonly placed on course reserve lists in university libraries (for example, Keesing 1975), as well as in critiques of sociobiology in the light of cross-cultural findings (Sahlins 1976, Chapter 2); but it is clear that these works were never read by E. O. Wilson and Richard Dawkins, or until recently by contemporary Darwinians writing on the evolution of kinship.

85 Malinowski (1922) explicates his method in the Introduction to *Argonauts*. Michael W. Young (2004; Young and Malinowski 1998) provides valuable biographical detail and historical context. The descriptions of Trobriand society and the quotations in this section are from Malinowski (1966: 77–79).

86 Reynolds (1976). Psychological attachment theory came into primatology through the work of John Bowlby (1969) and Harry Harlow (1971). Their research shows that primate infants are born with the motivation to establish social relationships with caregivers and that adult primates (when properly socialized and motivated) have a predisposition to respond.

87 Smuts (1999), especially the summation on p. 231.

88 Kimbrell (1993), Sault (1994, 1996).

89 There is a good deal of theoretical overlap between sociobiology and its companion field of evolutionary psychology. McKinnon (2005) makes a good case that the "innate" modules of evolutionary psychology are a projection of Western cultural categories on to the brain. Gottlieb (2012), a former executive editor at *The Economist*, dismisses evolutionary psychology as just-so stories. In this chapter, I focus on Machiavellian intelligence, formulated by Byrne and Whiten (1988), Whiten and Byrne (1997).

90 Hauser (1988).

91 Dawkins (1976).

92 Quoted by Sapp (2003: 260) from Hrdy (1983: 21).

93 Ibid.

94 Hrdy (2009: 4).

95 Ibid. 5.

96 Ibid. 7.

97 Reynolds (1993).

98 McGrew and Feistner (1992).

99 Burkart et al. (2007).

100 Hauser et al. (2003). Hauser bills himself as an expert on the evolution of deception. Significantly, the dean of arts and sciences at Harvard University investigated him for "eight instances of scientific misconduct" that "involved problems of data acquisition, data analysis, data retention, and the reporting of research methodologies and results" (Wade 2010). Hauser resigned his professorship in 2011.

101 Lancaster and Kaplan (2009).

102 De Waal (1996: 33-34)

103 Ibid. 95.

105 Midgley (1979, 1983).
105 De Waal (1996: 33-34).
106 McGrew (1998), Wrangham et al. (1996).
107 West-Eberhard (2003: 5).
108 Ibid.

References

Agar, M. E., and Gary Mitchell. 1975. Behavior of free-ranging ddult rhesus macaques: a review. In *The Rhesus Monkey*, vol. 1, edited by G. H. Bourne. New York: Academic Press.

Altmann, Stuart A. 1962. A field study of the sociobiology of rhesus monkeys. *Annals of the New York Academy of Sciences* 102: 338–435.

———, and Jeanne Altmann. 1973. *Baboon Ecology: African Field Research*. Chicago: University of Chicago Press.

Avital, Eytan, and Eva Jablonka. 2000. *Animal Traditions: Behavioural Inheritance in Evolution*. Cambridge and New York: Cambridge University Press.

Axelrod, Robert, and William D. Hamilton. 1981. The evolution of cooperation. *Science* 211 (4489): 1390–96.

Bernstein, Irwin S. 1964. The integration of rhesus monkeys introduced to a group. *Folia Primatologica* 2: 50–63.

———. 1970. Primate status hierarchies. In *Primate Behavior: Developments in Field and Laboratory Research*. New York and London: Academic Press.

———. 1974. Aggression and social controls in rhesus monkey (*Macaca mulatta*) groups revealed in group formation studies. *Folia Primatologica* 21: 81–107.

———, T. P. Gordon , and R. M. Rose. 1974. Factors influencing the expression of aggression during introductions to rhesus monkey groups. In *Primate Aggression, Territoriality, and Xenophobia*, edited by R. L. Holloway. New York: Academic Press.

———, and W. A. Mason. 1963a. Group formation by rhesus monkeys. *Animal Behavior* 11 (1): 28–31.

———, and William A. Mason. 1963b. Activity patterns of rhesus monkeys in a social group. *Animal Behavior* 11: 455–60.

Bird, Douglas W., and James F. O'Connell. 2006. Behavioral ecology and archaeology. *Journal of Archaeological Research* 14 (2): 143–88.

Bird, Rebecca Bliege, et al. 2012. The hierarchy of virtue: mutualism, altruism, and signaling in Martu women's cooperative hunting. *Evolution and Human Behavior* 33 (1): 64–78.

Boesch, Christophe. 1996. Hunting Strategies of Gombe and Taï Chimpanzees. In *Chimpanzee Cultures*, edited by Richard Wrangham et al. Cambridge, MA and London: Harvard University Press.

———. 2002. Cooperative hunting roles among Tai chimpanzees. *Human Nature* 13 (1).

Bowlby, John. 1969. *Attachment and Loss*. New York: Basic Books.

Burkart, Judith M. , Ernst Fehr, Charles Efferson, and Carel P. van Schaik. 2007. Other-regarding preferences in a nonhuman primate: common marmosets provision food altruistically. *Proceedings of the National Academy of Sciences of the United States of America* 104 (50): 19762–66.

Butynski, T. M. 1982. Vertebrate predation by primates: a review of hunting patterns and prey. *Journal of Human Evolution* 11: 421–30.

Byrne, Richard W., and Andrew Whiten. 1988. *Machiavellian Intelligence: Social Expertise and the Evolution of Intellect in Monkeys, Apes, and Humans*. Oxford: Oxford University Press / New York: Clarendon Press.

Carmena, Joseph M., Mikhail A. Lebedev, Craig S. Henriquez, and Miguel A. L. Nicolelis. 2005. Stable ensemble performance with single-neuron variability during reaching movements in primates. *Journal of Neuroscience* 25 (46): 10712–16.

Chance, M. R. A., and R. R. Larsen, eds. 1976. *The Social Structure of Attention*. New York: John Wiley and Sons.

_____. and Clifford J. Jolly. 1970. *Social Groups of Monkeys, Apes, and Men*. New York: Dutton.

Cheney, Dorothy L., and Robert M. Seyfarth. 2007. *Baboon Metaphysics: The Evolution of a Social Mind*. Chicago: University of Chicago Press.

Crook, Paul. 1994. *Darwinism, War and History: The Debate over the Biology of War from the "Origin of Species" to the First World War*. Cambridge and New York: Cambridge University Press.

Darlington, Philip J. 1981. Genes, individuals, and kin selection. *Proceedings of the National Academy of Sciences of the United States of America* 78 (7): 4440–43.

Darwin, Charles. 1871. *The Descent of Man*. 1st ed. 2 vols. London: John Murray.

Dawkins, Richard. 1976. *The Selfish Gene*. Oxford University Press.

de Waal, Frans B. M. 1982. *Chimpanzee Politics: Power and Sex among Apes*. New York: Harper and Row.

_____.1996. *Good Natured: The Origins of Right and Wrong in Humans and Other Animals*. Cambridge, MA: Harvard University Press.

_____. 2001. *The Ape and the Sushi Master: Cultural Reflections of a Primatologist*. New York: Basic Books.

_____. 2009. Was "Ardi" a liberal? *Huffington Post*, 2009 Oct. 18.

Deets, Allyn C., and Harry F. Harlow. 1974. Adoption of single and multiple infants by rhesus monkey mothers. *Primates* 15 (2-3): 193–203.

Desmond, Adrian, and James Moore. 1991. *Darwin: The Life of a Tormented Evolutionist*. New York: W. W. Norton.

DeVore, Irven, ed. 1965. *Primate Behavior: Field Studies of Monkeys and Apes*. New York: Holt.

_____, et al. 1961. *Baboon Behavior.* Dept. of Anthropology, University of California: Released by Educational Film Sales, University Extension, University of California.

Dolhinow, Phyllis. 1968. *Primates: Studies in Adaptation and Variability.* New York: Holt.

_____. 1972. *Primate Patterns.* New York: Holt.

Dunbar, Robin. 2008. Kinship in biological perspective. In *Early Human Kinship: From Sex to Social Reproduction*, edited by Nicholas J. Allen et al. Malden, MA: Blackwell.

Ehardt, C. L., and Irwin S. Bernstein. 1986. Matrilineal overthrows in rhesus monkey groups. *International Journal of Primatology* 7 (2): 157–81.

Endicott, Kirk M., and Karen L. Endicott. 2008. *The Headman Was a Woman: The Gender Egalitarian Batek of Malaysia.* Long Grove, IL: Waveland Press.

Erdal, David , and Andrew Whiten. 1996. Egalitarianism and Machiavellian Intelligence in human evolution. In *Modeling the Early Human Mind*, edited by P. Mellars and K. R. Gibson. Cambridge and Oakville, CT: McDonald Institute for Archaeological Research /Oxbow Books.

Estioko-Griffin, Agnes, and P. Bion Griffin. 1981. Woman the hunter: the Agta. In *Woman the Gatherer*, edited by F. Dahlberg. New Haven, CT: Yale University Press.

Franklin, James. 1994. David Stove (1927–1994). *Australian*, June 21, 1994.

Friedman, Milton, and Rose D. Friedman. 1962. *Capitalism and Freedom.* Chicago: University of Chicago Press.

_____, and Richard T. Selden. 1975. *Capitalism and Freedom: Problems and Prospects; Proceedings of a Conference in Honor of Milton Friedman.* Charlottesville: University Press of Virginia.

Goodall, Jane. 1965. Chimpanzees of the Gombe Stream Reserve. In *Primate Behavior: Field Studies of Monkeys and Apes*, edited by I. Devore. New York: Holt.

_____. 1971. *In the Shadow of Man*. Boston: Houghton Mifflin.

_____. 1986. *The Chimpanzees of Gombe: Patterns of Behavior*. Cambridge, MA: Harvard University Press.

Gottlieb, Anthony. 2012. "It ain't necessarily so." *The New Yorker*, 17 Sep.

Gust, D. A., T. P. Gordon, M. E. Wilson, A. Ahmed-Ansari , A. R. Brodie, and H. M. McClure. 1991. Formation of a new social group of unfamiliar female rhesus monkeys affects the immune and pituitary adrenocortical systems. *Brain, Behavior, and Immunity* 5 (3): 296–307.

Harlow, Harry F. 1971. *Learning to Love*. San Francisco: Albion.

Hauser, Marc D. 1988. Minding the behavior of deception. In *Machiavellian Intelligence II: Social Expertise and the Evolution of Intellect in Monkeys, Apes, and Humans*, edited by A. Whiten and R. W. Byrne. Cambridge: Cambridge University Press.

_____, M. Keith Chen, Frances Chen, and Emmeline Chuang. 2003. Give unto others: genetically unrelated cotton-top tamarin monkeys preferentially give food to those who altruistically give food back. *Proceedings of the Royal Society of London* 270 (1531): 2363–70.

Hausfater, Glenn, and Sarah Blaffer Hrdy. 1984. *Infanticide: Comparative and Evolutionary Perspectives*. New York: Aldine.

Hawkes, K., J. F. O'Connell, and N. G. Blurton Jones. 2001. Hadza meat sharing. *Evolution and Human Behavior* 22: 113–42.

Hrdy, Sarah Blaffer. 1977. *The Langurs of Abu: Female and Male strategies of Reproduction*. Cambridge, MA: Harvard University Press.

_____. 1983. *The Woman That Never Evolved*. Cambridge, MA: Harvard University Press.

_____. 2009. *Mothers and Others: The Evolutionary Origins of Mutual Understanding*. Cambridge, MA: Belknap Press of Harvard University.

Hofstadter, Richard. 1963. *Anti-intellectualism in American life*. New York: Knopf.

Imanishi, Kinji. 1960. Social organization of subhuman primates in their natural habitat. *Current Anthropology* 1 (5/6): 393–407.

Isaac, Glynn. 1978. The food-sharing behavior of protohuman hominids. *Scientific American* 238 (4): 90–108.

_____. 1989. *The Archaeology of Human Origins: Papers by Glynn Isaac*. Cambridge: Cambridge University Press.

Jarrell, Holly, et al. 2008. Polymorphisms in the serotonin reuptake transporter gene modify the consequences of social status on metabolic health in female rhesus monkeys. *Physiology and Behavior* 93 (4-5): 807–19.

Jones, Daniel Stedman. 2012. *Masters of the Universe: Hayek, Friedman, and the Birth of Neoliberal Politics*. Princeton and Oxford: Princeton University Press.

Kappeler, Peter M., and Carel van Schaik. 2006. *Cooperation in Primates and Humans: Mechanisms and Evolution*. Berlin and New York: Springer.

Kaufmann, J. H. 1967. Social relations of adult males in a free-ranging band of rhesus monkeys. In *Social Communication among Primates*, edited by S. A. Altmann. Chicago: University of Chicago Press.

Kawamura, S. 1958. On the rank system in a natural group of Japanese monkeys. *Primates* 1: 111–30.

Keesing, Roger M. 1975. *Kin Groups and Social Structure*. New York: Holt.

Kimbrell, Andrew. 1993. *The Human Body Shop: The Engineering and Marketing of Life*. New York: Harper Collins.

Koford, Carl B. 1963. Rank of mothers and sons in bands of rhesus monkeys. *Science* 141: 356–57.

Koyama, N. 1967. On the dominance rank and kinship of a wild Japanese monkey troop in Arashiyama. *Primates* 8: 189–216.

Kummer, Hans. a1968a. Two variations in the social organization of baboons. In *Primates: Studies in Adaptation and Variability*, edited by P. Dolhinow. New York: Holt.

————. 1968b. Social organization of hamadryas baboons: a field study. *Bibliotheca Primatologica* (6): 1–189.

Lancaster, Jane B., and Hillard S. Kaplan. 2009. The endocrinology of the human adaptive complex. In *Endocrinology of Social Relationships*, edited by P. T. Ellison and P. G. Gray. Cambridge, MA: Harvard University Press.

Lee, Richard B. 1979. *The !Kung San: Men, Women, and Work in a Foraging society*. Cambridge: Cambridge University Press.

————, Irven DeVore, and Wenner-Gren Foundation for Anthropological Research, eds. 1969. *Man the Hunter*. Chicago: Aldine.

Lewis, Rebecca J. 2002. Beyond dominance: the importance of leverage. *Quarterly Review of Biology* 77 (2): 149–64.

Lewontin, Richard C. 1993. *Biology as Ideology: The Doctrine of DNA*. New York: Harper Collins. First U.S. edition. Original edition Canada 1991.

————, Steven Rose, and Leon J. Kamin. 1984. *Not in Our Genes: Biology, Ideology and Human Nature*. New York: Pantheon/Random House.

Lindburg, D. G. 1971. The rhesus monkey in North India: an ecological and behavioral study. *Primate Behavior* 2: 1–106.

_____, ed. 1980. *The Macaques: Studies in Ecology, Behavior, and Evolution.* New York: Van Nostrand Reinhold.

Loy, James. 1970. Behavioral responses of free-ranging rhesus monkeys to food shortage. *American Journal of Physical Anthropology* 33 (2): 263–71.

Maestripieri, Dario. 2007. *Machiavellian Intelligence: How Rhesus Monkeys and Humans Have Conquered the World.* Chicago: University of Chicago Press.

Malinowski, Bronislaw. 1922. *Argonauts of the Western Pacific: An Account of Native Enterprise and Adventure in the Archipelagos of Melanesian New Guinea. Studies in Economics and Political Science, no. 65 in the series of monographs by writers connected with the London School of Economics and Political Science.* New York: Dutton.

_____. 1966. *Crime and Custom in Savage Society.* Totowa, NJ: Littlefield, Adams. First published in 1926.

Marsden, Halsey M. 1968. Agonistic behavior of young rhesus monkeys after changes induced in social rank of their mothers. *Animal Behavior* 16: 38–44.

Marshall, Lorna. 1976. *The !Kung of Nyae Nyae.* Cambridge, MA: Harvard University Press.

Maslow, Abraham. 1936. The Role of dominance in the social and sexual behavior of infra-human primates. *Journal of Genetic Psychology:* 28–29.

Mauss, Marcel. 1954. *The Gift: Forms and Functions of Exchange in Archaic Societies.* Translated by Ian Cunnison. With an introduction by E. E. Evans-Pritchard. Glencoe, IL: Free Press.

McGrew, William C. 1998. Culture in nonhuman primates? *Review of Anthropology* 27: 301–28.

_____ and Anna T. C. Feistner. 1992. Two nonhuman primate models for the evolution of human food sharing: chimpanzees and callitrichids. In *The Adapted Mind: Evolutionary Psychology and the Generation of Culture*, edited by J. H. Barkow. Oxford: Oxford University Press.

McKinnon, Susan. 2005. *Neo-liberal Genetics: The Myths and Moral Tales of Evolutionary Psychology.* Chicago: Prickly Paradigm Press.

Midgley, Mary. 1979. Gene-juggling. *Philosophy* 54 (210): 439–58.

_____. 1983. Selfish genes and social Darwinism. *Philosophy* 58 (225): 365–77.

Missakian, Elizabeth A. 1972. Genealogical and cross-genealogical dominance relations in a group of free-ranging rhesus monkeys (*Macaca mulatta*) on Cayo Santiago. *Primates* 13 (2): 169–89.

Napier, John Russell, and P. H. Napier. 1967. *A Handbook of Living Primates: Morphology, Ecology and Behaviour of Nonhuman Primates.* London and New York: Academic Press.

Nicolelis, Miguel A. L. 2006. Rhesus brain controls robot arm. *Science News*, 92, Feb. 11.

Patterson, F. G., J. D. Bonvillian, P. C. Reynolds, and E. E. Maccoby. 1975. Mother and peer attachment under conditions of fear in rhesus monkeys (*Macaca mulatta*). *Primates* 16: 75–81.

Power, Margaret. 1991. *The Egalitarians, Human and Chimpanzee: An Anthropological View of Social Organization.* Cambridge and New York: Cambridge University Press.

Rawlins, Richard G., and Matt J. Kessler, eds. 1986. *The Cayo Santiago Macaques: History, Behavior, and Biology.* Albany: State University of New York Press.

Reynolds, Peter C. 1976. The emergence of early hominid social organization. I: The attachment systems. *Yearbook of Physical Anthropology* 29: 73–95.

_____. 1993. The complementation theory of language and tool use. In *Tools, Language, and Cognition in Human Evolution*, edited by K. Gibson and T. Ingold. Cambridge: Cambridge University Press.

Ridley, Matt. 1997. *The Origins of Virtue: Human Instincts and the Evolution of Cooperation*. New York: Viking/Penguin.

Roughgarden, Joan, Meeeko Oishi, and Erol Akçay. 2006. Reproductive social behavior: cooperative games to replace sexual selection. *Science* 311: 965–69.

Rowell, T. E., and R. A. Hinde. 1962. Vocal communication in the rhesus monkey (*Macaca mulatta*). *Proceedings of the Zoological Society of London* 138: 279–94.

Sade, Donald, S. 1967. Determinants of dominance in a group of free-ranging rhesus monkeys. In *Social Communication among Primates*, edited by S. A. Altmann. Chicago: University of Chicago Press.

Sahlins, Marshall D. 1965. On the sociology of primitive exchange. In M. Baton, ed., *The Relevance of Models for Anthropology*. ASA Monographs 1. London.

_____. 1972. *Stone Age Economics*. Chicago: Aldine-Atherton.

_____. 1976. *The Use and Abuse of Biology: An Anthropological Critique of Sociobiology*. Ann Arbor: University of Michigan Press.

Sapolsky, Robert M. 2001. *A Primate's Memoir*. New York: Scribner.

Sault, Nicole. 1994. How the body shapes parenthood: "surrogate" mothers in the United States and godmothers in Mexico. In *Many Mirrors: Body Image and Social Relations*, edited by N. Sault. New Brunswick, NJ: Rutgers University Press.

_____. 1996. Many mothers, many fathers: the meaning of parenting around the world. *Santa Clara Law Review* 36 (2): 395–408.

Slocum, Sally. 1975. Woman the gatherer. In *Towards an Anthropology of Women*, edited by Rayna R. Reiter. New York: Monthly Review Press.

Smith, Grafton Elliot. 1933. *The Diffusion of Culture*. London: Watts & Co.

Smuts, Barbara B. 1999. *Sex and Friendship in Baboons: With a New Preface*. Cambridge, MA: Harvard University Press.

_____, and Dorothy L. Cheney, Robert M. Seyfarth, Richard W. Wrangham, and Thomas T. Struhsaker, eds. 1987. *Primate Societies*. University of Chicago.

Soltis, Joseph. 2004. Mating systems. In *Macaque Societies: A Model for the Study of Social Organization*, edited by B. Thierry, M. Singh, and M. Kaumanns. Cambridge: Cambridge University Press.

Southwick, Charles H., M. F. Siddiqi, M. Y. Farooqui, and B. C. Pal. 1974. Xenophobia among free-ranging rhesus groups in India. In *Primate Aggression, Territoriality, and Xenophobia*, edited by R. L. Holloway. New York: Academic Press.

Stanford, Craig B. 1998. The social behavior of chimpanzees and bonobos: empirical evidence and shifting assumptions. *Current Anthropology* 39 (4): 399-420.

_____. 2001. The ape's gift: meat-eating, meat-sharing, and human evolution. In *Tree of Origin: What Primate Behavior Can Tell Us about Human Social Evolution*, edited by F. B. M. de Waal. Cambridge: Harvard University Press.

Stove, David. 1995. *Darwinian Fairytales*. Aldershot, England, and Burlington, VT: Ashgate.

_____. 2006. *Darwinian Fairytales: Selfish Genes, Errors of Heredity, and Other Fables of Evolution*. Edited and with an Introduction by Roger Kimbal. New York: Encounter Books.

_____. n.d. A new religion. *Royal Institute of Philosophy*. http://www.royalinstitutephilosophy.org/articles/article.php?id=27 (Accessed July 2007).

Strum, Shirley C., and Linda Marie Fedigan, eds. 2000. *Primate Encounters: Models of Science, Gender, and Society*. Chicago: University of Chicago Press.

_____, Deborah Forster, and Edwin Hutchins. 1988. Why Machiavellian intelligence may not be Machiavellian. In *Machiavellian Intelligence II: Social Expertise and the Evolution of Intellect in Monkeys, Apes, and Humans*, edited by A. Whiten and R. W. Byrne. Cambridge: Cambridge University Press.

Sussman, Robert W. 1999. The myth of man the hunter, man the killer and the evolution of human morality. *Zygon* 34 (3): 453–71.

Teleki, Geza. 1973. *The Predatory Behavior of Wild Chimpanzees*. Lewisburg: Bucknell University Press.

Thierry, Bernard, and James R. Anderson. 1986. Adoption in Anthropoid primates. *International Journal of Primatology* 7 (2): 191–216.

Tomasello, Michael. 2008. *Origins of Human Communication*. Cambridge, MA: MIT Press.

_____. 2009. *Why We Cooperate*. Cambridge, MA: MIT Press.

_____, and Julianne Kaminski. 2009. Like infant, like dog. *Science* 325: 1213–14.

Toth, Nicholas, and Kathy Schick. 2009. The Oldowan: the tool making of early hominins and chimpanzees compared. *Annual Review of Anthropology* 38: 289–305.

Tutin, Caroline E. G. 1979. Mating patterns and reproductive strategies in a community of wild chimpanzees (*Pan troglodytes schweinfurthii*). *Behavioral Ecology and Sociobiology* 6 (1): 29-38.

Virgo, H. B., and M. J. Waterhouse. 1969. The Emergence of attention structure among rhesus macaques. *Man: Journal of the Royal Anthropological Institute* 4: 85–94.

Wade, Nicholas. 2010. Harvard finds scientist guilty of misconduct. *New York Times*, 20 Aug.

Washburn, S. L., and Wenner-Gren Foundation for Anthropological Research. 1961. *Social Life of Early Man*. Viking Fund Publications in Anthropology 31. Chicago: Aldine.

———, and C. K. Lancaster. 1968. The evolution of hunting. In *Man the Hunter*, edited by R. B. Lee and I. Devore. Chicago: Aldine.

Watts, David P., et al. 2006. Lethal intergroup aggression by chimpanzees in Kibale National Park, Uganda. *American Journal of Primatology* 68 (2): 161–80.

West-Eberhard, Mary Jane. 2003. *Developmental Plasticity and Evolution*. Oxford and New York: Oxford University Press.

Whiten, Andrew, and Richard W. Byrne. 1997. *Machiavellian Intelligence II: Extensions and Evaluations*. Cambridge and New York: Cambridge University Press.

Wilson, Edward O. 1975. *Sociobiology: The New Synthesis*. Cambridge, MA: Belknap Press of Harvard University Press.

Wrangham, Richard, W. C. McGrew, Frans B. M. de Waal, and Paul G. Heltne, eds. 1996. *Chimpanzee Cultures*. Cambridge, MA, and London: Harvard University Press. Original edition 1994.

———, and D. Peterson. 1996. *Demonic Males: Apes and the Origin of Human Violence*. Boston: Houghton Mifflin.

Wright, Robert. 1994. *The Moral Animal : The New Science of Evolutionary Psychology*. New York: Pantheon Books.

Yerkes, Robert M. 1937. Primate coöperation and intelligence. *American Journal of Psychology* 50 (1/4): 254–70.

Young, Michael W. 2004. *Malinowski: Odyssey of an Anthropologist, 1884–1920*. New Haven, CT: Yale University Press.

———. and Bronislaw Malinowski. 1998. *Malinowski's Kiriwina: Fieldwork Photography, 1915–1918*. Chicago: University of

Chicago Press.

Zihlman, A. L. 1981. Women as shapers of the human adaptation. In *Woman the Gatherer*, edited by F. Dahlberg. New Haven, CT: Yale University Press.

Zuckerman, Solly. 1932. *The Social Life of Monkeys and Apes*. New York: Harcourt, Brace and Company.

Chapter Seven

Darwin's Contributions

Charles Darwin is most famous for things he did not do. He was not the discoverer of organic evolution, nor did he coin the phrase "survival of the fittest." At the same time, Darwin has received insufficient credit for many things that he did do that have had profound and long-lasting effects on Western society. These, contributions, however, are not in biological science but in the realm of state religion, materialist philosophy, and education.

Charles Darwin and his cohort

    • replaced the dominant ideology of the universities, namely Christianity, with the belief system of philosophical materialism (Chapters 2 and 3);

    • facilitated the takeover by the capitalist corporation by postulating competition and self interest as the source of the moral order and evolutionary change (Chapter 3);

    • saved the myth of Progress by maintaining that Malthus's Law of Population produces evolutionary winners who are better adapted than those who cannot effectively compete for scarce resources (Chapter 3);

    • helped to establish the biomedical technocracy (Chapters 4) while institutionalizing the educational infrastructure needed to support it (Chapter 3);

• institutionalized eugenics as the scientific way to improve the human species and ensure social Progress (Chapter 5).

In spite of these achievements, Charles Darwin is usually presented as the natural scientist who discovered the mechanism of organic evolution, not as the intellectual architect of a moral order congenial to corporations and technocracy. The moral order is arguably his greater achievement, for natural selection has limited explanatory power for primate social organization and cultural adaptation (Chapter 6). Moreover, evolutionary theory is so comingled with the Darwinist *a priori* (defined by the four tenets of PHAGe^G) that it is often hard to tell where the science ends and the capitalist ideology begins, as with the concept of the selfish gene.

Yet it is not anthropology's task to assess the scientific adequacy of natural selection as a general theory of organic evolution—that is the responsibility of biologists. But anthropology *is* in a position to describe the theory's ideological functions and its social implications. To this end, I have argued that Darwin's work is best understood as a projection of the values and beliefs of corporate capitalism and British imperialism onto organic nature.

When Marx Read Darwin

Darwin explicitly states his capitalist premises ("the doctrine of Malthus, applied to the whole animal and vegetable kingdoms"), but it was Karl Marx who immediately understood the ideological implications of natural selection. As Marx wrote in a letter to Engels at the time: "It is remarkable how Darwin rediscovers, among the beasts and plants, the society of England with its division of labour, competition, opening up of new markets, 'inventions' and Malthusian 'struggle for existence'."[2] Yet Marx buried this insight in his private correspondence, thus giving Darwin's theory of natural selection an implicit imprimatur.

Darwin and Marx, the intellectual architects of the dominant world systems of the twentieth century, spent their working years within a short train ride of each other, yet neither had a discernable effect on the other's thinking. Darwin never mentions Marx in print, while Marx's only published words on Darwin are two footnotes in *Das Kapital*. Except for a thank-you note that Darwin sent to Marx for an unsolicited copy of *Das Kapital*, they never corresponded either. It is probable that Darwin never even looked at Marx's magnum opus, for it was found in Darwin's library with the pages still uncut.[1]

Nonetheless, the world systems of Darwin and Marx are locked in a timeless pas de deux. Both have an unmistakable nineteenth-century character: the same corrosive materialism, the same emphasis on struggle, the same hostility to religion, the same pretension to universality, and the same appeal to the possibilities of progress grounded in purportedly scientific laws of evolutionary development. Yet Darwin's theory is based on self-interest and competition, whereas Marxism presumes social consciousness and the common good, making these two world systems incompatible in a deep way.

Since the publication of *Origin* in 1859, the left has seen Darwin as an ally in the fight for materialism and irreligion even while criticizing many aspects of Darwinian thought, including Social Darwinism, eugenics, and "Weismannism" (that is, genetics based on Weismann's[G] barrier).[3] But with the exception of Stalin, who banned population genetics and reinstated Lamarckism, the left never doubted Darwin's carefully-crafted persona of the apolitical biologist floating above the fray. It was not until the emergence of postmodernism in the second half of the twentieth century that Marx's observation of natural selection as a projection of capitalism could be taken at face value.

To say that a belief system functions as an ideology is not to judge it to be false. As discussed in Chapter 1, truth is usually a more persuasive and enduring foundation for ideology than is falsehood. Yet the ideological use of scientific findings is potentially destructive of science itself, since science presumes skepticism not belief. When a science is based on culturally-specific notions of human nature, then the potential for distortion is much greater. Once a science becomes the foundation of the moral order, then it is essentially impervious to criticism.

Much of the power of a dominant ideology is the widespread conviction that it is incontrovertibly true. And the more institutional power that the ideology underwrites, the harder it is for anyone to doubt its fundamental tenets. Yet the more massive the edifice that the ideology has to support, the more unstable the erection becomes. Thus, to even raise the question of the scientific veracity of Darwinism is to begin the process of disestablishing Wall Street and Silicon Valley, Big Science and the corporate academy—to name only the most prominent beneficiaries of a human nature construed as a vehicle for competition, consumption, and technical Progress.

In the next section, I take advantage of the newly-cleared shelf space to explore the social implications of the thought of Wallace and Kropotkin—two Victorian evolutionists who were sidelined more than a century ago by the apotheosis of Darwin. Neither man saw any incompatibility between biological evolution and socialism, but neither was a doctrinaire follower of Darwin either. In reassessing their contributions, I present my personal vision of a postcapitalist society based on Christian ethics and democratic socialism: not a roadmap but a road sign pointing in the direction of life without Darwin.

Notes

1 Stack (2000).

2 Marx to Engels, 18 June 1862. http://www.historyisaweapon.com/defcon6/works/1862/letters/62_06_18.html

  Also quoted by Crook (1994: 13) with a slightly different translation but with the same meaning.

3 Stack (2000).

References

Crook, Paul. 1994. *Darwinism, War and History: The Debate over the Biology of War from the "Origin of Species" to the First World War.* Cambridge; New York: Cambridge University Press.

Stack, D. A. 2000. The first Darwinian left: radical and socialist responses to Darwin, 1859-1914, *History of Political Thought* 21 (4): 682-710.

Chapter Eight

Postcapitalism

In 1898, the co-theorist of natural selection, Alfred Russel Wallace, noted that the experience of the nineteenth century:

> has fully established the fact that, under our present competitive system of capitalistic production and distribution, the continuous increase in wealth in the possession of the capitalist and landowning classes is not accompanied by any corresponding diminution of the severity and misery and want or in the numbers of those who suffer from extreme poverty.[1]

Wallace's assessment is as true today as it was then. In the 1990s, as the American[G] empire was expanding into the former Soviet Union, the American economy was experiencing a major concentration of wealth. The income of the middle class in the United States, when measured by purchasing power, had been falling steadily since the 1980s, while the net worth of the rich had significantly increased.[2] These trends were made dramatically clear early in the twenty-first century by a report from the Organisation for Economic Co-operation and Development.[3] The OECD is not a socialist think tank but was set up in 1961 to foster capitalist development in the free world. The OECD member countries include America's economic peers: all major European nations as well as all major industrial countries with the exception of Taiwan and BRIC (Brazil, Russia, India, and

China). Yet by 2008 the United States had "the highest inequality level and poverty rate" of any member country, with the exception of Mexico and Turkey.[4]

Moreover, when the world's richest nations are ranked by the
gap between rich and poor, the United States wins the bronze
medal, surpassed only by Hong Kong (gold) and Singapore (silver), making a continent-sized country socially equivalent to a
city-state run by the superrich. A more recent study by the bank
Credit Suisse, done with slightly different statistical measures,
shows a similar pattern. In the words of these authors: "The bottom half of wealth holders collectively accounted for less than
1% of total global wealth in mid-2019, while the richest 10%
own 82% of global wealth and the top 1% alone own 45%."[5]

In a similar vein, the top seventeen capital management firms
in the world (as measured by the dollar value of their assets),
corporations such as Morgan Stanley and Blackrock, controlled
over 41 *trillion* dollars in 2017. These firms invest on behalf of
the 36 million millionaires and 2,400 billionaires that comprise
the world's richest one percent, and they are heavily invested in
each other.[6]

Even more astonishing, only a few hundred people serve on
the boards of directors of these companies. A population that
could fit in an auditorium sets the priorities of capital investment worldwide. As one professor of international relations has
argued, the United States now satisfies the definition of a plutocracy,[G] a society governed by and for the rich.[7] At the same time,
the top one percent and their global institutions comprise what
Robinson calls a transnational capitalist class (TCC) that is beyond the law of any one country.[8]

These long-term trends should not surprise us. That twentieth-century engine of American middle-class affluence—consumer capitalism—was never about sharing the wealth. Rather,
it was a way of not having to. Instead of establishing a society

in which everyone gives according to his ability and receives according to his need, consumer capitalism promises everyone the prospect of more consumer goods through an ever-expanding pie. *Everyone* gets to eat champagne and lobster. Expansion of the pie requires a society-wide commitment to economic growth. Growth means increased consumption, which in turn requires more energy and raw materials. Also, energy consumption has environmentally destructive effects of its own such as heat, carbon dioxide, and nuclear waste. Capitalism's supposed remedy for a more inequitable distribution of wealth is environmental degradation.

At this point, the technocrat steps in and promises more bang for the buck by means of improved technology. Sure, the pie has to keep getting bigger, but a capitalist economy selects for new technology and process improvements that make production more efficient, providing increased growth at less environmental cost.[9]

Unfortunately, technology is only as sustainable as the society in which it is embedded. Even in cases where sustainable technology is widely adapted, such changes do not necessarily lead to a more ecologically sustainable society. The dream of Progress tells us that the old is obsolete and the new desirable, so technical innovation creates new, unsatisfied desires that can only be fulfilled by the latest and greatest. Also, by the time you and I buy it, the billionaires have moved on, so we need to throw out the old and buy something more up to date. At the same time, capitalist society increases desire in general through fashion and advertising so the satisfaction of material needs can never be stabilized nor achieved.

Under the values of capitalism, the well-being of other people is relevant only to the extent that the latter are useful for satisfying one's own interests, whether as employees, sales prospects, or investors. Where the traditional moral order is measured by how we treat other people, capitalism is based on the solipsistic motivations of envy, greed, and competition. Significantly, the motivations that are treated as virtues by capitalism are considered by traditional religion to be vices that fragment human community and endanger the human soul.

In short, the corporation's notion of morality is diametrically opposed to the moral order of real human beings, for whom the effect of one's action on others is the primary consideration. Indeed, as some theologians have argued, not only the corporation but all of capitalism is an inherently immoral form of social organization because it exalts profitability as the highest value while replacing moral judgment with putative market forces.[10] Indeed, it is hard for anyone to morally defend a system that takes collective wealth that has been created by large numbers of people working together and makes it the property of a few individuals.

From a moral point of view, the bounty made possible by industrial production, instead of being used to eliminate poverty and ameliorate suffering, was used to expand a competitive system of status display at the expense of the planet earth.

Indeed, capitalism is barely an economy at all. An economy distributes goods and services to the populace, but capitalism is better understood historically *as a way of converting a class system based on the hereditary control of land to one based on the competitive control of money.* It functions to concentrate wealth at the top of a social hierarchy, not to redistribute it. Some poor individuals do get wealthier by participating in the capitalist system (the rags to riches story); even more people live comfortable lives as its apologists and functionaries. But distributing wealth to anyone except to fellow investors as capital gains was never part of the system's charter, so the statistics of income disparity in countries where capitalism has free rein should come as no surprise.

As for the aspirations of social reformers, capitalism has never had the will or the means to deliver them. It is impossible for a system that is designed to concentrate wealth in the hands of a few to lift the masses out of poverty. It is also impossible for a capitalist corporation, which is legally charged with maximizing profit for its owners, to serve as an instrument of general well-being. The primary "duty" of the capitalist corporation is to maximize profit for its owners while ignoring the social and ecological consequences of its actions.[11]

In 2019 the heads of some of the largest corporations in the world met to improve the corporation's image. They added some nonprofit goals to the time-honored share-holder's return on investment—such as protecting the environment, investing in employees, and dealing fairly and ethically with suppliers.[12] This agreement, however, is nonbinding; and the value of corporations on the stock market is still being measured by profitability.

Prominent capitalists have recognized the moral vacuum at the heart of their institution. In the words of Kevin W. Sharer, longtime head of Amgen Inc., one of the world's largest biotech/pharmaceutical firms, and now on the faculty of the Harvard Business School: "Global capital doesn't have a social conscience. It will go where the returns are."[13]

The economic and social conditions of the twenty-first century mirror those of the Gilded Age, but there is a big difference in the public reaction to the situation. A century ago, there was a massive push to reform capitalism or to replace it with something better.[14] There were sit-down strikes in factories and demonstrations of worker solidarity, inspired by a powerful socialist critique. There were also marches in the streets that drew widespread public support for the socialist cause.

In the United States, this ferment led to the reforms initiated during the Progressive Era, such as increased voter registration, the extension of the vote to women, and eventually citizenship for American Indians. In addition there was legislation to strengthen the moral fiber of the nation, including eugenic sterilization of the biologically unfit and a nationwide ban on alcohol.

The First Hippie

No one better personifies the radical politics of the Progressive Era than a young college dropout, Dorothy Day.[15] She became an activist while still in her teens, inspired by the socially-conscious literature of the Victorian period and motivated by her own passion for social justice. Dorothy was first arrested as a teenager while demonstrating for voting rights for women. She would be arrested many more times in her life, fighting for social equality on a variety of fronts.

In 1916 Dorothy left college after two years and moved from the state of Illinois to New York City. There she supported herself as a journalist, working for socialist publications. She smoked cigarettes, had affairs with a succession of men, protested against the war (World War I), and may have taken illegal drugs (alcohol). She also practiced her own brand of spirituality and advocated a return to the land. Abbie Hoffman, the Sixties icon, is said to have called Dorothy Day "the first hippie."[16]

When Dorothy was twenty years old, the Communists seized power in Russia, and like many other middle-class intellectuals in the capitalist West, she was attracted to its revolutionary ideals. Although Dorothy never joined the Communist Party, her friend Helen Gurley Brown would later become the head of the Party in the United States, while her best female friend from college would later die prematurely in the 1930s while studying at the Lenin Institute in Moscow.[17]

In April 1917, the U. S. government entered World War I over the objections of most of the American people and the U.S. secretary of state, who resigned in protest.[18] At the same time, the government launched a campaign to suppress opposition to the war and to prevent any repeat of the Russian revolution at home. It arrested pacifists, Communists, and labor organizers.[19]

After the war, Dorothy Day married on a rebound from a bad relationship, and she and her husband went on their honeymoon to Europe, where they lived for a time in England and on the island of Capri. The marriage lasted less than a year. When Dorothy Day returned home to Chicago, she found herself in the middle of the anti-Red purge. As Dorothy notes in her autobiography, it was a time when the Communist Party was leading a precarious existence underground, "when meetings were held in the Michigan woods, when there were hundreds arrested."[20]

Dorothy had always been drawn more to the Wobblies than to the Communists. One night, Dorothy and a female companion sought shelter at a hospitality house in Chicago maintained by the Industrial Workers of the World. That night the two of them were arrested in one of the police raids:

> The ugly fact remained that we were two young girls arrested by four plain-clothes men who refused to leave the room while we got up and dressed for fear we would try to get away by the fire-escape. These were the days of the Palmer red raids when no one was safe. Those were times of persecution for all radicals.[21]

The United States government was cracking down on partying as well. In 1920 as a consequence of an amendment to the Constitution, the federal government put into effect a national ban on the manufacture, importation, and sale of alcohol. This dry period known as Prohibition lasted from 1920 to 1933. Although it did decrease alcohol consumption, its unintended effect was to glamorize drinking, which led to widespread flouting of the law. People who were normally law-abiding citizens made bathtub gin and went to speakeasies. The black market for alcohol nurtured criminals and corrupted the police. This era of fast cars, easy money, and illicit booze is known as the Roaring Twenties.[G 24]

While in Europe, Dorothy had written a novel, more autobiographical than literary; to her surprise, a movie studio bought the film rights. Although the movie was never produced, Dorothy used the proceeds to buy a fisherman's cottage on Staten Island, N.Y. It was a bucolic scene in those days, with woods behind the cottage and a view of the bay in front. For several years, she lived there with her new lover, Forster Batterham, a man about whom little is known except that he was an anarchist and biologist who liked to fish. While cohabitation is commonplace nowadays, in the 1920s only bohemians shared a home without benefit of matrimony. Dorothy referred to Batterham as her common-law husband.

In 1925, Dorothy found herself pregnant by Batterham. A few years earlier, at the insistence of a previous lover, Dorothy had an illegal abortion. The experience was so traumatic that this time Dorothy resolved to keep the baby. Batterham, however, was uninterested in being a father and politically opposed to marriage.

To make matters worse, Dorothy was increasingly drawn to religion, especially to the Catholic Church. Hatred of religion united the warring factions of the left. Marx had denounced religion as the opiate of the masses while Bakunin had written a screed vilifying Christianity.[25] Dorothy's friends were shocked and dismayed by her sudden change in direction, yet she had never been opposed to religion. Dorothy had been raised Episcopalian, and as a child she read the Bible and sang in the choir. Unlike many other Protestant denominations, the Episcopalians retain a number of Catholic practices, including the priesthood and high-church rituals, so Dorothy's interest in Catholicism was not as anomalous as it appeared.

Dorothy's embrace of religion alienated Batterham, and when he refused to attend the baby's baptism, the couple went their separate ways. Like so many women nowadays, Dorothy struggled to strike a balance between caring for her daughter and meeting the demands of her career. She experienced the economic precariousness of a single parent and the social stigma of an unmarried mother.

Like many single mothers, Dorothy was poor—and in the United States, poverty is a sin. Poverty means that you have not lived up to the American Dream and have failed to take advantage of the great opportunities that the country has given you. In the Land of Desire, each man (and woman too) is captain of his soul and master of his fate.

Dorothy's new-found religion, the Catholic Church, has a very different take on poverty from that of the American Dream. In Catholicism, poverty is a virtue provided that it is voluntarily embraced. Poverty that is consciously embraced can be a spiritual discipline, an example to others, and an expression of solidarity with the poor. However, privation has no value in itself and is the cause of physical and psychological maladies. It is every Catholic's obligation to help the poor.

Many activists, Catholic or not, live lives of de facto voluntary poverty in that they get paid much less than if they used their skills in the service of big business, which their commitment to social justice prevents them from doing. Voluntary poverty of the de facto kind distinguishes activist organizations from many institutional charities.

In the United States, big business is mirrored by big charity. In a stratagem popularized by Andrew Carnegie, millionaires who had made their fortunes through cut-throat capitalism and had doggedly fought collective efforts to humanize their businesses, began to give away millions of dollars to worthy causes, usually by chartering a legal entity whose income is derived from an endowment of corporate stock. Corporate foundations are charities from the viewpoint of the U.S. government's tax collectors, and gifts to the foundation are tax deductible. Yet these organizations typically pay handsome salaries to their executives. The president of the Bill and Melinda Gates Foundation, for example, is paid at a "market rate" of a million dollars a year.[26] The chief investment officers at universities and private foundations are often paid far more.

In the United States, corporate philanthropy provides much of the funding for the arts, the humanities, and the think tanks that formulate public policy. As Giridharadas points out, corporate philanthropy works to prevent any fundamental changes in the system of power.[27] Foundation funding of public amenities such as museums ensures that exhibitions reflect corporate priorities, while the donor's name on a building legitimizes the donor's fortune, even when it was made by selling addictive drugs to the public.[28] In addition, corporate philanthropy enables the wealthy to influence the priorities of science, just as the Rockefeller, Carnegie, and Harriman fortunes imparted the trajectory of eugenic Progress to the nascent science of genetics (Chapter 5). The function of corporate charities such as the Gates Foundation is to reinforce the class system, not to end it.

Dorothy never saw herself as a million-a-year poverty czar. In the words of one commentator: "What she wanted was not just better wages and more reasonable working hours, but an upheaval and transformation of existing society, an entire revolution, but one carried out with love, the only weapons being education and mercy." [29]

The Chiefless Ones

Dorothy's socialism was inspired less by Marx than by Kropotkin. Peter Kropotkin was the nineteenth-century naturalist who argued that Mutual Aid has parity with Darwin's natural selection as an evolutionary principle.[30] Kropotkin was born into the Russian aristocracy in 1842 and groomed for a career in the military. As a young officer in the czar's army, he was chosen to lead an expedition to survey the natural resources of Siberia. In the course of his travels he made observations on the flora and fauna, and it was this experience that led him to question the uncompromising competitiveness built into Darwinian theory. At the same time, his exposure to western European thought prompted him to criticize the authoritarian society in which he had been raised. Like many socialists of that era, he became an exile, and never returned to his homeland until after the Russian Revolution.

As a teenager, Dorothy became entranced with Kropotkin's *Memoirs of a Revolutionist*. As she later wrote: "The call to my youth was the call of Kropotkin, and the beauty of his prose, the nobility of his phrasing, appealed to my heart...[he was] to me at that time a saint in his way."[31]

Dorothy would eventually become a saint in *her* way, even being mentioned four times by Pope Francis in his address to the United States Congress in September 2015.[32] Significantly, the pope did not tell America's assembled legislators, about half of them Republican, that Dorothy Day had at first been inspired by the cofounder of anarchism.

In the early 1870s, around the same time that Darwinists were engaged in their takeover of higher education, European socialists were debating the role of the state in their quest for a more egalitarian society. One faction, personified by Mikail Bakunin, judged the state to be an intrinsically immoral institution because it divides the human race into us/them categories while using war and capital punishment to achieve its objectives.[33] Another faction led by Karl Marx maintained that socialists should seize control of the state in order to use it as a vehicle for social revolution.

Americans tend to use the terms "state" and "government" synonymously, but they are not the same thing. A government is an institution responsible for leading and managing the collective activities of society. A state, in contrast, is a form of government that has a special relationship to collective violence.

A state is an institution with a monopoly on collective aggression within a specified territory, and whose aggression is sanctioned by the moral order.[34] Brawls by soccer hooligans and the executions of rivals by criminal gangs are certainly examples of collective violence, but they lack legitimation by the moral order. Rather, they are considered to be crimes, thus eliciting collective aggression by the state in the form of arrest, incarceration, and perhaps physical punishment. To be legitimate, collective aggression must be supported by the public and/or by the dominant class, such as legal imprisonment and the use of guns by the police. Even deadly force, such as warfare and capital punishment, is considered legitimate provided that it is sanctioned by the moral order.

Nonstatist Societies and Subsistence Economies

Since people in the twenty-first century have been living in states all of their lives, it is hard to appreciate the fact that a monopoly on collective violence is not the only way of organizing human society. All human societies undertake collective tasks, so they necessarily have some process for the coordination of social cooperation; but not all societies have collective aggression that is legitimized by the moral order. Extant gatherer-hunter bands do not have legitimized collective aggression (Chapter 6). In fact, many small-scale societies do not even have a government, in the sense of an institution with the right to coordinate other groups of people.

Nonstatist societies are typically associated with subsistence economies. There are variations in such economies, but they usually include common ownership of critical resources, labor recruited from extended[G] family groups, reciprocal exchange, and an egalitarian ideology.[35] Provided that the population is small and stable enough that people know one another, and especially if society is so organized that family and neighbors perform tasks together that are perceived to be in everyone's interest, then people readily work together cooperatively, without the imposition of any external authority.

I once visited an island located off the coast of Papua New Guinea (PNG) to film examples of cooperative work groups. Manam Island is in the Bismarck Sea about 13 km (8 miles) off the north coast of New Guinea. The island is small, only 10 km (6 miles) across; the land is the top of an undersea volcano, rising dramatically out of the sea to more than 1, 219 meters (4,000 feet). In 2005 the island was evacuated when the mountain began to erupt, but the Manam Islanders have since been coming back, though with one eye on the volcano.

The physical aspects of a culture—the houses, the clothes, the subsistence technology—can all be captured on film, but the core of a culture is accessible only through language. The people of Manam Island speak an Austronesian language, which is a language family that is spread across an enormous stretch of ocean, from Easter Island in the east to Madagascar in the West. For the description of Manamese life, I use the findings of the two anthropologists who did fieldwork there.[36]

The village that I visited in the 1970s was built in the traditional manner, with thatch-roofed houses raised on pilings. This ensures ample ventilation of the living area above while also providing a shady space below. Each family has its own vegetable gardens, which are a short walk from the village, and the canoes are drawn up within sight of the houses, so the commute to work is minimal.

There are about a dozen villages on the island, and each village consists of a number of households, each occupied by a man and one or more wives and their children. Each family has its own home or portion of a larger home, but a man's brothers and married sons typically have homes of their own nearby, so the houses of close patrilineal[G] kin form small hamlets. A number of hamlets comprise a village, which typically has fewer than 300 people.

In addition to their local lineage and their hamlet, people also belong to one of a number of patrilineal clans,[G] where a clan is a group of lineages whose members trace descent from the same ancestor. These clans are exogamous,[G] which is to say that one cannot marry a member of one's own clan, so people must seek spouses from other clans, either from their own village or from neighboring ones. Since men live near their close male relatives, brides leave their natal homes and take up residence in their husband's hamlet.

To add a further level of complexity, the Manamese have a class system with an aristocratic class that provides the hereditary chief of each village and lineage as well as a commoner class that accepts chiefly authority, especially in matters of public ceremony and ritual knowledge. In his ceremonial capacity, the chief has a garden that is worked by commoners to provide the food that he distributes during feasts. The role of chief is ascribed: that is, the current chief chooses one of his sons as successor.

In spite of the class system and the hereditary chief, the economy is egalitarian. The norm of reciprocity ensures that everyone shares food. On days when your fishing catch is poor, mine might be good, so I give you fish knowing that you will reciprocate. Also, generosity prevails within the household and lineage, so that everyone gets enough to eat. Dinner is a unique blend of take-out and cooking-in. Each married woman prepares dinner for her family, but she also puts portions of the food on hand-carved wooden plates and carries them to the homes of her kinfolk and neighbors. Simultaneously, in other houses, women are doing the same thing, so one can literally see circles of reciprocal exchange moving through the village. Thus, in each home the evening meal consists of one's own food as well as portions of the meals cooked by other households, so one is usually eating some fish and vegetables that one did not harvest or cook oneself. Such economies ensure that everyone in the local community gets enough to eat and that the old and infirm are provided for.

While on the island and on the adjacent mainland, I was able to observe people deploying a fish trap in the lagoon, butchering a pig, and roofing a house. All of the work is done cooperatively, with people pitching in as the task demands. In the roofing task, a number of men work side by side kneeling on the beam that supports the roof, each interlacing palm leaves together to make them watertight. Down below, a man tosses additional palm leaves up to the thatching crew as needed, while others are out gathering more raw material. Even when a society lacks specialized trades, there is always some role diferentiation and social exchange within face-to-face work groups, such as the palm leaf tosser versus the thatchers, even though such positions are not occupations.

In societies where people learn subsistence skills as children, there is much less need for management and supervision. Because work is out in the open, children can see what their parents do for a living, so there is much more scope for observational learning and less need for classrooms and manuals. Play consists largely of social games that incorporate some adult activity that will prove useful later in life. Children do actual work as well, such as helping to gather firewood and taking care of their younger siblings. Cooperative work relies on people's own understanding of the work that needs to be done, on their ability to work together, and on the process of complementation.[G]

Complementation is the ability to infer someone else's intention and perform the complementary action.[37] This enables people to do things that no one person could do alone, such as lifting a large refrigerator. In our society, parents do complementary tasks dozens of times a day without thinking about it, as when one parent lifts the toddler out of the stroller and hands off the child to the other parent in the car, who puts the child in the child seat.[37] Such cooperative face-to-face interactions are the foundation of a human level of technology, and they have little precedent in apes.

In subsistence societies, the basic life-support skills, such as food gathering and building a fire, are usually known to everyone, even children. However, there is usually a sexual division of labor as well, with men doing some tasks and women doing others. The sexual division of labor can be as basic as "men mostly hunt, women mostly gather," while other societies may have more complicated rules. Also, subsistence societies typically have people with specialized knowledge of various kinds as well, such as healers who know the most effective herbs or boat builders who may have a special skill for shaping the hull.

Nor is it the case that in subsistence societies women stay at home caring for children. Usually, they are too busy working—either producing society's main subsistence or helping the neighbors, which is essential for maintaining the network of reciprocal exchange. As for child care, there is plenty of it: other members of the extended family are always there to help, and the older children help care for the younger. Also, women often take the kids to work, such as to the garden to help weed or to the woods to help gather wild plants.

In some subsistence societies, women do most of the work and have the least amount of power, but this is often true of industrial societies as well. In contemporary societies, there is a great deal of variation in women's roles, ranging from the Nordic democracies to Saudi Arabia.[38] In a subsistence society, women provide the three most essential ingredients to the economy: 100% of the children to perpetuate the kin group, much of the food needed to feed them, and active participation in the network of reciprocal exchange that keeps goods and services flowing. In a society based on face-to-face relationships, these contributions give women a good bargaining position relative to men and a measure of autonomy—though this does not always translate into political power. The major difference between subsistence economies and capitalism is that in the latter the domestic sphere is peripheralized and unrewarded, robbing women of their respect and power.

Domestic activities quite literally count for nothing under capitalism. Capitalism counts only monetized transactions, that is, transactions denominated in money. Thus, the labor a woman expends at home caring for her children or helping an invalid neighbor is literally of zero value in capitalism. No wonder many women no longer want to do it.

In some subsistence societies, women had more power and influence than they did in the European societies that "discovered" them. For example, the Haudenosaunee (Iroquois) people of what is now New York state and southeastern Canada combined a kincentric system of clans and chiefs with representative democracy and power to women.[39] The social organization of the Haudenosaunee is important in both the theory of early socialism and the history of cultural anthropology.

In the mid-nineteenth century, Lewis Henry Morgan, an American lawyer with ethnographic tendencies, began inquiries among the Haudenosaunee who were living on a reservation in New York State. As he explains, "As far back as 1846, while collecting materials illustrative of the institutions of the Iroquois,

I found among them, in daily use, a system of relationships for the designation and classification of kindred, both unique and extraordinary in its character, and wholly unlike any with which we are familiar."[40] In 1871, Morgan published the first systematic description of a matrilineal kinship system—and thus helped to create cultural anthropology.

Friedrich Engels read Morgan's work and was impressed by the strong role that women played in Iroquois society.[41] Like Morgan, Engels thought kincentric societies represented an earlier stage of human social development, and he interpreted Morgan's data as evidence for a stage of primitive matriarchy.[G] It is now recognized that the Haudenosaunee political system, rather than being matriarchal, sees male and female roles as complementary and interdependent.

The Haudenosaunee are matrilineal, which is to say that people trace descent through their mother's line. In unilineal societies, all the people who trace descent back to the same ancestor are members of the same clan. The Haudenosaunee have clans named for bears, eels, herons, and a variety of other animals, who are accorded the respect due a relative. These names symbolize earth, water, and air respectively.

Haudenosaunee women retain their own property in marriage and pass it on to their children, who are of the mother's clan, not of the husband's clan. In unilineal[G] societies, the oldest members of one's lineage are accorded great respect, and they are often consulted for their influence and experience. Among the Haudenosaunee, the prominent women in a clan are called the clan mothers, and they have important roles in the political system.

At least a century before the English, French and Dutch arrived in northeastern North America, perhaps much earlier, the Haudenosaunee formed a political confederacy of five separate Iroquoian-speaking nations, what is known to historians as the Iroquois League or the Five Nations. This political organization was pivotal in the colonial period; and it still exists, though the people themselves have lost control of most of their traditional homeland and now live on reservations.

Each clan of the Five Nations sends a representative to the Grand Council. The clan mothers choose the man who represents the clan in the Grand Council. The clan mothers also choose the male chiefs for the local council, and they have the right to remove chiefs who are not representing the views of the community. Thus, women in Haudenosaunee society had much more power than in the patriarchal societies of preindustrial Europe, where, until the nineteenth century in England, a woman was a legal ward of her father or her husband and had no role in the political process unless she was the reigning monarch.

Haudenosaunee political philosophy seeks to maintain harmony by adopting policies that everyone can live with, so the decisions of government are based on consensus. Not even members of the Grand Council have the power to command: they have to rely on their interpersonal skills to persuade others. Political leaders in nonstatist societies are typically accomplished public speakers, negotiators, and conciliators who can appeal to the citizenry's self interest, emphasize the collective benefits, enlist the support of the moral order, and motivate a sense of group solidarity. They are leaders, not authoritarians.

The absence of command is unfathomable to people raised in European monarchies and bourgeois democracies. They think that without an army and a head of state human society will devolve into chaos. Thomas Hobbes stated this belief unequivocally in seventeenth-century England, but he was living in a society where a small ruling class imposed its will on the majority of the people without the consent of the governed. In such circumstances, Hobbes is probably right. In kincentric societies, however, people perceive themselves to be related to one another, so norms of generosity, harmony, and cooperation apply.

In subsistence societies, individual self-sufficiency is not a social ideal. Many Americans are raised with an ethos of individualism in which society is reduced to a nuclear family living on
its own island, as in the novel *The Swiss Family Robinson*, or to
the lone male survivalist as in *Robinson Crusoe*. In the latter story,
a single White man reproduces a European lifestyle on a desert
island, first by salvaging goods from a scuttled ship, then by finding a subservient savage to do the heavy lifting. Such stories are
fantasies created by colonialism.

Subsistence economies are not social isolates. Even when composed of related families, such communities still have ties outside
the community as well, not just with family members living in
other villages but with unrelated members of foreign groups, for
purposes such as trade and political alliances. On Manam Island,
for example, men (and high-ranking women) have trade relationships with men on the mainland. Trade is neither capitalistic
nor market-based but depends on personal relationships that are
handed down from father to son (a man calls his father's trading
partner "father"). Even so, trade is essential to the Manamese
way of life because the island is not self-sufficient in food. The
Manamese are dependent on sago from the mainland during the
dry season. In the 1930s, Wedgwood recorded that galip nuts,
pigs, taro, and tobacco were given by the Manamese in exchange
for sago, pottery, bamboo, and petticoats. Boars' tusks and dogs'
teeth, the materials used in status display, are also imported from
the mainland.

In Darwinian theory, nonstatist societies with subsistence
economies are called tribes[G] and regarded as the stage of social
development that precedes civilization. To Charles Darwin tribes
were a spent force of history that was yielding to the civilizing
efforts of Queen Victoria's subjects. Yet even the word "tribe" is
a remnant of Western colonialism. As recently as a century ago,
European colonial administrators would draw boundaries on a

map, assign territories to specific ethnic groups, and then appoint some favored natives as "tribal leaders" to govern on their behalf. The term tribe has been retained in American law, but anthropologists rarely use it nowadays because it lumps together a broad range of social organizations and subsistence strategies as if they were the same. The term nation,ᴳ which means the people born in the same place, has much the same meaning but without the implicit homogeneity and primitiveness.

Until the globalization of capitalism, subsistence economies were found throughout the world with a variety of subsistence strategies, but in the past few centuries their range has been much reduced. Where they still exist, their territories have been incorporated into states. Yet their existence is important because they provide clear evidence that socialism coexists with a wide range of political forms.

Subsistence economies differ from both capitalism and Communism in at least five ways. First, the family is a unit of production as well as consumption. Second, the efficient distribution of goods and services is ensured by the norms of reciprocity and generosity, not by buying and selling. Third, essential goods and services, such as food and child care, are shared among the local community. Fourth, land and other key natural resources are collectively owned by social units larger than nuclear families, such as a village or a clan. Fifth, economic relationships with other communities are also implemented through reciprocal exchange, such as traditional trade relationships and intermarriage. Since this complex of social characteristics is found all over the world and in every period known to historians, it is a perennial part of the human condition, constantly being reinvented; but under capitalism it has been been denigrated as primitive, socially peripheralized, and stripped of it productive functions.

The bifurcation of human history into tribal versus civilized has an obvious ideological function. How convenient for the

British Empire that societies with colonies, famines, and slave plantations are judged to be the most advanced on earth whereas those with local government, equitable distribution of goods, and common ownership of critical resources are dismissed as primitive survivals of an earlier stage of evolution!

The Enclosure of the Commons

Resources that are jointly owned and cooperatively managed are called the commons.[G] In premodern Europe, the commons coexisted with an aristocracy that owned the land and a peasant class that farmed it. Under feudalism, land was inalienable, so the lord could not sell it to someone else, while the peasantry had the right to farm the land where they were born even though they did not "own it" in the capitalist sense. In premodern Russia, each village allocated multiple strips of farmland to each family to ensure that everyone shared both the best land and the worst, as well as giving everyone access to multiple ecological zones.[42] The village also established rules for the use of collective resources such as water and firewood to prevent over-exploitation. This system was run by the peasants themselves through a council of male householders.

However, as modernity advanced, the state and aristocracy began to make their own claims on the commons, diverting it to their own use, a process called enclosure. By the eighteenth century in places such as Great Britain, the joint ownership of rights to resources, such as the right to graze one's livestock in the village meadow and fish in the local stream, had been largely commandeered by the elite. Although remnants of the commons still exist, capitalism has largely replaced it with private property.

Charles Darwin played no role in the enclosure process in England, which mostly happened long before he was born; but by reducing human society to individualism and competition, he gave moral approbation to the enclosures that were still going on in the colonies; at the same time, his individualist theory of human evolution was a stumbling block to reclaiming the communal ownership of property being advocated by socialists.

In 2009 Elinor Ostrom won the Nobel Prize in Economics for demonstrating to other economists that common ownership and cooperative management of shared resources are far from being primitive and inefficient.[43] To the contrary, in comparing agricultural projects in a wide range of countries, Ostrom found that when water for irrigation is managed by a local organization of farmers then the process performs at higher levels of efficiency, as measured by metrics such as water volume and number of recipients, than when managed as large-scale projects by state or international agencies.

Significantly, both Bakunin and Kropotkin were born into the Russian aristocracy at a time when a preindustrial system of production was still commonplace in that country. Even though there was a centralized Russian state that enforced the will of the land-owning class and sought to expand the empire, peasant villages had their own collective organization and rhythm of work that ensured that seed would be planted and grain harvested whether or not there were decrees from the imperial capital. Also, in the course of his travels through Eurasia, Kropotkin had the opportunity to observe cooperative work among nomadic herders and indigenous settlements. Early socialists were inspired by extant nonstatist societies.

In applying their observations to the European class system, Bakunin and Kropotkin argued for an economy based on cooperation instead of competition, one in which workers produce goods and services without exploitation by a capitalist class or coercion by the state. Even though both men were trained as military officers, in their theory of political economy, the state is inherently *anti*-socialist because its core competence is not cooperation but coercion. Socialists who emphasized the incom-

332 | Life Without Darwin

patibility of socialism with the state called themselves anarchists, from Greek roots meaning "without a chief."

To English speakers, anarchism sounds like anarchy, and this similarity was exploited by propagandists. At the end of the nineteenth century, after a high-profile assassination by an anarchist, the major powers convened an anti-terrorism conference that made no distinction between terrorists and anarchists. Cartoonists in major newspapers depicted anarchists as shaggy-bearded fanatics hurling bombs, not very different from the way in which Moslems are depicted today.[44] Thus anarchism went from being a descriptive term to a label used to smear opponents, just as "Communist" became a catch-all epithet during the McCarthy period. Nowadays, anarchists sometimes call themselves libertarian socialists to escape the connotations of anarchy and terrorism.

The anarchist vision—a nonstatist society composed of worker cooperatives with critical resources held in common—was threatening to aristocrats, capitalists, and Communists alike. The political strategy of the Communist Party presumed a state apparatus that could be seized by revolutionaries and used to forcibly install a classless society with the Communists in charge. The Communist plan was undercut by people such as anarchists who advocated the abolition of the state itself; what's more, such people claimed to be revolutionists too, fractioning the united front of the left. During the Spanish Civil War of the 1930s, the Communist Party took up arms against the anarchists, even though both were supposedly on the same side, while both Lenin and Stalin suppressed them in the Soviet Union.[45] Modernists and progressives were disturbed by the anarchist vision as well. To partisans of science and Progress, the cooperative village and the artisan's workshop, however picturesque, were emblematic of the primitive past they were striving to leave behind.

The State and the Moral Order

For many people in the United States, not just the religious[G] right but atheists and progressives as well, the state is considered the most appropriate vehicle for addressing moral issues, such as excessive alcohol consumption and women's access to abortion. As Kazin points out, a crusading faith and a democratic nation emerged together in American history, both born of the Second Great Awakening: "The synthesis of evangelical Protestantism and the ideology of grassroots democracy was found in no other nation—at least not with such passionate conviction and for such a long period of time."[46]

However, the notion of a moralistic state raises the question of whether a state can even in principle enforce morality. The state's mandate is enforcement of the law by means of coercion and punishment whereas moral solutions are rarely, if ever, achieved by imposing the power of the collectivity against the individual. The state can impose outward conformity of behavior by using the threat of fines and incarceration; it can enforce a punitive quid pro quo, such as an eye for an eye and a tooth for a tooth. But Christian morality involves moral consciousness, repentance, forgiveness, social justice, and the peaceful resolution of conflicts.

For over 1,700 years, autocratic rulers, from Roman emperors to Puritan divines, have tried to merge the state with Christianity; but even when this effort is so successful that prelates live in palaces like princes, it always makes for a troubled marriage. The state thinks of itself as the dominant power, whereas in the Christian religion, the moral order takes precedence over the law. In state Christianity, Henry VIII or his equivalent decides what is right and wrong; but in the Judeo-Christian tradition, right action springs from moral consciousness inspired directly by God. In the Bible, this idea is expressed as a story, as God speaking to Moses from the burning bush—an experience which gave Moses the moral courage to challenge the authority of the pharaoh.

Significantly, the two most prominent human beings in the Bible, Moses and Jesus, end up in conflict with state power. In the case of Jesus, the politicians and clergy conspire to kill him. The idea that the state is the enforcer of the moral order follows logically from the premises of a state religion, but it has little support from the Gospels.

As De La Torre argues, Christianity is exemplified by its praxis of love, especially in the service of people abused by state power, as was Jesus himself:

> The act of solidarity [with the oppressed] becomes the litmus test of biblical fidelity and the paradigm used to analyze and judge how social structures either contribute to or eradicate the exploitation of the marginalized.[47]

Early socialists experienced religion as the ideological arm of authoritarian states; but as Dorothy Day seems to have intuited, there is far more philosophical compatibility between Christianity and anarchism than Bakunin ever imagined.

Socialism, American Style

The Roaring Twenties ended abruptly in 1929 with the crash of the American stock market. Banks failed, businesses filed for bankruptcy, and millions of workers lost their jobs. The Republican administration in Washington tried to reassure the public that this calamity was just a temporary down-turn in the business cycle, of the sort that the country had weathered before; but the presidential election of 1932 gave the federal government a mandate to actively intervene in the economy. The Democratic Party under Franklin D. Roosevelt promised a New Deal that would get America moving again.

Roosevelt and his brain trust, many of whom were drawn from universities, applied the economic theory of John Maynard Keynes, who had argued that laissez-faire capitalism is inherently unstable, leading to cycles of boom and bust. Keynes maintained that the government needs to become an active partner in the economy, ensuring the stability that unrestrained capitalism had been unable to provide.

To doctrinaire free-enterprisers, any legislation that regulates business is by definition socialist and anathema (Milton Friedman wrote a book denouncing Keynes); but in 1932, many prominent members of the American capitalist class saw the New Deal as insurance against a socialist revolution. In 1917, revolutionaries installed a left-wing constitution in Mexico; later that same year, the Communists seized control in Russia. In the aftermath of World War I, Europe plunged into economic chaos, with unemployed ex-servicemen filling the streets and many of them supporting the Communists and socialists. In 1929, American prosperity ended with a jolt, and the growing economic Depression suggested to many that the United States was vulnerable to revolution.

Even blue-blooded plutocrats enlisted in Roosevelt's administration, men such as Averell Harriman, who first came to prominence as the twenty-something chairman of one of America's most successful companies, the Union Pacific Railroad. Harriman headed Roosevelt's outreach to big business and served in a number of key positions, including ambassador to the Soviet Union.[48]

The final result of the New Deal was a truncated welfare state, one with tax-supported old age pensions (though only for employed people who had paid into the plan in installments via their paychecks), electrification of the countryside, and price supports for farmers. The New Deal sought to reform capitalism; it did not seek to replace it.

In December 1932, the month before Roosevelt's inaugura-
tion, Dorothy Day was on assignment in Washington, D.C.,
covering a march to the White House by unemployed workers
that had been organized by an affiliate of the Communist Party.[47]
She recounts that while in Washington she prayed at the Basilica
of Our Lady of the Immaculate Conception, the patroness of
America, asking for guidance in her desire to use her journal-
ism skills in the service of the poor. When Dorothy returned to
New York, she found an unexpected guest waiting for her in the
kitchen. He was an odd, middle-aged man with a strong French
accent and the unaffected manner of a peasant. He had been
referred to Dorothy by the editor of a well-known Catholic magazine, *Commonweal*.[49] The man's name was Peter Maurin.

Maurin was born into a huge farming family in a rural re-
gion of France. As a child he had experienced the family farm
with its cooperative ethos and seasonal rhythms, a lifestyle not so
different from the village commons that Kropotkin knew from
Russia. Maurin was also a socialist and a devotee of Saint Francis
of Assisi. As Dorothy later expressed it: "Peter Maurin came to
me with Kropotkin in one pocket and St. Francis in the other!"[50]

Dorothy Day and Peter Maurin spent the first few months
talking to one another, sharing books and ideas. His views had
been shaped by his experience of village life and extensive reading
in Catholicism and socialism, hers by social activism and personal acquaintance with leading figures in the American left. Both
strongly agreed that no one should ever go homeless or hungry.

In her autobiography, Dorothy recalls the night that she spent
in a hospitality house run by the Industrial Workers of the World.
In the Wobbly tradition, they kept a giant pot of mulligan stew
bubbling on the stove. Every resident and guest would bring
whatever they could scavenge—a pound of potatoes, a bunch of
carrots, whatever—and give it to the kitchen for the communal
pot.

Dorothy contrasts this experience with the next night, which she spent in jail in Chicago after the police raided the Wobbly premises. The only food available in jail, namely coffee and a sandwich, had to be purchased from the matron for a dollar, a usurious price in an age when a cup of coffee cost a nickel and a steak dinner could be had for $1.25.[51] Without the generosity of other prisoners, Dorothy would have gone hungry.

At this point in her life, Dorothy felt she had to choose between the revolutionary insurrection promoted by the Communist Party and her own commitment to nonviolence.[G] Her break with Communism was signaled by the name chosen for the newspaper that she and Maurin cofounded: the *Catholic Worker*. The name was an unambiguous counterpoint to the official organ of the American Communist Party, the *Daily Worker*. To make the point emphatically clear, the first edition of the new newspaper hit the streets on May Day 1933.

Engagement with the Marginalized

Dorothy Day and Peter Maurin understood that the commitment to social justice is both personal and collective. In its collective aspect, social justice must ensure that everyone has the material necessities of life while neutralizing the self-serving collective violence wielded by the elite. This collective program is sustained by a personal moral praxis that bypasses both the punitive moralism of the state and the disengaged rationalism of the academy.

Throughout history, moral action has been motivated by a combination of altruism, empathy, and courage, not by rationalism and intellectual orthodoxy. The Quakers did not hope to gain financially by launching their successful movement to abolish the African slave trade.[52] Evangelical Christians in Nazi-occupied Holland risked their lives to hide Jewish children—but not because they hoped to see a tree planted in their honor in Israel.[53]

Catholic clergy in El Salvador, enjoying the amenities of an urban intelligentsia, chose instead to protect indigenous villagers—and were murdered for their effort.[54] In all countries, people from diverse ethical traditions, often at great risk to themselves, shelter victims of persecution.[55] In all these instances, strangers are treated as if they were kinfolk. Moral consciousness and intellectual reflection are not at cross purposes in the human mind, only in the ideologies of academe and state capitalism.

The Catholic Worker sought to create community through personal engagement with the poor. As with ethnographic fieldwork, day-to-day social interaction with the marginalized undercuts the outsider's privileged position, forcing mutual engagement that is experienced as neither judgmental nor punitive. This results in cooperative alliances that cross-cut the fault lines erected by the system of social stratification, making it harder for the state to divide and conquer. A personal moral praxis focused on engagement with the marginalized transcends the exclusionary categories that keep the classes apart.

Engagement with the marginalized is not coextensive with volunteerism and charitable giving. Volunteering as a docent at the art museum affirms and reinforces one's own class identity, while making a generous bequest to one's poor relations, however meritorious, keeps the money in the family. In both cases, social good results from the action, but neither qualifies as engagement with the marginalized.

As corporate philanthropists know, charity is a form of unilateral exchange that expresses asymmetries of power. Even so, there are situations when sending money is an essential moral act—situations where people have been reduced to helpless dependency and when time is of the essence, as in the case of the Great Famine of Ireland. Thus, charity has an essential role to play in the alleviation of suffering, but it does not alter the system of social stratification that is so often the cause of the misery.

To engage the marginalized one must seek them out where they live: in homeless shelters, prisons, and under bridges. Personal engagement with the marginalized can take many forms, such as giving bottles of water to Mexican immigrants in the deserts of America's borderland, which is a felony under U.S. law. One can also help build housing for the homeless, staff a mental health hotline, or inform a community about the effects of industrial pollution. The possibilities are endless. But whatever the personal cause, the critical factor is that the action be voluntary and interpersonal. The moral order is rooted in community: it is not enough to send money.

Engagement with the marginalized is not imposing one's own moral standards on the poor. In a socially stratified world, judging other people's lives by the standards of the elite reinforces the relationship of us-versus-them that insulates those in the dominant class from the moral implications of their own actions. As De La Torre expresses it: "Foremost for those who are marginalized is the ethical response to the use, misuse, and abuse of power rather than issues of character, values, virtues, and moral principles."[56]

In addition to engagement with the marginalized, the Catholic Worker movement was committed to nonviolence, a stance that distinguished it from the Communist left and the anti-Communist right. The emphasis on nonviolence set the tone for the Civil Rights movement that began in the late 1950s and the anti-Vietnam War movement that followed not long after. Dorothy Day participated in both.

From the viewpoint of the powerful, nonviolent resistance is the philosophy of the loser, but it is the only response to state oppression that does not escalate the conflict or reinforce the hierarchy. By using force against the state one provokes retaliatory aggression, an activity at which the state excels. On the other hand, to submit to state power reaffirms the class system and one's powerless position within it. But refusing to do what the state demands while expressing neither aggressive nor submissive signals in effect changes the game.

Nonviolent resistance requires a person of strong moral convictions and endurance, and it must be backed by widespread community support and well-organized groups with experience in nonviolent activism. Nonviolent resistance is not passivity. As a pacifist it is still permissible to break into a military base and pour human blood on the nosecones of nuclear missiles.[57] In pacifism, human life is sacred but corporate property is not—just the opposite of capitalism.

The Catholic Worker movement reaffirmed the three essential elements of social justice: social consciousness that is sensitive to the well-being of others, collective action that facilitates the well-being of the marginalized through one's own interpersonal engagement with them, and a personal moral praxis that furthers social consciousness and collective action.

Capitalism, in contrast, reduces human society to rugged individualists engaged in capital accumulation, while its institutions reward careerism over cooperative action for the common good. Capitalism destroys the communities in which the moral order is embedded by turning the populace into a collection of atomistic individuals in competition with one other for scarce resources. So before one can cultivate a moral order compatible with social justice, one must first establish the communities that can nurture it. To this end, the Catholic Worker built more than forty hospitality houses for the unemployed in major cites, as well as a number of worker-owned farms to ensure food security.

While a hospitality house is a good beginning, it falls short of a complete solution. When the poor in the hospitality centers get on their feet again, they have no choice but to seek employment in the class society that made them poor in the first place. Dorothy's hero, Peter Kropotkin, provides the next step.

Kropotkin's Postcapitalist Vision

Like Marx, Kropotkin wanted nothing less than reconstruction of industrial society on socialist principles, but unlike Marx, he envisioned a nonstatist society in which "all essential social activities were controlled and organized through voluntary associations and a network of autonomous federated communes"[58]—a supply chain composed of cooperatives instead of corporations. Kropotkin set forth his vision of political economy in a series of books that are still readable and relevant today.[59]

Kropotkin used the high technology of his day, namely railroads, to illustrate his imagined future:

> At Madrid, for example, you take a ticket for St. Petersurg direct. You travel along railways which have been constructed by millions of workers, set in motion by dozens of companies; your carriage is attached in turn to Spanish, French, Bavarian, and Russian locomotives; you travel without losing twenty minutes anywhere, and the two hundred francs which you paid in Madrid will be divided to a nicety among the companies which have combined to forward you to your destination.[60]

Railroads developed pari passu with telegraph lines, so they had the instantaneous communications needed to sustain this level of coordination. But in the nineteenth-century, transportation and communications were generally too slow for lateral integration to work effectively. In the twenty-first century, however, the global supply chain is already laterally integrated via telecommunications, computers, and the internet, enabling multiple companies to ship goods around the world so they can be used as parts and materials by other companies.

However, the social organization of the contemporary supply chain is straight out of Victorian England. Corporations are still the links in the chain, and their boards of directors are still controlled by financiers who are almost always men, while the employees are still bifurcated into a class system of labor versus management.

The contemporary supply chain, for all of its high technology, is still based on a global underclass that is functionally indistinguishable from the sweat-shop workers described by Jack London more than a century ago.[61] The garment-making factories have since been moved from London and New York to Malaysia and Bangladesh, but people are still being economically exploited in order to make clothes for England and the United States.[62]

By any measure, the twentieth-century attempt to reform capitalism through legislation has failed. Many safety-net services previously paid for by government have been privatized by the neocons, while wealth is now concentrated to an unprecedented degree. Clearly, it is time to think once again about alternatives to capitalism. However, Communism is not one of them. As some anthropologists and economists have argued, the social theory of anarchism is far more relevant to today's world than the Marxism-Leninism that dominated the twentieth century. Graeber captures the renewed interest in libertarian socialism:

> everywhere one finds the same core principles: decentralization, voluntary association, mutual aid, the network model, and above all, the rejection of any idea that the end justifies the means, let alone that the business of a revolutionary is to seize state power and then begin imposing one's vision at the point of a gun.[63]

Replace Corporations with Cooperatives

The successor to the Victorian corporation is some combination
of workplace democracy and employee ownership, what is called
a cooperative.[G 64] There is no social blueprint for a cooperative.
Provided that it ensures that the voices of all its members are
heard, that it performs its stated collective goals, and that it does
not enforce its will through collective violence, then the social
organization of a cooperative may combine elements from a wide
range of social models. These might include shares of ownership,
rights-in-use, voluntary labor, contract labor, management, elected offices, kinship status, consensual decision making, and so on.
In fact, there is no one ideal mix of social ingredients for cooperatives in postcapitalist society, since co-ops are adapted to the
functions they peform and the cultures in which they are found.
The cooperative is a social organization that exemplifies Ostrom's
Law: "If something can work in practice it can work in theory."

For more than a century, socialists have been quietly building
thousands of economic cooperatives under the nose of corporate capitalism. These cooperative institutions encompass a broad
range of human activities: public utilities, credit unions, farms,
factories, schools, transport services, supermarkets, and local
hospitals. Kropotkin's vision of economic production based on
the lateral integration of independent, democratic entities seems
even more feasible today given modern transportation, computers, and telecommunications.

Cooperative enterprises bring people together to work on a
collective product that no one person could do alone, so they are
able to produce complex products just as corporations do. They
also have management, budgets, and quality control. Like capitalist enterprises, co-ops are flexible and adaptive, since a handful
of individuals can get together and jointly found a cooperative
that fills a community need. Unlike a corporation, however, one
cannot crown oneself king by providing the bulk of the capital.

The rules of governance ensure that the workers have an effective voice in the decisions that affect them.

Consider, for example, the Park Slope Food Cooperative, a successful supermarket in New York City founded in the 1970s.[65] It looks similar to any other American supermarket in an affluent neighborhood, with thousands of food products for sale, including a wide array of fresh fruits and vegetables with an emphasis on the organically grown. The cheese section is truly international in scope, while the shelves display many brand names that American shoppers would find familiar.

Yet there are also striking differences. The prices are much lower than in comparable stores. Staff are available to help shoppers home with their groceries for free. There is also a supervised child care center, as well as a guarded parking area for bicycles. In most places in New York, such personal services are done by a subordinate class of underpaid workers who cannot afford to live in the neighborhoods where they work. But everyone who shops at the Park Slope Food Co-op is also a worker in the store. Only members are allowed to shop there, and every member works about three hours a month in order to make the enterprise possible. At last count (2019) there were 17,000 members—which is an upper limit imposed by the physical space of the building.

The Park Slope area of Brooklyn, now a sought-after neighborhood, was poor and run-down when the cooperative began decades ago, so the Co-op is not a boutique institution created by gentrification. The Park Slope Food Co-op uses many capitalist practices such as buying products from external suppliers and selling them for money; but unlike the capitalist enterprise, the goal is to provide lower food prices for its members, not to make a profit for an owner. The Co-op also has more than 40 employees who manage the infrastructure. This ensures that there is a core of people knowledgeable in a particular specialty and whose well-being depends on the continued success of the enterprise.

Yet all the critical day-to-day operations needed in a supermarket, such as food preparation, restocking shelves, and customer checkout, are done by members donating their time.

As with a corporation, there is a board of directors, but its members are themselves members who have been elected by other members. The function of the board is to maintain the integrity of the enterprise and its services to members—not to ensure profitability for a class of outside investors.

In a capitalist corporation, the watershed decisions, such as moving the factory from Illinois to Indonesia, are made by the board of directors, not by the people who work there. Had the United States had a socialist workplace, the massive offshoring of industry that impoverished the American working class in the late twentieth century would probably never have happened.

Community cannot be bought, hence Park Slope Food Co-op's insistence that every member work in the store. Nor is community compatible with anonymous customers and short-term employees, hence the membership requirement. Because members meet others face-to-face, the political process does not reward mass marketing and media personas. This avoids the fate of large not-for-profit organizations where membership can be purchased by money alone; such organizations often function as de facto capitalist enterprises.

The cooperative is unabashedly socialist, but it is the opposite of state ownership of the means of production. A common refrain of apologists for capitalism is that socialism requires a totalitarian superstructure that leads us down the "road to serfdom."[66] For example, in the words of the eminent economist Schumpeter: "I for one cannot visualize, in the conditions of modern society, a socialist organization in any form other than that of a huge and all-embracing bureaucratic apparatus."[67] Yet it would be hard to imagine a better framework for totalitarianism than the one already developed by state capitalism's Big Data.[68]

The cooperative, in contrast, is the cradle of democracy. Nowadays, the majority of people work in bureaucracies modeled on the army and governed by a chain of command; even the corner grocery store has been superseded by some national or international chain. Yet a democratic society is impossible if the majority of its citizens spend most of their lives conforming to directives by people they have never met and whose decisions cannot be questioned. In such circumstances, no one can acquire the social skills and political experience needed to live in a democracy, which requires joint responsibility and participation in collective undertakings. Contrary to the American experience, democracy does not consist of choosing between two corporate-funded candidates in a gerrymandered district. Democracy needs to be exercised in the workplace as well as in the polling place.

Cooperatives keep capital from accumulating in the hands of a few, thus preventing the formation of a plutocratic elite that controls the government through campaign contributions and hired lobbyists. Because ownership cannot be purchased, the co-op also prevents takeovers by other organizations.

While not definitively part of the cooperative model as it exists today, a modular approach to expansion retains the local control while providing economies of scale. Instead of building, say, the world's largest cooperative supermarket chain, with hundreds of stores and a managerial hierarchy, it would be more consistent with democracy to spin-off each store as a separate entity with its own system of governance adapted to local conditions. To ensure the purchasing power needed to remain competitive in a capitalist environment, the spin-off stores would all be members of a purchasing network whose job is to get fair prices from suppliers. This replicates the social structure that aready exists, since a cooperative supermarket is itself a buying network for its individual members.

As our cellphones covertly record which supermarket shelves we pause to look at, it is important to understand that there are alternatives to the capitalist system of production and distribution.[69] There is no reason in principle why a democratic system that functions effectively in an urban supermarket with 17,000 workers cannot be replicated in all the other entities in the global supply chain.

Deligitimize Deadly Force

Much socialist endeavor is based on the premise that a demoncratic state can reform capitalism; but as the founders of anarchism recognized, the state is primarily an instrument for preserving the privileges of a few, not for delivering social services to the many. States tend to be warlike and imperialist as well, set on expanding their own territory at the expense of their neighbors. Thus the possibility of a peaceful world is bound up with the future of the state.

In social science theory, the state is a late development in human history, coincident with the rise of civilization, agriculture, and settled communities.[70] This is consistent with the eighteenth-century evolutionist idea that societies evolve from the simple to the complex and from savagery to civilization. In the eighteenth century, Jean Jacques Rousseau reversed the polarity of Hobbes's primitive man, arguing that the first societies were peaceful and egalitarian, since creatures in a state of nature have few wants and less to gain by oppressing their neighbor.[71] Anthropological fieldwork among extant nomadic gatherer-hunters does indeed show that these societies are based on sharing and consensus, with no warfare and minimal internal aggression, with the added bonus of a workday that is much shorter than a farmer's. Rousseau's thesis that the most ancient human societies were peaceful and communistic appears to have been vindicated. However, this conclusion I think is premature.

States are a form of social organization characterized by status hierarchy, collective aggression, the right to command, and an ideology of legitimation. None of these properties are material, and they bear no intrinsic relationship to any particular subsistence strategy. Also, as discussed above, subsistence economies can coexist with different types of social organization, as different as nomadic hunters are from chiefdoms of farmers. In ancient societies that were living close to nature, small-scale statist societies would be invisible in the archeological record.

When I was living among the Batek De' in Malaysia, I was struck by the fact that the entire culture was archeologically invisible. The houses were made of bamboo and palm fronds. Ceremonial items were fabricated on the spot out of feathers and strips of palm fiber. The major tool was the steel machete traded from the Malays. In such a hot, humid climate, in fifty years there would be literally nothing left except stone tools, which they no longer used.

Generally speaking, the symbols of social hierarchy in kincentric societies do not fossilize because they are usually made out of biodegradable materials such as straw, feathers, and vegetable dye. Even when there are rock-hard indicators of rank, there is still the problem of recognizing them for what they are in the archeological record. On Manam Island, the aristocratic class gets to wear boar tusks while the commoners have to make do with dog teeth. [72] When excavating an ancient grave, how would the archeologist know that fossilized boar tusks and dog teeth mark the difference between aristocrats and commoners respectively?

The archeology of the state is complicated by the fact that social hierarchy and the right of command, even when present in a society, may be confined to the ceremonial sphere. For example, on Manam Island, the chief has control of a garden that is used to provide the food for the ceremonial feasts that are held periodically, and he depends on commoners to work it, so there is work by commoners in the service of an elite. There is also disparity between the classes in terms of intellectual property, as only the chief knows the magic and chants that are needed to make the ceremonies efficacious. Social roles such as the Manamese chief have clear relevance to our understanding of the priest-kings that are associated with early civilization, yet they leave no physical tracks whatsoever.

Nor is Manam Island an anomaly. The combination of hierarchically-ranked lineages, hereditary chiefs, and egalitarian subsistence economies are found throughout the broad belt of Austronesian languages, from Hawaii to the Indian Ocean. In his classic review of political systems in the precolonial Pacific, the anthropologist Marshall Sahlins argues that the Polynesian states of Hawaii and Tahiti could easily have developed from an aristocratic lineage of ritual experts that acquired the command of deadly force, even as the subsistence economy of familial production and reciprocal exchange remained largely unchanged.[73]

Thus, the thesis that the state is a late development in human history may be an artifact of preservation. Internal aggression and status hierarchy occur in many species of nonhuman primates, including our closest relatives, and both can be found in the majority of human societies today. Once agriculture and writing were developed, states would be in a good position to exploit these cultural developments, but there is no compelling reason to assume that the latter bear a causal relationship to the formation of the state. The definitive features of the state are much closer to the dynamics of primate fear and aggression.

Until the nineteenth century, there were large swaths of the planet earth populated by self-governing, nonstatist, kincentric societies. Indeed, states were often dependent upon the former for infusions of workers and resources, so there was a kind of political balance.[74] As states became more imperialistic, indigenous peoples would often retreat further into unoccupied areas, such as mountains or swamps, thus preserving their independence.

However, as industrialization advanced, this strategy of avoidance became increasingly untenable. In the United States, the deployment of the Gatling gun in the nineteenth century ensured that future battles would be heavily biased in favor of the Anglo colonizers at the expense of indigenous peoples.[75] During the same period, a similar transformation of the indigenous commons was taking place in Africa. In the Sudan, the British used the newly-invented machine gun to decimate thousands of indigenous horsemen who mobilized against them. Beginning in 1904, the German army in Southwest Africa began using machine guns, which wiped out Herero resistance to German occupation.

As states were colonizing the lands claimed by nonstatist societies, the forces of global capitalism were transforming the ecosystems on which indigenous peoples depended for their livelihoods. In the early nineteenth century in the United States, millions of acres in the South were deforested and turned into cotton fields worked by enslaved Africans.[76] The Indians who lived there were force-marched to reservations west of the Mississippi River. Within two decades of the American Civil War, tens of millions of buffalo were exterminated from the Great Plains and the prairie grass plowed under for farms. The people that depended on the buffalo were killed by the U.S. cavalry or confined to reservations, while their former homeland was crisscrossed with barbed wire. In the tropics, from the Indo-Pacific to South America, rainforest was cleared for oil palm and rubber tree plantations. The people living there, who had previously farmed their own land and governed their own communities, became an impoverished class of agricultural workers dependent on wages from global corporations.

In the twenty-first century, with ever-more efficient aerial surveillance and infrared sensors, not even the forest or the dark of
night provide adequate protection for people seeking to avoid
predatory states. Barring a collapse of the transnational class system, the long tradition of fleeing abusive power by migrating to
the margins of civilization appears to have come to an end.

Coincident with these changes, human collective action has
been scaled up to the point that it has begun to converge as
blowback and backwash, sweeping across the arbitary boundaries
imposed by colonial powers and industrial states, while moving
pollution and violence from someone else's country into yours.[77]
Many people think that the way to deal with these convulsive
changes is to make the state even stronger by building megalithic
walls and enforcing strict immigration policies; but it is often the
imperialist policies of sovereign states that create the waves of
migration in the first place.

The state's boundaries, far from reflecting ethnic realities, are
the historical product of wars, while its "nationalities" are often
political constructions designed to further its consolidation of
power. Moreover, the capitalist class has demonstrated that it
controls the governments of so-called democracies to the point
that it has rolled back the socialist reforms of the twentieth century and replaced them with "austerity" and "the Washington
consensus."

Given the deterioration of habitats on the planet earth, there
will certainly be calls to establish a "world government" to deal
with issues such as global warming. A single global state hatched
by the current superpowers will be no more concerned about
ecology than the regional ones are now, while a supranational
state would lack even the limited checks and balances of the current international system. Institutions expand by exploiting their
core competency; and the logical consequence of state power,

whether regional or global, is coercion and social stratification, not sustainability and peace.

Since there is nowhere to run and nowhere to hide, it is time to reexamine the premise that legally-constrained collective violence is the platform on which civil society should be built. Yet Hobbesians are not receptive to this idea. They believe that command and deadly force are essential in human society because people are aggressive and selfish by nature.

Culturally-constructed Xenophobia

The attribution of innate xenophobia to human beings has a basis in primatology. Nonhuman primate societies have a solidary[G] core and a xenophobic[G] perimeter, such that unknown individuals seeking to integrate into the group are often perceived as threatening and may elicit collective[G] aggression by group members.[78]

Also, the dynamics of aggression and fear are very similar in all species of primates. The agonism[G] of humans and simans is probably homologous in a biological sense, which is to say that these behaviors and motivations involve similar genes, brain mechanisms, and developmental pathways. Agonism employs similar behaviors across species as well, such as standing tall and striking the enemy versus crouching and running away. In humans, such pan-primate behaviors are made even more powerful by being integrated with cultural constructions and language, such as shooting with a gun or verbally begging for mercy.

Yet the commonalities of primate aggression are only part of the story, for human beings have three times as much brain as an ape of comparable size, indicating that thought matters. I have had several college-educated people tell me that warfare is natural because chimpanzees attack and kill strange chimpanzees that they encounter. It is a measure of the cultural penetration of Darwinism that many believe that the genes we share with chimpanzees carry more weight than the readily observable fact that we encounter strangers every day without murdering them. People even travel to foreign countries and come back alive. In human society, warfare is only one option on a broad spectrum of intergroup relations, any one of which might be invoked in specific situations: avoidance, trade, tourism, ceremonial events, athletic contests, hospitality, intermarriage, exploitation, and, last but not least, warfare.

Collective aggression in chimpanzees is more like a brawl than like warfare. Brawls are aggressive intergroup encounters that appear to develop spontaneously and, in the human case, run counter to the social norms of the population at large. For example, in 2019, three judges on the circuit court of the American state of Indiana got drunk at a conference and went looking late at night for a strip club.[79] Two men in a passing car shouted something derogatory, and one of the judges, the only woman in the group, responded with an obscene gesture. The two men got out of the car, and an altercation ensued, which resulted in a shooting that put two of the judges in the hospital. Brawls such as this often lead to death, but we don't call them warfare: we call the police. In warfare, collective aggression is controlled *by a system of authority and command,* not by the motivational state of the fighters.

Even when there is an incident that could easily provoke a war, such as one country's warship being attacked by the aircraft of another, a state of war is declared only if the political leaders of the aggrieved country judge the event to be an intentional provocation that is supported by the political leaders of the other.[80]

Collective aggression is not an aggregate of individual aggressive acts but *intentional action by a cooperative group to harm a common enemy.* A common enemy requires social communication that singles out someone as the target of aggression—"That's him!"—as well as attributes that make enemy status believable.

The common enemy must elicit enough fear and anger to motivate collective action to inflict harm. In chimpanzees, being a stranger might be enough to trigger this response, but among humans, it is society that ultimately defines who the enemy is. Typically, "the enemy" is an abstract category that requires communication to other members of society by means of language and the arts. A simian can attack a stranger, but only a human being can attack a communist or an infidel.

The fault is not in our genes but in the moral order. Both warfare and political repression require the *moral legitimation* of cooperative aggression, the *cultural shaping* of a suitable enemy, and *the support of the political authorities* in order to be translated into collective action. Whereas effective participation in a brawl requires instant response in the absence of reflection, both warfare and political repression require discussion, planning, resource allocation, and decision making, so they necessarily engage our rational and moral faculties in a way that a brawl does not. One does not need to eliminate anger in order to eliminate wars and repression by the state.

Warfare is but one point on a spectrum of intergroup hostility that ranges from ethnic slurs to the intentional killing of the enemy. The most extreme form of warfare is the genocidal[G] war, where the goal is kill the noncombatants as well as the warriors. In the latter situation, warfare is no longer a contest between warriors but a prelude to cultural and physical genocide. On the victim's side, genocide fosters xenophobia; on the aggressor's side, it requires the demonization of the enemy. A certain amount of ethnocentrism is normal in human beings, but genocidal warfare requires an invader who believes himself to be so morally righteous or racially superior that the enemy is vermin to be exterminated. Such beliefs are often implemented by soldiers so hardened by violence that they are indifferent to the suffering of others.

Paradoxically, genocidal aggression is facilitated by the dark side of moral consciousness, that is, by the belief that the victims "deserve it"—if not by what they have done then by virtue of who they are, be it Indians, Jews, or infidels. Some of the best-documented cases of wholesale slaughter of noncombatants can be found in the conflict between English-speaking colonists and the indigenous peoples of North America. The intentional extermination of Indians by Whites began with the Pequod War of 1637 and continued until the end of the nineteenth century. Since then, genocide has been implemented sporadically by means of conspiratorial murders and eugenic sterilization.[81]

Self-righteous callousness combined with the moral legitimation of violence enables other dehumanized institutions as well, such as plantation slavery and corporate capitalism. Significantly, plantation slavery, genocide, and capitalism were synergistic forces in American history. The expansion of plantation slavery required the extermination or removal of Indians from the American South, while the rise of industrial capitalism in New England was financed in large measure by the profits made from trade in cotton and slaves.[82]

The Triad of Social Justice

Yet there is reason for optimism. If collective violence can be legitimized, it can be delegitimized. Even institutional configurations that have existed for centuries, such as plantation slavery, have disappeared in an historical moment once their morality was questioned to the point that their presence became a political issue.

A just society depends on three mutually-supportive concepts —none of which are found in Darwinism.[83] These are community, commons, and a commitment to nonviolence.

Community is a population of people known to one another who participate in cooperative work groups instrumental to collective goals and who exchange goods and services through reciprocity. The social organization of extant gatherer-hunters has been influential on socialist thinking since Rousseau, but community cannot be scaled up to an industrial level because it depends on personal relationships among people who have a history of working cooperatively together. One can, of course, require everyone to address one another as citizen or comrade, but this is a theater of communitas. Communities are not made by fiat but by people living in proximity and working together in face-to-face groups on tasks of mutual need. Modernism sought to replace the local community, but the latter is especially important for ensuring that cultural practices are adapted to local conditions, thus ensuring a subsistence economy that is ecologically sustainable. Communities are inherently local.

The second concept, the commons, ensures collective ownership of critical resources, such as water and electricity, that no one person makes but that every person needs to have. The commons is a system of equitable ownership of collective resources. It is not a wilderness owned by no one. When *Homo sapiens* began its great diaspora during the last Ice Age, one could move through vast areas without encountering another person. But that was a long time ago. What European settlers to North America perceived as "empty wilderness" had in fact been someone else's commons for at least 12,000 years.

Such collectively-owned resources are managed for the common good, not for profit. Managing resources in common, however, requires the participation of the people who are affected by resource extraction as well as those who benefit from it.[84] This is a key difference between socialism and capitalism. In the latter, the capitalist buys the rights to extract the resources with no obligations to the local community or to people living downstream.

A democratic state can in theory regulate resource extraction and give voice to local concerns; but given the enormous income disparity between the capitalist class and everyone else, as well as the coercive power of the corporate state, this is unlikely to happen, except perhaps in Scandinavia. The commons needs to be locally managed within the constraints established by a larger, inclusive, democratic political process that integrates multiple communities—not as ranks in a hierarchical class system but as a network of independent but interconnected nodes.[74]

The third principle, the commitment to nonviolence, governs social relations both within the community and with other groups. Historically, state organizations have coexisted with the commons and local communities; and they have waged war against outsiders even as they have kept the peace within. But in my judgment such situations are inherently unstable since states, if not always predatory and repressive, can easily become so. As long as society is organized around a monopoly on collective aggression, there is always the danger that local communities will be turned into social classes and their commons absorbed by the elite, even as collective aggression gets redirected inward to maintain the privileges of the dominant class. Collective violence facilitates command, whereas democracy requires civility.

Wherever there are human beings there is the potential for conflict and aggressively motivated actions by individuals and small groups, some of which will be horrific; but systematic intergroup violence requires a political process of coordination by the government and a moral process of legitimation. If these collective prerequisites are not forthcoming, then brawls between face-to-face groups and hate by individuals cannot escalate to the scale of warfare.

Each of these variables—community, commons, nonviolence— is fragile on its own but together they form a stable social configuration. The societies of extant nomadic gatherer-hunters, such as the !Kung San and the Batek De' (Chapter 6), are proof of concept. These societies have survived for centuries by means of reciprocal exchange, cooperative work groups, shared access to critical resources, and a commitment to peace and consensual decision-making. But during this time, they also enjoyed a home range that had not yet been appropriated by imperialist states. The commons is necessarily the third leg of the triad of peace and justice.

The Flat Earthers

Consumer capitalism requires a population of atomistic individuals committed to personal gain, but social justice requires people who will work together for the common good. The international ecology movement provides one such critical platform, socialist activism another, and socially-conscious religion a third. Ultimately, both ecological awareness and moral consciousness depend on the collective realization that we are living on a sphere—together.

Science has proved that we are living on a sphere. More than two centuries before the Christian era, Eratosthenes assumed that the earth was spherical and measured its diameter; in 1519 Spain launched a successful expedition to circumnavigate the globe; in 1968 NASA astronauts shot an iconic photo of the earth as seen from outer space. Both ecological sustainability and the moral order are grounded in the realization that what goes around comes around.

Yet the ruling elite still consists of flat earthers. People for whom the earth is a spreadsheet invest in coal-fired power plants with confidence that the acid rain will never fall on them. People who equate human progress with technical proficiency think that faster algorithms will some day house the homeless. People who think that economic development is synonymous with the common good are compelled to transform a pristine coastline into the next Miami Beach.

What's more, the triumph of capitalism has so degraded the public forum that civilized discussion of contentious issues is all but impossible. Postman notes that public discussion has been preempted by capitalism's entertainment complex, while Giroux deplores the effects of Social Darwinism on the common good.[85] No one has expressed the Darwinist aspect of contemporary politics more succinctly than one of the best-known and long-standing Republican Party operatives, Roger Stone, since convicted for obstruction of justice: "'Politics is not about uniting people. It's about dividing people. And getting your fifty-one per cent.'"[86]

The social and ecological effects of flat-earth thinking are obvious to most people; but the world's top-tier capitalists, instead of trying to live sustainably where they are, plan to move to other planets. The youthful dream of Amazon's Jeff Bezos was colonizing outer space. As class valedictorian at Palmetto Senior High School in Florida, the future founder of Amazon revealed to the *Miami Herald* that he wanted to "'build space hotels, amusement parks, yachts and colonies for two or three million people orbiting around the earth.' Eventually, his grand plan included getting everybody off the blue planet and turning it into a big park of sorts."[87] Bezos and at least two other capitalist luminaries (Elon Musk and Richard Branson) now have their own space-flight companies with plans for tours and colonies.[88]

This raises a collective question: do we really want to live in a world where 10 percent of the people own 82 percent of the wealth, where dissent is suppressed through fake news and universal surveillance, and billionaires gaze down at us from the moon—the ultimate gated community? It is time we lived life without Darwin.

The twenty-first century is that period of history in which the human race will collectively experience living on a sphere. The goal of replacing national states with world-wide networking, local cooperatives, a global commons, and a strong peace movement, far from being a starry-eyed scheme at odds with political realism, is perhaps the only practical way of ensuring our collective freedom while surviving on a small planet.

The End

Notes

1 Wallace (1898), quoted by Young (1985: 19).

2 Organisation for Economic Co-operation & Development(2008).

3 ibid.

4 ibid.

5 Credit Suisse Research Institute. 2018. Global Wealth Report 2018. https://www.credit-suisse.com/about-us/en/reports-research/ global-wealth-report.html?utm_source=Tricontinental+subscrib- ers+single+list&utm_campaign=6df162e0d8-EMAIL_CAM- PAIGN_2019_10_30_05_31&utm_medium=email&utm_ term=0_bb06a786c7-6df162e0d8-190706649 Accessed Nov. 2019.

6 Phillips (2018). More recent sources (note 5 above) gives the num- ber of millionaires as more than 40 million.

7 Brenner (2018).

8 Robinson (2014).

9 David Schaller's newsletter has been tracking sustainable technol- ogy for almost twenty years: http://www.sustainablepractices.info/ There is now a growing movement within political economy that seeks to provide an alternative to continuous growth.

10 De La Torre (2014), especially pp. 67 ff.

11 An exception is the benefit corporation discussed in Chap.3.

12 See: David Gelles and David Yaffe-Bellany. 2019. Shareholder value is no longer everything, top C.E.O.s say. *New York Times*, 19 Aug. .

13 Quoted by Schwartz and Rappeport. 2017. Call to create jobs, or else, tests Trump's sway. *New York Times*, 23 Jan.

14 Fraser (2015) provides an overview of the anticapitalist movement in the United States in the twentieth century. Dorothy Day (1938) describes the first few decades of the twentieth century in the light of her own experience as an activist.

15 For biographical data on Dorothy Day, I have used Loughery and Randolph (2020), Forest (1986) and Day's spiritual autobiogra- phy (1938), available online at https://catholicworker.org. Diener (2016) has written a short and sensitive analysis of Dorothy Day's life and work. Ellsberg (2010) discusses her sex life. Klejment

(2009) has details I have not seen elsewhere. To get a better sense of Dorothy, I talked with people who knew her, and I listened to an interview she gave on KPFA, Pacifica Radio, in Berkeley, CA.

16 This is widely attributed to Abbie Hoffman.

17 For Dorothy's Communist friends, see her autobiography (Day 1938: Chap. 4). https://www.catholicworker.org/dorothyday/articles/204.html

18 William Jennings Bryan was the secretary of state under Wilson and resigned when war became American policy. See Kazin (2006), *A Godly Hero: The Life of William Jennings Bryan*. New York: Knopf. Except for the prohibitionism and the biblical literalism, Bryan's politics were a precursor of the New Deal.

19 Ackerman (2007) describes the Red Scare in detail. See also Allen (1997) chapter 3.

20 Day (1938: Chap. 9).

21 Ibid.

24 Allen (1997), writing in the early 1930s, describes the Roaring Twenties from the viewpoint of a historian who lived through it.

25 Socialism is basic to Christianity (Acts of the Apostles 4:32-37). But then Marx did not say exactly this, nor was he the first to say it: https://en.wikipedia.org/wiki/Opium_of_the_people

The canonical anarchist text on religion is Bakunin (1911), *God and the State*. https://www.gutenberg.org.

26 On not-for-profit salaries see:

(1) Kristi Heim. 2009. Gates Foundation chief earns top pay among foundation CEOs. *Seattle Times*, 1 Oct. https://seattletimes.com Accessed June 2019.

(2) Michael Edwards. 2016. Foundation CEOs shouldn't serve on corporate boards. *Chronicle of Philanthropy*, 2 Nov. https://www.philanthropy.com/article/Opinion-Foundation-CEOs/238284 Accessed Aug 2019

27 Giridharadas (2018).

28 (1) Holland Cotter. 2019. Money, ethics, art: can museums police themselves? *New York Times*, 9 May.
(2) Robin Pogrebin et al. 2019. New scrutiny of museum boards

takes aim at world of wealth and status, *New York Times*, 2 Oct.

29 Diener (2016): http://numerocinqmagazine.
com/2016/08/03/78027/

30 Morris (2018).

31 Day (2006: Chap. 4).

32 For Pope Francis's speech to the U.S. Congress, see: https://time.
com/4048176/pope-francis-us-visit-congress-transcript/ Accessed
June 2019.

33 Fiala (2018) places anarchism in the context of political philosophy. Shatz's translation of Bakunin (1990) contains a good biography. Bakunin was more a man of action than of letters, and he is at
his best with pamphlets:

(1) ttp://www.revoltlib.com/anarchism/the-immorali-
ty-of-the-state/view.php

(2) http://www.revoltlib.com/ anarchism/stateless-socialism-anar-
chism/view.php

34 The definition of the state as a monopoly on force is Max Weber's.

35 Sahlins (1972).

36 I base my description of Manam Island on ethnographic fieldwork
done by Camilla Wedgewood in the 1930s and by Nancy C. Lutkehaus from the 1970s to the present.

37 Reynolds (1993).

38 The World Economic Forum publishes an annual report that ranks
countries on a sexual equality score.

39 https://www.haudenosauneeconfederacy.com Accessed Sept. 2019.
This site has information on their culture as well as on the polity.
The latter shaped the U.S. constitution (Johansen 1982).

40 Morgan's (1851) fieldwork among the Haudenosaunee was important to the anthropological understanding of kinship systems,
but his most famous book *Ancient Society* is factually incorrect on
many issues and theoretically outdated.

41 Engels, Frederick. 1942. *The Origin of the Family, Private Property,
and the State: In the Light of the Researches of Lewis H. Morgan.* New
York: International.

42 Scott (2012).

43 Ostrom (1990). See Vollan and Ostrom (2010) for recent references. Ostrom reprises her life's work in a lecture: https://www.youtube.com/watch?v=T6OgRki5SgM

44 A classic example of the demonization of anarchists is Joseph Conrad's novel, *The Secret Agent* (1907), one of the prototypes of the thriller in English. It reads like a disinformation piece commissioned by British intelligence.

45 Orwell (1938) experienced the war between the Communists and the anarchists during the Spanish Civil War.

46 Kazin's (2006) essay on religion and American politics provides a quick background.

47 De La Torre (2014: 11).

48 https://millercenter.org/president/truman/essays/harriman-1946-secretary-of-commerce

49 https://www.catholicworker.org/dorothyday/articles/435.html

50 https://dorothyday.catholicworker.org/articles/538.html

51 https://www.khanacademy.org/humanities/us-history/rise-to-world-power/1920s-america/a/1920s-consumption

https://restaurant-ingthroughhistory.com/2016/02/21/when-coffee-was-king/ Both sites accessed Aug. 2019.

52 Hochschild (2005).

53 Klempner (2006).

54 Whitfield (1994).

55 Rabben (2011).

56 De La Torre (2014: 10).

57 Peace activists have broken into missile bases and used human blood as a form of expression—at much cost to themselves: https://kingsbayplowshares7.org/ Accessed Oct. 2019.

58 Morris (2004: 71).

59 Kropotkin (n.d., 1901, 1926).

60 Kropotkin (n.d: 10).

61 London (1903). There are still sweatshops in the United States, but the owners have to break the law: Natalie Kitroeff. 2019. Fashion Nova's secret: underpaid workers in Los Angeles factories, *New*

York Times, 16 Dec.

62 The anthropologist Aihwa Ong (2010) looks at the opposite end of the Silicon Valley supply chain—a factory in Malaysia.

63 Graeber (2004). See also Scott (2012) and Richard D. Wolff's podcasts, especially "Socialism in America": https://www.rdwolff.com

Graeber's (2014) treatise is essential for understanding capitalism.

64 (1) For the definition of a co-op: https://illinois.coop/about-coops/cooperative-principles/

(2) For the legal status of cooperatives in the USA: the Sustainable Economies Legal Center in Oakland, CA at https://theselc.org

(3) see also the Center for Cooperative Development: https://www.cccd.coop/

65 The information on the Park Slope Food Cooperative is based on my personal observation and interviews with members, including two of the founders. The article by Schwartz (2019) gives a sense of what it is like to work in the Co-op.

66 *The Road to Serfdom* is a book by Hayek; see neoliberalism in the Glossary, as well as Chap. 6 above.

67 Schumpeter (1950: 206). Physicist Richard Sonnenfeld calls this type of argument "proof by lack of imagination" (personal communication).

68 I have explored the social implications of Big Data in a suspense novel, *The Day Coyote Danced*: https://borderlandnorth.com

69 See: Michael Kwet. 2019. In stores, secret surveillance tracks your every move. *New York Times*, 14 June.

70 Scott (2019).

71 Jean Jacques Rousseau. 1910. *A Discourse Upon the Origin and the Foundation of the Inequality Among Mankind*. Harvard Classics, Volume 34. First edition 1755. https://www.gutenberg.org

72 Lutkehaus's (2013) paper describes the ceremonial intergroup relations among villages and the regalia of rank.

73 Sahlins (1963).

74 Scott (2017).

75 Ellis (1986).

76 Baptist (2016).

77 Johnson (2006).

78 Holloway (1974). Primates have not changed much since this book was printed.

79 Barbara Goldberg. 2019, Indiana judges suspended after brawl outside White Castle, 15 Nov.: https://www.reuters.com   Accessed Nov. 2019.

80 I have in mind the Israeli attack on the American spy ship *U.S.S. Liberty* during the Six Day War, but there are many other examples.

81 Grann (2018) describes the systematic murders of Osage Indians by White conspirators in Oklahoma in the 1920s, events that are close enough to us in time that he can make his case with photographs and FBI records. For the sterilization, see Alexandra Stern (in Chapter 5 references).

82 Baptist (2016).

83 Ryan (2009) sees collaborative relationships as resting on a mutually-supportive triad of persons. I have extended his concept to institutions.

84 Scott (1998) critically examines some large-scale projects that reflect the statist perspective.

85 Postman (1985), Giroux (2010).

86 Jeffrey Toobin quoting Roger Stone in http://www.newyorker.com/magazine/2008/06/02/the-dirty-trickster

87 (1) Luisa Yanez. 2013. Amazon.com founder and Palmetto High grad Jeff Bezos to buy Washington Post, *Miami Herald*: http://www.miamiherald.com/2013/08/05/3544596/jeff-bezos-a-rocket-launched-from.html#storylink=cpy Accessed May 2013.
(2) Eric Berger. 2019. Jeff Bezos unveils his sweeping vision for humanity's future in space, *Ars Technica*, 9 May. https://arstechnica.com/science/2019/05/

88 The following article deals with all three corporate cosmonauts: Richard Branson's Virgin Galactic prepares to go public, *The Guardian*: 9 July 2019.

References

Ackerman, Kenneth D. 2007. *Young J. Edgar: Hoover, the Red Scare, and the Assault on Civil Liberties*. New York: Carroll & Graf.

Allen, Frederick Lewis. 1997. *Only Yesterday: An Informal History of the 1920s*. First edition 1932. New York: John Wiley & Sons.

Bakunin, Mikhail Aleandrovich. 1900. *Statism and Anarchy*. Trans. and ed. by Marshall S. Shatz. Cambridge: Cambridge University Press.

Baptist, Edward E. 2016. *The Half Has Never Been Told*. New York: Basic Books.

Brenner, Michael. 2018. Plutocracy now! *Consortium News* Vol. 24, No. 250, 7 Sept.

Day, Dorothy. 2006. *From Union Square to Rome*. Maryknoll, NY: Orbis Books. 1st ed. 1938.

De La Torre, Miguel. 2014. *Doing Christian Ethics from the Margins*. 2nd ed. Maryknoll, NY: Orbis Books.

Diener, Laura Michelle. 2016. The habit of being passionate: Dorothy Day's radical mysticism. http://numerocinqmagazine. com/2016/08/03/78027/ Accessed July 2019.

Ellis, John. 1986. *The Social History of the Machine Gun*. 1st ed 1975. Baltimore: Johns Hopkins University Press.

Ellsberg, Robert. 2010. Dorothy in love: New letters reveal the frank sexuality of a possible saint. *America*, 10 Nov.

Fiala, Andrew, "Anarchism," *The Stanford Encyclopedia of Philosophy* (Spring 2018 Edition).

Forest, Jim. 1986. *Love is the Measure: a Biography of Dorothy Day*. New York: Paulist Press.

Fraser, Steve. 2015. *The Age of Acquiesence: The Life and Death of American Resistance to Organized Wealth and Power*. New York: Little, Brown.

Giridharadas, Anand. 2018. *Winners Take All: The Elite Charade of Changing the World*. New York: Knopf.

Giroux, Henry A. 2010. The disappearing intellectual in the age of economic Darwinism, *truthout.org*, 12 July.

Graeber, David. 2004. Anarchism or the revolutionary movement of the 21st century. https://zcomm.org/znetarticle/Anarchism-or-the-revolutionary-movement-of-the-twenty-first-century-by-david-graeber/ Accessed Nov. 2018.

_____. 2014. *Debt: The First 5,000 Years*. London & Brooklyn NY: Melville House

Grann, David. 2018. *Killers of the Flower Moon: The Osage Murders and the birth of the FBI*. New York: Vintage Books/Penguin Random House.

Hochschild, Adam. 2005. *Bury the Chains: the British Struggle to Abolish Slavery*. London: Macmillan.

Holloway, Ralph L., ed. 1974. *Primate Aggression, Territoriality, and Xenophobia: A Comparative Perspective*. New York: Academic Press.

Johansen, Bruce E. 1982. *Forgotten Founders: How the American Indian Helped Shape Democracy*. Boston: Harvard Common Press.

Johnson, Chalmers A. 2006. *Nemesis: The Last Days of the American Republic*. New York: Metropolitan Books.

Kazin, Michael. 2006. A difficult marriage: American Protestants and American politics. Dissent.http://www.dissent magazine.org/article/?article=159

Klejment, Anne. 2009. The spirituality of Dorothy Day's pacifism, *U.S. Catholic Historian* 27, Spring.

Klempner, Mark. 2006. *The Heart Has Reasons: Holocaust Rescuers and Their Stories of Courage*. Cleveland: Pilgrim Press.

Kropotkin, Peter. n.d. *The Place of Anarchism in Socialistic Evolution: An Address Delivered in Paris*. Trans. by Henry Glasse. New ed. enlarged. London: William Reeves. First published in *The Anarchist*, July 1887.

_____. 1901. *Fields, Factories and Workshops; or, Industry Combined with Agriculture and Brain Work with Manual Work*. New York: Putnam.

_____. 1926. *The Conquest of Bread*. New York: Vanguard Press.

London, Jack. 1903. *People of the Abyss*. London and New York: Macmillan.

Loughery, J. and B. Randolph. 2020. *Dorothy Day: Dissenting Voice of the American Century*. NY: Simon & Shuster.

Lutkehaus, Nancy C. 1990. Hierarchy and "heroic society"; Manam variations in Sepik social structure, *Oceania* 60 (3): 179-197.

_____. 2013. Bodily transformations: the politics and art of men as pigs and pigs as men on Manam Island, Papua New Guinea. *Pacific Arts* New Series 13 (1):5-13.

Morgan, Lewis Henry. 1997. *Systems of Consanguinity and Affinity of the Human Family*. Reprint of 1871 ed. Omaha: University of Nebraska Press.

Morris, Brian. 2018. *Kropotkin: The Politics of Community*. Oakland, CA: PM Press.

Ong, Aihwa. 2010. *Spirits of Resistance and Capitalist Discipline: Factory Women in Malaysia*. 2nd ed. Albany, NY: SUNY Press.

Organisation for Economic Co-operation and Development (2008). *Growing Unequal? Income Distribution and Poverty in OECD Countries*. Paris.

Orwell, George. 1938. *Homage to Catalonia*. London: Secker & Warburg.

Ostrom, Elinor. 1990. *Governing the Commons: the Evolution of Institutions for Collective Action*. Cambridge: Cambridge University Press.

Phillips, Peter. 2018 *Giants: The Global Power Elite*. New York: Seven Stories Press.

Postman, Neil. 1985. *Amusing Ourselves to Death*. New York: Viking.

Rabben, Linda. 2011. *Give Refuge to a Stranger: The Past, Present, and Future of Sanctuary*. Walnut Creek, CA: Left Coast Press.

Reynolds, Peter C. 1993. The complementation theory of language and tool use. In *Tools, Language, and Cognition in Human Evolution*, edited by K. Gibson and T. Ingold. Cambridge: Cambridge University Press.

Ryan, Paul. 2009. *The Three Person Solution: Creating Sustainable Collaborative Relationships*. West Lafayette, IN: Purdue University Press.

Robinson, William I. 2014. *Global Capitalism and the Crisis of Humanity*. New York: Cambridge University Press.

Schumpeter, Joseph A. 1950. *Capitalism, Socialism and Democracy*. 3rd ed. New York: Harper and Rowe.

Schwartz, Alexandra. 2019. The grocery store where produce meets politics, *New Yorker*. 25 Nov.

Scott, James C. 1998. *Seeing Like a State: How Certain Schemes to Improve the Human Condition Have Failed*. New Haven, CT: Yale University Press.

———. 2012. *Two Cheers for Anarchism: Six Easy Pieces on Autonomy, Dignity, and Meaningful Work and Play*. Princeton NJ: Princeton University Press.

_____. 2017. *Against the Grain: A Deep History of the Earliest States.* New Haven: Yale University Press.

Sahlins, Marshall D. 1963. Poor man, rich man, big-man, chief: political types in Melanesia and Polynesia, *Comparative Studies in Society and History* 5 (3):285-303.

_____. 1972. *Stone Age Economics.* Chicago: Aldine-Atherton.

Stanish, Charles. 2017. *The Evolution of Human Co-operation: Ritual and Social Complexity in Stateless Societies.* Cambridge: Cambridge University Press.

Vollan, Bjorn, and Elinor Ostrom. 2010. Cooperation and the commons, *Science*: 12 Nov. 330:923-924.

Wallace, Alfred Russel. 1898. *The Wonderful Century: Its Successes and Its Failures.* 2nd ed. London.

Wedgewood, Camilla. 1947. Trade and exchange of goods on Manam Island (summary), *Man*: 48:8.

_____. 1959. Manam Kinship. *Oceania* 29 (4):239-256.

Whitfield, Teresa. 1994. *Paying the Price: Ignacio Ellacuría and the Murdered Jesuits of El Salvador.* Philadelphia: Temple University Press.

Young, Robert M. 1985. *Darwin's Metaphor: Nature's Place in Victorian Culture.* Cambridge Cambridge University Press.

A Glossary
on the Intersection of
Religion, Society, and
Evolution

achieved social status: one that can be attained to some extent through one's own effort, such as Eagle Scout or salesman of the year. It contrasts to ascribed[G] social status.

adaptation: the thesis, developed in the empirical work of Charles Darwin, that the morphology of a species[G] is best understood as a product of both the physical conditions of the environment and the effects of the activities of other species in such roles as prey, predator, pollinator, and so on. See also cultural[G] adaptation.

adaptive radiation: the differentiation of a single ancestral species[G] into multiple daughter species each of which is adapted to a different geographical area or ecological niche.

adjunct faculty: part-time faculty at a university, often hired as independent contractors rather than as employees. They now comprise a majority of faculty at American universities.

agonism: in primatology, social interaction that expresses aggression and fear or a blend of both. See agonistic[G] display.

agonistic display: in primatology, social interaction that expresses aggression and fear but without the consummatory[G] behaviors of biting and fleeing respectively. When biting and fleeing become involved it is no longer considered to be display.

alpha: (adjective) denoting the highest-ranking position in a status[G] hierarchy, as for example the alpha male in a group of monkeys.

alternative splicing: the process by which a single gene can code for multiple distinct proteins by means of changes to the RNA transcribed from the gene. It contradicts the one gene/one protein theorem of the Central Dogma.[G]

altruism: doing something for another without any expectation of getting anything back. See generalized[G] altruism, parochial[G] altruism, and reciprocal[G] altruism.

American empire: the effort by the United States of America to dominate geopolitics after World War II, characterized by (1) multinational organizations to foster capitalism and anti-Communism, (2) military expansionism through a network of client states and foreign bases, (3) economic domination by U.S. corporations, and (4) an ideology of "freedom."

Anglican: (adjective) pertaining to the doctrines and practices of the Church of England, which was founded by the English monarchy in the 16th century; (noun) a member of that church.

apologetics: the use of rational argument to justify religious doctrine.

appetitive behavior: in ethology,[G] a sequence of actions that precedes and is instrumental to the consummatory[G] act of a motivational state, e.g. courtship is the appetitive behavior of copulation.

aristocracy: in Great Britain, a ruling elite composed of men with hereditary titles of nobility. A title specified one's rank relative to other members of the aristocracy, conferred rights to the lands associated with the title, and made one eligible for high positions in the military and government.[G]

ascribed social status: one that an individual is normally powerless to change, such as ex-convict or infant. Contrasts to achieved[G] status.

atomistic individualism: the premise, fundamental to both capitalism[G] and Darwinism,[G] that society is simply an aggregation of individual interests and has no properties or processes of its own.

band: in anthropology, a group of families that usually live together and travel as a unit. Bands are characteristic of contemporary gathering-and-hunting societies.[G]

belief system: those concepts that are accepted by a community of people as a true description of the world.

benefit corporation or **B corp**: in American law, a for-profit corporation[G] that can legally pursue a social good even if it reduces profit to its stockholders.

Benthamite: pertaining to the work of Jeremy Bentham (1748-1832), a social philosopher who promoted the thesis that the greatest happiness of the greatest number is the guiding principle of moral action.

biblical literalism: reading the Bible as if it were written as a naturalistic[G] description of past events.

Big Science: science dependent on massive state[G] funding, especially during and after World War II.

biogeography: the branch of biology that maps the distribution of organisms.

bio-immortality: my term for the belief that biological science can confer personal immortality by means of biotechnology.

bipolarity of science: my thesis that scientific institutions have a **factuality pole** that transforms empirical data into scientific facts by means of the scientific method and an **ideological pole** that uses such facts to promote science as an institution.[G] Both poles are needed for science to exist.

bourgeoisie: in Marxist terminology, the class[G] that owns the means of industrial production, that is, the capitalists.[G] The term derives from the medieval word for the free citizen of a town, as opposed to the serfs and land-owning aristocracy.

callitrichid: a monkey of the family Callitrichidae, native to South America. They are important to evolutionary theory because they share many social properties with humans, such as social[G] exchange and co-operative[G] parenting.

Calvinism: those branches of Christianity that derive historically from the polity established by John Calvin (1509–64) in Geneva or were influenced by his theology, as were Presbyterianism, Congregationalism, and Unitarianism. The New England intellectual establishment in the United States was heavily influenced by Calvinism through Puritanism.[G]

Calvinist substrate of Darwinism: my term for values and beliefs implicit in Darwinism[G] that reflect tenets of Calvinist[G] theology.

Cambrian: the geological period from 570 to 510 million years ago when the first distinct lineages (phyla) of multicellular animals appear in the fossil record.

capitalism: a social process in which (1) individuals (or fictive individuals such as corporations[G]) claim ownership of the products of human activity and the tools and natural resources to make them, and sometimes the human beings themselves, with (2) the intention of selling or renting them to others at a profit while (3) dismissing the social and environmental costs of the process as someone else's problem. In the modern period, capitalism is a way of converting a class system based on inherited rights in land to one based on the control of money. See also corporate[G] capitalism, consumer[G] capitalism, and state[G] capitalism.

capitalist: (adjective) pertaining to or exemplifying capitalism; (noun) a person who practices capitalism.

capitalist class: ✦ those people whose primary source of income is rents from real property and return on investments; ✦ in Marxist theory, those who own the means of production.

capitalist corporation: a corporation^G authorized by the state^G to issue shares of ownership and to engage in commercial activity.

catastrophism: a theory developed by Georges Cuvier^G (1769-1832) that was based on the study of the fossil record and geological stratification. It asserts that in the history of life on earth there have been multiple mass extinctions, which he called catastrophes, with corresponding discontinuities in the rock column, each of which is followed by a new era with new species.

Catholic Worker: a program launched in the United States in 1933 by Dorothy Day (1887-1980) and Peter Maurin (1877-1949) to ameliorate poverty. It published a socialist^G newspaper, established a network of hospitality houses to provide food and shelter to the destitute and homeless, and started cooperative farms to provide food security to the working class.

cell nucleus: a structure in the cells of eukaryotes^G where nucleic acid (such as DNA) is stored when the cell is not dividing.

cellular continuity: the finding that biological cells are descended from previous cells and are not produced by spontaneous generation or other discontinuous events.

Central Dogma of genetics: James Watson (1928-) and Francis Crick's (1916-2004) theory that a specific sequence of nucleotides^G in a DNA molecule determines a corresponding sequence of nucleotides in an RNA molecule which in turn determines the sequence of amino acids that comprise a particular protein molecule. That is, DNA → RNA → protein. Because genetics based on the Central Dogma initially ignored the role of other molecules on gene^G expression, the Central Dogma implicitly promoted genetic[G] determinism while providing an ideological rationale for the biotech industry.

Chicago School of economics: a version of laissez-faire[G] capitalism that came to prominence in the 1970s, associated with Milton Friedman (1912-2006) and his colleagues at the University of Chicago. It was influential in the promulgation of neoliberalism.[Soc]

clan: in anthropology, a group of lineages whose members trace descent from a common ancestor, who may be represented as an animal, plant, or feature of the landscape. See kinship[G] system.

class: one of the divisions of a class[G] society.

class society: a society divided into two or more subpopulations ranked by wealth and/or other symbols of status and in which the upper class [G] politically dominates the lower. Also called *social stratification*.

coevolution: changes in two or more species[G] that are due to each species adapting to the presence of the other, such as parasites evolving so as to more easily infect their hosts even as their hosts evolve better defenses against them. I use "coevolution" in this book as a descriptive term for social institutions that have a similar relationship to one another.

Cold War: the state of hostility that existed between capitalist and Communist countries between 1947 (when the United States adopted the Truman Doctrine) and 1991 (when the Soviet Union was dissolved), characterized by proxy wars in neutral countries in which both sides refrained from using nuclear weapons.

Cold War academy: an institution of higher education, typified by the elite universities of the United States during and after World War II, that is financially dependent on military funding and whose faculty members contribute to secret projects sponsored by the military and espionage agencies. This arrangement did not end with the Cold War.[G]

collective aggression or **collective violence**: when two or more people or groups cooperate to intentionally hurt a third party or person.

command: (noun) any social role that confers the right to tell members of a class of people what to do and to punish them if they don't do it. It is definitive of state[G]-based societies and authoritarian organizations.

commons (singular noun): property or resources that are collectively owned and cooperatively managed for the good of the whole community.

communism (not capitalized): an egalitarian society with property held in common. Compare with Communism.[G]

Communism (capitalized): the system of socialism[G] advocated by the Communist Party of the Soviet Union in the 20th century.

competition: (1) personal interaction between individuals to determine who will get what they both want, e.g. two runners competing to run the race in the shortest time. (2) the loss of needed resources to others for whatever reason, e.g. a plant that is crowded out by weeds. Darwin uses competition in both senses.

complementation: my term for when two or more individuals perform complementary actions that are instrumental to the same goal by inferring the intention of the other. It enables humans to perform tasks that cannot be achieved by one individual acting alone, e.g. you lift one end of the heavy box while I lift the other. Compare to parallel[G] activity.

congruent belief systems: my term for belief [G] systems that have substantially different content but which use similar modes of thought so that belief in one system facilitates and reinforces belief in the other, as for example, Darwinism[G] and capitalism.[G]

consort pair: in primatology, a temporary social group consisting of a sexually mature male and a sexually receptive female. Females of some primate species[G] may participate in multiple consort pairs in the course of a single estrus^G period.

consort turnover: when one male replaces another in a consort^G pair.

consumer capitalism: a class^G society in which one's social status is determined by the public display of goods and services that are promoted in the mass media as desirable acquisitions and are purchased (except by the wealthy) by borrowing money at interest from the capitalist^G class. See capitalism^G and corporate^G capitalism.

cooperative: (noun) a business or organization that is owned, staffed, and managed by its members who cooperate through shared work and democratic decision-making to produce a collective product or service.

cooperative parenting: when both parents participate in the care and feeding of the child, as exemplified by all human societies, a few species of mammals, and the majority of bird species.

corporation: an organization chartered by the state^G that is governed by a board of directors and enjoys the legal rights of an individual. In a capitalist ^G corporation, the board issues shares of ownership and governs the company so as to maximize profit to its owners. See also benefit^G corporation.

corporate academy: my term for an institution of higher education that is financially dependent on the production and commercialization of intellectual property developed by the faculty. It is sometimes called the *neoliberal*^G university.

corporate capitalism: a society in which capitalist^G corporations^G dominate the economy. It contrasts with capitalist societies composed of enterprises owned primarily by families, partnerships, and/or individual humans. See also state^G capitalism.

consummatory behavior: in ethology,^G any action that normally terminates or satisfies a motivated series of actions, e.g. copulation is the consummatory behavior of sex. Contrasts to appetitive^G behavior.

creationism: ✦ a school of Christian theology that interprets the Genesis account of creation as a naturalistic ᴳ description of past events; ✦ a political ideology in the United States that uses the Genesis account of creation to justify a crypto-racist, procapitalist, and authoritarian social agenda.

cross cousin: a child of an opposite-sex sibling of one's parents, e.g. my mother's brother's child. Compare to parallel ᴳ cousin.

cultural adaptation: adaptation to an environment by means of social organization and socially transmitted knowledge rather than by somatic change. In *Homo sapiens*, it presumes inference of intentionality, complementation,ᴳ observational learning, reciprocalᴳ exchange, generalizedᴳ altruism, cooperativeᴳ parenting, and language. Compare to adaptation.ᴳ

cultural anthropology: the process of learning about a foreign culture by means of participant ᴳ observation and making generalizations based on such findings.

Cuvier, Georges (1769-1832): the founder of vertebrate paleontology and a proponent of the theory of catastrophism.ᴳ

Darwinian theory: the use of the concepts formulated by Charles Darwin (1809-1882), such as adaptationᴳ and selection,ᴳ to explain biological processes in a scientific manner. Such content is typically found in university courses on evolutionaryᴳ biology. Compare to Darwinism.ᴳ

Darwinism: an ideologyᴳ consisting of four core beliefs: (1) **P**rogress through genetic change—whether selection, eugenics, or genetic engineering, (2) **H**ostility to religion,ᴳ (3) **A**tomistic ᴳ individualism, and (4) **G**enetic inheritance of social behavior. The initial letters of these four tenets make the mnemonic PHAGe, which rhymes with *page* as in paper. See also Social Darwinismᴳ and Darwin's ᴳ cohort. Compare to Darwinianᴳ theory.

Darwin's cohort: a human community that uses Darwinism[G] as a guide to social policy.

descent through modification: Charles Darwin's term for organic[G] evolution.

Devonian: the geological period from about 400 million to 360 million years ago when the first land animals appear in the fossil record.

diluvialism: the thesis that certain geological phenomena, such as fossil marine organisms found far from the sea, prove that Noah's flood was an historical event. Now a cornerstone of creationism,[G] it was important in the development of geological science in the 18th and 19th centuries. See English[G] school of geology.

design: the argument dating from pre-Christian times that great complexity in a natural system proves that it was intentionally designed by an intelligent creator. See intelligent[G] design.

diurnal rhythm: in primatology, the normal succession of activities in the course of a primate's day, such as active foraging for food in the morning followed by relaxed mutual[G] grooming in the afternoon.

dominance hierarchy: a type of status[G] hierarchy where rank is determined by aggressive competition for scarce resources.

English school of geology: a phase in the development of the earth sciences, centered at Oxford University in the 1820s, that accepted the Genesis account of creation as a naturalistic[G] description of past events and used it to make predictions about the fossil record.

epigenetic: anything that alters gene[G] expression without altering the sequence of nucleotides[G] in the DNA.

epigenetic inheritance: transmission via the germline[G] of changes that have been induced by epigenetic[G] causes, as, for example, by methylation.[G]

estrus: a state of physiological readiness for sex induced by periodic fluctuations in the level of sexual hormones.

ethnographer: someone who writes a description of a society and its culture based on the method of participant[G] observation. The work so produced is an ethnography.

ethology: the biological study of animal behavior, especially research that emphasizes innate behavior patterns and instinctual motivations.

eugenics: any attempt to improve the human species by altering the genetic composition of subsequent generations, such as selective breeding, sterilization, and germline[G] genetic engineering.

eukaryote: an organism whose genetic material is concentrated in chromosomes within a cell[G] nucleus. All multicellular animals, plants, and fungi are eukaryotes, as are some single-celled organisms such as amoebas and ciliates.

evangelical: Christians who believe in "personal conversion and a rigorous moral life, on the one hand, and concentrated attention on the Bible as a guide to conviction and behavior, on the other, with a special zeal for the dissemination of Christian faith so conceived." Quoted from Gabriel Fackre, 1983. "Evangelical, Evangelicalism." In *The Westminster Dictionary of Christian Theology*, edited by A. Richardson and J. Bowden. Philadelphia: Westminster Press.

evolution: See organic[G] evolution, social[G] evolution, progressive[G] evolution, and unilineal[G] evolution.

evolutionary: pertaining to processes of gradual development over geologic time and/or to evolutionist[G] theories.

evolutionary biology: biology that describes the process of organic[G] evolution by employing Darwinian[G] theory as the explanatory framework.

evolutionary psychology: a variant of Darwinism[G] developed in the early 1980s that asserts that human social life can be explained by innate modules in the human brain that were selected for during a hypothetical gathering-and-hunting[G] past.

evolutionism: the thesis that historical changes in human societies and changes in organisms over geologic time are both manifestations of a single process that can be explained by putative laws of progressive development. Evolutionism in this sense confounds cultural[G] adaptation with organic[G] evolution.

exogamy: the requirement that members of a particular social group or class marry non-members.

extended family: a family group consisting of relatives that extend beyond the nuclear family (e.g. grandparents, cousins, etc.) and who live together in the same residence.

fundamentalism: a movement in American Protestantism that began in the early 20th century that seeks to ameliorate the effects of modernism[G] and secularization by advocating a return to the "fundamentals" of the Christian faith, a list of which the founders provided. The term has since been generalized to anti-modernist movements in other religions.

Frankfurt School: a scholarly project in Germany after World War I to make available the little-known works of the young Karl Marx (1818-83) and to integrate them into Marxist theory.

gathering-and-hunting (synonymous with **hunting-and-gathering**): ✦ in modern anthropology, a subsistence[G] strategy based on the gathering of wild plants and the hunting of wild animals, and which may be mixed with other strategies, such as horticulture and trade; ✦ in Darwinian theory, the most primitive stage of human society to which the human mind and body are purportedly adapted.

gene expression: the processes that enable the information in a gene to be accessed, to be transcribed into RNA, and to produce effects on the phenotype.[G]

generalized altruism: in Darwinian theory, doing something for another without any expectation of getting something back of comparable value. It is equivalent to the word altruism in ordinary English.

genetic determinism: the belief that an organism and its behavior can be completely specified by the information encoded in its DNA.

genocidal war: the process of conquering another society by systematically killing its people, whether or not they are combatants.

genome: the entire sequence of nucleotides[G] in the genetic material of an organism or a species.[G]

genotype: the genes that are contained in an individual organism, especially genes with known variants in other individuals. Contrasts to phenotype.[G]

germline: a lineage of cells that gives rise to reproductive cells (such as eggs or sperm) and its continuation via sexual reproduction through multiple generations.

germline genetic engineering: intentional modification of genes found in germ cells (such as sperm or ova). It contrasts to somatic[G] cell genetic engineering, in which genes are altered in the body of a single individual but are not transmitted sexually to another generation.

Gilded Age: the period of American history between the end of the Civil War (1865) and the beginning of the Progressive Era[G] (1890s), characterized by rapid industrialization,[G] the mechanization of agriculture, the rise of corporate[G] capitalism, increased urbanization, great disparity of wealth, and the organization of the working class into unions.

government: any institution[G] whose primary function is to lead and manage the collective activity of groups or other institutions. A state[G] is one form of government. Compare with intergroup[G] coordination.

Great Awakening: a movement among Protestants in North America beginning in the 1730s, characterized by itinerant preachers, revival meetings, and sermons that appealed to the heart. Breaking with the key Calvinist ^G doctrines of predestination and the depravity of man, it offered the possibility of salvation for all through repentance for sin and acceptance of Jesus's saving grace. When pluralized, the term denotes a succession of revival movements that began in the 1730s, the 1780s, the 1840s, and, according to some authorities, the 1960s.

great chain of being: the thesis, dating from Classical times, that social groups and species can be ranked on a linear scale of perfection from superior to inferior forms. Also called the *scala naturae.*

Great Depression: the period in American history from the crash of the stock market in 1929 to the country's entry into World War II in 1941, characterized by a slump in manufacturing and wide-spread unemployment.

group selection: in Darwinian theory, the situation in which an individual organism's reproductive success is contingent on the success of the population to which it belongs.

heritability: the extent to which a phenotypic ^G trait can be attributed to genetic causes.

History: when spelled with a capital H, it denotes the belief that human history moves in some inevitable direction through the operation of laws akin to scientific laws.

Hobbesian: pertaining to the work of Thomas Hobbes (1588-1679) who argued that human society requires a strong, centralized authority because human beings are aggressive and selfish by nature.

Holy Orders: in the Catholic and Anglican churches, a religious ritual that gives a person the grace and spiritual power to perform the sacramental duties of a priest.

hominid: an ape-like primate that is anatomically adapted for bipedalism. Even though the term is no longer used by biological taxonomists, it continues to be useful in anthropology because it denotes a cluster of biobehavioral traits that chimpanzees do not have and which are important in the theory of human evolution. Compare hominin.[G]

hominin: denotes human beings, chimpanzees, and any extinct species in this lineage. The terminology is based on the finding that human beings are closer genetically to chimpanzees than to other apes. However, the term is also ideological in that it promotes the Darwinist premise that genes take precedence over gross anatomy, social organization, and behavior in the classification of organisms. Compare hominid.[G]

Homo: the genus that contains modern humans (*Homo sapiens*) as well as closely related species[G] that precede it in geologic time.

homology: body parts of different species that occupy the same position in the body plan and have detailed anatomical correspondences, e.g. the arm of a human and the wing of a bird.

horizontal gene transfer: genes that enter a genome[G] from an organism that is not its parent, including genes from other species.[G]

human ethology: the application of ethological methods to human behavior. See ethology.[G]

human evolution: the thesis that the human species has developed over geologic time from a non-human ancestral species[G] by means of a process of descent[G] through modification.

hunting-and-gathering: See gathering-and-hunting.[G]

ideology: any belief[G] system that is used to further a specific political or economic interest. An ideology is measured by its social efficacy and not by its truth or falsity.

inclusive fitness: any process whereby the fitness of the relatives with whom one shares genes increases one's own fitness. Kin[G] selection is an instance of inclusive fitness.

industrial: a society that is characterized by (1) the organization of labor in a factory system, (2) the use of machines powered by inanimate sources of power, and (3) and belief that technical innovation will produce increased material prosperity for all (Progress[G]). In the non-Communist world, it also promises (4) individual upward mobility within (5) a class[G] system defined by capitalism.[G] See consumer[G] capitalism.

industrialization: the process of creating an industrial[G] society.

instinct: in the tradition of European ethology,[G] any behavioral system that develops in animals reared in social isolation that is self-motivating and includes distinctive appetitive[G] and consummatory[G] behaviors.

institution: a social group that performs a critical function in society and inculcates its beliefs and practices in new members so that it can survive for multiple generations.

instrumental intelligence: a functional system in the primate brain that perceives, understands, and uses physical objects and causality while assessing the physical effects of intentional action on the physical world and on other animate beings. It is distinct from social[G] intelligence with which it is functionally integrated.

intelligent design: a movement within the creationist[G] school of theology that seeks parity with evolutionist science by using the argument from design[G] as a scientific explanation of life.

intergroup coordination: the process of leading and managing the collective activity and cooperative behavior of multiple groups. It is found in all human societies, whether or not they have states[G] or governments.[G]

keystone ideology: my term for an ideology[G] that is broad enough in scope that it can subsume more parochial ideologies, enabling collaboration among multiple institutions.^{G}

kin selection: the thesis in biology that individuals may act in a way that decreases their own survival provided that it is balanced by the survival of genetic relatives with whom they share genes. Kin selection implies that the probability of altruism^G is proportional to the degree of genetic relatedness. The thesis is exemplified by the quip attributed to J. B. S. Haldane (1892-1964) that he would happily give his life for two brothers or eight cousins.

kincentric society: any human society in which social life is primarily organized by a culturally-constructed kinship^G system. Such societies are usually supported by a subsistence economy based on common ownership of critical resources, labor recruited from family groups, reciprocal exchange, and an ideology of egalitarianism.

kinship system: categorizes people by means of kinship terms that recognize degrees of relatedness and descent from ancestors while conferring associated rights and responsibilities. Kinship relations as specified by language cannot be inferred from the degree of genetic relationship as determined by biology.

Kropotkin, Peter (1842-1921): a naturalist and socialist who argued that competition in organic nature is counterbalanced by Mutual^G Aid.

lac operon: a scientific model published by Francois Jacob (1920-) and Jacques Monod (1919-76) in 1961 that describes how genes in the intestinal bacterium *E. coli* interact so as to produce the enzymes that metabolize lactose, the characteristic sugar of milk.

laissez-faire economics: the thesis that the market functions best when government^G has no role in the economy. It is a key tenet of neoliberalism.^{G}

Lamarckism: ✦ the theory of organic^G evolution published in the early 19th century by Jean Baptiste Lamarck (1744-1829), who hypothesized that the habitual behavior of animals produces anatomical modifications in their descendants that better enable their activity; ✦ a pejorative term in 20th-century Darwinism[G] for any theory that asserts the inheritance of acquired characteristics.

lateral gene transfer or **lateral gene flow**: See horizontal[G] gene transfer.

Law of Population: Malthus's term for his conjecture that population increases geometrically (that is by doubling) while the food supply increases arithmetically (that is by increments).

Linnaeus: the Swedish botanist Carl von Linné (1707-78) who introduced the system of taxonomy that is used by modern biology, consisting of a genus name followed by a species name (e.g. *Homo sapiens*) with species arranged into a tree-like hierarchy based on degrees of similarity.

Machiavellian intelligence: In Darwinian theory, the use of social[G] intelligence to propagate one's genes.

Malthusian: pertaining to the thesis elaborated by Thomas Robert Malthus (1766-1834) that population increases faster than the food supply, making social equality impossible to achieve. He named this thesis the Law of Population.[G]

Marxism: a theory of politics and economics based on the writings of Karl Marx (1818-83) and Friedrich Engels (1820-95). Communism[G] is an ideology[G] and praxis[G] based on Marxism.

materialism: a school of philosophy, more precisely called philosophical[G] materialism, that asserts that only matter is real or knowable. See also methodological[G] materialism.

matriarchy: In Victorian social theory, a hypothetical stage of human social evolution in which women are the ruling class. Matriarchy should not be confused with extant matrilineal[G] societies in which women control their own property and hold important positions in society. Compare to patriarchy.[G]

matriline: in primatology, a multigenerational group whose members are descended from the same female and which functions as a cohesive social unit within the troop.[G]

matrilineage: the basic kinship group in a matrilineal[G] society.

matrilineal: in anthropology, a type of kinship[G] system in which descent is traced through a succession of female ancestors. It is distinct from matriarchy[G] and matriline.[G]

Mendel, Gregor (1822-84). The discoverer of Mendelian[G] genetics.

Mendelian genetics: genetic science as first formulated by Gregor Mendel: it asserts that (1) phenotypic[G] traits are controlled by discrete hereditary particles (genes); (2) sexually-reproducing organisms transmit two copies of each gene to the next generation (one from the mother and one from the father); and (3) only one gene of each pair (the dominant gene) controls the phenotypic[G] trait that is observed. Traits inherited in this way are called *Mendelian* traits.

meritocracy: a hierarchical social system that promotes people to positions of power by evaluating their performance using standards of ability that are supportive of the system of power.

methodological materialism: the thesis that the scientific method is applicable only to the study of matter. Compare to philosophical[G] materialism, which is the belief that only matter is real or knowable.

methylation: the process by which a methyl group ($-CH_3$) becomes attached to a DNA molecule, thereby preventing gene[G] expression. It is one mechanism of epigenetic[G] inheritance.

modernism: belief in the privileged status of scientific knowledge and the progressive nature of social change. The philosophies of positivism,[G] materialism,[G] and naturalism[G] are all supportive of modernism, while both Darwinism[G] and Marxism[G] incorporate modernist premises.

modernization: the process of instituting social changes that reflect recent innovations and ideas, often at the expense of older, more-established practices. It is a necessary correlate of modernism ^G and Progress.^G

molecular biology: the study of molecules that are essential to biological processes, especially DNA and RNA.

moral order: a culturally-specific complex of ideas about how to live that specifies (1) appropriate behavior towards oneself and other people, (2) the consequences of inappropriate behavior, and (3) the agents (whether human or supernatural) that make judgements of right and wrong.

mutate: the process of making a mutation.^G

mutation: any permanent change in genetic material that can be passed on to the next generation, such as a change in the sequence of nucleotides^G in a DNA molecule.

Mutual Aid: Kropotkin's^G alternative to Darwin's natural^G selection, in which organisms naturally cooperate.

mutual grooming: a common social activity of primates in which two or more individuals comb one another's pelage. It facilitates social relationships while improving health.

nation: derived from the Latin word *nacio*, for "born": a population consisting of people born in the same geographical area and who share cultural characteristics. See also state^G and tribe.^G

natural selection: the theory developed by Alfred Russel Wallace (1823-1913) and Charles Darwin (1809-82) that asserts that (1) organisms normally produce far more offspring than can survive, (2) not all offspring of the same parents are genetically identical, that (3) competition among members of the same and different species results in differential survival and/or the lack of an opportunity to breed, thereby (4) producing new species^G over time through incremental genetic change.

natural theology: theology based on the premise that one can develop some knowledge of God and/or prove the existence of God by studying nature.

naturalism: as used in this book, a description of something in accurate detail that emphasizes its observable features.

neocon: abbreviation of *neoconservative*.^G

neoconservative: those members of the Republican Party in the United States associated initially with the Project for the New American Century (PNAC) or, more generally, anyone who advocates global capitalism,^G deregulation of industry, privatization of public services, and the use of the U.S. military to enforce compliance.

neo-Darwinism: a theory developed in the 1930s and 1940s in England and the United States that explains organic^G evolution by means of population^G genetics.

neoliberalism: a school of economics that began in Europe in the late 1930s and is associated with the names of Friedrich A. Hayek (1899-1992), Karl Popper (1902-94), and Ludwig von Mises (1881-1973). It subsequently became American economic policy through the influence of the Chicago School.^G See also neoconservative.^G

neoliberal university: see corporate^G academy.

New Deal: The social and economic legislation introduced in the United States by President Franklin D. Roosevelt and the Democratic Party between 1933 and 1945.

Nonconformist: In England, any Protestant denomination that challenges the doctrines or authority of the Church of England.

nonstatist: a society that has no institution^G with a monopoly on collective^G violence. Equivalent to *stateless*. See state.^G

nonviolence: a philosophy and praxis that rejects the use of aggression to achieve collective goals.

nuclear family: a cohesive social group consisting of a father, a mother, and their children.

nucleotide: one of the repeating units (each unit consisting of sugar, phosphate, and base) that form the backbone of the DNA and RNA molecules.

operon: a group of two or more genes in bacteria whose transcription is controlled by a single promotor (that is, by a segment within a gene that initiates transcription). See lac[G] operon.

organic evolution: the thesis that (1) all life on earth is historically continuous with a small number of ancestral species; (2) a species may give rise to daughter species or become extinct; (3) daughter species have anatomical similarities inherited from a common ancestor; and (4) complex organisms develop from simpler ones. In this book, organic evolution is synonymous with Darwin's term descent[G] through modification.

origin myth: a story that describes events in the distant past that symbolically expresses the social relations of the present or social relations as people wish them to be. A myth is neither true nor false but socially efficacious.

paleoanthropology: the scientific study of the human past by means of the systematic excavation of fossils and artifacts, objective methods of dating, anatomical comparison of fossils, and interpretation of archeological finds in the light of cultural[G] anthropology.

pangenesis: a theory of genetics, held by Hipprocates and Darwin, that all the organs of the body shed small, hypothetical particles that migrate to the reproductive organs, where they are passed on to the next generation.

parallel activity: when two or more individuals perform the same activity at the same time, e.g. people running to escape from a fire. It contrasts to complementation[G] which is cooperation with complementary actions instrumental to a shared goal, e.g. when one hunter chases the prey out of the tree while the other kills it when it gets to the ground.

parallel cousin: a child of a same-sex sibling of one's parents, e.g. my mother's sister's child. Compare to cross[G] cousin.

parochial altruism: a concept in the theory of group[G] selection in which self-sacrifice by some members of one's own group increases the fitness of all members of one's group relative to that of other groups.

participant observation: the art and science of learning about a people by living among them, becoming fluent in their language, participating in their activities, and systematically inquiring into their beliefs and practices.

patriarchy: a class[G] society in which legal authority is vested in adult males, as in preindustrial Europe. Although some species of nonhuman primates have status[G] hierarchies in which males outrank females, in human society male power is reinforced by ideology[G] and institutions.[G]

patrilineal: in anthropology, a type of kinship[G] system in which descent is traced through a succession of male ancestors. It is distinct from patriarchy.[G] Compare to matrilineal.[G]

PHAGe: see Darwinism.[G]

Phase I Darwinism: from the 1870s until the 1940s: characterized by the establishment of Darwinism[G] as the founding ideology of the secular university by means of coevolution between evolutionist science and corporate[G] capitalism. This phase was concurrent with racial typology, neo-Darwinism,[G] and overt eugenics.[G]

Phase II Darwinism: from World War II to the mid-1970s, characterized by the development of molecular biology in conjunction with Big

Science.^G This phase was concurrent with the adoption of the Central Dogma,^G the public repudiation of eugenics,^G and the abandonment of overt racism^G (though both eugenics and racism continued covertly).

Phase III Darwinism: from the mid-1970s to the present: defined by the merger of biomedical science with state^G capitalism. This merger was concurrent with the Chicago School,^G neoliberalism,^G sociobiology,^G evolutionary^G psychology, and the development of genetic engineering.

Phase IV Darwinism: from 2000 to the present, characterized by the study of religiosity^G and the development of bio-immortality.^G

phenotype: the observable characteristics of an individual organism. It contrasts with genotype,^G which consists of the genes that program these characteristics.

philology: the comparative study of languages with the goal of discerning their origins and relationships. The term was superseded in the 20th century by historical linguistics.

philosophes: literally "lovers of wisdom," the term denotes those intellectuals in 18th-century France who developed the concepts of unilinear^G evolution, modernism,^G and Progress.^G

philosophical materialism: the belief that only matter is real or knowable. It contrasts to methodological^G materialism.

phonemic perception: the human ability to segment a continuous acoustic wave of speech into the discrete sounds that distinguish one word from another in a particular human language.

physical anthropology: the study of human beings as biological organisms, such as human anatomy and human genetics. It complements cultural^G anthropology.

Pleistocene: the geological period ending around 10,000 years ago that is characterized by successive phases of glaciation in middle latitudes.

It is the period when the genus *Homo* first appears in the fossil record.

Pliocene: the geological period beginning about 5 million years ago and ending with the Pleistocene^G when bipedal ape-like primates first appear in the fossil record.

plutocracy: a society governed by and for the wealthy.

political economy: an archaic term for the study of the political and economic institutions of society. Some scholars have suggested that the term be revived since it recognizes that political and economic organization are inseparable.

population genetics: the study of the genetic variation in natural populations of organisms based on the concepts of gene, gene pool, isolating mechanism, mutation,^G and selection^G pressure. See neo-Darwinism.^G

positivism: ✦ a school of philosophy that asserts that only what is demonstrable by science is true and that anything that cannot be proved scientifically is unfounded; ✦ a theory developed by Auguste Comte (1798-1857) that postulates three evolutionary stages in the development of human thought. The third stage is certainty based on science.

postmodernism: a school of social analysis developed in the late 1960s that questions objectified views of society inspired by the physical sciences.

praxis: the hands-on application of a belief system as opposed to its theoretical content.

precariat: a social class^G of financially-precarious workers who move from one short-term job to another.

predestination: the theological doctrine associated primarily with John Calvin that eternal salvation cannot be earned by human beings by their actions on earth; the term is derived from the Latin for "to make firm beforehand."

professoriat: a social class^G consisting of professional academics of professorial rank.

Progress: when written with a capital P, the belief that there are laws (whether of nature, history, or society) that ensure the increasing well-being of the human species over time.

progressive: (adjective) pertaining to Progress^G or progressive change; (noun) a person who believes in Progress or progressive change.

Progressive Era: a period in American history from the early 1890s until the early 1920s characterized by legislation to give the vote to more segments of the population, to mitigate the negative effects of big business, and to improve the moral fiber of the nation.^G

progressive evolution: the thesis that evolution produces more complex organisms over time. It is often conflated with Progress^G and unilinear^G evolution.

Puritanism: a religious reform movement in the 16th and 17th centuries that sought to purge the Church of England (Anglican^G church) of any remaining Catholic beliefs, iconography, and practices and/or to establish new churches that exemplify such purified Protestantism.

racism: the use of innate biological differences among human populations to rank people in a status^G hierarchy or class^G system. See White^G supremacy.

rationalism: the belief that reason and logic are the only valid criteria for human thought and action.

reciprocal altruism: sociobiological jargon for doing something for another's advantage with the expectation of getting back something of comparable value. Since the action is not altruistic at all, the anthropological term of reciprocal^G exchange is preferable. See also generalized^G altruism.

reciprocal exchange: doing something for another with the expectation of getting something back, exemplified by the expression: "You scratch my back and I'll scratch yours." Also called *reciprocity*.

reductionism: any attempt to explain the properties of a system in terms of the properties of its constituent parts.

religion: a collective system of beliefs and practices that establishes and maintains social relationships with supernatural beings and/or deceased humans.

religiosity: in Darwinian theory, a putative instinctive tendency in the human species to hold beliefs or engage in activities commonly associated with religion that Darwinists find irrational and objectionable.

religious right: an alliance of Christian clergy in the United States that seeks to give selective tenets of Christian morality the force of law while supporting an authoritarian social agenda.

retrovirus: an infectious virus made of RNA that can, with the help of a host cell, transcribe itself into DNA which may be incorporated into the host cell's genome.[G]

reverse transcriptase: a naturally-occurring enzyme that enables the transcription of RNA into DNA. Although not contradictory to the Central Dogma[G] as formulated by Francis Crick, it was widely perceived to be so at the time of its discovery in the 1970s; and it undercuts the simplified version of the Central Dogma that is used as an ideology[G] of genetic[G] determinism.

Roaring Twenties: the period in American history from the end of World War I to the stock market crash of 1929.

selection: see natural[G] selection and selection[G] pressure.

selection pressure: in Darwinian theory, anything that causes the frequency of one gene in a population to change relative to a competing gene.

sexism: the use of biological differences between the sexes to justify their rank in a class^G system or status^G hierarchy. See also patriarchy.^{G}

social anthropology: the name for cultural^G anthropology in the former British empire except in the United States.

Social Darwinism: the use of Darwinism^G and/or evolutionary^G biology to justify laissez-faire^G capitalism, class^G systems, sexism,^{G} and racism.^{G}

social exchange: when one individual intentionally transfers goods and services to another. When the process goes in both directions it is called reciprocal^G exchange.

social evolution: any theory that asserts that human social institutions develop and change over time in a systematic way. It is sometimes confused with unilinear^G evolution.

social intelligence: the ability to understand social phenomena, such as inferring the intentions of others and predicting the reactions of others to one's own action. Compare to instrumental^G intelligence.

socialism: ✦ a family of political movements beginning in the 19th century that seeks to replace capitalism^G with a more just form of social organization, whether state^G ownership of the means of production (Communism^G) or a nonstatist^G society composed of a network of worker cooperatives^G (anarchism^G); ✦ any of a number of Christian movements from the first century to the present that seek to live in accord with the principle expressed in Christian Scripture: "no one claimed that any of his posessions was his own, but they had everything in common" (Acts: 4:32).

sociobiology: a variant of Darwinian theory first promulgated in the early 1970s that asserts that all of social life can be explained by inclusive^G fitness and by individuals seeking to competitively propagate their genes.

solidarity: the willingness of members of a group to support one another in times of adversity or when in conflict with outsiders.

somatic cell genetic engineering: intentional modification of genes in the somatic cells of the body. Such changes are not transmitted to subsequent generations. Compare to germline[G] genetic engineering.

species: ✦ The lowest level in the Linnaean system of taxonomy, consisting of organisms that appear morphologically similar and are presumed to produce fertile offspring when interbred. A species may be optionally subdivided into subspecies on the basis of morphological differences among populations; ✦ in population[G] biology, that stage of the evolutionary process at which two actually or potentially interbreeding populations of organisms become separated to the point that the production of fertile hybrids between the two does not occur; ✦ in molecular biology, a population of organisms that maintains a coherent set of genetic traits in nature.

spiritualism: the belief that the spirits of the dead continue to exist after death and that it is possible to make contact with specific deceased individuals by using the services of a medium, that is, a person who is believed to have a special ability to make such contact.

state: an institution[G] that has the approval of the moral[G] order to exercise a monopoly on collective[G] aggression within a designated territory. A state may include subsidiary institutions with smaller territories and/or lesser degrees of authority.

state capitalism: a political system in which the state[G] and the capitalist[G] class work together to further the capitalist system at the expense of other interests. See also plutocracy,[G] which is the end result of this process.

state religion: any religious institution[G] that is funded and controlled by the state.[G]

status hierarchy: in primatology, a group whose members convey differences in social rank relative to one other through such processes as aggression, submission, agonistic [G] display, social[G] exchange, and coalition building, resulting in a situation in which some members outrank others. Compare to dominance[G] hierarchy.

stem cell: a cell taken from a multicellular organism that has not yet differentiated into its mature form and retains the capability of producing more copies of itself or becoming any one of a number of different cell types.

subsistence strategy: any combination of motor skills, technical knowledge, and social coordination that a social group uses to provide sustenance to its members.

technocracy: a system of political power based on the control of science and technology.

tribalism: in Darwinian theory, either (1) a putative stage of human evolution prior to civilization in which people were organized into tribes[G] or (2) any society that is organized by putative instincts for group identity and solidarity.

tribe: a human population with a common language and culture and no state[G] organization. The term is little used in contemporary anthropology due to its imprecision and colonial associations. See kincentric[G] and nation.[G]

troop: in primatology, a cohesive social group that moves as a unit and consists of at least one breeding adult male and one breeding female with her dependent offspring. In some species, such as baboons and macaques, troops can contain multiple breeding males and multiple breeding females and total hundreds of individuals.

unilineal: a kinship[G] system that traces descent from either the father or the mother but not both. A matrilineage[G] is unilineal.

unilinear evolution: the belief that human societies develop from the simple to the complex through an invariant sequence of stages. See progressive[G] evolution.

Weismann's barrier: the thesis of August Weismann (1834-1919) that the germ cells of multicellular animals are isolated from the rest of the body and that genes are passed unchanged (except by *mutation*[G] and recombination) from one generation to the next. The majority of animal species and all plants do not have such isolation.

Whigs: A political movement in Great Britain from the late 17th to the mid-19th centuries that advocated a Protestant monarchy that was subordinate to a strong parliament and the rule of law. By Darwin's day, the Whigs had the backing of the industrial class and had become a force for modernization.[G]

White supremacy: the belief that there is a biologically defined population called the White race that is superior to other races. See racism.[G]

X Club: an association founded in London in 1864 by Thomas Henry Huxley (1825-95) and a small number of colleagues. It had the goals of promulgating Darwinism,[G] professionalizing science, and replacing Christianity in British universities (then controlled by the Church of England) with a new curriculum inspired by evolutionist[G] science and positivist[G] philosophy.

xenophobia: fear provoked by the presence of a stranger. In nonhuman primates, it often takes the form of collective avoidance and sometimes collective[G] aggression.

Index of Persons Mentioned or Quoted in the Text

Acheson, Dean   154

Aristotle   79

Augustine   111

Baker, Sunny   22

Bakunin, Mikail   316,
319, 331, 334

Barton, Ruth   100

Batterham, Forster   316-17

Bauer, Bruno   105

Berger, Peter L.   25

Berkeley, George   113

Bezos, Jeff   159,
359

Blackburn, Simon   130

Blurton Jones, N.G.   255

Boulton, Matthew   48

Boyd, Robert   207

Branson, Richard   359

Brenner, Michael   310

Bridgewater, 8th Earl of   61-62

Brown, Helen Gurley   314

Buckland, William   59-62,
65-66

Bush, George W.   30

Busk, George   99-100

Calvin, John   2, 102,
104, 106, 108-09, 113, 121-23, 126, 229

Canning, George   52

Carnegie, Andrew   32, 185,
190, 317-318

Chalmers, Thomas   61

Chance, M.R.A.   237

Chandler, Harry   186

Cheney, Dorothy L.   238

Chernyshevskii, N. G.   71

Churchill, Winston   185

Claeys, Gregory   6, 11

Clark, Stephen R.L.   131

Commoner, Barry   177-
178, **322**

Comte, August   104-05

Condorcet, Marquis de   76

Cornell, Ezra   112-13

Crick, Francis   172-73,
179

Cuvier, Georges   38, 53-
55, 60, 81, 206-07

Dalai Lama   241

Darlington, Philip J.   227

Darnovsky, Marcy   195

Darwin, Charles   1-3,
5-16, 19, 25, 32-38, 48-49, 51-53, 56-58,
62-63, 66-71, 75-85, 99-100, 103, 105,
108, 117, 122-125, 127-132, 142-144,
147, 149-150, 164, 174, 180-185, 187,
189, 191, 195-196, 198-199, 208, 210,
226, 229-230, 249, 256-257, 259, 269,
274, 304-307, 318, 328, 330, 360

Darwin, Erasmus (Charles's brother)
9

Darwin, Erasmus (Charles's grandfather)
9, 48-52, 56-57, 62-63, 70-71, 108

Darwin, Leonard (Charles's son) 185

Davenport, Charles B.   185,
190, 192, 194

Dawkins, Richard   150,
158, 173, 204, 228-29, 273-74, 280

Day, Dorothy   314-
319, 334, 336-37, 339-40

Day, Matthew   105

Degler, Charles   83

De Gray, Aubrey   159

De La Torre, Miguel   334,
339

Dennett, Daniel   79, 150,
158

Desmond, Adrian J.   9, 37,
104, 124

DeVore, Irven   17

De Waal, Frans de   278-
280

Dickens, Charles   8

Dikötter, Frank   185-
186

Dobzhansky, Theodosius   201,
227

Dunbar, Robin   263-64
Eibl-Eibesfeldt, Irenäus   258-59
Elder, James H.   230-31
Eliot, Charles W.   115
Engels, Friedrich   71, 305,
  326
Epstein, Jeffrey   150
Eratosthenes   358
Erdal, David   259
Fisher, Ronald   184-85
Flandreau, Marc   142,
  148
Francis of Assisi   109,
  336
Frankland, Edward   99-100
Franklin, Rosalind   172,
  334
Fraser, Steve   147
Friedman, Milton   228,
  335
Galileo   27
Galton, Francis   19, 67,
  180-183, 193-194, 196, 199, 209
Gates, Bill   150
Gilman, Daniel Coit   115
Girihadras, Anand   318
Giroux, Henry A.   359
Gladstone, William Ewart   101
Goethe, Charles M.   189
Goodall, Jane   16, 230-
  31
Gopnik, Adam   80-81
Gorner, Peter   159
Gosney, Ezra S.   186
Graeber, David   342
Grant, Robert Edmund   49, 58,
  63, 101, 111-13
Gray, Asa   68
Gray, Aubrey de   159
Greeley, Horace   112
Greg, W.R.   180-82
Gross, Paul R.   116-17
Hadley, Arthur Twining   115
Haeckel, Ernst   191

Haldane, J. B. S.   189,
  226
Hamilton, William   225
Ham, son of Noah   65, 188
Harriman, W. Averell   185,
  318, 335
Haughton, S. H.   71
Hawkes, K.   255
Hegel, Georg Wilhelm Friedrich 108
Henry VIII, king of England   106
Hirst, Thomas Archer   99-100
Hitler, Adolf   28-29,
  186, 188-90
Hobbes, Thomas   242,
  327, 347, 352
Hoffman, Abbie   314
Hofstadter, Richard   5-6
Ho, Mae-Wan   179
Hooker, Joseph Dalton   99-100
Horn, Dara   159
Hrdy, Sarah Blaffer   274-75
Hutton, James   52
Huxley, Aldous   209-10
Huxley, Julian   131,
  189
Huxley, Thomas Henry   67-68,
  70, 99, 101-03, 105, 124-27, 161, 210
Isaac, Glynn   254
Jacob, Francois   175
Jefferson, Thomas   51, 111
Jenkin, Fleeming   69
Jesus   2, 67,
  105, 108, 334
Jones, Daniel Stedman   226
Jordan, David Starr   115
Joseph Priestly   48
Josiah Wedgewood   48
Kallis, Aristotle A.   188
Kant, Immanuel   108
Kaplan, Hilliard   277-79
Kazin, Michael   333
Keesing, Roger   227
Kellogg, Vernon   184
Kelvin, 1st Baron (William Thomson)

69

Keynes, John Maynard   335

Kropotkin, Peter   70, 307,
318-19, 331, 336, 340-41, 343

Kühl, Stefan   190

Lamarck, Jean Baptiste   53, 55-
57, 62, 68, 70-71, 82, 195, 203, 206-07

Lancaster, Jane   17, 276-
79

Leach, William   162-
163

Leacock, Eleanor   25

Levitt, Norman   116-
117

Lewontin, Richard C.   226-27

Linnaeus, Carl   125

London, Jack   342

Loye, David   124

Lubbock, John   99, 143-
144, 146, 148-49, 196

Luckmann, Thomas   25

Lyell, Charles   36

Lyon, Jeff   159

Macintosh, James   129

Maestripieri, Dario   262

Malinowski, Bronislaw   18, 25,
266-69

Malthus, Thomas Robert   6-9,
12-13, 19, 25, 70-73, 75-78, 81, 84, 117,
123, 129, 182, 304-05

Margulis, Lynn   202

Marsden, George M.   109-10,
114-15

Martineau, Harriet   9

Marx, Karl   2, 25-
26, 69, 73, 103, 305-06, 316, 318-19, 341

Maurin, Peter   336-37

McCarthy, Joseph   24, 332

McCosh, James   68

McLellan, David   25

Mendel, Gregor   79, 203

Midgely, Mary   280

Millikan, Robert A.   186

Mivart, St. George   69

Monod, Jacques   175

Moore, James R.   9, 37

Morgan, Lewis Henry (anthropologist)
325-26

Morgan, Thomas Hunt (biologist)
189, 310

Moses   333-34

Mother Teresa   150

Muller, Hermann J.   189-90,
192

Musk, Elon   359

Napoleon   51, 56

Nissen, Henry W.   231

Nixon, Richard   191

Noah   60, 62,
65, 188

O'Connell, J.F.   255

Osborn, H. F.   82

Ostrom, Elinor   331,
343

Paley, William   55-56,
58, 61, 68-69, 84-85, 105, 229

Pasteur, Louis   38, 175

Pearson, Karl   184

Petersen, William   7-8

Pinker, Steven   130,
150

Pliny the Elder   61

Polonius   163

Pope Francis   319

Postman, Neil   359

Priestly, Joseph   48

Rampelburg, Joanne   21

Reagan, Ronald   20, 75,
157

Reich, David   193

Richards, Robert J.   129-30,
187

Richerson, Peter J.   207

Ridley, Matt   193

Robinson, William I.   310,
328

Rockefeller, John D.   189-90,
192, 318

Roosevelt, Franklin D.   334-36

Rousseau, Jean Jacques   72, 347-

-48, 356
Rose, Michael | 35, 6,
26, 57
Sagan, Dorion | 202
Sahlins, Marshall | 226,
249
Sapolsky, Robert | 34, 235
Sapp, Jan | 35, 275
Sault, Nicole | 159
Schrecker, Ellen | 24
Schumpeter, Joseph A. | 345
Sedgwick, Charles | 131
Seyfarth, Robert M. | 238
Shapiro, Beth | 193
Sharer, Kevin W. | 313
Silver, Lee M. | 161,
194-95
Smith, Adam | 71
Snow, C. P. | 61
Sonneborn, Tracy | 203-
204
Spencer, Herbert | 5-6, 9,
11, 70, 99, 191
Spielberg, Steven | 160
Stalin, Josef | 25, 30,
306, 332
Stanford, Craig B. | 246-
253
Stanford, Leland Jr. | 114
St Hilaire, Etienne Geoffroy | 63
Stone, Roger | 359
Stove, David | 229
Strum, Shirley | 235-36
Tappan, Henry P. | 111
Thatcher, Margaret | 20, 75,
157
Thiel, Peter | 159
Todes, Daniel P. | 71
Travers, Robert | 150,
230
Turner, Frank Miller | 101
Tutin, Caroline | 236
Tyndale, William | 58, 68
Venter, Craig | 178

Victoria, queen of England | 66, 328
Wade, Nicholas | 158
Wallace, Alfred Russel | 13-15,
34, 52, 70-71, 180-81, 183-84, 307, 309
Walton, Sam | 119
Wanamaker, John | 163
Ward, James | 115-16,
327
Washburn, Sherwood | 16-17,
253-55
Watson, James | 158,
172-73, 175, 177-79, 192-93, 195, 200,
203
Watt, James | 48
Weaver, Warren | 192
Weber, Max | 121
Wedgewood, Josiah | 48
Weikart, Richard | 187-88
Weismann, August | 173-74,
306
Weissman, Irving | 30-31
Wells, H. G. | 209
West-Eberhard, Mary Jane | 280-81
White, Andrew Dickson | 67
Whiten, Andrew | 259
Wilson, E. O. | 102,
124, 130, 158, 191, 207, 225-27, 256,
259, 274, 280
Wilson, Woodrow | 115
Yerbury, Hilary | 25
Yerkes, Robert | 230-31
Young, Robert M. | 68, 83

Index of Topics

aggression, war, dominance

African slave trade   11, 188, 337

agonistic   236

alpha   235, 237, 240-241, 245, 261

American Revolution   50-51

British Empire   11, 99, 143, 148, 330

class system   50, 65, 75, 120, 164, 189, 194, 200, 249, 312, 318, 322, 331, 339, 342, 351, 357

collective aggression   253, 320, 348, 353, 357

dominance   56, 230, 233-234, 236-237, 243-247, 252, 255-256, 258, 272-274

French Revolution   7, 53, 55, 63, 65, 131

Great Famine of Ireland   8, 74, 182, 338

imperialism   36, 188, 225, 253, 347, 351, 358

Napoleonic era   51, 56, 63

racism   26, 186

Russian Revolution and Soviet Union 30, 180, 257, 309, 315, 319, 332, 335

social stratification   155, 338, 352

status hierarchy   33, 163, 237-238, 240, 243-244, 247, 348-349

warfare   67, 73, 258, 320, 347, 352-354, 357

World War I   25, 180, 266, 314, 335

World War II   20, 149, 151, 154-156, 184, 190

xenophobia   252, 352, 354

altruism, sharing

altruism   122-123, 150, 208, 226, 243, 259-260, 269, 271-272, 274, 276, 279, 337

charity   8, 11, 72, 121, 127, 317, 338

cooperative parenting   208, 276, 278

cross-fostering   261-262

grooming   204-205, 234, 236, 242, 248-251, 259-261

philanthropy   318

belief systems

(see also capitalism, Darwinism, religion, socialism)

agnosticism   104, 114, 126

American Dream   317

bio-immortality   158-161

congruent systems of belief   32-34, 132-133, 149, 227

Enlightenment   31, 54, 63, 72, 125, 131, 147, 195

Great Chain of Being   54

ideology   3, 12, 15, 24, 26-30, 35, 64-66, 74, 85, 98, 116, 121, 132, 142, 145-147, 149, 151-152, 160, 162, 164, 188, 195, 200, 209, 227, 252, 271, 273-274, 304-305, 307, 321, 333, 348

individualism   2, 32, 34, 127, 161, 196, 207, 242, 269, 275, 280, 328, 330

materialism   32, 56, 117, 124, 147, 151, 158, 161-162, 184, 304, 306

modernism   3, 133, 209, 269

myth, mythology   31, 37, 73, 126, 304

naturalism   194

Progress, myth of   2, 10,
  12, 29, 31-32, 34, 54, 57, 63-64, 78, 85,
  112, 125-127, 129, 131, 146-148, 160-
  161, 164, 180, 182, 187, 189, 195-196,
  198-199, 209, 227, 275, 304-307, 311,
  318, 332, 358

rationalism   10, 102,
  104, 109, 133, 158, 337

capitalism

(Chapters 1, 4, 8)

bourgeoisie   64, 71,
  327

City of London (finance)   144,
  146-148

consumer capitalism   162-
  164, 310-311, 358

corporate academy   156-
  157, 307

corporate capitalism   3, 5-6,
  10, 15, 20, 22-24, 26, 32-36, 63, 66-67,
  59, 74, 118-122, 132-133, 142, 147-
  151, 155-158, 161-164, 179, 196-198,
  226-227, 253, 271, 305-306, 310-313,
  317, 325, 329-330, 335, 338, 340, 342-
  343, 345-347, 350, 355-356, 358-359

corporations   15, 20-
  22, 118-120, 132, 157, 160, 305, 310,
  313, 341-343, 351

enclosure   330

entrepreneur   157,
  196

Gilded Age   5, 147,
  313

initial product offering (IPO)   21, 23,
  156

laissez-faire   62, 74,
  78, 98, 132, 157, 226, 335

neoliberal   192,
  226

New Poor Law   8, 71, 84

plutocracy   180,
  310

railroads, role of   106,
  144, 185, 341

Silicon Valley   21, 23,

                                    156, 307

state capitalism   150,
  161, 164, 338, 346

Wall Street (finance)   119,
  156, 307

Whigs   7-11,
  85, 117, 129, 149

creationism

design, argument from   55

diluvialism   60, 62,
  67

English school of geology   60, 62

natural theology   55, 58,
  61, 69, 83-84, 118, 229

Darwinism

adaptation   1, 81-
  83, 202, 208-209, 231, 305

adaptive radiation   82-83,
  123

atomistic individualism   2, 34,
  196, 207, 226, 244, 340, 358

competition   1, 5,
  9-11, 23, 32-33, 36, 66, 70, 75-76,
  82, 123, 125, 161, 164, 207, 226, 233,
  235-236, 243, 246, 258-259, 274-275,
  304-307, 312, 330-331, 340

coevolution with capitalism   (see
  Chapter 4); 142, 149-150, 202, 207

Darwin industry   35

Darwin's cohort   149-
  150, 210

eugenics (see Chapter 5); 1, 127, 151,
  154, 159-160, 180, 184-187, 189-196,
  198-199, 209, 305-306

evolutionary psychology   150,
  196

generalized altruism   208,
  260, 269, 276

genetic determinism   176-
  179, 184, 199, 201-202, 204, 207-208,
  227, 263, 272-273, 280

GenRich   161,
  194

group selection   123,
  163

heritability of IQ   154
H.M.S. Beagle   9, 34,
66, 77, 129, 144
H.M.S Rattlesnake   103,
144
inclusive fitness   226-
227, 255, 260, 263, 270
kin selection   226,
260, 276
Law of Population (see also Malthus);
6-7, 9, 71-73, 78, 81, 304
meme   207,
228-229
natural selection   1, 6-7,
9, 11-16, 19, 25, 32, 35-38, 52, 66, 69-
71, 76-84, 98, 123-124, 129, 132, 147,
180-182, 184, 187, 193, 195-196, 198,
200, 209, 227, 229, 279-280, 305-306,
309, 318
neo-Darwinian synthesis   202
On the Origin of Species   7, 11-
12, 14, 36, 66-70, 76, 78, 80, 82, 84, 103,
117-118, 174, 195, 229, 306
reciprocal altruism   150,
260
selfish gene   1, 157,
228-229, 305
sexual selection   82, 234,
274
sociobiology   102,
157, 164, 176, 191, 196, 225-229, 243,
249, 254, 262-263, 270, 278-281
The Descent of Man   15, 36-
37, 124, 128, 132, 151, 180, 187, 196,
226, 259
The Voyage of the Beagle   66, 77
twin studies   200
unconscious selection   35, 80,
83
Weismann's barrier   174
X Club   99-101,
103, 105, 131, 142-143, 146, 149, 208

evolution

(see organic evolution)

moral order

(see Chapters 3, 6, 8; also religion)
moral legitimation   354-
355
moral order   3, 85,
99, 125-133, 148, 161-164, 267-268,
278-280, 304-305, 311-312, 320, 327,
333-334, 339-340, 354, 358
nonviolence   337,
339-340, 355, 357
social justice   160,
314, 317, 333, 337, 340, 355, 358

organic evolution

(see also Darwinism)
bio-engineering   177
cell nucleus   176-
177, 202-203
cellular continuity of life   38
Central Dogma of genetics   173,
175-179
descent with modification   (see
Chapter 2); 123
epigenetic inheritance   202,
204-206
ethology   128,
227
gene expression   176,
178, 204-205
genome   160-
161, 174, 177-178, 197, 202, 205, 207,
225
genotype   199,
206
homology   50
methylation   204-
205
molecular biology   154,
156, 172-176, 192, 203, 228
mutation   83
nucleotide   178,
204-205
phenotype   199,
206-207
population genetics   151,
207, 306

reductionism 197
reverse transcriptase 174, 176
stem cells 31-32, 157, 160, 177
symbiosis 202

religion

(see also creationism, moral order)
Anglican (Church of England) 57-58, 61, 72, 100-102, 106, 117, 122, 124, 146-147
apologetics 56, 68
Bible 19, 56, 58-60, 62, 65, 67-68, 71, 79, 101, 105, 122-126, 146, 160, 188, 316, 333-334
Calvinist 102, 104, 108-109, 113, 121-123, 126, 229
Christian 3, 56, 62, 55, 67, 69, 98, 104-106, 109-111, 114, 122, 133, 146-147, 151, 161-162, 304, 316, 333-334
evangelical 104, 122, 124-125, 333, 337
fundamentalist 61, 124, 126
Great Awakening 109, 333
Nonconformist 124, 146
nonsectarian 67, 107-108, 110-114, 146
predestination 122
Presbyterian 111, 113
Protestant (when not otherwise specified) 58, 106, 109, 113, 124, 333
Puritan 104, 122, 124, 161, 229, 333
Roman Catholic 57-58, 101, 104, 110, 123, 162, 186, 316-317, 336-340
Society of Friends (Quaker) 48, 112, 124
state religion 101, 161, 334
Unitarian and Universalist 102, 105, 108-110, 114

social science

(see also aggression, belief, capitalism, socialism)
achieved status 72, 74, 163, 179, 242, 244, 311, 333
anthropology 2, 16-18, 21, 25, 116, 144, 148, 181, 190, 226, 228-229, 239, 254, 258, 266, 276, 280, 305, 325-326
ascribed status 155, 241, 322
Batek De' 256-258, 348, 358
Big Science 156, 307
cultural adaptation 209, 305
cultural anthropology 20, 35, 84, 105-106, 111, 116, 159, 162, 188, 200, 207-209, 229, 239, 243, 251-252, 260, 263-264, 276-277, 305, 325-326, 349, 352-354, 356
ethnography 18, 254, 325, 338
famine 8, 72-75, 182, 205, 234, 338 (see also Great Irish Famine under Aggression)
gathering-and-hunting 36, 255-259, 347, 356-357
government 6, 21, 24, 51-52, 74-75, 106-107, 111-112, 118-119, 144-148, 151, 155, 178, 185, 191, 314-315, 318, 320, 327, 330, 334-335, 342, 346, 351, 357
Haudenosaunee 325-327
human adaptive complex 277
hunting hypothesis 253-254
institution 29, 55, 59, 65, 107, 113, 116, 132, 145, 192, 313, 319-320, 344
kinship 48, 239, 263-265, 267, 269-271, 278, 326, 343
Manam Island 321, 328, 348-349
matriline 240-241, 250
matrilineal 267, 326
participant observation 18, 24, 266

patriarchy   251-
  252, 327
philology   67, 105
phonemic perception   18
political economy   6, 9,
  36-37, 70, 77, 149, 331, 341
postmodernism (see Chapter 1); 306
praxis   334,
  337-338, 340
primate (nonhuman) societies (see
  Chapter 6; also troop); 17, 19, 198, 230,
  234, 236, 239, 241, 243, 249, 252, 273,
  276, 352
reciprocal exchange   208,
  226, 260, 278-279, 321, 323-324, 329,
  349, 358
state   5-6, 8,
  12, 30, 32-33, 54, 101, 106, 111-113,
  118-119, 121, 126, 129, 132, 142, 150,
  154, 161, 164, 180, 183, 186, 191, 193,
  225-227, 230, 235, 248, 280, 306, 314,
  319-320, 325, 327, 330-335, 337-339,
  342, 345-349, 351-354, 357, 359
subsistence economy (see Chapter 8);
  72, 245-246, 256-257, 320-321, 323-
  325, 328-329, 348-349, 356
tribe   125,
  328-329
Trobriand Islands   266-
  269
troop (nonhuman primate)   232-
  233, 235-242, 244, 246, 261, 278
unilinear   147,
  187, 195

community   2,
  29-30, 77, 110, 119, 123, 133, 142, 145,
  149, 162, 187-188, 200, 237, 246, 252,
  258, 264, 268, 270-271, 279, 312, 323,
  327-329, 338-340, 343, 345, 355-357,
  359
cooperative (noun)   343,
  346, 353
Industrial Workers of the World (IWW,
  Wobblies)   315,
  336
Marxism   25, 62,
  161, 306
Park Slope Food Cooperative   344-
  345
socialism   3, 161,
  163-164, 253, 307, 318, 325, 329, 332,
  334, 336, 342, 345, 356
solidarity   125,
  163, 270, 279, 313, 317, 327, 334

socialism

(see Chapter 8)
anarchism   316,
  319, 332, 334, 342, 347
Catholic Worker   337-
  340
commons   330,
  336, 350, 355-358, 360
Communism   24, 154,
  329, 337, 342
Communist Party   75, 204,
  314-315, 332, 336-337

About the Author

Peter C. Reynolds has a doctorate in anthropology from Yale University and an A.B degree from the University of California at Berkeley. He was a visiting fellow at the Salk Institute for Biological Studies and a postdoctoral fellow at Stanford University Medical Center. His first book, *On the Evolution of Human Behavior*, was published by the University of California Press.

As a research fellow at Australian National University, he did ethnographic fieldwork among villagers in Papua New Guinea and among gatherer/hunters in the Malaysian rainforest. Subsequently, as a manager in the computer industry, he observed capitalists at work in Silicon Valley. Peter is also the author of a political suspense novel, *The Day Coyote Danced*.

**You can purchase copies of this book
directly from our web site.**

https://www.borderlandnorth.com

www.ingramcontent.com/pod-product-compliance
Ligatning Source LLC
Chambersburg PA
CBHW022131020426
42334CB00015B/840